Learning to Rule

STUDIES OF THE WEATHERHEAD EAST ASIAN INSTITUTE,
COLUMBIA UNIVERSITY

The Studies of the Weatherhead East Asian Institute of Columbia University were inaugurated in 1962 to bring to a wider public the results of significant new research on modern and contemporary East Asia.

For a complete list of books in the series, see page 259.

Learning to Rule

COURT EDUCATION AND THE REMAKING
OF THE QING STATE, 1861–1912

DANIEL BARISH

Columbia University Press

New York

Columbia University Press
Publishers Since 1893
New York   Chichester, West Sussex
cup.columbia.edu
Copyright © 2022 Columbia University Press
All rights reserved

Library of Congress Cataloging-in-Publication Data
Names: Barish, Daniel, author.
Title: Learning to rule : court education and the remaking of the Qing state, 1861-1912 / Daniel Barish.
Other titles: Court education and the remaking of the Qing state, 1861–1912
Description: New York : Columbia University Press, [2021] | Series: Studies of the Weatherhead East Asian Institute, Columbia University | Includes bibliographical references.
Identifiers: LCCN 2021023383 (print) | LCCN 2021023384 (ebook) | ISBN 9780231203296 (trade paperback) | ISBN 9780231203289 (hardback) | ISBN 9780231554961 (ebook)
Subjects: LCSH: China—History—Qing dynasty, 1644-1912. | China—Politics and government—19th century. | Education of princes—China—History—19th century. | China—Kings and rulers—Education—History—19th century. | Tongzhi, Emperor of China, 1856-1875. | Guangxu, Emperor of China, 1871-1908. | Puyi, 1906-1967.
Classification: LCC DS761 .B37 2021 (print) | LCC DS761 (ebook) | DDC 951/.035—dc23
LC record available at https://lccn.loc.gov/2021023383
LC ebook record available at https://lccn.loc.gov/2021023384

Cover design: Julia Kushnirsky
Cover art: True picture of crowning ceremony of the emperor of the great Qing empire, color lithograph, 43.1910.

FOR MY TEACHERS, PAST AND PRESENT

CONTENTS

Acknowledgments   ix

Introduction   1

1. New Forms of Learning for a New Age of Imperial Rule, 1861–1874   27

2. The Malleability of Youth: Guangxu in the Classroom, 1875–1890   55

3. Putting Lessons Into Practice: Guangxu on the Throne, 1891–1898   83

4. Cixi's Pedagogy: Female Education and Constitutional Governance, 1898–1908   109

5. Learning to Be a Constitutional Monarch, 1908–1912   137

Conclusion: Emperor and Nation in Modern China   163

Character Glossary   183
Notes   187
Bibliography   229
Index   249

ACKNOWLEDGMENTS

In the years since I first began this project, I have been continually overwhelmed by the generosity offered to me by a range of people, some of whom I knew well, but also many others to whom I was a relative stranger. It is an understatement to say that this book would not exist without the contributions of an extraordinary group of teachers, colleagues, friends, and family. It gives me great pleasure to offer brief thanks here.

This book had its first incarnation in graduate school at Princeton. My advisor, Benjamin Elman, was a model of support and rigor. Whether in class, during office hours, or over dinner in Shanghai and Tokyo, he consistently pushed me to ask big questions grounded in careful research. I cannot thank him enough for his time and dedication. Even before I arrived on campus, Janet Chen was a constant source of enthusiasm and encouragement. From reading endless drafts of my writing to lunchtime conversations about teaching, she routinely went above and beyond as a mentor. Coursework with Tony Grafton, the hours we spent talking in his Firestone Library hideaway, and his infectious enthusiasm for learning inspired me to expand the scope of my research. I am immensely grateful to Elisabeth Kaske for her careful reading of, comments on, and framing of my work in ways I had not yet seen or understood. She inspired many of the new questions that I seek to answer with this book.

In courses and casual conversations, Jeremy Adelman, Nicola Di Cosmo, Sheldon Garon, Federico Marcon, and Susan Naquin all contributed to my development as a scholar by expanding the scope of my interests and my knowledge. Whether they know it or not, they gave me the ambition and tools to pursue the research and writing of this book. Before arriving at Princeton as well, I was fortunate to work with unforgettable teachers. While I was an undergraduate at Emory,

Joachim Kurtz lit a passion for studying China and set me on the path to a Ph.D. His suggestion to move to China after graduation with no plan or expectations remains the single most valuable piece of advice I have ever received. Over the years he has remained a frequent source of counsel and friendship. At Columbia, Eugenia Lean, Gray Tuttle, and Madeleine Zelin nurtured my interests and introduced me to the professional study of history. In seminars and in feedback on research papers, they showed me how to transform my interests into scholarship by critically examining sources and questioning received narratives. Although not all have seen this book—and none should be tied to its faults or limitations—I know the full depth of the debt I owe to my teachers, and I cannot thank them enough.

At every stage of my education, I was fortunate to be surrounded by supportive peers whose work helped to inspire my own. First at Columbia, the members of my M.A. cohort, and the Ph.D. students to whom we looked up, provided an extraordinary model of community—both intellectual and social. With ping pong matches in Kent Hall and late-night conversations in Starr Library, Ashton Briganti, Glenda Chao, Jae Won Chung, Anatoly Detwyler, Meng Fan, James Lin, Weiwei Luo, Sixiang Wang, Luke Weiss, and Lan Wu convinced me that historians were my people. Somehow, the community of East Asian scholars at Princeton lived up to the lofty ideals established at Columbia. John Alekna, David Boyd, Daniel Burton-Rose, Kent Cao, Ying-kit Chan, Kjell Ericson, Yulia Frumer, Elijah Greenstein, Jinsong Guo, Songyoul Han, Reut Harari, Mike Hatch, Tom Mazanec, Seiji Shirane, Alexis Siemon, Mårten Söderblom Saarela, Wayne Soon, Dror Weil, W. Evan Young, Xue Zhang, and Bingyu Zheng shared meals, ideas, sources, and laughter in ways I will never forget.

With my home in the History Department at Princeton, I was privileged to share the classroom, the softball field, and evenings at the Ivy Inn with the most collegial and intellectually rigorous people I have known. In particular, Olivier Burtin, Katlyn Carter, Patrick De Oliveira, Christian Flow, Tommi Lankila, Nikhil Menon, Morgan Robinson, and Sean Vanatta each read more of my writing than could be reasonably expected of any friend or colleague. I'm lucky to call them both. Andrew Collings, Merle Eisenberg, Diana Andrade Melgarejo, Lee Mordechai, Randall Pippenger, Fidel Tavarez, and Ian Ward as well always made my returns to New Jersey from trips abroad feel like coming home.

Much of the research and writing of this project took place overseas. In Tokyo, Oki Yasushi and Haneda Masashi welcomed me to the Institute for Advanced Studies on Asia at the University of Tokyo. The list of people to whom I owe thanks in China is nearly endless. Archivists and librarians at many institutions, particularly the First Historical Archives in Beijing and the Shanghai Municipal Library, went out of their way to help me navigate their collections. In Beijing as well, Huang Aiping, Liu Zhengxian, Xiang Xuan, Zheng Yunyan, and Zou Ailian generously offered their time and support for my work, discussing my early ideas, opening doors at archives, and showing me the best places for a hearty bowl of noodles after a long day of transcribing documents. In and around Shanghai, Cao Nanping, Dong Shaoxin, Duan Zhiqiang, Ge Zhaoguang, Jiseo Kim, Lin Qiuyun, Lu Minzhen, Lu Xushuang, Xiong Yuezhi, Zhang Qing, Zhang Xinyuan, Zhao Ying, and Zheng Yuan all welcomed me into their research communities, indulging my questions and sharing their expertise about sources, scholarship, translations, and more.

While in Shanghai I was also fortunate to be part of a lively group of graduate students who enriched my time there in more ways than one. For museum trips, Beijing duck Thanksgiving dinners, and everything in-between, I'd like to particularly thank Nicco Athens, JM Chris Chang, Heng Du, Katie Grube, Yiyi Hsieh, Peiting C. Li, Tom Mazanec, and Stephanie Tung. For their comments on conference papers, sourcing material, and other help over the years, I'd also like to thank Peter Barber, Mark Elliott, Teresa Davis, Tineke D'Haeseleer, Andreas Eckert, Christina Florea, Luca Gabbiani, Martin Heijdra, Hansun Hsiung, Xi Ju, Lex Jing Liu, Zhenzhen Lu, William Ma, Kate Merkel-Hess, Ken Meyer, Emily Mokros, Richard Morel, Kiri Paramore, Ke Ren, Isso Shimamoto, Wang Go-Weng, Christina Welsch, Frances Wood, and Bingyu Zheng. Each one made the experience of presenting at a conference or arriving at a new archive rewarding professionally and personally in equal parts.

As this project made its way to becoming a book, numerous scholars generously offered feedback and helped to refine both my thinking and my writing. Pamela Crossley, Tobie Meyer-Fong, R. Bin Wong, Chuck Wooldridge, Peter Zarrow, and an anonymous reviewer for Columbia University Press all went out of their way to provide insightful and instructive comments. Their careful attention to the sources, scope, and significance of the research both challenged and inspired me. Peiting C. Li commented on my first conference paper in graduate school, was a frequent source of inspiration through our time in Shanghai, and, in the final stages of completing the book, generously read chapters and offered discerning comments that brought me across the finish line. Over the past several years, I have been fortunate that Xia Shi has read nearly everything I've written, and her questions and comments on sections of the final manuscript were invaluable. In Waco, Elesha Coffman, Jacqueline-Bethel Mougoué, and Dan Watkins offered frequent advice and support.

Over the years, my research has been generously supported by a variety of institutions. Funding from Princeton University and a Fulbright IIE Dissertation Research Fellowship allowed me to spend many fruitful years in archives abroad. The Baylor University College of Arts and Sciences, Stanford University Center for East Asian Studies/U.S. Department of Education International and Foreign Language Education Office, University of Chicago Center for East Asian Studies, and University of Michigan Lieberthal-Rogel Center for Chinese Studies also provided critical support. I thank them all for their trust and investment in me and their support of the project.

Sections of this book have been previously published as "Empress Dowager Cixi's Imperial Pedagogy: The School for Female Nobles and New Visions of Authority in Early Twentieth Century China," *Nan Nü: Men, Women, and Gender in China* 20, no. 2 (2018): 256-284, and "Han Chinese, Manchu, and Western Spaces: The Changing Facade of Imperial Education in Qing Beijing," *Frontiers of History in China* 14, no. 2 (2019): 212-42. I would like to thank Harriet Zurndorfer and Brill at *Nan Nü* and Limeng Weng and Higher Education Press at *Frontiers* for their permission to reuse the material here.

Even after all the years spent researching and writing, I had very little idea about what it took to produce a book. At Columbia University Press, Caelyn Cobb, Monique Briones, Marisa Lastres, and Anita O'Brien have been wonderful in guiding me through the publication process. I can't thank them enough for their expertise and patience. At the Weatherhead East Asian Institute, I owe deep thanks to Eugenia Lean and Gray Tuttle for first suggesting the series as a potential fit, and to Ariana King for patiently helping a nervous first-time author navigate the process.

Over the past several years, when I encountered roadblocks and needed words of encouragement, when I encountered success and needed prodding to celebrate, or when I didn't know what I needed, no one has been there more, or in more ways, than Christina Lee.

Finally, not a day goes by that I don't feel the love and support of my family. My parents, Ken and Harriet, my sister Rachel, and the extended Barisklewtzky clan have always believed in me, even when I couldn't see why. From the very start they trusted that my hard work would pay off and encouraged me to keep going at the times when it might have been easier to give up. Working on this project has been a great adventure, one that would have been impossible without the knowledge that they always have my back. My family never questioned my choices, from traveling around the world to spending endless hours trying to decipher handwriting from a century ago with no certainty that anything would come of it. They never pressured me to do anything else, even when it meant missing years of Seders and Super Bowl parties.

I grew up in a house overflowing with books, and I owe my family more thanks than I can do justice describing here for instilling in me a deep love of learning—even if, as they will surely tell you, it is a love that took a *long* time to develop. Having now completed my own book, nothing makes me happier than knowing the pride and joy my family will feel adding it to their shelves.

Learning to Rule

INTRODUCTION

On August 19, 1861, Weng Tonghe (1830-1904) met with friends for dinner in Beijing. One of the men at the gathering, a certain Lu Shenpei (dates unknown), told the group of the disaster recently befallen his hometown. Rebels had overrun the city, laying waste to everything in their tracks. To spare themselves the torture and indignity of submitting to the chaotic army, entire families had thrown themselves into the river to drown. Weng could hardly bear to hear the tales of such misery. That night after dinner, he wrote in his diary, "Our people are deep in an abyss of suffering, yet those in charge are at peace and know no sympathy. Destiny has brought us here. I say that there are no more capable men in the empire!"[1]

Weng came from an eminent family of officials with a long tradition of service in the Qing court, and yet his lament was emblematic of decades of growing crises—both natural and manmade—around the country, and of growing alienation between scholar-officials and the imperial house. Scholarship on the nineteenth century in China has long identified a range of issues around the turn of the century that caused unrest throughout the Qing Empire. From population growth and a growing scarcity of arable land to inflationary pressures and maladministration, a combination of what William Rowe has called "secular change" and "cyclical decline" threatened Qing rule.[2]

In part driven by these challenges, the turn of the nineteenth century also saw an increase in domestic uprisings, with revolts such as the White Lotus Rebellion stretching the capacity of the Qing state.[3] The widespread rebellions created opportunities for local gentry to take ever greater control over their communities, and reformist writings in the period increasingly stressed literati activism, with a focus on local issues. As historians have shown, this emphasis on local affairs was in part an outgrowth of strained relations between scholars and the imperial house emerging from the late Qianlong period, as many officials blamed Heshen (1750-1799) for unduly monopolizing power and undercutting scholarly influence at court.[4] In the middle of the century, adding to these challenges came the menace of imperialism from newly industrialized countries of the West, increasingly using both drugs and violence to seek profit from trade with China.[5] By midcentury, then, the Qing faced numerous threats to the security and sovereignty of its empire.

When Weng complained that the empire was in crisis and lacking leaders with the ability to respond, he thus spoke both to long-term challenges as well as more immediate emergencies. To put it simply, when Weng wrote in 1861, the Qing Empire appeared to be on the verge of collapse. Half the country was cut off from the capital as the Taiping Rebellion (1850-1864) ravaged the southern countryside and cities. Beijing, meanwhile, was on fire as an allied army of British and French forces entered the city and looted the Summer Palace. The Xianfeng emperor (r. 1850-1861) was forced to flee to an isolated mountain retreat. Just three days after Weng's lament, the emperor died and the throne was passed to his only heir, a five-year-old boy. For Weng and countless others around the empire, it seemed all was lost, and his lament might fit easily into traditional accounts of dynastic decline and the crumbling of the Qing state.

At the same time, however, Weng's life is also emblematic of another dimension of the long nineteenth century and the post-Taiping period. As officials and local leaders around the country began the arduous process of suppressing rebellions and rebuilding their communities, the enthronement of a series of young children as emperors brought debates about the course of reconstruction into the heart of the capital. Over the next fifty years, officials with divergent visions of the future all found a home inside the emperors' classroom, battling over the seeming minutiae of the curricula and scheming to exclude their intellectual and political rivals. From the amount of time allotted each day for Tongzhi (r. 1861-1875) to study Manchu language and archery to the hiring of tutors from outside the bureaucracy for Guangxu (r. 1875-1908) and the inclusion of classmates with experience studying abroad for Xuantong (r. 1908-1912), debates surrounding the education of the three late Qing emperors became proxy battles for divergent visions of how to best restabilize the country.

In fact, less than six months after Weng Tonghe bemoaned a lack of central leadership, his father, Weng Xincun (1791-1862), proudly stepped into the Forbidden

City as part of the group of scholars assembled to lead the new Tongzhi emperor's education. Each of the tutors was promised that in guiding the young emperor's schooling, they would have a chance to shape the country's future.[6] Meanwhile, scholars from around the empire were invited to participate in the emperor's education and the project of dynastic renewal, as candidates at the Palace Examination were asked what books should be added to the emperor's curriculum to train the young boy to lead the country.[7] As a tutor to both the Tongzhi and Guangxu emperors himself after his father's death, Weng Tonghe shared the classroom with allies and enemies, fighting to instill the young rulers with the knowledge, values, and skills he believed were critical for the country's future. Many from outside the bureaucracy as well sought to use Weng's connection to the emperor to gain imperial sponsorship for their ideas, as groups from reformist Chinese intellectuals to foreign powers worked to have their texts and agendas placed in the curricula of the young rulers. In the decades following his lament, Weng thus became a central figure in the effort to reinfuse the imperial center with learned and capable leaders, starting with the emperor himself.

Learning to Rule explores the ways in which, from the precarious days of the 1861 coup that brought Empress Dowager Cixi (1835–1908) to power through the early twentieth-century constitutional reform movement, the presence of young children on the throne suggested to Chinese scholars, Manchu officials, the domestic press, and foreign powers that the battle for China's future could in part be fought from inside the emperors' classroom. During their youth, when the emperors spent their time studying rather than holding audiences with high officials, the court actively presented the Tongzhi, Guangxu, and Xuantong emperors as empty vessels rival parties could fight to fill. By taking part in the youthful emperors' education, scholars hoped to create a future imperial sponsor for their program of learning and reform. Despite varying perspectives on how to restabilize the country, each group hoped to use the power of the emperor—both his functional role within the bureaucracy and his symbolic role as a model for people around the country—to promote change.

The many groups involved in the emperors' education thus worked both to bring the new texts and new fields of learning that were emerging outside the capital into the emperors' curricula and to use the example of education reforms inside court classrooms to inspire more widespread change outside the Forbidden City. Over the course of the era, the constellation of ideas surrounding court education grew as the Qing worked to infuse its rule with new forms of learning and power from around the world. In this way, court education provides a valuable new window into a cluster of intersecting trends of the late Qing. Debates about the introduction of Western learning, the fate of the Manchu Way, the place of women in society, early twentieth-century notions of constitutionalism, and emergent conceptions of national identity were all reflected in discussions surrounding the education of the final three Qing emperors.

Neither the tutors nor outside commentators believed that changes to the emperors' education were the only thing needed to rebuild the country, and many of the problems facing the Qing were outside the control of even the most powerful ruler. But, as Pierre-Étienne Will has argued, despite the many limitations on their personal power, because of the symbolic place emperors held within late imperial ideals of governance, both the personal behavior of the ruler and his knowledge of the affairs of the country and the world at large had serious ramifications for the workings of the state.[8] Yet despite a rich body of scholarship on the institutional, educational, financial, and military reforms that took place in the post-Taiping era, giving new life to the Qing while setting the stage for state-building projects of later regimes, scholarship has revealed little about how changing ideas regarding education or governance made their way into the emperors' classroom.[9] By focusing our attention on debates surrounding the appropriate texts, tutors, and rituals for the education of the three late Qing emperors, this book shows multiple conceptions of strength and stability present in the era and the ideas and policies that different groups thought were needed to revive the dynasty. Moreover, it suggests new ways to understand how the powerholders of the period, particularly Cixi, managed court politics in a changing domestic and international landscape.

As will be elaborated, the debates that run through the story of this book took place in the context of a long domestic tradition of a complex relationship between court education and ideals of rulership in China and the challenges, both structural and contingent, that relationship faced in the post-Taiping era. The education of the late Qing emperors, however, also took place in a new global age in which changing ideals of governance—notions such as constitutionalism and national identity—led to reforms in the education of leaders around the world. These were not simply changes to the curricula of princes and monarchs, but new notions of the very aim of their educations. As countries experimented with the imperial form, rulers were presented as models of new modern identities, used to teach the people what it meant to participate in emperor-centered national communities. Situating the education of the final three Qing emperors in both these contexts contributes new understandings to the post-Taiping era and the history of modern China. It also places the Qing court in conversation with other states of a late imperial world order, revealing both the flexibility and fragility of the Qing emperorship as it, along with a variety of new voices seeking power and influence, continuously renegotiated the "relationship between the ruler and the ruled" in a new age of domestic unrest and global change.[10]

COURT EDUCATION AND THE EMPERORSHIP

As Pamela Crossley has argued, Qing rule was long based on a model wherein a variety of people, institutions, and rituals—the totality of which is referred to as the emperorship—worked in concert to govern the empire.[11] Even the most powerful emperor, therefore, was only ever one part of a complex ruling structure. Though there are many other components of the system worthy of investigation, as Harold Kahn has shown for the Qianlong (r. 1735-1796) era, the education of the emperor both was an important part of the emperorship and offers historians a window into the ecosystem as a whole.[12] That is to say, for scholar-officials at the time, the personnel and texts of court classrooms provided an opportunity to guide the state and influence the emperor's understanding of his role in the system. For historians today, meanwhile, those same issues offer insight into the variety of competing beliefs regarding the appropriate balance of power between monarch and minister and what forms of learning were understood as capable of bringing order to the empire.[13]

In the tumultuous summer of 1861, when the five-year-old Tongzhi took the throne, both the emperorship and court education took on a new form, with periods of regencies granting the empress dowagers ultimate authority while the emperors were in the classroom. The regencies of the Tongzhi, Guangxu, and Xuantong eras were explicitly temporary, and the court continually promised that when the emperor came of age and completed his education, he would assume personal control over the state.[14] While in the end the emperors would hold personal power for only around ten of the fifty years under examination in this book—and thus examples of their attempts to deploy functional power in the mold of their High Qing predecessors are rare—those involved in court education continually planned for times when the emperor would indeed put his classroom lessons into practice from the throne.[15] In this way, the regencies made the classroom a vector for reform while granting Cixi and her allies additional influence via their management of court education. In the second half of the nineteenth century, therefore, the place of education in the emperorship again provides insight into how changing ideas of governance were debated and how power was distributed within the system.

To understand the debates and changes of the post-Taiping era discussed in the chapters to follow, it is therefore important to briefly trace the long history of connections between education and governance. Scholarship has long shown that court education was an important component of the emperorship in the late imperial period, playing a particularly strong role in drawing scholars into service and regulating the relationship between monarch and minister. However, historians have yet to consider the reverberations of that relationship in the post-Taiping period. By exploring these issues, *Learning to Rule* reveals how Chinese scholars and a variety of other groups drew on China's long dynastic history, the distinct customs of the Manchus, and the statecraft tools of imperial powers in the attempt to remake the emperorship.

From early in Chinese history, scholars produced specific texts and imperial courts created separate institutions for the education of emperors, not simply because there was a belief that emperors needed a special education, but also because scholars recognized the education of emperors as a unique opportunity to help shape the state.[16] Moreover, as Jack Chen has shown, once on the throne, emperors from Taizong (r. 626–649) to Qianlong worked to shape their image not only through their writings but also in the texts they produced for the education of their heirs.[17] At the same time, as the case of Qianlong makes clear, court education was also an opportunity for scholars to mold emperors. In his iconic study of eighteenth-century rulership, for example, Kahn described the multiple forces and voices that influenced the young Hongli during his education, leading the prince to create an idealized image of power that he would attempt to put into practice as the Qianlong emperor.[18]

This fusion of education and politics came together perhaps most clearly beginning in the Northern Song (960–1127) with the creation of the Classic Mat (*jingyan*), ritual performances of learning where scholar-officials presented interpretations of the Classics to the emperor.¹⁹ The texts at the heart of these lectures, particularly the *Daxue* (Great Learning), suggested an intrinsic connection between devotion to learning and good governance. The Song scholars such as Cheng Yi (1033–1107) who designed the Classic Mat argued that since the emperor was not naturally more virtuous than the common people, he had a responsibility to surround himself with scholar-officials and listen to their teachings in carrying out governance of the empire.²⁰ Thus, as Marie Guarino argues, the Classic Mat saw the inauguration of a "new conception of political authority that bound the legitimacy of the emperor's political authority to his personal effort to become a learned individual."²¹ This idea continued into the Ming dynasty (1368–1644). Under the Ming, as scholar-officials and the emperor navigated an often-times thorny (and violent) relationship of power sharing, Classic Mats were held twice a year. And, as Chu Hung-lam has shown, as each side sought to advance its views via interpretations of classical texts, the lectures "were not purely educational, not merely learning sessions devoted to the classics and histories," but in fact "revealed tensions in the ethics of government."²²

The Qing adopted and adapted this model from the Song and Ming, leaving their own mark on the Classic Mat as the Manchu rulers negotiated their relationship not only with Chinese scholar-officials but also with the throne's other constituencies, particularly the Manchu and Mongolian communities. Qing Classic Mats, for example, added sacrifices to Manchu ancestors alongside Confucius as well as Manchu-language lectures to those delivered by Chinese scholars.²³ Starting in the Shunzhi reign (1644–1661), Qing emperors held Classic Mat sessions 184 times before mid-nineteenth-century crises disrupted the practice.²⁴

While the Classic Mat sanctioned the right of scholars to participate in governance and largely positioned the emperor as student, discourses of political legitimacy in late imperial China also suggested that the emperor played a key role as teacher, the ultimate arbiter of classical knowledge and an exemplar for the realm. Ming texts, for example, said that the dynasty's founder, Zhu Yuanzhang (1328–1398), "was not just a ruler; he was also a teacher . . . the first ruler-teacher to govern China since the golden age of antiquity itself."²⁵ Therefore, while the Classic Mat provided scholars an opportunity to take the leading role, other occasions, such as Imperial Lecture (*linyong jiangxue*), reversed the position and placed the emperor at the center.

The Imperial Lecture originated in the Ming and was an opportunity for selected high officials to present an interpretation of a passage from the Classics, but, more important, for the emperor himself to deliver an authoritative explication to an audience representative of the full body politic of the empire.[26] The lecture was attended by members of the imperial family, officials from all departments within the government, students from imperially sponsored schools, examination candidates in the capital, descendants of Confucius and other ancient sages, and many others. At a lecture by Qianlong in 1785, for example, several thousand officials and over three thousand students gathered to hear the emperor's teachings in which Qianlong described his efforts at moral cultivation as an example for future generations.[27] For the Manchu rulers, seeking to assert their authority over the bureaucracy, the Imperial Lectures were critical milestones in articulating the power of a newly enthroned emperor, and the court worked to arrange the event at the beginning of each new reign.

The long history of court education thus makes clear that, despite professions of their own grandeur, emperors in late imperial China functioned within a volatile system of power sharing with scholar-officials, what historians in recent years have begun to refer to as China's constitutional system.[28] Over the course of the late imperial era, scholars and the emperor thus battled for power and control in what Phillip Kuhn relatedly terms the "bureaucratic monarchy."[29] In this fight, education often played an important role, and scholars worked to increase their power in affairs of state in part by advancing interpretations of the Classics that privileged their role as mentors to the throne. For scholars beginning with Zhu Xi (1130–1200), the phrase "the learning of the emperor" (*diwang zhi xue*) thus came to symbolize the importance of scholarly guidance of imperial action, providing lessons from history that would enable the ruler to perpetuate good governance around the empire while providing scholars the opportunity to shape the emperors' very notion of what good governance entailed.[30]

NINETEENTH-CENTURY FLEXIBILITY AND FRAGILITY

Yet, as discussed earlier, at the turn of the nineteenth century scholar-officials increasingly directed their attention to local affairs as the Jiaqing (r. 1796–1820) and Daoguang (r. 1820–1850) era courts ceded significant authority to literati in managing their communities.[31] With the influence and power of the court seemingly in a position of irreversible decline at the start of the century, historians have thus largely looked to the provinces for the roots of both the reform and revolution that came in the decades that followed.[32] Contrasting the long-standing connections between court education and imperial power with the epochal changes of the nineteenth century, Kahn therefore wrote that after Qianlong, "never again would the emperor, and hence his education, be at the center of Chinese history."[33] This book suggests the need to rethink that perspective.

Critically, many of the same scholars who argued for literati activism were also adamant that the emperorship and constitutional system worked only with a charismatic and virtuous throne at the center.[34] Their own power was legitimated through the emperor, and throughout the nineteenth century scholars simultaneously pushed to expand their influence while rebuilding the throne. When Xianfeng came to power in 1850, for example, scholars took the opportunity to argue for a more robust educational apparatus at court to ensure that they would play a central role in governance. Scholars called on Xianfeng to devote himself to the study of the Classics, with officials such as Zeng Guofan (1811-1872) arguing for a revival of the Kangxi (r. 1661-1722) era practice of Daily Lectures (*rijiang*) in the palace.[35] Zeng said that although Kangxi had held the lectures for many years, if Xianfeng did them for just a short time and concentrated on his education and moral cultivation, peace and order would return to the empire.[36]

Throughout his reign, Xianfeng indeed sought to draw on the traditional institutions of court education to both solidify his relationship with officials and repair the authority of the throne, holding both Classic Mats and Imperial Lectures despite the frequent threat of war and rebellion. After several decades of tumult in the provinces—and a childhood education in which his tutor Du Shoutian (1788-1852) had repeatedly stressed the threat of foreign powers on the coasts—Xianfeng saw court education as an important component of the project to stabilize Qing rule.[37] In response to Zeng Guofan's call for Daily Lectures, for example, the newly enthroned emperor said that after the mandated period of mourning for his father, he would immediately reinstate the practice, dormant since the Kangxi era.[38] Surrounding himself with the empire's most renowned scholars and donning the garb of both teacher and student, Xianfeng sought to rebuild the throne and restore order to the empire.[39]

Yet Xianfeng would be the last emperor to hold the Classic Mat or deliver an Imperial Lecture. His reign was in many ways characterized by an acceleration of the rise of local interests and the regionalization of military power during the

Taiping Rebellion. Even with the suppression of the Taipings, the youth of the final three Qing emperors, each coming to the throne before the age of six, forced changes to the traditional institutions of court education and its connection to the rest of the emperorship. Throughout the post-Taiping era, scholars frequently argued (to no avail) for a revival of the Classic Mat and other rituals and institutions designed to guarantee their place as mentors to the throne. The absence of such events in the context of expanding provincial power bases perhaps suggests that the emperorship itself "no longer functioned."[40] Despite these challenges, however, the presence of children on the throne in fact provided new opportunities for scholars to help guide the state and remake both the emperorship and empire.

At the very start of the Tongzhi era, the court issued an edict that suggests a focus on court education may shed light on a variety of efforts undertaken to stabilize and rebuild the country. Writing in the young Tongzhi's name, the court said, "I have ascended the throne at a young age. It is therefore especially important that I devote myself day and night to my studies."[41] In the meantime, the edict said, scholar-officials should prepare texts for the empress dowagers, explaining the history of other female-led courts throughout Chinese history. The court presented an image of rule that would draw on the expertise of scholars and knowledge of history to inculcate virtue and wisdom in both the emperor and empress dowagers. For the moment, the empress dowagers would lead the fight to restore the country, but the emperor would soon take his rightful place at the head of the system. This rhetoric was repeated throughout the Tongzhi, Guangxu, and Xuantong reigns, as the court consistently described the emperors' childhood education as the basis of imperial achievement, good governance, and the health of the empire. Through all the turmoil of the era, the court told the country that the emperor and his teachers were diligently working to mold him into a virtuous leader.

Moreover, in an era of an expanding repertoire of fields of learning and debates about how to balance traditional texts with new knowledge, the court invited such discussions into the emperorship through the emperors' classroom. In announcing the start of the Tongzhi era, the court promised that scholars, regardless of previous appointment, would be considered for a job as imperial tutor, given the chance to convince the emperor to embrace their vision of the future, and allowed to help lead a top-down reform movement.⁴² This open call to service was part of the larger process of coalition building and balancing of competing factions that would come to define much of the era.⁴³ By involving competing constituencies in decisions surrounding the emperor's education, Cixi and her allies shifted the power aspirations of different factions from the present to the future, drawing adversarial groups into service of the court and the project of dynastic reconstruction. Meanwhile, the presence of these competing voices and the multiple forces trying to shape the emperors led to a volatile politics surrounding court education, and battles in the classroom threatened the stability of the emperorship on multiple occasions throughout the era—not to mention producing an often times rocky pedagogy as the tutors fought among themselves.

Over the course of the next several decades, the education of young emperors thus not only became a battleground for traditional scholars but also provided new groups an opportunity to attack those very same scholar-officials and argue for alternative visions of the future. Throughout the period, a growing range of voices writing in the burgeoning domestic press proposed curricular reforms and claimed the right to pass judgment on imperial tutors. These new intellectuals sought to reform the emperor's education such that he would break free from what they described as the influence of conservative officials. For those outside of power, the emperor's personal education came to be seen as a potential launching pad for countrywide reform projects, using imperial modeling and sponsorship of new programs of learning to bypass perceived obstacles in the traditional bureaucracy. Foreign powers as well sought to use the emperor's education to enhance their influence in the country, encouraging the emperor to study English and other subjects of Western learning to enable him to cast aside advisors and translators and personally engage with the foreign community.

Critically as well for our understanding of the era, it was not just scholar-officials or reformist Chinese intellectuals who sought to mold the young emperors in their image or use them for their political projects. Manchu officials too worked to reassert the martial prowess of the early Qing by creating curricula for Tongzhi, Guangxu, and Xuantong that focused on mastering Manchu, Mongolian, and mounted archery. These proposals were grounded in early Qing conceptions of rulership that posited a direct connection between individual proficiency in the "Manchu Way" (a matrix of skills and values such as Manchu language proficiency, archery, horseback riding, and frugality) and the survival of the dynasty.⁴⁴ Moreover, as Edward Rhoads has shown, the post-Taiping period saw a newfound importance of imperial princes in the workings of the state, and in arguing for a revival of the Manchu Way in the emperors' curriculum, officials sought to present the emperor as model to the imperial family (and Manchu community as a whole) to prepare them for the roles they were to play in rebuilding the empire.[45]

Despite the challenges facing the Bannerman community in the era, the court consistently described Manchu as the "root of the dynasty" in plans for the education of the late Qing emperors, and the Manchu tutors fought bitterly throughout the period to increase their time in the classroom and influence at court. By revealing the continued importance of Manchu learning and identity to court education, *Learning to Rule* thus builds on the insights of a generation of scholarship highlighting not just early Qing conceptions of a distinct Manchu culture but the continual importance of those ideas throughout the latter course of the dynasty.[46] Thus, counter to the classic understanding produced by Mary Wright, the reconstruction of the Tongzhi Restoration period cannot be understood as simply a "Chinese" project, as debates around court education show the resilience of the ideals of the Manchu Way in the post-Taiping era.[47]

In this period of regencies dominated by Cixi, court education also offers new insights into the power of the empress dowager. Although the regencies were defined as temporary, Cixi's role in both the private operation and public image of the emperorship grew over the period. As scholars have previously shown, Cixi had a talent for building and rebuilding coalitions and balancing factions.[48] With young emperors in the classroom, control over the appointment of tutors was another tool in her toolbox. In addition, Cixi worked to co-opt the language and rituals of court education for her own purposes. By holding lectures for herself at court, she drew scholars into service by offering them an opportunity to serve as her tutors. The publication of these efforts and the attempt to distill a narrative of devotion to learning, meanwhile, worked to undercut political opponents by positioning Cixi as an honorable inheritor to a long tradition of sage rulership in China.

Throughout the period as she sought new forms of power, Cixi positioned herself as a patron of multiple fields of learning, from Manchu and Mongolian to the Chinese Classics and Western learning. Particularly in the decade after the abortive 1898 reforms, Cixi actively worked to place herself not just at the center of politics but also at the forefront of a new image of the Qing state. Through personal diplomacy, painting and photography, and the promotion of female education, she presented herself as the leader of a new type of empire, one that drew its strength not only from the domestic intellectual traditions of the Manchu Way and Confucian Canon but also from a global language of modern governance. At the start of the twentieth century this was a language that included both examples of strong female leaders and an increasing attention to widespread female education. A focus on Cixi's participation in court education thus also suggests the need to reevaluate the role of the court in expanding educational opportunities for women around the turn of the twentieth century.

The growing presence of Cixi in public presentations of the emperorship also highlights how, despite contentious struggles inside the classroom, by investing in the education of young rulers, scholar-officials, intellectuals, and foreign powers gradually magnified the imperial family as symbols of potential unity around the country. Scholar-officials had long argued that court education was an important link between the throne and bureaucracy, but in the late nineteenth century, as the Qing studied the nationalizing monarchies of countries such as Japan and Germany, they also began to argue that court education should play a role in uniting the people. Particularly in the aftermath of the Sino-Japanese War of 1894-1895, a wide range of writers suggested that the emperor's curriculum should be modernized so that he could be presented to the country as a model of reform. Later, with the creation of the national school system and the transition to a constitutional monarchy, writers argued both for a new curriculum for the emperor and new rituals for schoolchildren to help teach ruler and ruled how to participate in an emperor-centered national community.

COURT AND COUNTRY IN POST-TAIPING CHINA

In this way, *Learning to Rule* adds to our understanding of modern China by highlighting how changing ideas of education and governance intersected with a push for a renewed imperial center and national unity after decades of unrest. In this era of dramatic change, few have in fact considered the place of the emperor. In contrast to the rich body of scholarship on the Qing emperorship in earlier eras, we know comparatively little about court life in the final decades of Qing rule.[49] As Mariame Bastid describes, "Victim of the disrepute which befell the institutions of a fallen regime, the function of the emperor during the last decades of the Qing dynasty, after the Taiping Rebellion, has rarely been the object of scholarly research."⁵⁰ In her own study of the gradual secularization and statutization of imperial authority, Bastid notes that, as had often been the case in eras long past, "for high officials at the end of the Qing, the essential role of the Son of Heaven was to preserve the unity of the country."⁵¹ But how was he to do that? Ho-fung Hung has recently suggested that despite the many crises of the first decades of the nineteenth century, the "moral legitimacy" of the emperor had in fact recovered from its late eighteenth-century nadir, and others have shown that an idealized figure of the emperor remained a powerful symbol in uniting people during times of war and famine well into the latter parts of the dynasty.⁵² Yet few have built on Bastid's project of exploring the place of the emperor in the post-Taiping period, and despite recent scholarship revealing unexpected successes in the recentralization of power, provincial identities and local leaders still dominate our understanding of the era.⁵³

This book is indeed indebted to a rich field of scholarship on the post-Taiping period that has revealed an expansive group of leaders and intellectuals who drove policy changes around the country. Much of that scholarship, and this book as well, is inspired by a perhaps simple question: in the face of the environmental, social, and economic ravages of the first half of the nineteenth century, how did the Qing Empire manage to survive and, in some cases, resolidify its power? Mary Wright was the first to seriously explore this topic, arguing that a nearly miraculous recovery and reunification around the imperial center took place in the 1860s thanks to the ways in which officials "rallied around the lately discredited throne with virtually unanimous loyalty."⁵⁴ As she wrote, the "Chinese emperor was always more important as a function than as a personality," and in this new era, according to Wright, simply an occupied throne was enough to bring "men of outstanding ability" to positions of high authority and undertake the work of restoring order and unity.⁵⁵ Building on this insight, scholars have subsequently produced a rich literature on this postwar generation of powerful Chinese officials—as well as other forces such as the interests of foreign powers and the court's efforts to win domestic loyalty by conflating its own interests and identity with those of the larger Chinese population—that helped to prop up the dynasty.⁵⁶

Yet at the same time, Pamela Crossley has brilliantly shown how the story of modern China can in fact be examined without much reference to the court in the post-Taiping era. Focusing instead on "regional power structures" such as the Beiyang Intendancy and leaders such as Li Hongzhang (1823-1901) and Yuan Shikai

(1859-1916), Crossley reveals the centrality of new provincial institutions and organizations to the economic, political, and military innovations of the period.[57] An outgrowth of empowering local militias and local decision-making in the process of suppressing the Taipings, these new leaders outside the court then led a variety of reconstruction efforts in the postwar period, effectively creating "a new regional state within the empire."[58] These local powers only grew over the course of the post-Taiping period. Much scholarship has therefore suggested that this dynamic, and the ways in which the provincial interests of an expanding group of activists around the country clashed with those of the imperial court, would eventually destroy the dynasty.[59]

While Crossley's approach differs from that of Wright in that it highlights a devolution of central power and moves our focus away from the imperial center and toward the "militarization" of local power, the two in fact share a foundational assumption that the emperor, unlike in earlier eras of the Qing, was not a part of the post-Taiping story.[60] This idea is further explored by Prasenjit Duara, who shows that the imperial state was only one component of the power structure in Chinese, particularly rural Chinese, society, and even powerful figures such as Yuan Shikai had to negotiate with other claimants to authority when pushing reforms.[61] Finally, focusing on the epochal intellectual changes of the era, scholars such as Peter Zarrow have shown how thinkers and activists outside the court or traditional bureaucracy such as Kang Youwei (1858-1927) and Liang Qichao (1873-1929) challenged the very notion of the dynastic state.[62]

This study suggests not that the historiographic focus on men such as Li, Yuan, or Kang is misguided in delineating the power dynamics of the era or in uncovering the source of new intellectual ideas, but rather that, to date, scholarship presents an incomplete picture of how those men sought to deploy their power or spread their ideas in projects of reform. By exploring court education, this book shows how those very same men and many more like them sought to use both the empirical power of the throne in the bureaucratic state and the symbolic power of the emperor in the country's culture to promote change. Be it Prince Chun (1840-1891) urging Tongzhi to master Manchu language and archery so he could model behavior to the Bannermen community (chapter 2), or Yan Fu (1854-1921) suggesting that Guangxu study abroad and bring back the best practices of states from around the world to help transform China the way Peter the Great (1672-1725) had Russia (chapter 3), scholars and officials in the post-Taiping period believed that an emperor who embraced a set of teachings could both demand change through the ink of his imperial edicts and inspire change through his personal example. Thus, while taking the initiative to rebuild their local communities and accumulating vast regional military and economic power, scholars and officials simultaneously sought to enlist the emperor in the fight, hoping he would adopt a program of learning and use all forms of his power to initiate countrywide reforms from the capital.

Put another way, the focus of scholars and intellectuals on the emperor in the post-Taiping period was a component of the larger project to "reform the people" through education.[63] A wealth of scholarship has shown how the development of new educational institutions in the second half of the nineteenth century and the Qing attempt to build a national school system in the first decade of the twentieth century were born from a desire to create a citizenry with both the technical skills and patriotic sentiments needed to make the county strong.[64] As Roger Thompson succinctly described in his study of local councils and regional leaders, "as the twentieth century began, the Chinese government, through administrative, political, and educational reforms, tried to transform the emperor's subjects into a constitutional monarch's citizens."[65] This late Qing project was then expanded on by the Republic, which, as scholars such as Robert Culp and Henrietta Harrison have shown, saw the creation of patriotic citizens as one of the core aims of Republican education.[66] Yet, as with other reforms of the late nineteenth century, scholarship has largely focused attention on how these changes spread in communities outside of the capital.[67] *Learning to Rule* shows that not only did these same ideas influence the emperors' education, but many saw the creation of a modern monarch as a critical step in the production of the nation. The subjects of a multiethnic empire needed to learn how to be citizens of a nation, but so too did the emperor need to learn how to be a constitutional monarch. A history of court education thus also provides new insights into the broader history of education and citizenry in China.

For example, as Wen-hsin Yeh described in her majestic study of Republican-era higher education, when the Qing court established the School of Combined Learning (Tongwen Guan) in 1862, the decision raised the ire of many high officials in the capital. Yeh lays out how this opposition was "led by Woren, the Mongol Neo-Confucian moralist, tutor to the emperor, head of the Hanlin Academy, and president of several of the Six Boards in succession."[68] In Woren's long list of government positions, it is his job as tutor to the emperor that invites a closer examination of court education. As chapter 1 shows, Woren used his position in the emperor's classroom to fight the spread of Western learning and advocate for a curriculum for the young ruler that sought to mold him into the image of a traditional sage-king. Yet many of Woren's colleagues in the classroom and the bureaucracy, as well as intellectuals writing in the press, had other ideas, and they fought to fuse Western learning with the Classics in court education. In effect, they sought to make the emperor's classroom a miniature Tongwen Guan and a laboratory for a new type of hybrid education for both ruler and ruled that would help make the country strong. Thus, while Yeh suggests it was not until decades later in the modern school system that topics such as foreign languages and science were fused with Chinese and the Classics in a single curriculum, *Learning to Rule* shows how that process in fact first took place in court education, and how those involved in the process imagined themselves as both training a modern monarch and setting the mold for the creation of a new citizenry.[69]

The perspective on the dynamic among scholars, the press, and the throne provided by an examination of court education thus adds a new dimension to our understanding of the late Qing as well as research focused on state-building across revolutionary divides, showing how local reform projects were woven into a national framework of reconstruction. While officials worked to rebuild the institutions of governance around the empire, they simultaneously sought to cultivate the emperor and restore a powerful presence to the throne who could sponsor their programs and lead through his example. As scholars from Wright on have shown, the field of actors involved in reform projects beginning in the Tongzhi era expanded in part because of the youth of the emperor.[70] What this book uniquely shows, however, is the special place court education held in that process, as competing groups sought to influence the future of the Qing in part by molding those young emperors in their image. Throughout, the book suggests that the post-Taiping era was not simply a time of dynastic decline but also one of dynastic reinvention.

PERFORMING RULERSHIP IN THE LATE IMPERIAL WORLD

At the turn of the twentieth century the Japanese statesman Itō Hirobumi (1841–1909) said of his own royal family, "It is really very hard luck to be born a crown prince. Directly he comes into the world he is swaddled in etiquette, and when he gets a little bigger he has to dance to the fiddling of his tutors and advisors."[71] Much as Itō observed about Japan in the Meiji era, court education in China had long sought to control as much as it did empower, as scholar-officials worked to create an emperor who, as Gu Yanwu (1613-1682) had once put it, was a "cultural giant" but a "political dwarf."[72] In the post-Taiping era, this long-standing negotiation over imperial power was first joined with debates in the Tongzhi and early Guangxu periods about how to balance multiple fields of learning in the effort to restabilize the country, and then in the late nineteenth and early twentieth centuries by efforts to join the global movement to nationalize monarchies. Throughout, multiple groups sought to shape the future of the country in part by pulling the strings of court education. This book suggests, therefore, that although the monarchy is often seen as incompatible with political modernity, an emphasis on the figure of the emperor rightly places the Qing within a global movement to transform dynastic sovereignty for the modern era.[73]

In the post-Taiping period, Chinese and Manchu officials were in fact not the only participants in the effort to rebuild the Qing and gain influence through the emperors' education. Foreign powers—invested in the survival of the Qing to preserve their own interests—were often the most enthusiastic promotors of emperor-centered reform. As James Hevia has argued, the foreign powers "thought of imperialism and colonialism as pedagogical processes, one made up of teaching and learning by means of gun and pen."[74] In attempting to teach China how to behave in this European world, foreign powers sought access to the young emperors, hoping to transform them into allies and advocates.

For many of those seeking to influence late Qing emperors and mold them into willing participants in the Western world order, Emperor Meiji (r. 1868-1912) of Japan was a frequent object of comparison. Long before Japan defeated China in the 1894-1895 Sino-Japanese War, foreign commentators pointed to changes in Japanese court education as evidence of a reforming state.[75] Newspapers in China as well frequently reported on the educational activities of the Japanese imperial family, and Meiji was lauded as an example not just of changes in personal education but also in creating new links between ruler and ruled. Foreign commentators suggested that China should learn from both of these changes, and when rumors began to circulate that the emperor of Japan might visit China, the *North China Herald* (*NCH*) enthusiastically supported the idea of Meiji visiting Guangxu, saying that "it will result in a pro-Asiatic alliance for the conservation of the integrity of China and Japan, and that the Emperor of Japan may be able to persuade his brother at Peking to come out of his Palace and see something of the outside world."⁷⁶ The *NCH* did not simply argue that Guangxu should embrace new forms of learning. Rather, it suggested that he should be publicly paraded as a model of modern education and national unity. If Guangxu could be transformed into a symbol of the nation and encourage reform, the paper argued, then China would be stable and foreign privileges secure.

The focus on the education and public presentation of these emperors speaks to a global late imperial moment wherein imperial families were invested with new forms of symbolic power as their political influence waned. Although ideas of popular sovereignty and expanded political participation spread widely across the century, even at the start of World War One, Europe was home to only three republics, and the Qing existed in a world dominated by nationalizing monarchies.⁷⁷ In the late nineteenth and early twentieth centuries, emperors across the world were being removed from the inner workings of the state and elevated above it as sites of unity. What David Cannadine has called a "cavalcade of impotence" in Britain and Takashi Fujitani has described as the "Splendid Monarchy" of Japan saw the imperial family invested with new symbolism in the attempt to construct a national identity.⁷⁸ Abandoning court robes for military uniforms and parading around their countries, monarchies looked to remold the underpinnings of their authority and fashion a new image that embraced the knowledge and styles of the modern world. The project clearly did not work everywhere, as Jeroen Duindam has observed, and in Europe monarchies were upheld as the enemies of the nation as often as they were lauded as its symbol.⁷⁹ Yet in each context the emperor as symbol of the nation was a modern creation, not a timeless tradition.⁸⁰

Here, too, a focus on court education helps to reveal many of the dynamics of the era. As states embarked on projects to centralize and nationalize education systems and project new images of power, a reeducated imperial center was a powerful tool in presenting a model for the country. Just as "peasants" had to be taught to become "Frenchmen," so too did the kaiser, the tsar, and the emperor need to learn to be German, Russian, or Japanese.⁸¹ In Russia, for example, princely education took a sharp turn toward emphasizing the national myth at the expense of engagement with European intellectual traditions.⁸² In Germany, the future Kaiser Wilhelm II (1859–1941), after a strict course in Greek and Latin, spent time in public school in order to understand the "thoughts and feelings" of the people he would one day lead.⁸³ Emperor Meiji, meanwhile, after a thorough education in the Confucian Classics, began to read Samuel Smiles's *Self Help* in 1871 as part of

Westernizing education reforms.[84] In each case the newly educated monarch was presented to the country as an example to follow and as a symbol of national unity. In countries such as Japan and Siam, the project took on an additional layer of importance as court education reforms were meant not just to foment unity among the domestic population but also to position the countries as participants in a Western world order as a defense against imperialism.[85]

The Qing court was not a passive recipient of this pedagogy. The efforts to stabilize Qing rule were an active engagement with both Manchu and Chinese conceptions of rulership and the contemporary world of imperial statecraft and knowledge regimes. That is to say, in an era of imperialism, learning to rule increasingly came to include not only studying from an expanded set of texts but also learning the forms and styles of European monarchies.[86] In particular, in the years following the Sino-Japanese War, some Chinese intellectuals increasingly argued that the emperor's education should bring him out from inside the classroom and into the lives of the people of his empire. In the early Qing, emperors had in fact toured the empire and presented themselves as the center of authority as part of what Michael Chang has described as the attempt of ethnically infused "patrimonial domination" over the Chinese bureaucracy.[87] But these events produced as much backlash as power. By the nineteenth century, as much of the world was busy watching imperial parades, the Qing had explicitly rejected public displays of pageantry. This was a victory for Confucian scholars and a point of pride for many officials. As Zhang Zhidong (1837–1909) wrote in 1898, in the past emperors would travel around the empire at great expense to the people of the realm, but now Qing emperors worked diligently in the palace, leaving only when necessary to inspect public works.[88]

Despite his preference for this more private sovereign, however, Zhang was concerned by what he saw as a paradox: Western rulers, he said, were not as virtuous or benevolent as Qing emperors, yet people in China did not love their sovereign as much as those in the West loved theirs.[89] How could the people be made aware of the emperor's benevolence and virtue without the costs and hardships associated with tours of the empire? For Zhang, the long-standing ideal in China of the emperor as patron of education offered an answer. If the emperor embraced educational reforms for himself, he could then be presented to the country as a model and a rallying point for reform. In edicts and announcements regarding his education, and in the ceremonies invented to celebrate his studies, the emperor's classroom thus became analogous to what Fujitani has called in the context of Japan a "mnemonic site"; that is, "material vehicles of meaning that either helped construct a memory of an emperor-centered national past that, ironically, had never been known or served as symbolic markers for commemorations of present national accomplishments and the possibilities of the future."[90] And as in Japan, where students were frequently called on to line the streets for imperial parades and ceremonies, so too in the final decades of the Qing did the court seek to bind students and emperor in the production of a national community.[91]

As the editors of the *World's Chinese Students' Journal* (*Huanqiu Zhongguo xuesheng bao*) wrote in 1909, "Happy is that nation whose ruler is a true statesman and possesses those essential powers conducive to the well being of a country"—men, the journal said, like George Washington, Peter the Great, Napoleon, Meiji, and Kangxi.[92] The students were writing at the start of the Xuantong era amid debates over the young emperor's education in a time of constitutional transition and multiple threats to the safety and sovereignty of the country. In many ways, however, they echoed the complaints of scholars such as Weng Tonghe from fifty years earlier, bemoaning the current crop of high officials and urging the employment of men of talent under the leadership of the new emperor. Were this to happen, they said, China might yet be able to accomplish the "Herculean task" of building a "modern nation."[93] The calls for Xuantong to lead like Kangxi or Meiji were thus not simply about increasing the autocratic power of the throne. Rather, they suggested that the country needed an emperor with a broad education and trained in the ways of the world; one who could push change through the bureaucracy, but also one who would provide a model at the center for the people to emulate in their own educations. With a young emperor taking the Qing throne, this was a model—the students hoped—they might help to shape.

ORGANIZATION OF THE BOOK

This book is not a comprehensive history of the late Qing. It does not suggest that the emperors' education was the only component of the attempt to rebuild in the aftermath of the Taiping Rebellion, nor that there were not many groups simultaneously working to upend Qing rule and overthrow the dynasty. A focus on court education, however, helps to highlight several key dynamics of the post-Taiping period, including a push for a renewed imperial center after years of turmoil, the incorporation of new fields of learning into Qing conceptions of governance, and the attempt to construct an imperial-centered national identity. This was not a smooth process, and the many battles fought within the emperors' classroom were emblematic of both long-standing tensions within Qing rule and new challenges of the era. As scholarship on the post-Taiping period has noted, however, many officials believed that reforms at court and removing rival scholars were essential to the success of other projects of reconstruction.[94] *Learning to Rule* shows how many of those same officials saw the education of the emperor as an opportunity to advance these causes, claiming power for themselves while helping to rebuild the country.

To explore how the personnel shifts and curricular battles of the emperors' classroom were connected to broader changes around the country, this book proceeds chronologically from the ascension of the Tongzhi emperor in 1861 through the Qing abdication edict signed in 1912. It draws on a broad range of sources, including the diaries of Qing officials, archival materials related to the staffing of classrooms, public pronouncements from the court such as edicts, as well as newspapers and journals in both the Chinese and international press. Over the course of the book, the chapters highlight themes such as the perceived malleability of youth, the importance of female regency as a form of rule in the post-Taiping period, the increased public visibility of the emperors' education, the place of foreign models in education reforms, an expansion of actors seeking to claim a role in influencing court education, and an evolving perception of the relative importance of the emperor's education for his empirical and symbolic roles in the state.

Chapter 1 opens with the death of the Xianfeng emperor and examines how, amid civil war and factional infighting, the empress dowagers reached out to a range of ideological and political factions, who in turn sought to transform the young emperor into a symbol of divergent visions of the country's rejuvenation. Whereas the post-1861 emperorship defined the emperors' youthful education as a period of regency with power vested in the empress dowagers, the chapter begins by examining Cixi's efforts to embrace the rituals and language of classical education, cultivating an image of a female sage-ruler. In all these efforts, the past was key, as scholars and imperial leaders drew on the history of earlier eras in China when female-led regencies had guided the state while the emperor pursued his studies to justify the new Cixi-dominated emperorship. All the while, the chapter shows how the young emperor's classroom became a volatile site of competition between advocates of Chinese, Manchu, and Western learning.

Chapter 2 examines how, although Tongzhi disappointed his teachers and alienated many in the bureaucracy, his death in 1875 created an opportunity to once again imbue a young and malleable emperor with new forms of learning. As new ideas and technologies flowed into China, Tongzhi's failings could have depleted the emperorship of its political valence. Yet despite the challenges of the previous decade, there was hope that the Guangxu emperor would help rejuvenate the dynasty. That hope was largely premised on the frequent analogy to the reign of another child who had come to power in tumultuous times, the Kangxi emperor. A flood of commentary in the 1870s argued that the threats of the current day were similar to those faced by Kangxi, and that it was in part the young emperor's multifaceted education that had enabled him to bring peace to the empire. Unlike in Kangxi's era, however, debates over the content of Guangxu's education took place in full public view, as an enlivened domestic press joined scholars at court in arguing over the primacy of different subjects in the emperor's curriculum. Intellectuals outside the government made use of new tools of communication in an attempt to sideline the bureaucracy by presenting the emperor with new knowledge, encouraging him to embrace a wide range of teachings and then take direct action to lead the country. In the early Guangxu era, then, the discourse of the emperor's education became the focus of national and international conversations.

Chapter 3 analyzes the early years of Guangxu's personal rule and examines the challenges that arose as the now adult emperor sought to put his lessons into practice and as the Qing faced a new set of challenges. In particular, the emperor's decision in 1891 to study English sent waves through the bureaucracy and challenged the power of many within the government. Then, in the aftermath of the Sino-Japanese War, proposals for Guangxu to study abroad placed court education firmly at the center of national politics. These calls were part of the larger program of reforms during the summer of 1898, a hundred-day period that ended with the removal of Guangxu from power and the emergence of Cixi as the dominant public face of the emperorship.

Chapter 4 covers the final decade of both Guangxu's and Cixi's lives, examining the post-Boxer attempt to integrate the Qing into a global community of monarchies. Having sidelined Guangxu (and temporarily replaced him with another malleable heir), Cixi's personal diplomacy and image were key to this project. Equally important was the Qing promise to transition into a constitutional monarchy and the effort to establish schools to educate a new group of Qing noblewomen as symbols of a refashioned imperial authority and vanguards in the construction of a Qing national community. By creating a hybrid education for nobles and expanding the role of women in the state, the court sought to ground its legitimacy not only in Manchu and Confucian traditions but also in a transnational language of modern rulership. With the creation of the national school system as well, the court worked to teach students around the country about their connection to Cixi and other members of the imperial family, hoping to build new forms of loyalty for the coming constitutional monarchy.

Chapter 5 takes the narrative through the final years of the dynasty, the short reign of the Xuantong emperor. Even as assassination attempts and revolutionary plots unfolded around the country, a vigorous debate took place surrounding the design of the young emperor's education. Integrating Manchu and Chinese traditions with foreign models of court education, the Qing debated adding classmates with experience studying abroad, teachers with foreign degrees, and other reforms to transform Xuantong into a constitutional monarch. To bring the young monarch into the lives of his subjects, the court also created new rituals for the start of Xuantong's education, teaching not just Xuantong to be an emperor but people around the country what it meant to be a part of the new constitutional monarchy.

The conclusion highlights the long-standing connection between court education and governance in Chinese history and the ways in which the challenges of the post-Taiping era affected that relationship. By focusing on the late imperial discourse of the "learning of the emperor," the conclusion suggests some of the ways in which attention to court education can thus shed light not only on the specific question of the emperors' education but also on broader themes of modern China, including the relationship between emperor and nation. In particular, I explore the curious postimperial life of Puyi (1906–1967) and the many regimes which sought to reeducate the former emperor in the hopes of deploying him as a symbol of their cause.

The cover of this book shows a print issued by a Japanese publishing company in 1910 celebrating the recent ascension of Puyi to the Qing throne as the Xuantong emperor. In the center of the picture, he is flanked on either side by Empress Dowager Longyu (1868–1912) and Prince Regent Zaifeng (1883–1951) as a large group of officials stand in the foreground. The upper-right corner shows a portion of a plaque that was hung in the Palace of Heavenly Purity (Qianqing gong) with calligraphy written by Qianlong, copying his grandfather Kangxi's script. The phrase is an allusion to passages from the *Shangshu* (*Classic of History*) that describe the emperor as a model for the entire world and therefore urge him to be wholeheartedly devoted to his education and moral cultivation.[95]

This, in many ways, is the story at the heart of the book. Scholarly focus on the emperor was driven by a variety of forces, and the attention on him and his education was multidimensional. In part, it was propelled by his functional role in the bureaucracy and his ability to, à la Qianlong, insert his will and effect change from his pen.[96] But it was also driven in part by his symbolic role throughout the empire. The emperor had always been, as the phrase from the *Shangshu* suggested, a model for the people. But this idea gained new significance in the post-Taiping era (and particularly in the aftermath of the Sino-Japanese War), as the Qing looked to the example of other countries where reeducated emperors had been effectively used as icons of reforming imperial regimes. Although the print celebrating Puyi's ascension is not indicative of the balance of power in the late Qing as it erases the role of provincial leaders in driving many of the changes of the era, it nonetheless suggests an opportunity to reflect more fully on the place of the emperor, the court, and education in the culture and politics of modern China. *Learning to Rule* is my attempt to do just that.

1

NEW FORMS OF LEARNING FOR A NEW AGE OF IMPERIAL RULE, 1861–1874

Early in 1862, Woren (1804–1871), a Mongol official and 1829 *jinshi*, wrote that the learning of the emperor was key to peace throughout the empire and the link between the imperial house and the people.[1] In fact, Woren had long believed this to be the case, having told Xianfeng in 1850 that, upon assuming the throne, his first priority should be to devote himself to studies.[2] When Woren wrote at the start of the Tongzhi era, however, his comments appeared as a harsh critique, as the empire faced crises all around. Yet throughout the decade, as local and provincial officials began building arsenals and academies, and as regional armies fought to suppress rebellions, a group of officials in the capital seized on changing ideas about education and competing visions for the future of the dynasty. They sought to impart those ideals in the young emperor's education and, as Woren suggested, help to repair ties between ruler and ruled and strengthen the country.

In the months before Woren wrote, the Qing Empire faced multiple existential crises. Ruling from Nanjing, Hong Xiuquan (1814–1864) and his Taiping rebels controlled key southern commercial and agricultural regions. In the North, British and French armies marched on Beijing, looting the Summer Palace and forcing Xianfeng to flee the capital. The emperor's absence created a crisis in the city. Officials described scenes of chaos in the capital, and in hundreds of memorials they beseeched Xianfeng to return, writing that the absence of the imperial body from Beijing was an omen of impending collapse.[3] Only the emperor, they argued, could restore peace and order to the capital and country.

But Xianfeng would never return to Beijing. He died on August 22, 1861, passing the throne to his only heir, a five-year-old boy named Zaichun (1856–1875).[4] With only a child on the throne, why did the Qing not succumb to the Taiping

Rebels, the foreign imperialists, or the long-term forces of devolution and regional interests pulling the country apart? How did it attract scholar-officials back into its service? In what ways did the variety of ideas for reform and self-strengthening emerging around the country make their way into the Forbidden City?

Several generations of scholarship have revealed the diversity of activities associated with the reform efforts of the final fifty years of Qing rule, from innovation in local administration to industrialization, fundraising, foreign relations, and other fields of governance.[5] By focusing on debates surrounding the education of the new emperor—including the teachers, texts, and rituals of his classroom—this chapter adds a new perspective to scholarship on the era of the Tongzhi Restoration, revealing how the variety of paths that scholars and officials pursued to revive the dynasty played out not only in the development of provincial institutions or local endeavors but also at the traditional center of power as a contest to control the emperor's curriculum.

The emperor's youth was an important element of this dynamic, as multiple groups of scholars saw him as a blank slate they could work to form in their own image. During Xianfeng's reign, and particularly during his exile in Rehe, multiple factions had emerged, jockeying for power and influence. Xianfeng's embrace of one of those factions—the brothers and imperial family members Sushun (1816-1861) and Duanhua (1807-1861)—left much of the bureaucracy disaffected.[6] Xianfeng's death and the enthronement of his five-year-old son therefore provided an opportunity for the court to reach out to those estranged by the politics of Xianfeng's reign as the process of reform and reconstruction began at the capital and around the country. This chapter shows how part of that process included the broad invitation to help mold the next ruler of the Qing Empire.

At the start of the era, the empress dowagers invited imperial family members, Manchu officials, and Chinese scholars to join in the task of educating the emperor and ruling the empire during his minority. Each group understood the structure as temporary, with the promise that when the emperor completed his education, he would assume personal control and authority. Implicit in the model, therefore, was the ideal that the emperor's childhood education would provide the foundation for his vision of leadership and ideas for the country's future. The emperor's classroom, therefore, was one of the many sites in the contest between scholarly and political factions and their attempts to rebuild the empire in accordance with their own ideals. These battles reveal the struggle to balance traditional Chinese and Manchu sources of identity and authority with new forms of learning.

This chapter explores a variety of attempts during the Tongzhi era to use court education to advance different visions of the future, each with the emperor intended to be the chief patron and model of that vision. Because of Empress Dowager Cixi's central role in court politics beginning in this era, the chapter also examines her own use of classical learning and the instruments of court education in the aftermath of Xianfeng's death. Finally, it charts the immense struggles in Tongzhi's education and his brief but tumultuous period of personal rule after the completion of his studies.

BRINGING CIXI AND TONGZHI TO POWER

The summer of 1861 has long been considered a turning point in Qing history, with the "Xinyou Coup" and rise of the empress dowagers to power seen as an irrevocable break with tradition and the start of a precipitous decline in imperial authority.[7] This understanding, however, obscures much about both the way in which people at the time saw the crises as well as the creative solutions put forth over the next several decades. While Xianfeng was in exile, Sushun and his allies had exerted increasingly tight control over the court, angering many members of the imperial family.[8] At the same time, officials in Beijing grew disdainful of Sushun for keeping the emperor away from the capital and outside scholarly influence. The power struggle and coup that emerged after Xianfeng's death, therefore, was the result of—and an attempt to mend—long-simmering factional struggles within the governing structure, not simply a product of Cixi's personal ambitions.

When Xianfeng died in Rehe, Sushun took control over the emperorship as head of a council of advisors for the new boy emperor (giving him the reign name Qixiang). In the following days, Sushun issued a series of edicts that set the timeline for the court's return and the enthronement of the emperor in Beijing. Sushun's edicts, however, failed to appease capital officials. The timeline for the court's return left several months with an empty throne in Beijing. As one official, Li Ciming (1830-1894), wrote in his diary, "The country should never be without a ruling emperor for a single day. There is no precedent for the present situation."[9] Li went on to mock Sushun for issuing edicts in the young boy's name, writing that he "is only a boy of six. How could he write and issue an edict himself? Our descendants will laugh at this farce, for a long, long time." Scholar-officials such as Li depended on the emperor to legitimate their position in government, and Sushun's ventriloquist act and refusal to return the emperor to Beijing created widespread dissatisfaction with the ruling council.

Both scholars in Beijing and members of the imperial family feared that Sushun and his fellow council members would cut off access to the emperor and monopolize power. Yet, with a child on the throne, the council could not simply be cast aside. Sushun's enemies needed to replace him with someone of equal or greater authority in the imperial system. For those in the bureaucracy seeking to oust Sushun, therefore, Cixi and Ci'an (1837–1881) provided the most useful of possible allies. The position of empress dowager came with deep-seated authority and respect but also a long-standing history of strict limits to the exercise of power.[10] Although female-led regencies were not common in Chinese history, they were not unprecedented, and officials who supported replacing Sushun with Cixi and Ci'an mined history to argue for the virtues of female rule.[11] In particular, the dowager-led regency structure was justifiable by analogy and reference to the pre-conquest and early Qing periods when female regencies were more common.[12] Empress Dowager Xiaozhuang's (1613–1688) role in Shunzhi's (r. 1644–1661) court as well as Kangxi's early life is the prime example of women in the early Qing helping to guide the education of a young ruler but eventually yielding power.[13] In 1861 Cixi, as mother to the emperor, was the perfect replacement for Sushun: respected and justifiable through tradition but not seen as a threat to monopolize power.

The first suggestion for these new roles did not come from the empress dowagers, but rather from an official named Dong Yuanchun (dates unknown). In calling for the empress dowagers to replace Sushun and his eight-man council, Dong argued that in this time of crisis, Cixi and Ci'an had a stronger claim to the physical embodiment of imperial power and thus would be able to "bind the hearts of the people" and unite the country.[14] With the empress dowagers at the center of government, Dong argued, "the people may know where to direct loyalty and obedience."[15] Dong's insistence on the importance of a unitary embodiment of imperial power was a direct attack against Sushun and his allies, who, convincing Xianfeng to flee Beijing, had split the court and drained its symbolic power. To heal that divide, however, Dong did not simply argue for the empress dowagers to take charge. Rather, he called for the new government to incorporate scholars alienated by both Xianfeng and Sushun. Dong therefore urged the selection of new tutors for the young emperor, arguing that Sushun unfairly monopolized influence over the emperor in part by controlling his classroom.¹⁶

With the support of officials such as Dong, Cixi, Prince Gong (Yixin, 1833–1898), and their allies moved against Sushun. In a November 2 edict describing the takeover, the empress dowagers blamed Sushun and his clique for forcing Xianfeng to flee Beijing against his will and then for preventing him from returning when he had desired.¹⁷ Removing the imperial body from Beijing (i.e., outside the reach of most officials) was thus the most fundamental of Sushun's crimes. In additional announcements, the empress dowagers expanded the list of Sushun's wrongdoings, including entering the palace without invitation, demanding audiences with the empress dowagers, using imperial porcelain, and even having dared to sit on the imperial throne.¹⁸ The narrative drew on the memory of other great "villains" in Chinese history—from Wei Zhongxian (1568-1627) to Heshen—men who aggrandized themselves at the expense of scholar-officials and the emperor.¹⁹ Having been painted in this light, Sushun was beheaded in front of a large crowd on November 10, 1861. The empress dowagers presented the punishment as an act of both power and grace: though killed, Sushun was spared the initial sentence of death by a thousand cuts.²⁰

To inaugurate the new era, the dowager-led court then embarked on a multifaceted campaign to simultaneously present the empress dowagers as legitimate and learned rulers while drawing the bureaucracy into service. In part, this latter task was accomplished by highlighting the emperor's youth and the opportunity to mold the imperial mind. In edicts describing the start of the era, the court repeatedly described how the empress dowagers would simultaneously rule, care for the emperor's learning, and pursue their own education, inviting scholarly participation into each endeavor.²¹ The discourse of court education thus presented both the emperor and empress dowagers as empty vessels the bureaucracy could fight to fill.²²

Just as Xiaozhuang eventually receded as the young Kangxi asserted his own authority, there was thus little reason to think that the 1861 coup would result in nearly fifty years of female rule. While some at the time speculated that the new reign name "Tongzhi" itself meant "joint rule" and thus evidence of Cixi's grand ambitions, that is almost assuredly not the case. In the view of many at the time, "Tongzhi" was not meant as "joint rule," but rather as "to return to (or see restored) together a state of order."²³ As officials all around the country worked to rebuild their communities, in the capital, the project of returning order to the empire included the task of educating the young emperor.[24]

LEARNING TO BE A (FEMALE) SAGE-KING

As a part of her political maneuvering after assuming a central role at court, Cixi now worked to educate herself and, equally important, to promote an image of a classically learned and legitimate steward of the Qing intellectual and cultural tradition. While in later years opponents attacked her by saying she was the latest of many illegitimate female rulers in Chinese history, at the start of the Tongzhi era, Cixi and her allies drew on dynastic history to argue that female rulership was a legitimate incarnation of the emperorship.[25] The final fifty years of the Qing elaborated on those earlier models to establish and normalize a new form of imperial government, one wherein female regents simultaneously ran the emperorship and educated the emperor until he came of age.

Cixi's educational ventures consisted of two main projects: The first, a crash course in classical education, sought both to draw scholars into service by offering them an opportunity to serve as mentors to power and to provide the empress dowager with the vocabulary of rulership necessary to effectively hold court. The second project, the publication of these efforts and the attempt to distill a narrative of devotion to learning, was intended to undercut political opponents by positioning Cixi as an honorable inheritor of a long tradition of sage rulership in China.

There are no contemporary records that document Cixi's early education. That fact is easy to understand: when she was born in 1835, there was no indication that she would lead a historically significant life. Yet in later years, once Cixi had established herself as a political force, commentators took great interest in reconstructing her early childhood and education. In fact, the empress dowager herself actively participated in constructing myths regarding her studies and training. Around the turn of the twentieth century, an image of Cixi's early education coalesced that described her as part autodidact and part recipient of imperial favor, transforming her from an illiterate concubine into a sagely ruler.[26] One common anecdote is that Xianfeng had himself tutored Cixi, teaching her how to read memorials and allowing her to assist in sorting through court communications. Yet, rather than shedding light on Cixi's actual education, the anecdote instead speaks to the importance that projecting an air of learning played in her strategy of legitimation and political authority: the evidence for Xianfeng tutoring Cixi seems to stem from Cixi herself, nearly half a century after the supposed events would have occurred.[27] Although the event is not recorded in state-sponsored texts, its presence in popular writings and the frequency with which Cixi was described as a "female Yao or Shun" in the Chinese press suggests that the *image* of the empress dowager as a diligent student of government indeed played a role in maintaining support for her place in the emperorship.[28]

Though narratives of Cixi's education prior to 1861 are largely an after-the-fact imagining, her and Ci'an's educational activities in the immediate aftermath of seizing power are well documented, both in private sources and in state-sanctioned historical records. The empress dowagers had taken power in part predicated on the claim that they best represented the tradition and authority of the Qing emperorship, an institution whose leadership was tied to its ability to define, propagate, and mobilize the classical canon. Therefore they quickly and actively worked to educate themselves and bring scholar-officials into service of the court.

To begin their education, the empress dowagers first turned to the Old Manchu Veritable Records and the Qianlong era compilation *Yupi lidai tongjian jilan* (Comprehensive mirror of dynastic history with imperial commentary).[29] To continue their studies as well as co-opt the tradition of imperial sponsorship of scholarship, the empress dowagers then ordered the compilation of their own "historical mirror," to be called *Zhiping baojian* (Precious mirror for governance and peace). The empress dowagers had officials "compile records of the political affairs of past emperors and kings and of previous times in history of women ruling from behind the screen."[30] In lessons based on the book, the empress dowagers and their tutors discussed many of the same women whom memorialists presented in 1861 as evidence of the historical precedent justifying female regency.[31] After the completion of the *Zhiping baojian* lecture series, Ci'an and Cixi continued their education in other ways, including several years of lectures on the Classics, historical subjects, and issues of governance such as land registration and taxation.[32]

In all these lessons, the empress dowagers relegated themselves to the position of student. The pair brought in a wide array of scholars to lecture them, creating space for scholars in the emperorship and providing officials the opportunity to argue for different understandings of good governance. In this way, the empress dowagers placed limits on their own power and invited the cooperation of the bureaucracy in the project of restoring the throne and the empire. Some of the scholars assigned to lecture the empress dowagers were at the same time serving as the emperor's tutors, and the empress dowagers would often end their own lessons by asking the tutors to report on the emperor's progress.[33] Scholars thus moved back and forth between the three imperial bodies, working to inculcate them all with the different types of knowledge they hoped would help to lead the empire.

Just as Cixi's education at court was in part a mechanism of outreach to scholars, so too did she draw on traditions of artistic production to more broadly cultivate an image of sagely rule. That is to say, Cixi's engagement with the Classics was not limited to textual study. In the years after 1861, Cixi spent considerable energy producing art and calligraphy, strategically deploying her works as imperial gifts to scholars throughout the bureaucracy.[34] These scholars, in turn, produced the state-sponsored sources that portrayed the empress dowager as devoted to the study and practice of good governance. Her embrace of learning also became a part of the visual representation of imperial power in the second half of the nineteenth century: a Tongzhi era portrait of Cixi depicts her reading, the first portrait of its kind for an imperial woman.[35] By presenting Cixi as devoted to learning, scholar-officials were in part glorifying themselves for providing the education and working to restore the authority of the throne. But they were also contributing to Cixi's protracted campaign of legitimation based on the projection of scholarly bona fides while arguing for the dowager-led emperorship as a legitimate form of rule.

COMPETING TUTORS AND TEXTS IN TONGZHI'S CLASSROOM

The rule of the empress dowagers, however, was always understood as temporary. As the edicts and pronouncements emanating from court at the start of the Tongzhi era discussed earlier said, the emperor would assume control once he completed his education. Thus the court continually assured the country that just as the empress dowagers were being educated, so too was the young emperor. The rhetoric of Tongzhi's education suggested that he would be molded into a strong imperial presence who could both lead efforts of reform within the bureaucracy and unite the country behind the throne as it began projects of self-strengthening.[36] As Prince Gong wrote, "The son of heaven is he who follows the way of the ruler and the way of the teacher. He transforms the people and reforms their customs. It is said that he pacifies them with virtue."[37]

In the initial edict announcing the start of Tongzhi's education, the empress dowagers said that the learning of the emperor was not simply found in explicating words and phrases from the Classics. Rather, what was most important for Tongzhi was to serve the people by cultivating himself to bring peace to the empire.[38] Yet there was no agreement about the appropriate course for the Qing to chart to reach that peace. The crises of domestic rebellion and foreign imperialism that rocked the Qing world in the first half of the nineteenth century set off a vigorous debate about how best to strengthen the country and return the dynasty to its former glory. With a young child on the throne in 1861, the emperor's curriculum emerged as a focal point of these discussions, as different groups argued for Tongzhi to be trained in the disciplines they believed were key to molding him into a leader for the new era. Tongzhi's Manchu teachers fought to preserve the Manchu core of the emperor's education, arguing for a throne heavily invested in the linguistic and martial traditions of the early Qing; scholar-officials argued for the primacy of Confucian texts in restoring order; still others pictured Tongzhi opening the country to the knowledge and practices of the Western world.

Each of these visions of the future was now represented in Tongzhi's classroom, both the physical space as well as the texts and tutors. When Tongzhi began his education in 1861, the Hongde Hall (Hongde dian, Hall of Promoting Virtue) became the emperor's classroom, and officials assigned to instruct him were given the concurrent title Official of the Hongde Hall (*Hongde dian xingzou*). In the early Qing the hall had played a central role in court education: until the twenty-fifth year of the Kangxi era when the Hall of Literary Brilliance (Wenhua dian) was repaired, the Hongde dian hosted the Classic Mat.[39] By placing Tongzhi's classroom in the former site of the Classic Mat, the court made several arguments about the education of the new emperor: it would, like the Classic Mat, be a venue for scholar-officials to participate in governance by offering their interpretations of classical texts, and it would be a fusion of Chinese and Manchu expressions of authority. Sitting in the rooms and looking up during class, the young Tongzhi would have seen warnings in the form of calligraphic plaques from his great-great-grandfather to be mindful of the accomplishments of the ancients and continue the work of sages and kings who "Bestowed the Three Impartialities" (*feng san wu si*).[40]

Imperial calligraphy on the walls of the Hongde Hall in fact played a large role in efforts to shape the atmosphere of the classroom. The couplets looking down over the young Tongzhi drew on the wide range of intellectual traditions that formed the composite nature of Qing ideology and the history of court education. Through the brushes of illustrious Qing emperors, the court urged Tongzhi to be diligent in his studies: the Confucian Classics were extolled as the heart of good governance, and the Avatamsaka Sutra was used to encourage a thorough immersion in reading. This syncretic tradition and a focus on introspection were crucial components of the Hongde Hall's calligraphy. A couplet inked by Qianlong, for example, counseled the young emperor to listen to a wide range of opinions, discover the faults in himself, and work to correct them to conform to the will of heaven and the people. The couplet contains illusions from the *Classic of History*, the *Zhuangzi*, and the *Zuozhuan* (Commentary of Zuo), among other texts, foreshadowing both the curricula and moral lessons that awaited the young student.[41]

In this way, the couplets in Tongzhi's classroom served a variety of pedagogical tasks. The fusion of Confucian, Buddhist, and Daoist imagery signaled the breadth of intellectual traditions the young emperor must master in his education and mobilize in his rule. The persistent message of dedication to learning, meanwhile, helped to create an austere environment and indicated the seriousness of the task at hand. Finally, that the couplets were inked by Tongzhi's eminent predecessors reminded both student and teachers alike of the rewards that potentially awaited them at the end of the educational program. The calligraphy thus transformed the walls of the Hongde Hall into an ever-present system of encouragement and surveillance.

Outside the walls of the classroom, edicts issued shortly after the start of the Tongzhi era emphasized the importance of seizing the moment to begin his childhood education to establish a foundation for his personal reign.[42] In highlighting his youth and outlining a direct link between his studies and future rule, the court therefore suggested that the job of tutor was an opportunity to shape the future of the country. Over the course of Tongzhi's education, a variety of officials would move in and out of the classroom, serving as tutors for varying lengths of time. The officials who would come to serve in the emperor's classroom were a combination of imperial princes, Manchus, and Confucian scholars—many of whom had been previously forced out of government by Sushun—who together represented the variety of views within the Qing on the type of education appropriate for the moment.

In his final will, Xianfeng—or Sushun (the authorship of the document being a contested issue)—had appointed tutors for his young son. But after the 1861 coup, the empress dowagers brought new officials into the service of the court by expanding the group named to serve in the emperor's classroom. Xianfeng's original instructions had tasked Li Hongzao (1820-1897) with instructing the young emperor in the Classics. With Sushun out of power, Li was allowed to keep his job, but he was now joined by Qi Junzao (1793-1866), Weng Xincun, and Woren. By so greatly expanding the number of teachers focused on the traditional canon, the dowagers signaled to the Confucian bureaucracy that the era would be one of cooperative governance. These new tutors also represented key constituencies the empress dowagers sought to draw back into service of the court after the tumult of the Xianfeng era. In particular, the appointment of Qi and Woren was meant to assure the participation of the "veteran literocrats" of the Southern City clique, who, as James Polachek has shown, were consistently hostile to the idea of peaceful engagement with Western powers or adopting the learning of foreign countries.[43] These scholars were also some of the most vocal opponents of Sushun and the policy decisions of the late Xianfeng reign, and with their new positions as imperial tutors, the court assured that their views would be heard in the emperor's education.

In fact, both Qi and Weng had personally jarred with Sushun, particularly over matters of foreign affairs. Qi, for example, had earlier served on the Grand Council and as head of the Palace School for Princes (Shangshufang). Early in Xianfeng's reign Qi was made grand secretary, and he was a central participant in Xianfeng's Imperial Lecture in 1853. Yet by the middle of the 1850s Qi clashed with Sushun, and in 1855 he retired from government service.[44] Throughout his career, Qi was a vocal proponent of taking aggressive postures toward the rising British threat on China's coast.[45] Qi was also famously weary of the growing power of regional officials and regional armies, and he argued that the future stability of the country rested on employing upright officials at the center of power.[46] He had long worked to advance the careers of his like-minded brethren through the examination system, and he now gained direct access to the throne as one of the emperor's tutors.[47]

Weng Xincun was one of those like-minded men who had earlier benefited from Qi's patronage. Weng had been a prominent official early in the Xianfeng era, serving as president of the Board of Civil Appointments and Board of Revenue in the mid-1850s. Similar to Qi, however, Weng battled with Sushun over the latter's efforts to raise funds through extralegal means, and Weng was forced into retirement in 1859.[48] By bringing men such as Qi and Weng out of retirement and into the emperor's classroom, the empress dowagers gave legitimacy to their views on foreign affairs and the syncretic classicism they promoted.[49]

At the same time, however, the new group of tutors added by the empress dowagers also suggested that it was not just the Confucian Classics but also the Manchu martial and linguistic traditions of the early Qing that might serve as the foundation of the dynasty moving forward. In addition to the new Confucian tutors, the empress dowagers tripled the number of Manchu instructors (*anda*) in the emperor's classroom. Xianfeng had originally appointed Woshenhunbu (1797–1866) for the job, but he was now joined by Yijinga (1811–1866) and Airen (1794–1863). The empress dowagers ordered Woshenhunbu, Yijinga, and Airen to instruct Tongzhi in the Manchu language, what they described as the "root of Our Dynasty," to build a base for the restoration of the dynasty's illustrious past.[50]

Confucian ideals certainly played a large part in Tongzhi's education, but a closer look at the texts of his curriculum demonstrate that Manchu materials and ideals in fact occupied a central space. Not only did Tongzhi read from a Manchu version of Kangxi's *Shengzu Ren huangdi tingxun geyan* (Aphorisms from the familial instructions of the Kangxi emperor), known in Manchu as *Šengdzu gosin hûwangdi-i booi tacihiyan-i ten-i gisun*, but he also read Manchu-language versions of the *Classic of Filial Piety* and the *Analects*.[51] In this way, the personnel and texts of the emperor's classroom suggest that the significance of a distinct ethnic identity of the Qing and the traditions of the Manchu Way extended well into the nineteenth century as the court searched for ways to restabilize its rule. Early Qing conceptions of rulership argued that there was a concrete relationship between individual proficiency in the Manchu Way and the survival of the dynasty, an idea that appears to have persisted in the classrooms of the late Qing emperors.[52]

Critically as well, the teachers were all put under the direct supervision of imperial family members Prince Gong and Prince Chun. The empress dowagers tasked Prince Chun with overseeing Tongzhi's Mongolian, horseback riding, and archery lessons, while Prince Gong was responsible for overall supervision of the emperor's education. Placing the imperial princes in charge of the emperor's education reflected the desire to mold Tongzhi into an effective expression of imperial authority rooted in the traditions of the Qing imperial lineage. The ideology and personnel of Tongzhi's education thus helped to set the stage for the "reimperialization" of government in the second half of the nineteenth century, as members of the imperial family took on greater responsibilities for the everyday functioning of the state.[53]

THE EARLY DAYS OF TONGZHI'S EDUCATION

Clashes between proponents of these different ideas were a major part of life for those inside the emperor's classroom in the nineteenth century, as the groups constantly fought to oust their rivals and secure for themselves the leading role in molding the emperor.[54] Everything from the arrangement of personnel to the schedule of lessons created acrimony between the imperial tutors, and far from a place of solemn instruction, the emperor's classroom appears to have often been a hotbed of conflict and controversy.

On the first day of Tongzhi's formal studies in 1861, the emperor went to the Hall of Sages inside the Palace School for Princes early in the morning to make an offering to Confucius while the tutors stood guard.[55] When the emperor completed his offering, he proceeded to the exterior of his classroom building where a large group of officials were seated awaiting his arrival.[56] As Tongzhi ascended the steps of the hall, they all rose and bowed three times, knocking their heads on the ground nine times. Then, "when His Majesty rose to enter the room, the officials kneeled."[57] But theirs was not simply a relationship of subordination: just as princes were required to clasp their hands and reciprocate greetings when meeting a teacher, emperors had to similarly respect their tutors.[58] Before entering the classroom, therefore, "His Majesty clasped his hands and bowed and addressed the teachers."[59]

The arrangement of teachers in this daily ritual exercise reinforced both the hierarchies and tensions in Tongzhi's education. Awaiting the arrival of the emperor outside the classroom each day, the tutors lined up on the southern wall with the Chinese scholars granted superior positions to the Manchu *anda*.[60] Yet, although they received the place of honor in preclass rituals, the Chinese teachers were unnerved by the ways in which the Manchus dominated Tongzhi's education. For example, while the Chinese teachers were given ritual precedent in the lineup, Manchu was given priority in the day's lessons, and each morning started with lessons in the Manchu Way.⁶¹ Once inside the classroom as well, the seating arrangement and position of teachers suggested to Chinese scholars that their Manchu colleagues had the upper hand. While giving their lessons, the *anda* sat facing the emperor, but the Chinese tutors taught standing at a distance. The Chinese teachers resented the closer ties their Manchu colleagues had with the emperor, and they sought to mobilize ritual protocols to level the playing field. Multiple times throughout the era, along with other allies at court, they memorialized arguing that the *anda* were breaching etiquette by sitting and facing the emperor, violating the appropriate separation between minister and ruler.⁶²

Friction between Manchu and Chinese teachers over the rituals in Tongzhi's classroom mirrored similar battles between scholars and officials in guiding the direction of the country. Maintaining differences between their Han and Manchu subjects remained a central component of the court's governing philosophy throughout the nineteenth century. Surrounding the young emperor with this ritually segmented body of officials and insisting on enforcing different sets of rules for Manchu and Han teachers, the court presented the emperorship as definitively, perhaps defiantly, Qing in the face of rising Chinese influence.

The place of Manchu lessons was in fact a constant source of conflict among Tongzhi's teachers and officials at court. Tutors frequently debated the attention different subjects should be allotted in the curriculum and jealously guarded time for their respective subjects. For example, regulations set out for Tongzhi's education stipulated that Manchu schoolwork should take up the first forty-five minutes of class each day.⁶³ Yet Weng Tonghe's diary is peppered with complaints about the Manchu tutors exceeding their time limit and encroaching on his lessons. One day in October 1867, for instance, Tongzhi arrived for class at 10:00 a.m., yet the Manchu lessons did not end until 12:30.⁶⁴ Weng was irritated to say the least. But aside from his diary, he had few outlets to vent his frustration. The day after the *anda* stole Weng's time, Prince Gong came to the Hongde Hall to inspect the emperor's Manchu schoolwork and talk with all the teachers. Weng complained in his diary that "Gong was partial toward Manchus, and the Manchu *anda* and I were not without rancor, but it was pointless to mention."⁶⁵ The situation continued, and with Weng unable to prevent the *anda* from overstepping their allotted time, he continued to fill his diary with bitter notes deriding his Manchu colleagues.

These interpersonal conflicts reveal a major tension throughout the era as different tutors sought time and influence within the emperor's classroom. At the beginning of Tongzhi's education, the court had promised that scholars would all have the chance to mold the young emperor's views, but the ways in which Weng believed he was being isolated from the emperor gradually undermined that idea. Weng therefore went to the empress dowagers, asking them to intervene on his behalf in the classroom. Fearful of alienating the Confucian scholars at court, Ci'an and Cixi sided with Weng and ordered that from then on Manchu schoolwork should not exceed one hour every day. Although this was an extension of the original time limit, it was nonetheless a conciliatory gesture toward the Chinese officials who had played a central role in bringing the empress dowagers to power. The *anda* did not go down without a fight, however, and did everything they could to add Manchu lessons at the expense of Chinese.[66] In the end, they raised the ire of the empress dowagers, who said, "We ordered that Manchu schoolwork should be set to forty-five minutes, how is it that it's still going on after sixty or ninety minutes?"[67] Ci'an and Cixi called in the Manchu tutors and ordered them to stop adding time to the Manchu lessons. In an effort to deflect the dowagers' criticism and maintain their good standing, the *anda* extolled the emperor's progress in his education and development before promising not to exceed ninety minutes with their lessons.[68]

In the second half of the nineteenth century, however, the intellectual world of the Qing was not limited to Chinese and Manchu knowledge. All around the country in the 1860s, new ideas, texts, curricula, and institutions were spreading elements of Western learning as scholars and officials debated how to incorporate new fields of knowledge.[69] The emperor's classroom was not isolated from this debate, and officials battled over the place of Western learning in molding Tongzhi into a strong leader. Prince Gong, for example, believed that incorporating new fields of learning, particularly those from the West, was critical to the future of the Qing. When he wrote in a Manchu-language memorial at the very start of Tongzhi's education that the emperor and his teachers would work to exhaust their studies in all fields of learning (Manchu: *tacin*), he clearly imagined a broader definition than did others at court.[70]

In fact, Gong's career typifies the struggle to incorporate new fields into the emperor's classroom and plans for the future of the dynasty. In the immediate aftermath of the 1861 coup, he had been empowered with overseeing the emperor's education. Over the course of the next few years, however, Gong's advocacy of Western learning and associated ideas for reform earned him many enemies. Inside the emperor's classroom, the prince's colleagues began to resent the direction he seemed to be steering the emperor. Weng, for example, wrote in his diary in April of 1865 that "at the start when Prince Gong was acting as Regent Advisor, he was diligent and cautious. Yet now he is self-important and domineering. He relies on nobles to increase his power. He thinks little of the emperor, taking advantage of His Majesty's youth to make him do his bidding."[71] Weng and other Confucian scholars had been promised the chance to mold the imperial mind. But they now found themselves being pushed out of power by the prince. Over the course of the year, the prince's relationship with the empress dowagers become rocky as well, as more at court seemed to echo Weng's critique that Gong was using the emperor to do his bidding. At the end of 1865 Gong was dismissed from his posts, including management of the emperor's classroom.[72]

When they removed Prince Gong, the empress dowagers ordered a thorough review of Tongzhi's curriculum, creating an opportunity for others to assert their vision of the country's future and the appropriate course of study for Tongzhi.[73] One of the major proponents of removing the prince, and beneficiaries of his sacking, was the tutor Woren.[74] Woren was a major figure at court, holding a variety of concurrent positions while tutor, including president of the Board of Works and chancellor of the Hanlin Academy (Hanlin yuan).[75] In all these posts, he was a vocal opponent of the introduction of Western learning into China, opposing, for example, the opening of the Tongwen guan.[76] In the midst of that debate, Woren famously said that "it is better for a state to be established on ceremonies and on ethical codes than on tactics and clever contrivances. The basic need of China is not technical skill, but cultivation of the heart."[77] For Woren, the path to restabilizing imperial power and ensuring the future security of the Qing was found in values such as frugality and piety, and, as has been noted of his overarching approach to education, he "uncompromisingly rejected all borrowing from the West on the grounds that if the Western learning were let loose in China, the Chinese learning would not stay safely screened off and unsullied."[78] This was true in the case of the emperor's education as well, as Woren fought to oust Prince Gong and proponents of Western learning from Tongzhi's classroom.

Despite his many roles in government, Woren considered his post as the emperor's teacher to be his top priority.[79] From the start of Tongzhi's education, Woren had used his position to advocate for the primacy of classical learning and exclusion of subjects of Western learning in the emperor's curriculum. Woren even worked to have his own writings included in Tongzhi's studies.[80] One text in particular, *Qin xin jin jian* (Golden mirror for the instruction of the heart)—a collection of classical stories and aphorisms related to righteous ancient emperors with Woren's own annotations—was singled out for praise by the empress dowagers, who said it contained classical wisdom particularly suitable for the education of the young emperor.[81] The text was in fact a compilation of two separate editorial projects by Woren: the first focused on sage kings and emperors (*Diwang cheng gui*) and the second on exemplary scholars and officials (*Fubi jiamo*). Together, the texts presented Tongzhi with the message that the source of China's strength in the future could be found in its past, not in the new ideas and texts circulating in the treaty ports or in projects sponsored by men such as Prince Gong.[82] Placing his own texts in the emperor's curriculum was only part of the larger battle, and Woren fought to oust Prince Gong and other supporters of Western learning not just from Tongzhi's education but from power at court.[83] When Gong was dismissed, therefore, Cixi's appointment of Prince Chun as the new head of Tongzhi's education was a victory for Woren.[84] In this way, the dismissal of Prince Gong was emblematic of a larger debate around the country over the place of Western versus Chinese learning in strengthening the dynasty.

THE ALLURE OF KANGXI

In this fight over educational values and ideas for the future, however, all sides turned to the past to make their argument. Qing officials and outside observers who sought to mold Tongzhi into a Manchu Warrior, a Confucian Sage, or a scholar of Western studies each called on the example of the Kangxi emperor to make their case. In the minds of each group, Kangxi stood as the model of a young emperor whose education had enabled him to become a strong and effective leader, taking command of the Qing at a time of great peril and leading it into a prosperous age. He was the standard against which all others were judged, and his voluminous record of cultural production offered commentators no shortage of material with which they could either denounce or praise the contemporary sovereign. In particular, Kangxi's eclectic education—combining Manchu, Chinese, and Western subjects—provided partisans on all sides an opportunity to engage in a type of mental gymnastics, selectively highlighting elements of his reign and contorting them to create a model of imperial leadership for the nineteenth century.[85]

Reform-minded Chinese officials, for example, highlighted Kangxi's patronage of Western knowledge to argue that Tongzhi should set an example by adopting new forms of learning to strengthen the country and protect itself against imperialism. In a memorial discussing the possibility of holding examinations on astronomy and mathematics early in the Tongzhi era, the Zongli yamen (Office of Foreign Affairs) appealed to Kangxi's wisdom to make their case, reminding the young Tongzhi that Kangxi had employed foreigners in the imperial observatory.[86] The idea that Kangxi's successors had turned inward and failed to live up to their ancestor became a common explanation for the dynasty's decline. For these officials during the Tongzhi reign, then, the formula to assert the authority of the emperorship and strengthen China was for the emperor to follow the model of Kangxi in seeking knowledge from around the world.

Many others at court, however, rejected the idea that turning to the West was the best way for China to regain its strength and standing in the world. For these officials, the problem seemed to be that the Manchu court had forgotten its origins and the sources of its success. They therefore argued that it was crucial for Tongzhi to focus his education on mastering the Manchu Way. Here, too, the example of Kangxi proved to be fertile ground in which to root the argument. Officials suggested that if the emperor would master Manchu, Mongolian, archery, and horsemanship, he would reinvigorate the imperial family, the Bannermen population, and the empire as a whole. To be sure, Tongzhi needed to read the Four Books and the Five Classics, and learn from the lessons of Chinese history. But in the eyes of other officials, above all else the moment called for a Qing monarch steeped in the martial tradition of his ancestors and illustrious early Qing rulers.

Prince Chun, for example, drew a direct line between the emperor's progress in learning archery and the security of the empire. Restoring the Banner forces from their current state of disrepair would be a monumental task. In the mind of Prince Chun, however, the work started with establishing Tongzhi as a model Manchu to lead the restoration. The prince suggested that he and a Mongolian prince personally instruct Tongzhi in horseriding and archery every morning to combine Manchu- and Mongolian-language learning with training in martial skills in the emperor's daily routine. According to Prince Chun, Qing emperors had long emphasized military affairs, and it was important that the emperor personally excel at horsemanship and archery.[87] The prince's memorial was in fact written in both Chinese and Manchu. Yet in the Manchu version, an additional note explained that in the future the emperor's guard should take up the responsibility of training the imperial army, and Prince Chun argued that instructing the emperor in archery and Mongolian were matters that should be considered together with the training of the army. In this way, Tongzhi's education would serve as a model for others to emulate and, when completed, would enable him to be an effective leader of a rejuvenated Qing army.

Tongzhi indeed spent time practicing the martial skills necessary for ideal Qing rulership. To teach him to ride, the Imperial Household Department built wooden horses of three different sizes to spare the young emperor from the danger of falling off a live animal.[88] Weather permitting, Tongzhi's schooldays started with archery practice in the courtyard, and his progress in these skills often excited his tutors, even those tasked with instructing him in the Classics.[89] As Weng described one day's lessons in 1869: "His Majesty stood facing west, about ten paces away from the official. Yishan shot first. Then His Majesty drew the bow and shot three arrows, two hit the target. All the officials were elated."[90] And despite his fights with Tongzhi's Manchu teachers, Weng carefully monitored the boy's progress in that part of his education and seemed to take pride when Tongzhi performed well in his Manchu lessons.[91] For the emperor to ultimately be useful to any of the competing groups at court in asserting their vision of reform, he would need to command respect. Thus, although the tutors disagreed on the best course of study, the shared goal of restoring the throne made any progress Tongzhi exhibited a cause for celebration. There were, however, few such occasions.

STRUGGLES IN HIS EDUCATION

As it had under Kangxi, the Qing faced great threats to the security of its empire and claims of universal rulership early in the Tongzhi reign. Looking back at that earlier period, nineteenth-century writers frequently credited Kangxi's childhood education for establishing the foundation of his later successes, and they hoped the same would be true for Tongzhi. But in the 1860s and 1870s, all was not well. Tongzhi was frequently sick and absent from school.[92] When he did attend, the young boy was rarely attentive in class, and his tutors were at their wits' end trying to educate the juvenile ruler.⁹³ Weng, for example, complained in his diary that Tongzhi was a poor disciple, writing that it was impossible to stimulate the boy's interest in the classical texts and that he was more interested in playing with eunuchs than studying.⁹⁴ Weng's colleague in the classroom, Xu Tong (1819-1900), shared the concerns, and together they memorialized asking that Tongzhi not be allowed to watch operas or consort with eunuchs.⁹⁵ The tutors were of course taking part in the long Confucian tradition of blaming eunuchs and other pleasures for corruption and dynastic decline, and we should be wary of reading their complaints as literal reflections of Tongzhi's conduct.⁹⁶ At the same time, however, their concerns were not simply about educating a single child. The rhetoric surrounding Tongzhi's education frequently claimed a link between the emperor's classroom and the broader project of dynastic reconstruction. For Weng and his colleagues, therefore, Tongzhi's disinterest in the classroom foretold danger to the dynasty's future.

Cixi as well expressed concern that the young boy was not making sufficient progress in his studies. Throughout Tongzhi's youth, Cixi argued for the importance of returning the emperor to power and warned that his education was not adequately preparing him for the job.⁹⁷ She frequently pressed not just the Confucian scholars but also the *anda*, demanding in particular that they do a better job teaching the emperor Manchu and the other tools needed for Qing rule.⁹⁸ Her queries to Tongzhi's teachers—and her criticisms of their job performance—reinforce the idea that the period of regency was always intended as a temporary situation while also suggesting that Cixi believed she had a central role to play in rejuvenating the country. In February 1870, for example, in an audience with a group of fifty-eight officials lined up ten rows deep, Cixi said that although Tongzhi would take over the government in only three years, "the emperor's study of the sages is not complete. He is not yet even able to read memorials; how can he take over the reins of government?" She then told that crowd that "it is the responsibility of all officials to encourage the emperor's learning."⁹⁹

Weng was standing in the eighth row of officials that day, and he must have felt the pressure of hundreds of eyes glaring with disapproval at the imperial tutor and his student. Despite these warnings, however, Tongzhi did not seem to improve, and Weng complained for the rest of the year about his student's poor performance. Writing with a sense of deep frustration one day after a particularly poor showing, Weng said that Tongzhi "sat in the classroom for an hour and couldn't even write a single character. Then we tried to compose a poem and the poem was terrible. Under these circumstances, what can I do? What can I do?"[100]

TONGZHI'S ASCENSION TO PERSONAL RULE

Just two years later, and notwithstanding his struggles in the classroom, the court declared that it was time for Tongzhi to take his rightful place as the ultimate embodiment of authority within the Qing Empire. The functioning of the emperorship required public rejection of the widely known internal truth: Tongzhi had not been transformed into a sagely ruler. Therefore, despite the contentious debates and difficulties in educating him, the court presented a triumphant image in signaling the end of his education and his assumption of power. The court described both the empress dowagers and the emperor as diligent in their duties and framed the course of Tongzhi's education in entirely positive terms.[101] The empress dowagers issued an edict saying that "the emperor having made great progress in his studies, and being now in the prime of life, ought to assume the government of the empire."[102] After eleven years inside the Hongde Hall, in the courtyard practicing archery, and sitting beside the empress dowagers in audiences, it was time for Tongzhi to take the throne. Observing the situation from Shanghai, the editors of the British-owned *North China Herald* wrote that Tongzhi's assumption of power was a time of great hope for the foreign community, as many believed that now with the "leading strings" of his childhood education cut away, Tongzhi might embrace the ideas of his more Western-oriented teachers and ministers and lead a countrywide reform movement.[103]

Yet the empress dowagers and officials knew full well that Tongzhi's childhood education had not been successful for any of the groups who had hoped to mold him in their image. Moreover, because their place in the constitutional framework required an emperor committed to continued studies, Tongzhi's ascension to the throne was accompanied by widespread calls from scholars for the emperor to continue his education while running the country. The end of the formal period of his education did not mean that his studies would stop, nor that the empress dowagers would end their engagement in political affairs. In handing over power, Cixi and Ci'an declared that Tongzhi must continue to consult with his childhood teachers so as to never forget the lessons learned and to continue in his pursuit of knowledge.[104]

The empress dowagers also used other elements of Tongzhi's ascension—particularly his marriage—to ensure that both they and scholar-officials remained connected to the throne. In announcing the selection of his bride, they said, "It is now our duty to select a virtuous woman to be his consort and empress, so she may aid him in cultivation of imperial virtue and assist him in regulating the affairs of the palace."[105] In choosing Tongzhi's wife, not only did the empress dowagers argue for women to play a role in the emperorship even after they themselves stepped down, but they also continued to use access to the emperor as a political tool: the bride-to-be was the daughter of assistant imperial tutor Chongqi (1829-1900). Chongqi was the only Mongolian *zhuangyuan* (optimus) in Qing history, earning his degree in 1865. Like Woren, he was confident in the ability of classical learning to revive the fortunes of the Qing and a fierce opponent of Western learning. Later in life Chongqi would become famous for his bellicose positions vis-à-via Qing-Chosŏn relations and, more prominently, his role supporting the Boxer attack on Beijing.[106] A decade and more before these more infamous manifestations of his antiforeign attitudes, the selection of Chongqi's daughter as Tongzhi's wife signaled to those worried by the spread of Western learning that the court was not abandoning its traditional bases in the projects of court education or dynastic reconstruction.

Still, many officials seemed concerned that the end of Tongzhi's formal education might ultimately diminish their influence at court, and they called on the emperor to emulate his venerated ancestors by continuing to pursue his studies after taking the throne.[107] Just as had been the case during his childhood education, however, groups called on Tongzhi to pursue different fields of learning and model divergent ideals of imperial leadership to the country. For example, Prince Chun emphasized the need for the emperor to set aside time each day for his studies while on the throne, focusing on the importance of regularly communicating in Manchu with Bannermen officials and practicing horseback riding and archery to maintain his health and Qing traditions. Prince Chun also urged Tongzhi to embrace his role as lead pedagogue and exemplar. In describing times from his own youth when he had been inspired by the sight of the Daoguang and Xianfeng emperors practicing archery, Prince Chun exhorted Tongzhi to similarly serve as a model of the Manchu Way.[108]

The prince was by no means alone in this line of thinking. Many Chinese officials similarly suggested that the health of the empire started with the personal conduct of the emperor. They argued, however, for Tongzhi to be an exemplar of Confucian values. In March 1873, for example, one official described his hopes for Tongzhi's personal rule by calling on ideals from *The Analects*:

> The emperor is the pattern which all the officers and the myriads of the people must follow in their conduct. If the emperor's example be according to rectitude, then he is not under the necessity of issuing any commands; the model which he presents is sufficient to ensure obedience. If on the contrary his example is not according to rectitude, then although he may issue orders forever, yet no one will think of obeying them.[109]

Most evidence, however, points to the conclusion that Tongzhi would surely have been a bad example, be it of the Manchu Way or Confucian Sage Kingship, for others to follow. Rumors in Beijing described the emperor as frequently sneaking out of the palace to indulge in all types of forbidden pleasures, and the impatience he exhibited as a child in the classroom did not dissipate while on the throne.[110]

THE LIMITS OF TONGZHI'S POWER

Over the course of his decade in the classroom, a variety of scholars had sought to impart Tongzhi with ideals and knowledge they believed would be needed for the Qing to survive in an increasingly hostile world. Yet when Tongzhi took personal power on February 23, 1873, it was unclear what, if anything, the emperor had taken from his education and in what direction he would seek to lead the country. In part to mitigate the fears of scholars that the opportunity to influence the emperor was over, the edict announcing Tongzhi's ascension promised that he would continue his studies and thus guarantee scholars a voice in the halls of power.[111] And yet his short personal reign would come to be marked by frequent conflict between the throne and his officials. In many ways, the emperor's inability to overcome the opposition of the bureaucracy—and the ways in which many components of the larger emperorship cooperated to oppose him—demonstrates the fiction of grandeur and limits of imperial power inherent in the system. It also highlights the point raised by the official in the earlier quote: Tongzhi had failed to establish himself as a positive model, and hardly anyone was willing to follow him, regardless of the direction he sought to lead.

For example, as Emily Mokros has explored, one of Tongzhi's first acts upon assuming control was to order the reconstruction of the Garden of Perfect Brightness (Yuanming yuan), a decision that raised the ire of much of the bureaucracy. Tongzhi framed the call as an act of filial devotion, honoring the empress dowagers for their help in steering his education and running the country. In his classroom, Tongzhi had read the *Classic of Filial Piety* and accounts of the dedication of his ancestors to their mothers. Throughout the course his education, he was trained to perform respect to the empress dowagers in daily visits to their chambers. Yet now, ascending the throne, his efforts to put his learning into practice were met with resistance and condemnation. Officials opposed the Yuanming yuan project for a variety of reasons, with many highlighting the burden it placed on an already tight budget.[112] But Tongzhi persisted, arguing that the empress dowagers had provided a great service to the empire and deserved a place to rest. He urged members of the imperial family and Bannermen population to contribute funds for the project. Among Chinese officials, only Tongzhi's tutors did so, perhaps attempting to curry favor with their newly empowered pupil.[113]

Yet, in the end, it was also the tutors who offered some of the harshest criticisms of the construction. On July 3, 1874, Li Hongzao (Tongzhi's original and primary tutor) memorialized, writing that the Yuanming yuan project was distracting from more important matters. Li said that while Tongzhi was on the throne, his two main duties were to continue his studies and manage affairs of state. According to Li, the current project fell under neither category, and he thus urged Tongzhi to drop the idea and go back to work. A week later an assistant tutor, Li Wentian (1834–1895), also urged Tongzhi to stop, saying that continuing the project would not only impoverish the people but also contribute to banditry and increase the threat from imperialists in the region.[114]

The tutors were not alone in opposing Tongzhi's ambitions, as other members of the emperorship similarly voiced their displeasure with the emperor's decisions. On August 27, Prince Gong wrote a devastating memorial, using controversy over the construction project to criticize nearly everything about Tongzhi's rule. Prince Gong chastised the emperor for neglecting important affairs of state while indulging in selfish behavior. The prince said that when Tongzhi took the throne there had been a spirit of "restoration and self-strengthening" among officials. But now, a year into his personal rule, the emperor had disappointed everyone and that spirit was dissipating.[115] The situation was dire, and without immediate changes, Prince Gong predicted total collapse for the empire. He therefore outlined a six-point plan for the emperor to rectify his behavior. Among the suggestions, Prince Gong linked devotion to learning and effective governance. He told Tongzhi:

> Studying and managing state affairs are actually two sides of one coin. If one does not keep on studying, his knowledge cannot increase. Studying, therefore, should be a daily habit, and will undoubtedly aid you in reading and commenting on state business, such as memorials and petitions. Your Majesty has spent too much time on other activities. This is an ominous sign. I hope that Your Majesty will, from now on, concentrate on study which will also aid Your Majesty in nourishing your moral virtues.[116]

For Prince Gong, the emperor's continued education was a key mechanism through which scholar officials and men such as himself were able to participate in the governance of the empire. By urging the emperor to concentrate on studies, the prince was in effect urging him to embrace the bureaucracy and guidance of officials.

Reading Gong's memorial, Tongzhi was livid. In an audience with high officials a few days later, the emperor and Prince Gong reportedly got into a shouting match, and shortly thereafter Tongzhi, furious at his teachers for opposing his will, issued an edict dismissing Prince Gong, Prince Chun, Li Hongzao, and others from their posts.[117] However, as soon as Tongzhi dismissed the group, Cixi stepped in and reversed the decision. She said that "for the past ten years, without Prince Gong how could we have survived until today? His Majesty is young and inexperienced. The edicts he issued yesterday will be nullified."[118]

Tongzhi's clash with his officials brings into focus the precarious place of the emperor within the larger emperorship in this period. During the emperor's youthful education—the period of regency—representatives from different schools of learning each sought to mold a powerful imperial presence that could then act as their benefactor and lead the country in the direction they desired. Yet as an adult, having taken control of the state, when the emperor's personal will clashed with those groups, there was no simple way to circumvent him without draining the system of the useful fiction of a strong and virtuous throne. In the case of the

Yuanming yuan, in rallying against Tongzhi's desires, scholars, princes, and the empress dowagers cracked the illusion of power that had been promised to the emperor. Instead, they insisted that the strength of the Qing came from the continued participation of men such as Gong, Chun, and Li.

And yet almost immediately after they ruptured the image of Tongzhi as a powerful and unifying figure, the empress dowagers and other high officials at court worked to reconstruct that ideal. Despite the difficulties in his childhood education and personal reign, Chinese and Manchu officials continued to hope that the emperor's authority would provide them with the patronage they desired for their visions of reform. They therefore worked to maintain the useful fiction that Tongzhi was a dutiful student and leader, thereby protecting the emperorship and empire from the failings of the emperor.

This was perhaps most true in death. In late 1874, shortly after the Yuanming yuan conflict, Tongzhi was stricken with smallpox, and by December a council of princes assumed day-to-day operations of the state as the emperor lay dying. When he died in January 1875, the court, despite the clear disdain many high officials held for him personally, eulogized the deceased emperor in glowing terms: "For not a single day, in reverence for heaven and in obedience to the ancestral pattern, did he cease to be inspired with devotion in the cause of government and love on behalf of his people. He gave the charge of office to the attached and wise. He vanquished and subdued the great revolt. The welfare of the people and the policy of the state were ever present in his inmost thoughts."[119] Clearly this was not the Tongzhi described in this chapter, the one whose tutors struggled to educate and whose princes lambasted for selfish behavior. But it was the outward projection of the ideal of imperial authority and leadership. In fact, the final state-sanctioned description of Tongzhi (in the preface to the Veritable Records of his reign) declared that he was "respectful of his teachers" and "fond of learning" and singled out his tutors for praise in helping to mold the young student and for bringing a measure of peace to the empire.[120] Just as Woren had suggested years earlier, the text linked court education and dynastic reconstruction while allowing scholar-officials to argue for their continued power.

In the 1860s and 1870s, as local officials around the empire started to rebuild their communities in the aftermath of war and rebellion, the presence of a young emperor on the throne in Beijing suggested to some an opportunity to advocate for different visions of strength and stability for the Qing via Tongzhi's childhood education. In pronouncements from court and the writings of high officials, the promise of youth and the ability to influence the future of the empire through the emperor's education were common themes throughout the era.

In fact, this was the case not just for the Chinese, Mongolian, and Manchu officials discussed in this chapter but for commentators around the world, eagerly watching the Qing and urging it to reform. In 1863, two years into the reign of the then seven-year-old Tongzhi, for example, the *North China Herald* translated an article originally written in French and published in the *Chinese and Japanese Repository*. Titled "The Past and Future of China," the article described China as stuck in a point of development similar to that of mid-fourteenth-century Europe: "Surrounded by the greatest nations," the article read, China "must be re-animated by entering into profitable relations with them and by following their example in many things." Despite that current situation, however, the author held great hope for Tongzhi and the Qing, writing that the "present reign, succeeding to detestable and ruinous ones, begins under the most favorable auspices." The "most favorable auspice" was in fact that the paper recognized that the Tongzhi era began not under the leadership of an emperor but under that of a regency. Singling out Prince Gong for praise, the article trumpeted his progressive views and suggested that he would soon transform Tongzhi into a proponent of Western learning and lead the country toward a new future.[121]

Though the paper referred to Prince Gong as the man pulling the strings, widespread belief among Chinese officials that the empress dowagers had the clearest claim to authority (yet posed little risk of monopolizing power for themselves) helped to galvanize support for rule by the women until Tongzhi came of age. Once in power, the empress dowagers, particularly Cixi, built a diverse coalition of Chinese, Manchu, and Mongol officials to assist in their rule. Many of these officials—men such as Woren, Prince Gong, and Weng Tonghe—held a variety of important concurrent positions within the bureaucracy. As they worked to rebuild the institutions and infrastructure of the country through the Board of Rites, Grand Council, and other agencies, they also sought to transform the young emperor into a symbol of divergent visions of the country's rejuvenation while serving as "Officials of the Hongde Hall." The politics of appointment to the emperor's classroom, as well as management of his curriculum, were thus one of the tools the empress dowagers could deploy in managing court politics as they solidified their rule.

Even in this era of growing local activism and new theories of the state, an active and virtuous emperor was critical to Qing conceptions of rulership and the balance of power between throne and bureaucracy. Therefore, despite the personal deficiencies of Tongzhi in the classroom and on the throne, the ideal of the emperor remained alive at the center of power. Thus, just as Xianfeng's death had been an opportunity for new visions of education and reform to compete from within the emperor's classroom, Tongzhi's death suggested an opportunity for new groups to help guide the next young emperor and his empire. That project is the focus of chapter 2.

2

THE MALLEABILITY OF YOUTH

Guangxu in the Classroom, 1875–1890

When the Tongzhi emperor died in January 1875, the Qing faced a number of crises. Tongzhi's short personal reign had left many in the bureaucracy embittered, yet when he died with no heir, the throne was left precariously vacant. Who would replace Tongzhi, and, after the tumult of his reign, how would scholars conceive of their relationship to the throne? How would the traditional structures of court education and the training of the emperor respond to the dynamic changes at new educational institutions, translation bureaus, and a growing press around the country?

When it came to replacing Tongzhi, there were in fact several candidates for the job as the new emperor. Both Prince Gong and Prince Dun (Yicong, 1831–1889) were powerful figures at court and had sons who had studied in the Palace School for Princes in the late 1860s, granting them some claim to the learned authority required to assume the throne. Yet as adults who had already undergone years of training, it was difficult to present either as the empty vessel that had been central to the discourse of youthful education and regency during the Tongzhi era. Furthermore, the boys were tainted by the suspicion that they had contributed to Tongzhi's "hedonistic tendencies" and were thus partially responsible for the soured relationship between the former emperor and his officials.[1]

In choosing the new emperor, therefore, Cixi and her fellow regents sought out someone whose ascension could signal to groups of officials with competing visions of the future that, as had been the case at the start of the Tongzhi era, all were welcome to take part in the education of the emperor and, in that way, help guide the country. For this job, Prince Chun's (Yihuan, 1840–1891) young son Zaitian (1871–1908) was an attractive candidate. While Prince Chun was respected among officials, he was said to have little interest in personal power and therefore would not be tempted to unduly influence the emperor. As for the boy, the first public description of Zaitian came in a posthumous edict issued in Tongzhi's name, describing his successor as "virtuously disposed and filial, and endowed with bright intelligence."[2] Yet it was not Zaitian's "bright intelligence" that made him an attractive choice. Rather, it was his youth and the ability, in Cixi's words, to be educated to meet the challenges of the times that made him the most attractive candidate.[3]

Yet Zaitian's enthronement as the Guangxu emperor also caused serious conflict within the bureaucracy. Enthroning a boy of the same generation as the deceased emperor violated ritual norms regulating the ceremonies of ancestral worship, and protest memorials from many officials flowed into court. The solution—naming Guangxu as adopted son of Xianfeng and suggesting that Guangxu's first son would then be made the adopted son of Tongzhi—left many unsatisfied. In fact, the controversy continued for many years, reaching a climax in 1879 when an official named Wu Kedu (1812-1879) committed suicide in protest of the decisions both to appoint Zaitian as the new emperor and to name him Xianfeng's heir.[4]

With the controversy surrounding Guangxu's enthronement ongoing, the court worked to take control over the situation by formally inscribing the Tongzhi era as an unfinished success and presenting the new reign period as a chance for scholars to remain at the heart of governance. Part of this strategy was a discourse that emphasized the ways in which the progress of the Tongzhi reign was built on the cooperation of a wide array of officials, and in particular, those who had been tasked with educating the young emperor. As one edict described, when Tongzhi "first acceded to the throne, he labored diligently, day and night, under the direction of the benign maternal counsels, to accomplish his studies, under the tutelage of learned ministers. In the course of a few years, the rebels of the South and the roving bandits of the North were wholly subdued, and the provinces of the South and West once more enjoyed tranquility."[5] In this narrative, the work of regional armies and officials such as Zeng Guofan to bring a measure of peace back to the empire was tied to Tongzhi's (supposed) dedication to learning and the counsel of his teachers.

Similarly, in a posthumous edict, "Tongzhi" told the country that, having taken the throne as a child, he depended on the advice and teachings of others, and because of that, all around the empire rebellions had been quashed. Though the education of the emperor had clearly been only part of the constellation of reform efforts around the country over the past decades, these edicts placed great importance on the role that the activities of the emperor's classroom played in the era. But, Tongzhi said, "though the miseries of war have ceased, the wounds of our people are not yet healed."[6] Thus at the start of the new era both monarch and ministers would need to dedicate themselves to the project of reconstruction.

By stressing Tongzhi's reliance on the counsel of others, the empress dowagers transformed the deceased emperor into ventriloquist puppet voicing legitimacy for their continued power. At the same time, Tongzhi's death and the ascension of another young emperor were described as an opportunity for officials to again play a leading role in shaping the future of the country. As an edict in the name of the new Guangxu emperor put it: "Grave in our mind is the trust bequeathed, the burden of which is charged upon our unworthy person; yet we know that we are able to depend, in our capital and throughout the empire, upon our ministers and servants, high and low, in the ranks of the civil and military administration. Unitedly they will strive in uprightness and loyalty to maintain on our behalf an ever-improving rule."[7] To cement the throne's ties to the bureaucracy, the empress dowagers also issued a call for officials from around the empire to memorialize with advice for the new emperor while encouraging them to act diligently in their own posts.[8] As "Guangxu" said, "It behooves you, princes, nobles, and ministers, and officers high and low, to put forth your strenuous efforts, striving one and all in uprightness and loyalty to yield with joint accord support to an ever-improving rule." Working together on the shared task of restabilizing the dynasty, Guangxu said, would "give comfort above to the soul in heaven of His Majesty now departed and gratify below the hope of our subjects within the limits of the seas."[9] Through the combination of these edicts from the deceased Tongzhi, the young Guangxu, and the empress dowagers, the youth of the emperor was transformed from a perilous situation of uncertain authority and leadership into a call for service at court.

In the days and weeks following Tongzhi's death, the empress dowagers worked to formally reestablish the framework of regency that had guided the emperorship during Tongzhi's minority. Scholar-officials called on Cixi and Ci'an to again lead the government while the young Guangxu emperor was educated. The empress dowagers agreed while emphasizing that control would be returned to Guangxu as soon as his education was complete.[10] The period of female regency was therefore once again an explicitly temporary situation, and the task of educating Guangxu was understood as an open competition to mold the imperial mind. Even enemies were given a place, as Wu Kedu's memorial and other documents surrounding the debate over Guangxu's ascension were included among the texts that officials planned to use in the new emperor's education in the years to come.[11]

This chapter examines that education and explores how, although Tongzhi disappointed his teachers and alienated many in the bureaucracy, his death in 1875 created a renewed focus on court education. Throughout the 1870s and 1880s, scholars competed to impart their vision of the future onto the curriculum of the new emperor while an enlivened domestic press joined in arguing over the primacy of different subjects in the emperor's curriculum. All the while, Cixi worked to maintain the balance of power at court, both by presenting herself as a learned ruler and by ensuring that rival groups had access to the emperor's classroom.

REBUILDING THE IMPERIAL CLASSROOM

At the start of Guangxu's reign, the empress dowagers said that, because he had ascended the throne at a young age, "he must take the opportunity to begin his studies as soon as possible such that his continual progress to enrich his steadfast nature will carry over and become the foundation of governance."[12] In part, this meant studying classical texts and developing the moral, martial, and linguistic skills needed to perform the tasks of governance. Guangxu's tutors were therefore urged to exhaust themselves in educating the young emperor to prepare him for rule. But it also meant restoring the ties between throne and bureaucracy and officials throughout the state. Guangxu's schooling was thus interwoven into the ritual relations and the functioning of the emperorship. Regulations for his education described the need for him to participate in celebrations of events such as the birthdays of the empress dowagers, his own birthday, and other traditional festivals and sacrifices. Guangxu also needed to be trained to serve as the head of the imperial family, and the regulations for his schooling further outlined banquets and other events to establish his relationship with his Manchu service nobility, in addition to mandating that his days start with lessons in archery, Manchu, and Mongolian.[13] While he would not wield functional power in his youth, his participation in these events enabled him to serve as the symbolic link between the imperial center, the Manchu community, and an ever-fractious bureaucracy.

In planning Guangxu's education, the court thus continued much of the rhetoric of Tongzhi's classroom. But, perhaps because of the failings of Tongzhi's education and to signify the new era, when Guangxu started his schooling, the physical classroom was moved out of the Hongde Hall to a venue that would hopefully inspire a more diligent student. During the Guangxu reign, the Yuqing Palace (Yuqing gong, Palace of Nurturing Joy) became the central site of court education.[14] Beginning in 1709, the Yuqing Palace had been used as a residence and study hall for imperial princes, and both the Qianlong and Jiaqing emperors recorded their memories of living in the palace with their brothers before reaching the age of marriage.[15] By the time Guangxu took the throne, in addition to the main room dedicated for use as a classroom, there were also specialized waiting rooms for the imperial tutors where teachers would await the arrival of their student each morning.[16]

Inside, calligraphy from the young emperor's ancestors kept close watch over Guangxu as he progressed in his studies, tying the activities of the classroom to larger goals and projects of reconstruction around the empire. Much of the calligraphy placed in the Yuqing Palace was written by Jiaqing and was explicit in linking the specific place with the broader task of governance. In one passage, for example, Jiaqing recalled his own childhood education and asked future princes to sincerely comply with the laws and rituals of the dynasty to ensure that the Yuqing Palace would be a place of great strength and success for the dynasty. Jiaqing continued that theme in another couplet, writing that whereas princes must always be concerned with carrying forward the accomplishments of their ancestors to make sure the dynasty flourished, the Yuqing Palace was not a place to relax or take things lightly. Most concretely, Jiaqing wrote that "although this is just a room, it is the place from which the glory of the country will be continued. At all times think of nothing but comforting the people."[17]

Those tasked with helping to guide Guangxu in that process included both veterans of Tongzhi's classroom and a variety of new officials. Despite the failures of Tongzhi's education, Weng Tonghe was retained as Guangxu's primary tutor. Throughout the Tongzhi era, Weng had been a faithful servant of the empress dowagers. As noted in the previous chapter, Weng's father owed the resurrection of his career to the 1861 coup, and Weng frequently stressed the importance for Tongzhi to be filial in devotion to the empress dowagers. His loyalty was now rewarded with another posting as imperial tutor.

At the start of Guangxu's education, Weng was joined in the classroom by another strong proponent of the classical canon, Xia Tongshan (1831–1880). Xia earned his *jinshi* in 1856 and had served under Zeng Guofan during the Taiping

Rebellion. Yet Xia was generally opposed to the self-strengthening policies of officials such as Li Hongzhang and was aligned with the "Qingliu" scholars in the 1860s and 1870s, who urged the court to focus more on relief efforts for the population than on investing in new technologies from the West. Xia and his compatriots saw a breakdown in the relationship between the court and the domestic population—not foreign armies—as the greatest threat to the Qing, and they therefore argued for policies to focus on issues such as famine relief before arsenals.[18]

In many ways, Xia saw personal imperial virtue as crucial to strengthening the country. For example, in 1867 he heard a rumor that the young Tongzhi would be traveling outside the Forbidden City with other members of the imperial family to visit imperial gardens. Xia was greatly concerned by this idea, and along with Sun Yijing (1826–1890), he remonstrated against the trip. Among other things, Xia argued that as the emperor was young, this was no time to distract him from studies with tour or travel. He urged that the emperor should stay behind and focus on his studies to cultivate his imperial virtue.[19]

As other monarchies around the world were beginning to augment their power through public displays of splendor, Xia argued that the authority of the Qing was in fact rooted in the sovereign's frugality. He believed that the country was looking to the emperor for leadership, and the court must avoid doing anything that might sully the imperial reputation. For Xia, pronouncements describing the emperor's devotion to his education would be more effective than trips or tours in cultivating loyalty. Inviting Xia to serve in Guangxu's classroom sanctioned such views, and the empress dowagers once again provided Confucian scholars a platform in the center of power from which they could disseminate their ideals of rulership and reform around the country.

Xia's co-memorialist Sun Yijing as well would later gain a posting as one of Guangxu's tutors. Sun earned his *jinshi* in the late Xianfeng era, and after having been granted a position in the Nanshu fang (Southern Study) early in the Tongzhi reign on the recommendation of Woren, he served in a variety of educational institutions including the Guozijian and Hanlin Academy. Sun also held positions in key ministries such as the Board of Rites and Board of Revenue in the years before his appointment to Guangxu's classroom. Although he did not clearly identify with a single school or clique, throughout his career Sun emphasized the teachings of the Classics to meet the challenges of the day and—like his mentors and colleagues Xia and Woren—saw Confucian moralism and values such as frugality as key to stabilizing Qing rule. Along with his other roles in the state, his eventual posting in Guangxu's classroom gave Sun an opportunity to advance that view.[20]

But Qing rule rested on more than the Classics. The court therefore promised that the restoration project would include reinvigorating the martial and linguistic skills of the Qing founders and reestablishing the emperor as the leader of a mighty Manchu army. The empress dowagers tasked Prince Chun with overall supervision of the classroom and, in particular, urged him to ensure competent instruction in Manchu, Mongolian, horseback riding, and archery.[21] In fact, nearly every discussion of Guangxu's education closed by asserting the importance of Manchu as the "root of Our Dynasty," and just as the emperor's classroom was deployed to attract the service of Confucian scholars, so too was it used to assure Manchu officials of their place in the system.[22] In rhetoric and in the selection of personnel, the court remained committed to its uniquely Qing conception of rulership and authority based on maintenance of the Manchu Way and mastery of the Confucian Canon.

Over the next few years, a variety of teachers moved in and out of Guangxu's classroom, with representatives of different schools of thought, ethnic groups, and political cliques all among the staff. The group included Sun Jia'nai (1827–1909), Zhang Jiaxiang (1827–1885), Songgui (1833–1907), Chongqi (1829–1900), and Shiduo (1843–1914). While all these men were respected scholars, they also represented different factions within the government and presented the emperor with different worldviews that sought to pull him in different directions. Chongqi, for example, had been an assistant in Tongzhi's classroom who, as discussed in chapter 1, was critical of foreign engagement and would come to bitterly oppose the Hundred Days Reforms as well as support the Boxers. Sun Jia'nai, on the other hand, argued for the introduction of Western learning and the creation of imperially sponsored institutions to teach those new subjects. During and after his years as one of Guangxu's tutors, Sun played important roles in compiling and editing new encyclopedias of world knowledge and advocating for centrally planned and managed institutions for Western learning.[23]

The group of teachers also continued the trend from the Tongzhi era of placing imperial family members in critical roles within the central state. Songgui, for example, was a member of the Manchu Irgen Gioro clan and earned a translation degree in 1860. Shiduo, meanwhile, was a member of the Aisin Gioro family and holder of a hereditary princely rank. Placing Songgui and Shiduo in the classroom worked to assure imperial princes of their own place in the constitutional balance of power while negotiating the tension between bureaucratic and patrimonial styles of rule.[24]

At the start of Guangxu's education, however, a new group of voices emerged that sought a place in the young emperor's classroom in the hope of shaping the direction of the country. The burgeoning domestic press, based largely in the foreign concessions of Shanghai, became vocal participants in the discourse of court education.[25] For example, *Shenbao*, the country's leading daily newspaper founded just a few years prior, argued for the importance of surrounding the emperor with good advisors and sought to influence the appointment of officials involved in the emperor's education. While the paper would have much to say about the texts and teachers involved in Guangxu's formal studies, it also argued for the importance of overall character development in the young ruler and sought to ensure that his education extended beyond the walls of the classroom. For example, highlighting the malleability of the emperor in his youth, the article demanded that, in choosing the eunuchs and servants who would surround Guangxu, the court pick people who would instill in the emperor a passion for learning without pursuing personal benefit.[26] Not only did the paper hope to influence the choice of servants, but it also sought to shape Guangxu's curriculum, urging the emperor to read stories of loyal and virtuous eunuchs from the Han, Tang, and Ming while cautioning against the potential danger to the emperor caused by unethical advisors from those same dynasties.[27]

Being named the emperor's teacher not only put an official center stage in molding the imperial mind, but the tutors frequently had private audiences with the empress dowagers and had direct access to the halls of power. Therefore *Shenbao*, by claiming the power to pass judgment on those involved with Guangxu's education and hold them accountable for the proper development of the emperor's virtue, asserted that the press and voices outside the traditional bureaucracy had an important role to play in shaping the future of the country.

HOPES AND CHALLENGES AT THE START OF SCHOOL

Against the backdrop of nationwide reform efforts and a tenuous relationship between the throne and bureaucracy, Guangxu's informal lessons began on March 16, 1876. That morning, Weng Tonghe gathered with the other teachers and a group of princes in a small room on the east side of the Hall of Mental Cultivation (Yangxin dian), awaiting the young emperor's arrival.[28] After Guangxu took his seat facing south, the officials "set up a short table and unfolded paper writing instruments and books. I [Weng] took an ink brush and wrote the four-character phrase, 'The World is at Peace' (*tianxia taiping*). I also wrote the four characters, 'Rectitude and Honor' (*zhengda guangming*)."[29] These were ideal visions of the world and the practice of government that would be difficult to transform into reality in the classroom or around the empire.[30] As Weng described, "His Majesty was a little unsmooth with his control of the brush."[31]

The process of emperors learning to write involved a wide range of people and care. When writing phrases such as those Weng described, a tutor or *anda* would first write the character on a piece of paper. Next, an artisan would carve out the character and sprinkle white powder into it. The white powder would leak out onto a separate piece of paper providing an outline of the character for the emperor to trace.[32] On Guangxu's first day of school, when Weng had him write these inspirational phrases, the young emperor used vermillion ink to trace the characters onto red checkered paper, reminiscent of past—and promising future—monarchical power.[33]

After writing the two Chinese phrases, the Manchu teachers "used Manchu script to write one word. His Majesty looked at it and said 'A,' the first word in Manchu."[34] Returning to Chinese work, the tutors wrote "The Virtue of an Emperor" (*dide*), which Guangxu then read aloud. Weng then taught Guangxu the opening lines from the *Dijian tushuo* (Illustrated mirror for the emperor).[35] For Weng, this was the most exciting moment of the day: "His Majesty was really interested in this and he reached out his finger to touch [the pictures of] Yao and Shun."[36] Guangxu's engagement with the material provided hope that the emperor would in fact be different from Tongzhi, who years earlier had shown no interest in that same text. For Weng and his fellow tutors, the rise of a plastically virtuous emperor would ensure their continued prominence at court, and so for these scholars the Guangxu era began on an auspicious note.

Weng might have left the classroom that day in a good mood, but he was clearly nervous throughout the lesson. As he got up to leave the emperor's classroom, Weng bent over and realized that sweat had soaked through all his clothing.[37] It was indeed hard work. From that first day until the more formal opening of Guangxu's education two months later, Weng and the other tutors arrived at the palace every morning at three o'clock, never knowing if their student would show up for class that day.[38]

When Guangxu began his formal studies, Weng entered the palace and waited for the emperor to complete ceremonies inside the Hall of Sages. Then, around five o'clock in the morning, with Guangxu sitting on the throne inside his Yuqing Palace classroom, Weng and the other officials kneeled and performed several kowtows. When the officials had completed their greetings, Guangxu stepped down from the throne and, just as Tongzhi had done years before, bowed with his hands clasped toward his tutors and began the day's lessons. Unlike the informal beginnings of Guangxu's lessons, however, on the formal inauguration of the emperor's education, the Manchu Way took precedence in the curriculum: the lesson began with archery and a few sentences of Mongolian and Manchu. Weng then punctuated four Chinese sentences for the emperor to read. Weng wanted to give him four more, but the teachers were under instructions from the empress dowagers not to overwork the young emperor, and Guangxu seemed a bit tired.[39]

The early days of Guangxu's education provided officials with hope that the emperor was perhaps following in the footsteps of his technical ritual ancestor Xianfeng and not that of his immediate predecessor, Tongzhi. Weng wrote frequently in his diary describing Guangxu as a diligent student and extolling the emperor's progress in both his Manchu and Chinese studies.[40] But Guangxu was still just a child, and he sometimes frustrated his tutors with petulant or obstinate behavior when he had difficulty completing the day's assignments.[41]

More dramatically, a few years into Guangxu's education, one of his tutors, Sun Jia'nai, proposed that each day the tutors should record all the emperor's mistakes in a book he called the *Neixing lu* (Records of introspection). The book would be sent to the empress dowagers so that they could keep closer watch over the progress of the emperor's studies. From Sun's perspective, this was a clever political strategy of ingratiating himself to the empress dowagers. Sun was reaffirming the place of Cixi and Ci'an at the center of court power while demonstrating his own commitment to the development of the young emperor. At the same time, the book was a potential weapon in Sun's battle with other tutors in the classroom. Should the *Record* contain evidence of poor performance by Guangxu in subjects tasked to Sun's colleagues, Sun would have an argument for their dismissal.

Sun's plan, however, ran into a perhaps unexpected obstacle: the idea enraged the young emperor, and Guangxu threw what amounted to an imperial temper tantrum, refusing to attend class until Sun's idea was aborted. Weng took Guangxu's side, making the point to Sun, as he had to Xu Tong years earlier fighting over disciplining Tongzhi, that harsh criticisms were unlikely to be effective motivation.[42] Perhaps reflecting a genuine belief or perhaps an attempt to forestall Sun's political maneuverings, Weng nonetheless refused to support his fellow teacher in this particular form of pedagogy. Guangxu revealed himself to be a skittish pupil in other ways as well. Although Prince Chun was tasked with overseeing his son's education, the father's presence in the classroom apparently made the young emperor too nervous to focus or read new books, and so the prince often did not attend the lessons.[43]

More fundamentally than disputes over motivational techniques in the classroom, the overall content of Guangxu's lessons was an open question as new ideas and groups competed for dominance around the country. The Self-Strengthening Movement, the founding of new educational and technological institutions, as well as the first cohort of Chinese students studying abroad throughout the 1860s and 1870s had introduced new strains of learning into the repertoire of governance around the empire.[44] Moreover, now in the Guangxu era a greatly expanded press—both in Chinese and foreign languages—offered new space for debates about the imperial curriculum. As the court and high officials in Beijing struggled with how to incorporate new systems of knowledge into the practice of empire, the press in Shanghai sought to empower the throne, and themselves, with new forms of learning. Writers outside the ranks of officialdom and removed from access to power proposed curriculum reforms that they hoped would sideline scholar-officials at court, freeing the emperor to sponsor policies and programs proposed by intellectuals in the press.

Though there were many different ideas about the content of Guangxu's lessons, arguments were frequently framed as returning to the ideals of the Kangxi era. In the newly expanding Chinese press, for example, Kangxi played the foil for Guangxu from the very beginning of the emperor's reign. In 1876, just after Guangxu took the throne, *Shenbao* ran an article titled "Dixue lun" (On the learning of emperors) that traced the history of imperial education from the Yellow Emperor to the current day. After describing the importance of teachers to illustrious figures such as Yao and Shun, the article focused on the Kangxi era to make its argument for Guangxu's education. It suggested, for example, that Guangxu's classroom model its rituals and seating arrangements for teachers and students on Kangxi's time.[45] The paper told its readers that if Guangxu would respect teachers and learning in the way that Kangxi had, he would bring order to the empire and China would regain its strength.

Chinese officials also made the analogy between the youth of Kangxi and Guangxu, calling for a revival of the Kangxi era Daily Lectures and Classic Mat to expose Guangxu to a variety of teachers, create new links between the throne and the bureaucracy, and visibly demonstrate an imperial commitment to learning. These were key tenets of the scholarly conception of legitimate participation in government, and as Guangxu pursued his studies, officials used the emperor's education to advance their role in the state. Time and time again in these memorials, officials referred to the Kangxi era as the model for the Classic Mat lectures and as the ideal relationship between a young monarch and his ministers.[46] For these officials, the Kangxi era was particularly productive because it was not until the Qianlong era that the emperor added the "imperial comment" (*yulun*) portion of the event, giving himself the final say over interpretation of the Classics and asserting his dominance over scholars in the rituals of education.[47] In this way, the Kangxi era Classic Mat still suggested a balance of power in favor of scholar-officials in their role as teachers to the emperor. In trying to mold Guangxu into their model monarch then, these officials sought an ideal of imperial action guided by the tutelage of scholars.

Many within the foreign community in China also believed that a strong emperor was critical to the stability of the Qing state and its ability to uphold treaty obligations and other spoils of imperialism. During the early years of Guangxu's reign, therefore, the foreign press frequently sought to influence the young emperor's education by exalting Kangxi's learning. In particular, foreign writers drew on Kangxi's patronage of Jesuits and his interest in Western learning to argue for an expanded curriculum for Guangxu. They suggested that a Qing throne empowered by the knowledge of the West would restore China to a position of greatness. In late 1881, for example, the *Chinese Recorder and Missionary Journal* described the "appearance of decay" that "everywhere meets the eyes of the traveler in China." The paper nonetheless found reason for hope in precedent. When Kangxi ascended the throne, it argued, the country was in a similarly perilous state: the population was depleted, and the treasury nearly emptied by war and rebellion. Yet, "with an energy worthy of his high position, and with a wisdom and prudence that was not expected of one so young, he [Kangxi] set himself to work to promote the recuperation and prosperity of the country," enacting administrative reform, promoting frugality, reviving the educational system, and personally producing great works of scholarship.[48]

The Guangxu emperor was only ten years old when this article appeared. But the message was clear. If China were to regain its strength and prosperity, it needed an emperor like Kangxi to lead the country toward similar reforms. Just as *Shenbao* and the variety of scholar-officials proposing the renewal of the Classic Mat argued, the foreign press suggested that Kangxi offered Guangxu the "true course to be pursued" in the current day "in order to secure a similar recuperation from the present state of decay and impoverishment."[49] Yet at the same time, each group's image of the ideal emperor differed in how the throne would relate to other component parts of the imperial system and the types of learning they suggested were necessary to secure a stabile future for the Qing.

LANGUAGE AND POWER

In this context, language training in the young emperor's curriculum emerged as a flashpoint in debates surrounding how to best rebuild the power of the throne and reclaim the Qing position within the world community. For example, in 1876, one year into Guangxu's reign when he was five years old, *Shenbao* published several articles urging the empress dowagers to include English in the emperor's curriculum. Were the emperor to learn English, the paper contended, he would free himself from the restraints imposed by translators and personally interact with foreign diplomats. *Shenbao* was owned by the British merchant Ernest Major, and the paper's Chinese employees seemed to be advocating the long-standing British belief that Beijing was filled with antiforeign and antitrade officials who were holding the country back from reform. In their minds, adding English to Guangxu's curriculum would enable him to bypass these officials and strengthen the country by changing its relationship with the outside world.

This argument was made most forcefully in a February 15, 1876, article titled "Lun renjun yi tong taguo yuyan wenzi shi" (On the suitability of the sovereign learning languages of other states), which argued for the importance of educating the young emperor in a way that would prepare him to exercise his empirical power in the emperorship and play a central role in Qing foreign relations. After describing the delight that scholars inside and outside China felt upon hearing the news that the empress dowagers and the Imperial Astronomy Bureau

(Qintianjian) had selected an auspicious date for the emperor to begin his schooling, the author reproduced (or imagined) a conversation with foreigners about the emperor's education: "When foreign scholars ask me what books it is that the Emperor of China reads, I say they are the Writings of the Sages, the Classics, the Histories, and the Collected Writings. When they ask me what he does in addition to reading books, I tell them that he also studies our Qing dynastic language, Mongolian language, as well as horsemanship and archery." In this narrative, the emperor was taught to master multiple traditions of learning to cultivate his authority among different communities within the empire. He studied Manchu, horsemanship, and archery so as not to forget the roots of the dynasty. By speaking to the Mongols in their own language, the emperor was able to communicate without the need for an interpreter, thus demonstrating his close personal sentiment with groups that played an integral part in the founding of the country.[50]

But times have changed. Mongol, Manchu, and Chinese officials were not the only communities with which the emperor needed to communicate. Therefore, the article argued that the emperor ought to add knowledge of English to his diplomatic toolbox. To make his point, the article described the education of European monarchs, arguing that their early educations set the foundation for productive diplomatic engagements:

> All the countries of the Far West in the land of Europe, when their rulers are Crown Prince, they study all the languages of the various countries of the continent. Because of this, no matter how far away they might be from each other, the leaders of each country are able to have a thorough understanding of the ruler of other countries. When they meet in person there is no need for an interpreter, and they can speak face to face.

What's more, the author said, the leader of Russia, which lies between Europe and Asia, has mastered the languages of both continents, and the ruler of Japan has adopted Western methods while continuing to study Chinese Classics.[51] Extolling the virtues of polyglot monarchs around the globe, the article condemned translators as often-greedy troublemakers.[52] To productively engage with the foreign community, then, the emperor needed to learn English, discard the officials around him, and take personal control.

This was more than a question, however, of engaging with foreign powers. *Shenbao*'s proposal was an attempt to undermine the power of the scholar-officials in charge of the emperor's education and replace the influence of men such as Weng Tonghe with their own. Thus while we might interpret the growing domestic press as a forum for oppositional politics, the education of a young emperor provided an arena for writers outside of power to attempt to reshape, not undo, the emperorship.[53]

At court in Beijing, meanwhile, there were no signs that officials agreed that Guangxu learning English was the answer to China's problems. Rather, many continued to insist on the importance in the imperial curriculum of not only the Dynastic Language (*Guoyu*, i.e., Manchu) but also Mongolian (*Menggu yuyan wenzi*) in order to preserve the authority of the Manchu throne.[54] In 1884, for example, officials proposed that members of the three upper banners adept at Mongolian should be selected to train Guangxu in the language.[55] A similar proposal suggested examining members of the Plain Yellow and Plain White Banners in their Mongolian language abilities in order to select teachers for the emperor.[56]

Concern over the emperor's Mongolian-language competency was directly tied to his ability to communicate with officials, carry out his functional role within the emperorship, and lead the empire. Reminiscent of the Tongzhi era when Cixi had castigated officials for the emperor's inability to read Chinese or Manchu memorials, now in 1885, Cixi reprimanded the princes in charge of Guangxu's education for his apparent inability to read Mongolian-language memorials. The Mongolian-language instructors were warned to be diligent in their duties and ensure the emperor made daily progress in his studies so that he would understand all the information flowing into court and be able to carry out his rule.[57] Prince Chun, meanwhile, ordered officials in the emperor's presence to ask and answer questions in Manchu. He also outlined a plan for Guangxu's training in Manchu, Mongolian, archery, firearms, and horseback riding to ensure his mastery of the Manchu Way.[58] Guangxu was apparently an adept student of Manchu, and just a few years later he continued the unhappy tradition of his ancestors of having to castigate Manchu officials from the provinces for their own deficiencies in the dynastic language.[59] In fact, despite ways in which Chinese had become the dominant language of court affairs, Manchu still played an important role in the outward projection of the image of the Qing Empire. At audiences with foreign envoys, for example, both Tongzhi and Guangxu spoke Manchu.[60]

In many ways, therefore, language was critical to the functioning of the emperor's power within the bureaucracy and the projection of his authority around the empire. *Shenbao*, in urging Guangxu to learn English—and the empress dowager in insisting that he master Mongolian—argued that the emperor needed to play a personal role in the governance of the country. The editors at *Shenbao* took the argument further than Cixi in suggesting that Guangxu ought to circumvent officials and personally learn from other countries. In this way, the paper argued, he would strengthen his position in the government and China's place in the world. Critically as well from *Shenbao*'s perspective, English and other curricular reforms would reduce the power of scholar-officials in Beijing, creating space for the participation of new groups of intellectuals through the growing domestic press.

CIXI'S STEWARDSHIP OF STATE AFFAIRS DURING GUANGXU'S STUDIES

During Guangxu's youth, the court frequently reminded the country that the emperor was diligently pursuing his studies. However, despite clearly indicating that the emperor would take over control of government once his education was complete, during the period of his minority it was the empress dowagers who were described as handling state affairs.[61] For Cixi, this meant a combination of learning and violence to maintain ties to the bureaucracy while retaining primary control over decisions at court.

Artistic production and imperial gift giving, for example, remained central in maintaining relationships with officials. In 1882 alone, the Imperial Workshop mounted over one hundred of Cixi's paintings, many of which were then presented as gifts to key political allies.[62] Cixi's ability to cement the loyalty of the bureaucracy was deeply embedded in her ability to speak the language of Confucian moralism and project the aesthetic values of scholar-officials. While in the years following the 1861 coup she dutifully performed the role of student to draw scholars into her service, she now rewarded them with gifts, proving her continued devotion to their cause.

At the same time, Cixi worked to oust critics and strip authority from officials whose status threatened to disrupt the power balance either inside the emperor's classroom or within the larger state apparatus. This struggle was acutely revealed during the Sino-French War (1884–1885) as Cixi worked to balance the interests of multiple factions with competing foreign policy perspectives. During two years of start-and-stop fighting with France over influence in Vietnam, Qing foreign policy was largely driven by Prince Gong and Li Hongzhang, both of whom advocated a peaceful settlement. Their tentative posture angered many others in the bureaucracy, notably those grouped under the *qingyi* (pure discussion) banner, junior officials without direct access to the throne. These were the same types of officials that Cixi had used as her power base during 1861, when she rewarded members of the "Southern City" clique with prominent positions, including as tutors in the imperial classroom. When Qing forces were routed at Bac-ninh in March 1884, Prince Gong's tentative position enraged *qingyi* officials and threatened to sever their participation in the state. On April 8, 1884, therefore, Cixi dismissed Prince Gong, the entire Grand Council, and half of the Zongli yamen, promising new groups a voice in foreign policy affairs.[63]

In announcing the dismissal, however, Cixi did not focus on specific policy disagreements with Gong and his allies. Instead, she accused the group of forming a clique, acting in their own self-interest, and attempting to monopolize power. In an edict issued in the emperor's name, Cixi said that Prince Gong "and those associated with him were in the first instance fairly careful in their conduct and zealous in the assistance which they rendered, but as time went on, they became self-satisfied and thought only of securing their own aggrandizement."[64] This was precisely the critique of Prince Gong from the Tongzhi era, when officials such as Weng Tonghe accused him of manipulating the emperor for his own benefit. Just as Cixi had earlier pacified scholar-officials by removing the prince from Tongzhi's classroom, she now reached out to *qingyi* officials while ensuring power for herself by ousting Gong from the Grand Council.[65]

With Prince Gong now securely cast aside, Cixi led the court in advocating an aggressive stance against France, a position that won her much support and admiration among *qingyi*-aligned officials in Beijing. As Li Ciming—who had mocked Sushun in 1861 for his pretensions to speak for the young emperor—wrote in his diary:

> Cixi anxiously and diligently seeks good rule, a hundred times more than a female Yao or Shun. Since March 1884, she has single-mindedly advocated war. She summoned the members of the Grand Council to court and decreed to them: "the Xianfeng Emperor regarded the war of 1860 with great remorse, but He died with an ambition unfulfilled. Now we ought to wipe out the humiliation for the former Emperor."[66]

Li thus cheered the dismissal of the Grand Council and Cixi's embrace of the new foreign policy position. In his private thoughts, Li showed the power of Cixi's earlier efforts to cultivate herself in the mold of the sage-kings of old. Even greater than a female Yao and Shun, for Li, Cixi embodied the assertive imperial authority that had been missing since Xianfeng's exile.

Li's writing also suggests the degree to which the idea of a female-led regency had become an accepted model of governance. In Lloyd Eastman's classic analysis, Cixi's embrace of the aggressive policies of the *qingyi* group was born largely from her tenuous claims of authority, a situation that in later years prevented the court from leading more widespread reform.[67] Yet for several decades after Xianfeng's death, it was in fact Cixi's embrace of the role of scholar-officials in the emperorship that allowed the Qing to stabilize and work toward rejuvenation. In replacing Prince Gong with Prince Chun, for example, Cixi ensured officials that Chun would not interfere in day-to-day operations, and that his position was only temporary until Guangxu finished his education.[68]

At the same time, Cixi was not simply abdicating the power of the throne to the control of officials. In the aftermath of the war, despite the devastation of the Fuzhou Naval Yard and other Qing losses, when peace came in 1885 Cixi presented herself as a triumphant defender of the empire's frontiers. She did so primarily by highlighting successes in putting down rebellions in other provinces. In 1885, for example, Cixi commissioned paintings to honor Qing victories in the Taiping Rebellion and Nian Rebellion, as well as Muslim rebellions in Yunnan, Guizhou, Shaanxi, Gansu, and Xinjiang. In sixty-seven paintings depicting the battles, Cixi presented the Qing as a forceful empire and, through her patronage and commemoration, claimed personal credit for the success.

For these war commemorations, Cixi positioned herself as heir to Qianlong and his grand projects of war commemoration paintings. More than Qianlong's heir, in fact, Cixi claimed that she had in some ways supplanted the illustrious ruler in their shared imperial project: her paintings were hung in the Pavilion of Purple Light (Ziguang ge), replacing paintings commissioned by Qianlong to similarly celebrate success on the battlefield (that is, until they were unceremoniously looted from the pavilion by the allied imperialist forces in 1900).[69] The paintings were intended as a testament to the strength of Cixi's leadership, as she now declared that she was ultimately responsible for the court's military successes and an irreplaceable component of the emperorship. Cixi would give scholars access and power, but she retained possession of the key tools of imperial charisma and bureaucratic appointment that sustained the system.

BRINGING GUANGXU TO POWER

Just as Qianlong retired and nominally passed on power to Jiaqing, however, as the Sino-French War ended in early 1885, there were signs that the period of Guangxu's minority and Cixi's regency were coming to an end. This was the promise at the heart of the rhetoric of his education over the past decade: the eventual return of the emperor to power, and through him the implementation of the types of reforms advocated by one of the competing groups of scholars represented in his classroom.

Throughout 1885 Cixi issued edicts that reminded the population of the temporary nature of Guangxu's isolation to his classroom and her power at court, highlighting plans for the emperor to take up the responsibility for Grand Sacrifices and other key rituals in the coming years.[70] To begin the transition to personal rule, in 1886 Guangxu began to make comments on secret palace memorials in the same vermillion ink he had used to trace characters as a child with his tutors. Later that year, Cixi declared that ever since the emperor ascended the throne at a young age, he had been diligent in his studies and made daily progress in his learning.[71] Now, after all that hard work, his education was complete, and he was able to judge the past and present and distinguish right and wrong. It was therefore time to take up the reins of government.[72] The transfer of power back to the emperor brought with it potential for the throne to recuperate the unity of its authority under the personal rule of Guangxu. The rhetoric of his education had always suggested this was the goal, but, as with Tongzhi, it remained to be seen what that would mean in practice.

As it had done after Tongzhi's death as well, the court worked to cement a narrative of the past decade. While in Tongzhi's case the priority was to sustain the fiction of a diligent and virtuous emperor, as Guangxu prepared to take the throne, the primary task was to depict his childhood regents—and particularly Cixi—in the best possible light. To accentuate the image of Cixi as dutiful servant to the larger cause of the emperorship, the court publicized a variety of edicts in which Cixi displayed a desire to retreat from politics now that Guangxu had come of age. To start, Cixi reminded her audience that she and Ci'an had assumed power only at the behest of officials and for the good of the state until the completion of the emperor's education. More elaborately, Guangxu begged Cixi to stay in power and allow him to continue his studies and delay assuming power until his learning was even greater. Cixi rejected Guangxu's pleas and reminded him and officials that the period of regency was always intended to be temporary. Cixi said Guangxu was well prepared because "we have taught and guided the emperor in the inner precincts of the Palace, watching with pleasure his progress towards completion of his studies."[73] What's more, just as with Tongzhi, Guangxu was to continue his studies from the throne, and Cixi assured both the emperor and officials that she would continue to provide teaching and guidance whenever necessary.[74] Through these obsequious writings from officials and the emperor asking for the continuation of her rule, Cixi carved a new role for herself in the political system, a pedagogue emeritus who could be called on to adjudicate difficult situations or shift the balance of power in case of a stalemate.

In fact, the stress on Guangxu's continued education and reliance on Cixi meant that the emperor's ascension did not strictly follow the Tongzhi model. For two years, Guangxu operated under a system of "political tutelage" (*xunzheng*) wherein the "retired" Cixi still advised on important matters of state. This was not unprecedented in the history of the Qing. When Kangxi had taken over personal control in the seventeenth century, edicts similarly stated that whereas the country faced great challenges, the empress dowager would continue to provide guidance to the still-young emperor.[75] The specific phrase *xunzheng*, meanwhile, was co-opted from the early Jiaqing era, where it and other related terms were used to describe how the "retired" Qianlong continued to exercise authority. The period of "tutelage" thus in part promised to forestall the risk of the emperor quickly choosing sides in factional battles and alienating large swaths of the bureaucracy. The court promised everyone an opportunity to guide the young emperor and transform him into a powerful ally. Now that he was growing up and might attempt to exercise that power, officials feared the consequences of ending up as an enemy of the emperor's agenda. During the transition to Guangxu's personal rule, therefore, Cixi drew on earlier imperial models to reserve a role in the inner workings of power for herself and her allies.

In these early years of Guangxu's personal rule, Cixi worked to cement that space by continuing to model herself on earlier Qing rulers while cultivating relationships with members of the bureaucracy. As she had in 1885 with the battle paintings, Cixi again drew on Qianlong in her retirement. When Qianlong abdicated in 1796, he began construction on a palace that was to serve as his new home in retirement, the Palace of Tranquil Longevity (Ningshou gong).[76] Now in her own retirement, Cixi moved into the same palace. Once there, Cixi continued to emulate Qianlong, for example ordering that some of the former emperor's paintings be hung in the palace so she could study his brushstrokes.[77] Cixi also spent time copying the Heart Sutra, a favorite activity of Qianlong, not only mimicking his style but also going so far as to copy his seal.[78]

Other Qing rulers too provided Cixi with potential models of rulership, and she portrayed herself as learning from them, both artistically and politically. In 1889, for example, Cixi copied one of the Shunzhi emperor's paintings. This was not simply a private interest but rather part of Cixi's politics of authority. After Cixi copied Shunzhi's painting, she invited officials to view her work, and men such as Yuan Chang (1846-1900) dutifully composed verse to commemorate the experience. Cixi also continued painting and presenting those paintings as gifts to key officials around the country, such as Zhang Zhidong.[79] In this way she ensured that although Guangxu was at the center, she never left the emperorship.

Still, Cixi's rule and the era of regency were fundamentally built on a rhetoric of impermanence, and, having completed his education, Guangxu would ultimately take control of government. In 1889, therefore, after two years of tutelage, Guangxu began to reassert his imperial presence in the rituals and imagery of the monarchy. In his wedding and the other events such as the field-plowing ceremony and sacrifices around Beijing that Guangxu now led, the court presented the emperor as the focal point of power.[80] Education—both Guangxu's and that of people around the empire—was one of the tools in the consolidation of imperial authority back into the hands of the emperor. When his longtime tutor, Weng Tonghe, was granted several months leave to repair his family's cemetery, for example, Guangxu ordered that because of the great benefit to the country produced by the teacher's work, Weng "should travel at the public expense."[81] Guangxu argued that Weng's efforts to train the emperor into a learned leader would enrich the people, and they should therefore reward him.

At the same time, Guangxu's assumption of personal power was linked with the idea that not just Weng but a wide body of scholars would have the opportunity to serve the throne and inform the decision-making process. For example, on January 9 it was announced that there would be an extra examination for the *juren* degree around the country. Also in January, officials seized on the occasion of the emperor's assumption of power to propose changes to the military examinations.[82] A few months later, Guangxu personally received the *jinshi* winners, congratulating his newest officials and effecting bonds of loyalty.[83] Similarly, he now worked to extend his imperial presence through the brush and build ties throughout the bureaucracy. In 1890, as part of celebrations for his twentieth birthday, Guangxu gave high officials gifts of calligraphy. In addition, he sent gifts of his calligraphy to commemorate the opening of new temples around the country.[84]

But Guangxu also took steps to discipline the bureaucracy, transitioning from his role as student to that of teacher. In 1889, for example, he cracked down on abuses at the Palace Examination and personally supervised military examinations. In both instances, he sought to reassert the emperor's traditional role as final arbiter of both classical and military knowledge in the Civil Examination System. In one case, he went as far as to declare that a group that had recently passed the military *jinshi* was in fact deficient in their skills. The emperor personally held a reexamination of the class, failing at least seven of the candidates and punishing their original examiners.[85] Guangxu's step into the limelight was marked by a simultaneous retreat of Cixi from her role as the embodiment of political power. In March 1890—for the first time in thirty years—Cixi performed sacrifices with other imperial women at the Temple of Goddess of Sericulture. Juxtaposed with reports from the summer regarding Guangxu's activities at the military exams, her act suggested a partial return to the gender dynamics at court before Xianfeng's death and the emergence of female regency.[86]

Guangxu's ascension to the center of educational activities and politics culminated in the fall of 1891 when he announced plans to reform the empire-wide readings of Kangxi's Sacred Edict (*Shengyu*). For years, officials had urged Guangxu to emulate Kangxi, and now assuming personal control of court, he indeed worked to claim his place among the dynasty's illustrious rulers. In a September edict, he described how he had recently read a work in Manchu composed by the Shunzhi emperor. Guangxu said that the text's "exhortations to good works were directly inspired from Heaven and were transmitted in such cogent, clear, and exhaustive terms as to form a suitable instrument for reforming a degenerate world and leading it back to the paths of virtue." He therefore ordered that the book *Hani-i araha sain be huwekiyebure oyonggo gisun* (Important speech admonishing good deeds, composed by the khan) be translated into Chinese, printed by the imperial printing house, and distributed to every province to be read alongside the Sacred Edict in the twice-monthly performances.[87] In effect, Guangxu said that he was taking lessons from his own education and spreading them around the country in order to restore the fortunes of the Qing.

In the wake of the Taiping Rebellion, local leaders had temporarily taken up the job of delivering lectures on the Sacred Edict.[88] In adding the imperially authored text, Guangxu sought to reclaim the throne's position as chief pedagogue around the country. He also presented the text, known in Chinese as the *Yuzhi quanshan yaoyan* (Imperially commissioned exhortations to good deeds), as gifts to several high officials, including Li Hongzhang.[89] In this way, Guangxu also made clear that Chinese provincial officials did not hold a monopoly on ideas for reform and strengthening the country. Finally, by adding a text that up to that point had been available only in Manchu, Guangxu reminded his officials of the unique role of the Qing heritage in governing the empire. The battle to sustain Manchu language and ideals had been one of the major flash points of controversy within the emperor's classroom, as Manchu and Chinese officials battled for time and influence. Upon assuming the throne, Guangxu thus used the Confucian moralism of the Sacred Edict with the new addition of a classic Manchu text to assuage both groups.

THE PLACE OF SCHOLARS IN GUANGXU'S EMPERORSHIP

In some ways, Guangxu's flurry of activity and the seriousness with which he seems to have approached matters of governance fulfilled the lofty ideals set out by his tutors. He was combining both traditional Manchu components of Qing strength and the adopted Confucian Canon to create a model of vitality and virtue at the center of the empire. Critically, however, Guangxu's embrace of this type of personal leadership threatened to undermine the place of scholar-officials in the balance of power. Would Guangxu, now imbued with all the knowledge his teachers had offered, continue to rely on their counsel? Or would he, like Zhu Yuanzhang centuries before, purge the bureaucracy of those who sought to assert their role in the state?

As Guangxu assumed power, a wide range of scholars and officials grew concerned about their role in the emperorship. To argue for their continued relevance and influence at court, many officials therefore called for a revival of the long dormant Classic Mat and Daily Lecture rituals. As they had argued for many years, officials hoped that the events would guarantee their place in the ritual functioning of the state and their power within the emperorship. In this new era, however, in pressing for a revival of the events, officials focused on the need for Guangxu to master new fields of learning to meet the demands of his rule in changing times. Both Manchu and Chinese officials suggested to the emperor that a revival of the institutions would allow him to gain valuable new knowledge about the outside world, affirm his ties to the bureaucracy, and demonstrate his devotion to learning to people around the country.

In 1891, for example, a Manchu official named Wenyu (dates unknown) argued that reinstating the Classic Mat would be the best way to unite the emperor and the people. In urging Guangxu to reinstate the ceremonies, Wenyu drew on the example of the Kangxi emperor, quoting an edict from the twelfth year of Kangxi's reign that described devotion to studies as the first duty of a newly ascended emperor.[90] Yet Wenyu was not arguing for a simple imitation of the Kangxi era Classic Mats. Instead, he urged Guangxu to study current affairs. The lessons of the Classics were not sufficient to solve the problems of the current day, and so Wenyu called for Guangxu to continue his work as a student, expanding the scope of his learning. In this way, Wenyu used the revival of the Classic Mat with an expanded curriculum to ensure the continued role of officials serving as teachers at court. Wenyu told Guangxu said that if the emperor restored the Classic Mat and employed officials to instruct him in current affairs, "the imperial virtue will be rejuvenated, and the successes of government restored."[91]

Wenyu's sentiment was shared by some of his Chinese colleagues at court. The same year, Gao Xieceng (1841-1917) submitted a memorial asking to revive the Daily Lectures. Like Wenyu, Gao framed his argument in terms of bringing the current reign in line with the precedent of Kangxi. Gao wrote that beginning in the ninth year of his reign, Kangxi established the Daily Lectures and held them continuously for the next seventeen years, even while leading military campaigns and suppressing rebellions around the country. Kangxi thus laid a foundation for his descendants that ensured peace in the empire. As Gao said, "In following this practice, for over two hundred years, the influence of education has set a good moral example for the younger generations."[92] Like Wenyu, however, Gao did not want to simply imitate Kangxi's model. Instead, he wanted the lessons to focus on new fields of learning so that Guangxu could adjudicate the appropriate place of Western learning in the country's rejuvenation.

Here, Gao called on both Guangxu's functional and symbolic roles in the emperorship, asking him to both drive policy decisions and set an example for others to follow. Gao said that while some foolishly rejected all the new texts pouring into China, others blindly venerated the new fields of "Western studies," causing great confusion around the country. In Gao's mind, the only solution to this problem was a revival of the Daily Lectures wherein the emperor would be exposed to a wide variety of teachings and reestablish order to the confused state of learning. Gao thus urged the emperor to select an auspicious date to revive the Daily Lectures, promising that they would bring great benefit to the ruler and the empire.[93]

Like Wenyu, Gao was arguing for the importance of the emperor continuing to perform his role as the lead student of the empire while on the throne. This was partly a question of how best to incorporate new fields of learning into the governance of the country. But Gao and Wenyu were also fighting to ensure their continued place in the emperorship now that Guangxu's formal education had ended. During the emperor's youth, the regency structure had offered scholar-officials influence not only by granting them traditional postings in various state ministries, but also as tutors in the emperor's classroom. Leaving the classroom, taking the throne, and adopting the position of teacher himself, however, Guangxu threatened to mitigate that scholarly influence.

Guangxu's reaction to Gao's proposal in fact suggests that the fears of these officials—that the end of his education meant the end of their influence—were justified. The emperor flatly rejected the calls to revive the Classic Mat and Daily Lectures. In reply to Gao, Guangxu wrote:

> In taking over personal rule of the government, every day I call in ministers and officials for audiences. As far as the virtue and talent of officials and the gains and losses of policies, I consider them all with an open mind. I seek truth from facts from my readings of the Classics and Histories and have classes and discussions with the officials of the Yuqing Palace.... As for the request from the Imperial Censor to have officials give rotating lectures ... actually this is merely a nominal practice, and the corrupt practices are many.[94]

While claiming that he was in fact a dutiful student by continuing to consult with teachers from his childhood classroom, Guangxu nonetheless dismissed the notion that he needed more scholarly voices to aid him in the governance of the country. The edict rejecting reinstatement of the Daily Lectures pointed out that they were originally canceled by Qianlong, who found that lecturers were deviating from their lessons in the Classics and offering advice on topics outside their purview.[95] Rather than an asset to the edification of the throne, therefore, Guangxu claimed the events were ploys by officials to weasel their way into power.

Though the 1891 rejection of calls to reinstate the Classic Mat and Daily Lectures was hardly a dramatic affair, it nonetheless reveals a crucial tension at the heart of the post-Taiping emperorship. With children on the throne, officials had an opportunity to argue for their understandings of good governance and visions of the future through the emperors' youthful education. When the period of minority and regency ended, those officials could seek to use the traditional institutions of learning (such as the Classic Mat and Daily Lectures) to retain a degree of power over the emperor. When Guangxu rejected their calls, however, the officials were not content to simply acquiesce and abandon their claims to authority. If Guangxu would not allow them to influence affairs through the Classic Mat and Daily Lectures, the officials would search for other sources of power to authorize their participation in the state. In the coming years, these officials would turn to Cixi—the power inherent in her position as empress dowager and the cache of authority she built through years of cultural production—to champion their cause at the expense of Guangxu's personal power. In this way, the explosive events of the Hundred Days Reforms of 1898 (to be discussed in the following chapter) were rooted in the long-term tension of the post-Taiping emperorship and both the promise and peril of children ascending the throne. For years, scholars and officials had been told to look to the future for their aspirations of power, focusing in the moment on the task of educating the young emperor. But the end of Guangxu's education and the sidelining of scholarly voices at the start of his personal rule suggested to some that their future might never come.

After Tongzhi's short but tumultuous personal reign, some officials viewed the beginning of the Guangxu era as a second chance to cultivate a child emperor and transform him into a leader, both for dynastic renewal and as patron for their positions in power. But the question of exactly what type of emperor was needed for this project was a hotly contested issue. The Manchu Way, Confucian moralism, and Western learning all had their proponents, and both officials and intellectuals outside of the bureaucracy used the emperor's curriculum as a proxy for battles over the future direction of the country.

For these scholars, the emperor's childhood education was one of the ways in which they sought to both retain access and power and help shape the future direction of the country. Therefore, regardless of the content of the curriculum, officials constantly urged the young emperor to be diligent in his studies. For example, in 1881, following the death of Empress Dowager Ci'an, Guangxu was slow to return to school. Chen Baochen (1848-1935) memorialized, arguing that emperors did not have the luxury of abandoning studies. He told Guangxu that the best way to mourn and demonstrate his filial piety would be to return to class.[96] An active throne, empowered by learning (both civil and martial), was critical to the power of the emperorship.

This idea was captured that same year in a lengthy poem by the Qing official Huang Zunxian (1848-1905). Reflecting on the closing of the Chinese Education Mission to the United States, Huang recounted a time when the emperor was respected as a patron of learning, when China's educational system was revered around the world, and when international relations were conducted on China's terms. Describing men from around Asia coming to study at the Imperial Academy in Beijing, Huang marveled at the former glory of the emperor's culturally learned authority and prestige in the region. Huang said: "When the emperor visited the Hall of Classics, amid the magnificent display of court etiquette, epigraphic copies of canonical texts were taken out of boxes, treasured canopies were stretched over the temple yard where students read standing with books open, while numerous barbarians stood around in the outer court. What a manifestation of grandeur!" But, now wrote Huang, "Alas, it has become only a memory of the distant past."[97] "Ever since the court fled the capital," in 1860, Huang said, "our country has been weak and powerless to defend ourselves. The world powers now watch us like vultures."[98]

Huang viewed the power of the emperor and the educational system as inherently linked to China's position in the international world order. This was a view that emerged from both traditional notions of rulership in China and Huang's time serving as a Qing envoy in Japan. As in China, the Japanese emperor was positioned as a patron of learning and key to unity and strength.[99] Over the course of the 1890s, with Guangxu on the throne, Japan and the Meiji emperor would in fact emerge as a primary example through which reformist intellectuals such as Kang Youwei and Liang Qichao argued for dramatic reforms in China. For these men, as for Huang, the prospect of an emperor steeped in the Classics and promoting new fields of learning across the country was key to restoring China's glory and stature in the world. But in the effort to convince Guangxu to promote their particular vision, these scholars stretched the limits of the emperorship and fractured the constitutional balance of power. This contest, and particularly the role of Cixi, language, and foreign models of court education, is the subject of the next chapter.

3

PUTTING LESSONS INTO PRACTICE

Guangxu on the Throne, 1891-1898

On the morning of December 1, 1891, the Beijing skies were crowded with clouds threatening snow.¹ But for Zhang Deyi (1847-1918) and Shen Duo (dates unknown), the day began long before the sun would rise, and it is hard to imagine they had much time to worry about the chilly weather. They must have been nervous, probably excited too. Shortly after midnight, Zhang and Shen left their homes, passed through one of the imposing gates of the Imperial City, and walked through the Meridian Gate to enter the Forbidden City. It was a trip they had made before. Graduates of the Tongwen guan (School of Combined Learning), they had traveled around the world as translators and diplomats for the Qing court in the 1870s and 1880s.² But the walk must have felt different this time, because that day Zhang and Shen took on a new role, one that surely brought them pride and angst in equal measure. As they stepped into the Yuqing Palace on the east side of the inner court, Zhang and Shen were transformed from mere bureaucrats and placed at the center of power in the Qing emperorship.³ Because, on December 1, 1891, Zhang Deyi and Shen Duo became the emperor's teachers, the first in Chinese history to instruct the Son of Heaven in English.⁴

It started off innocuously enough. A few days earlier, on November 26, the Guangxu emperor had been late to school. After spending a little time looking at a map, Guangxu told one of his tutors that he wanted to learn English.⁵ The imperial bureaucracy reacted quickly, and just a few days later, Zhang and Shen left their homes in the dark of the night, making the trip to the Forbidden City to deliver the emperor's first English lesson from 4:00 to 4:30 a.m.⁶

From the very start, Qing emperors were polyglot rulers who, in speech, writing, and artistic production, crafted a variety of simultaneous images of authority, performing differentiated models of legitimacy to the various groups within and without their empire.⁷ In this sense, that Guangxu wanted to learn English is not surprising. He was following the precedent of his ancestors, adding another linguistic layer to the projection of imperial authority to existing Manchu, Mongolian, Tibetan, Uyghur, and Chinese realms. Early in the Qing, emperors had in fact needed to devote considerable energy to learning Chinese, and many Chinese officials in turn studied Manchu to benefit their careers under the new dynasty. The model of a Qing emperor fluent in all the languages of his empire was articulated by the Qianlong era pentaglot dictionary, the *Yuzhi wuti qingwen jian* (Imperially commissioned mirror of the Manchu language with five kinds of script placed together).⁸ While Qianlong, with his study of Tibetan, probably came closest to the ideal, it remained just that, and no single emperor ever actually managed to learn all the languages. Nevertheless, the model of the Qing emperor as a ruler educated in all the languages of his realm persisted throughout the nineteenth century.

As discussed in the previous chapter, the emperor's linguistic abilities and the place of language training in his education had serious ramifications for his relationship with the bureaucracy. Proficiency in Manchu and Mongolian was important in order to keep watch on frontier affairs and ensure the loyalty of his Inner Asian constituencies, while mastery of the Chinese Classics connected the throne with his body of scholar-officials. Yet in the 1870s, as intellectuals outside of the bureaucracy began to make use of the burgeoning domestic press to put forward their own ideas for the emperor's curriculum, some now argued that English held the key to unlocking the true power of the emperor. By studying English, these writers argued, Guangxu would be able take an active and personal role in Qing foreign relations, using his language abilities to bypass those very officials whom the press blamed for obstructing broader change around the country. For reformers outside of the bureaucracy, therefore, fighting to add new languages to the emperor's curriculum was seen as the first step in a larger battle over the future of the country.

This chapter examines that battle, opening with what many at the time interpreted as a seminal moment in the spread of Western learning and the coming of a new age in China: Guangxu's study of English. China's loss in the Sino-Japanese War in the middle of the decade temporarily punctured that utopian vision. At the same time, that loss brought forth a new dynamic in discussions of court education, as writers increasingly argued that the emperor's personal education should be used as a model of hybrid learning and reform for the rest of the county.

Then again in 1898, calls for Guangxu to study abroad and the emperor's push for reform placed court education at the center of national politics. While in the first two chapters the youth of the emperor suggested to scholar-officials the opportunity to argue for different visions of the future through his curriculum, this chapter explores both the flexibility and the fragility of the post-Taiping emperorship with an adult stepping out of the classroom and onto the throne. Throughout the decade, officials disaffected by Guangxu's patronage of particular scholars, fields of learning, or policies looked to the empress dowager to assert her influence to protect their power within the system by curtailing the young emperor. The chapter closes at the end of 1898 when officials alarmed by Guangxu's reform decrees called on Cixi to take power and restore them to the heart of governance, in effect demanding an end to Guangxu's personal reign.

ENGLISH AND DREAMS OF REFORM

To many foreign observers in 1891, Guangxu's study of English was categorically different from the language-learning efforts of his predecessors. In their minds, this was not about a Qing emperor continuing the tradition of his ancestors and building his authority through mastery of the world's knowledge. News about Guangxu's study of English and interest in Western books inspired telegrams, letters, newspaper stories, and monographs that indiscriminately picked up every bit of rumor and gossip together with facts. At the eye of the storm was a belief that the emperor's interest in English signaled a transformative moment in the history of internal development in China and its relationship to the world.[9]

In perhaps the most hyperbolic, yet not unique, reporting of the news, the *New York Times* carried a story on February 4, 1892, with the headline: "China Waking Up: That Is the Meaning of the Emperor Learning English."[10] Describing the start of the emperor's English class as the "greatest change in the history of China," the article promised that the language lessons would "probably do more toward removing the shackles of conservatism" than any other reform measure because it would inspire the entire country to open their minds. Writing with little sense of the epochal changes undergone in China over the past few decades, the *Times* concluded that "the meaning of the Emperor bending to the study of a foreign language must be that he and his advisors consider that the time for China to retain her Government and customs, founded 3,000 years ago, has passed, and that to deal with the powers of the present day she must alter her system accordingly." Since the Opium Wars, Western powers had been waiting for this moment, the time when their "pedagogy of imperialism" would pay dividends.[11] No longer metaphorical, Guangxu's actual English lessons made many believe that China had finally learned its lesson.

Despite such extravagant pronouncements of impending change, Guangxu's desire to learn English was both more complicated and less dramatic than the foreign press suggested. Guangxu's longtime tutor, Weng Tonghe, for one, was mildly bewildered as to why the emperor wanted to learn the "meaning of the characters of the Far West."[12] Yet Weng wasn't opposed to the emperor learning about foreign countries or incorporating new knowledge into his curriculum. In fact, Weng was responsible for introducing books about world history and geography, such as Wei Yuan's (1794-1857) *Illustrated Gazetteer of the Maritime Countries* (*Haiguo tuzhi*), into the emperor's studies.[13] Weng also presented Guangxu with the far more radical writings of Feng Guifen (1809-1874), describing them as "appropriate for the moment."[14] Yet just as Weng had fought bitterly in Tongzhi's classroom with the emperor's Manchu tutors for taking up too much time, he worried that adding a new subject to Guangxu's curriculum would not leave enough time for his continued study of the Classics, particularly given that Guangxu had now also taken over daily operations of the state.

But Guangxu was determined, and so the hunt for an English teacher began. It seems that Yan Yongjing (1838-1898) was the first person approached about the job. A native of Shanghai, Yan was educated in missionary schools in China before traveling to the United States, where he eventually graduated with a B.A. degree from Kenyon College in 1861. Returning to China, Yan worked as a translator for a variety of governmental and missionary organizations before joining the inaugural faculty at St. John's College in Shanghai in 1879.[15] However, Yan declined the offer to teach Guangxu. He is said to have refused the post for a variety of reasons, including his belief that it was too drastic a reform, not wanting to leave his missionary work, not wanting to get involved in politics, and on account of his personal deficiency in the language.[16]

The court then turned to W. A. P. Martin (Ch. Ding Weiliang, 1827-1916), head of the Beijing Tongwen guan, to select suitable teachers. It was Martin who chose Zhang Deyi and Shen Duo.[17] Though he obliged in providing men for the job, Martin worried about the efficacy of English language pedagogy at court. He did not, for example, have full faith that the teachers would be able to muster the courage to correct their august student if he made errors in speech or composition. Furthermore, Martin was not satisfied with Zhang's and Shen's own conversational English. He therefore instructed the pair to give him each of the emperor's exercises to personally correct before the teachers brought them to Guangxu.[18]

This may have solved some of the pedagogical problems, but there were other issues in the early days of Guangxu's English class. For instance, on one occasion either Zhang or Shen (it is not clear who instigated the incident) complained to Martin that the other had the habit of pulling his sleeve and correcting his English pronunciation to the emperor, causing great embarrassment to the teacher. Martin chastised the pair, saying, "I warned them that where doctors disagree the consequences are always bad, especially where the pupil is an emperor."[19] Perhaps because of an acrimonious relationship between the two teachers or because of the stress of the job, from then on Zhang and Shen taught the emperor on alternate days.[20]

While the English-language press was quick to point to the emperor's study of English as proof-positive of the triumph of Western civilization, the Chinese-language press did not see the lessons as particularly newsworthy. Reading the

FIGURE 3.1 Guangxu's English teachers, Zhang Deyi (*left*) and Shen Duo (*right*). Photos from William Alexander Parsons Martin, *A Cycle of Cathay* (New York: Revell, 1900), 316, 318.

New York Times, the *North China Herald*, or the *Times of London*, one might get the impression that Guangxu had abandoned the whole of Chinese civilization to study English. Yet reading only the Chinese-language press, one would be easily forgiven for not noticing this supposed seismic shift. In fact, British-owned *Shenbao*, China's largest paper at the time, does not seem to have made any mention of the emperor's English lessons, despite the fact that it had advocated for this very thing in 1876.

The most extended treatment given to the news by the Chinese language press was in *Wan'guo gongbao* (A review of the times)—a periodical edited by Reverend Young John Allen (Ch. Lin Yuezhi, 1836-1907) in Shanghai. The journal's February 1892 edition ran an article by Reverend Timothy Richard (Ch. Li Timotai, 1845-1919) that described the many benefits the emperor's study of English would have for the country. Titled "English in the Imperial Palace" in English but "Gongji daqing dahuangdi xuexi yingwen shi" (A respectful record of the grand emperor of the Great Qing's study of English) in Chinese, the article opened by noting that the news had been widely reported in the Western press, suggesting that it might still be novel information to his Chinese readers.[21] Richard lauded the emperor's selection of English as his foreign language of choice, saying it would give him access to information from both England and America, as well as familiarize him with the dominant language of the treaty ports and commerce in China.

Richard then described the four main benefits of the emperor learning English. The first concerned access to information:

> After obtaining knowledge of English, with just a single glance the Emperor will be able to learn for himself from books written by British and Americans authors. He will have personal knowledge of all the affairs of various countries, the pros and cons of government policies, the rise and fall of nations, the means by which the military can be enhanced, how commerce might flourish, how education can be spread, and all policies that might benefit the nation.[22]

Access to information had long been a tension and tool in the power struggle between the emperor and bureaucracy in Chinese political thought and practice. Here, Richard argued for the need to use knowledge of English to shift the balance of power back toward the throne. With all this new information at his disposal, Richard said, the emperor would learn from the experience of other governments to select the best policies from around the world. He would then be able to take

China from a state of weakness and poverty to strength and wealth. Learning English, Richard said, would also enable Guangxu to communicate directly with the ministers of foreign countries, and it would ultimately inspire the rest of the country to embrace Western learning. In this sense, Richard—like many Manchu and Chinese officials before him—connected the emperor's education to both his functional and his symbolic roles in the emperorship, empowering him in matters of daily governance while empowering others around the country to pursue similar educational reforms thanks to the tacit seal of imperial approval.

Interestingly, although Chinese newspapers did not report on the lessons at the time, the benefits of the emperor learning English that Richard described were the same as those articulated by *Shenbao* in 1876 when the paper proposed that the recently enthroned Guangxu should study the language. At that time, *Shenbao* suggested that Guangxu should study English to circumvent those in the bureaucracy opposed to the spread of Western learning, the opening of translation academies, and other projects of self-strengthening. It hoped that Guangxu would embrace the ideas circulating in treaty ports such as Shanghai, where *Shenbao* was based, and allow new ideas to break through the walls of officialdom in Beijing.

Now, in 1891, aided by printed reports such as those in the *New York Times* and *Wan'guo gongbao* and the rumor mills of the Beijing legations and Shanghai concessions, news of the emperor's English lessons—and more generally his interest in things foreign—spread quickly among officials in Beijing, across the country, and around the world. Some in the bureaucracy followed on Guangxu's heels and began to study English.[23] This led to a rise in demand for both textbooks and teachers and created a new economy of English inside the Imperial City.[24] The desire for dictionaries, textbooks, and reference works meant big business for companies such as Shanghai Commercial Press (Shanghai shangwu yinshuguan), a major pipeline of books to the court.[25]

Nowhere was Guangxu's study of English received with more enthusiasm than within the missionary community. While the 1876 proposals seemed motivated by commercial and political interests, in 1891 many foreigners saw Guangxu's study of English as a sign of imminent conversion, and they reported the news with messianic fervor. For example, missionary Isaac Taylor Headland described, with no shortage of glee, the start of the emperor's English lessons. Headland recalled that Guangxu "was in such a hurry to begin that he could not wait to send to England or America for books," and so another missionary, Dr. Marcus Taft, volunteered his young daughter's primer for the emperor's use. Not only did Guangxu want books to study English, but, in the minds of missionaries, he also wanted "every book that had been translated from any European language and published in Chinese."[26]

In 1891, several years before the supposed "awakening" of China after the Sino-Japanese War, many in the foreign community saw this apparent appetite for foreign books as the dawn of a progressive age in which education reforms spurred on by the emperor would lead to the conversion and "civilizing" of China.[27] As one group of female missionaries wrote, "A few years ago the instructors of a youthful Emperor would have scorned the idea of his studying anything besides their own sacred classics. Now the 'Sublime Ruler' is learning to read English from the same primary reader that is used by the little boys and girls in America." The female missionaries also assumed that because of W. A. P. Martin's background, Zhang and Shen would teach Guangxu using Christian texts. They concluded, therefore, that Guangxu "will become familiar with the story of Christ's life, and learn of the faith and courage of his disciples. This knowledge of the Holy Spirit can use to show the young Emperor that to worship and obey the foreigner's God is the highest good for himself and for the nation he rules."[28] Confident that the court curriculum would inspire change around the country, the missionaries, just as the *New York Times* did, saw the emperor's English class as emblematic of the triumph of Western civilization writ large, and Christianity in particular.

For those in both the Chinese and foreign press writing about Guangxu's English lessons and his interest in foreign subjects, the model of Japan and example of the Meiji emperor loomed large, and comparisons between Guangxu and his Japanese counterpart became common in the early 1890s. On January 21, 1893, for example, *Shenbao* reported on the recent start of lectures inside the Japanese emperor's palace: "On the morning of that day at 10 a.m., Classic Mat officials lectured on Japanese, Chinese, and Western Learning, as well as ancient Japanese learning and writing."[29] *Shenbao* here presented Japan as adopting a hybrid model of court education, combining elements of Chinese, Japanese, and Western knowledge to strengthen the country. The vocabulary of the Classic Mat as well as the inclusion of the Chinese Classics suggested that Guangxu need not abandon his traditional allies, only that he ought to create space for new teachers and fields of knowledge inside the palace. The American press as well covered the Meiji emperor's education, describing his study of English and French, the translation of foreign newspapers for him, and his active stewardship of the country.[30]

In this way, both the Chinese and foreign press viewed the imperial embrace of Western learning in Japan as central to the country's development, and they urged Guangxu to continue his own work in that direction. Those in China, such as Timothy Richard, meanwhile, couldn't wait for the day when Guangxu's study of English would allow the emperor to discard his advisors and translators and insert himself directly into Qing foreign affairs. This would mean the realization of *Shenbao*'s dreams from 1876, but it would also be a nightmare for the many officials within the emperorship who would be cut out of power.

EDUCATION WARS

This conflict came to a head in the years around the Sino-Japanese War. While scholars praised Guangxu for his diligence and commitment to learning, there nonetheless seemed to be a fear that his interests outside the classical canon were a potentially destabilizing force.[31] In particular, Guangxu's study of English and the hiring of Zhang Deyi and Shen Duo as tutors threatened the position of other scholars in the bureaucracy. In multiple memorials throughout 1893 and 1894, officials questioned the presence of Guangxu's English teachers in the palace. Zhang and Shen were repeatedly referred to simply as "translators," and their official bureaucratic ranks did not justify their new posts, let alone their frequent interactions with the emperor over the previous three years.[32] That is to say, Guangxu's interest in English was empowering a new group of officials, threatening the position of the scholar-officials who had sustained the emperorship over the previous decades.

When the Sino-Japanese War broke out in August 1894, there were thus already growing tensions over access to power and the emperor's assertion of independence from traditional scholar-officials. These rifts only grew throughout the year, and many at court—including Cixi—grew frustrated with Guangxu. In particular, the emperor and empress dowager clashed over matters related to his wife and concubine. The emperor disliked the wife Cixi had chosen for him, and by 1894 Guangxu was spending most of his time with a pair of concubines. The younger of the two, known as the Pearl Concubine, had reportedly begun to use her status to influence civil appointments and other affairs of the government. As it had been with Tongzhi, the choice of Guangxu's bride was a political calculation to cement loyalties within the bureaucracy. Guangxu's preference for other women and the power they drew from that favoritism therefore added a potentially destabilizing new force into the emperorship. By late November of that year, Cixi had seen enough, and she downgraded the status of the women and executed their eunuch ally.[33]

The larger problem, however, was reassuring officials in the bureaucracy that Guangxu was not going to abandon them and start relying on his new English tutors or other groups. Cixi therefore ordered that Guangxu's classroom activities be stopped entirely, directing him to concentrate full time on running the government—the primary task of which was the war against Japan. Guangxu pleaded to continue his studies, and the empress dowager backed down slightly from her original stance. She allowed Guangxu to return to the classroom, but with a strictly limited curriculum. Most important, in December 1894 the emperor's English lessons were halted, and Zhang and Shen were removed from their posts, victim to Cixi's pedagogy and the fears of the bureaucracy.[34]

Cixi's punishment of Guangxu and control over his classroom made clear that the empress dowager, despite her retirement, was never far from center stage and that she retained the political muscle to assert her will when needed. Perhaps even more important, many in the bureaucracy actively desired for her to do so. When officials saw their access to the throne threatened by the rise of new voices, they turned to Cixi to renew their promise of power. In this way, the bureaucratic opposition to Zhang and Shen—and the way in which it forced Cixi to act—foreshadows the more dramatic events of 1898. It also once again highlights how, because the post-Taiping emperorship was constructed with youths at the center and promised officials the ability to influence the emperor, the model struggled to cope with an adult on the throne no longer in need of tutors or tutelage.

The end of Guangxu's English lessons in the context of the Sino-Japanese War was not lost on foreign observers. Several months after the signing of the treaty of Shimonoseki in 1895, the Japanese newspaper *Yomiuri shimbun* published a short article on Guangxu's interest in English, writing: "According to the *North China Daily News*, His Excellency the Qing Emperor is passionate about the study of English. One would then expect that he should have read, on a daily basis, the *North China Daily News* and the *London and China Express*. However, it is said regarding his record over the past two years that he has been too busy seeing to affairs of state and has had no spare time to pursue his studies."[35] Cixi was absent from the Japanese newspaper's account, and in press reports around the world, the Sino-Japanese

War was frequently framed as a clash between two monarchs, Meiji and Guangxu, for supremacy in East Asia. The men were depicted as responsible for driving reform and leading their countries toward wealth and power. The 1894–1895 war appeared to show that Japan, and therefore Meiji, had won the race.

Education reforms, the adoption of Western learning, and English in particular were understood as both a fundamental component of the fight and a sign of Japan's victory. In the second half of the nineteenth century, English emerged as the language of international law, and Japan was quick to adopt what Alexis Dudden has described as the "fusion of power and words," embracing English to dislodge China from its place as the "arbiter of power" in East Asia.[36] In 1885, for example, when negotiating a convention in Tianjin with Li Hongzhang, Japan's representative, Itō Hirobumi, conducted the negotiations in English. Gone were the days of brush-talks, where literary Chinese served as the vernacular for scholars and statesmen across East Asia. When Li and Itō met again in 1895 to sign a treaty ending the Sino-Japanese War, there were three versions: Chinese, Japanese, and English. The agreement included a provision that stated any discrepancies between the versions would be adjudicated by reference to the English text.[37] Not only had China lost money and territory to Japan, but it also now relinquished control of the very language used to conceptualize its place in Asia and the world. In describing Guangxu as incapable of keeping up with his study of English, then, *Yomiuri shimbun* in effect argued that Japan had surpassed China as the leader of a new modern East Asia.

As is well known, China's defeat in 1895 shocked the national psyche and spurred calls for reform around the country. Having revealed herself as still central to the power dynamic at court and a vital ally in advancing an agenda and because of the image she had long cultivated as a ruler devoted to learning, Cixi was now sought out by both reform-minded officials in China and the foreign community for help in pursuing their goals. For example, as calls for education reform accelerated, proponents of female education appealed to Cixi and her self-fashioned image of scholar-student and heir to imperial tradition of educated women to promote their cause. In his essay "On the Education of Women" (Lun nuxue, 1897), for example, Liang Qichao argued that educated mothers were critical to the rearing of successful children. Written before the tumultuous summer of 1898, Liang's essay seemed to praise Cixi for her role in the educations of both Tongzhi and Guangxu. Shanghai businessman, official, and reformer Jing Yuanshan (1840–1903) was more explicit with his praise of Cixi in his efforts to promote female education, citing Xiaozhuang and Cixi as twin ideals of educated women. Jing further lauded Cixi's devotion to studying the Classics as the reason she had become the "mother of the realm." Foreign supporters of expanded educational opportunities for women echoed Jing's sentiment. Young John Allen, for example, cited Cixi's "devotion to learning as the reason she had been able to stabilize the realm and maintain China's harmonious relations with the foreign nations during her twenty years' regency."[38]

And finally, the empress dowager was, quite literally, the image of female education. The first issue of *Nü xuebao* (Journal of women's education) in July 1898 opened with a full-page picture of Cixi.[39] Articles in the journal frequently called on Cixi to lead the women of the country in the development of literacy and patriotism. In one essay, a female writer proposed that Cixi establish a variety of organizations for elite women to guide the spread of female education. In addition, the same author suggested that the empress dowager should travel the world to learn from the best practices of other countries and help transform China's women.[40] Having cultivated an image of sagely rulership based on devotion to learning in an effort to solidify her place at court since Xianfeng's death, Cixi now emerged as a focal point for those arguing that China's strength and renewal were best pursued through court-sponsored education reforms.

REEMPOWERING GUANGXU THROUGH EDUCATION

At the same time, China's defeat in the war galvanized Cixi's opponents to attack her leadership. These men, the so-called famous scholars (*mingshi*), focused their attention on Guangxu in hopes of finding a sponsor for their reform proposals. The slogan of the *mingshi* in their efforts to empower Guangxu, "the power of the sovereign is absolute" (*qiangang duduan*), harkened back to the High Qing when Kangxi, Yongzheng (r. 1722–1735), and Qianlong deployed the phrase to argue for the importance of undivided imperial authority and the prerogative of the emperor within the bureaucracy.[41] Now, the *mingshi* sought to convince Guangxu to use *his* "absolute power" to advance *their* reform efforts.[42]

The themes explored in the first two chapters of scholars seeking to infuse the emperor's curriculum with new forms of learning now took on a new sense of urgency as many throughout the country believed that only dramatic reform would save China. Scholars such as Kang Youwei, Liang Qichao, and Yan Fu argued that the country's future lay in Guangxu's hands, and that to strengthen China, the emperor needed to learn from the experience of other world leaders and personally embrace new forms of education. These men looked to transform the emperor into a patron of their cause by molding him in the image of other supposedly powerful monarchs, drawing inspiration from both Chinese history and the contemporary world. They also increasingly sought to explicitly and publicly tie court education to the education of the country as a whole, with the emperor presented as a model of new hybrid forms of learning for people around the empire.

Scholars first turned to the classical institutions of court education and domestic traditions in an attempt to bring new ideas to Guangxu's attention. Despite the emperor's rejection of proposals to restore the Classic Mat in 1891, for example, officials once again beseeched him to reinstate the practice. In an 1896 memorial to Guangxu advocating for the need to cultivate righteous officials to ensure the success of Self-Strengthening projects, Pan Qinglan (1848-?) cited an edict from the Shunzhi era in which the emperor said, "Since antiquity emperors have studied diligently and devised ways to effectively govern the country. We must establish Classic Mats and Daily Lectures to advise the king is a wise way."[43] Pan therefore urged Guangxu to order a variety of officials to take turns lecturing so that the emperor could learn from the best practices of the world and be equipped to select men of talent and virtue. Only with Guangxu personally leading the reform efforts, Pan said, would projects such as the opening of railways, mines, and warships actually bring benefit to the country.

Liang Qichao, too, found parallels in Chinese history for his ideal of modern leadership.[44] Extolling the military accomplishments of Kangxi and Yongzheng, as well as Tongzhi Restoration efforts to establish a navy and enter into trading relations with countries around the world, Liang painted a history of the Qing wherein the throne was strong and actively open to change.[45] But Liang saw the current state of affairs as an aberration from that history, as scholars were blocked from advising the emperor and presenting him with new ideas, thus imperiling China's future. To remedy the situation and make his case for the need of a reformed system of education for Guangxu, Liang called on the writings of early Qing intellectuals. For example, Liang was one of several writers who sponsored the republication of Huang Zongxi's (1610-1695) work *Mingyi daifang lu* (*Waiting for the*

Dawn: A Plan for the Prince). Completed in 1663, the work was banned in the early Qing. In the book, Huang offered a harsh critique of the imperial state beginning with the Qin (221–206 BCE), arguing that Confucian ministers were shut out of the decision-making process, and emperors were unduly influenced by the teaching and advice of empress dowagers and palace eunuchs. To remedy the situation, Huang proposed a variety of changes to the Classic Mat, demanding the emperor take a truly subordinate position to his teachers. In addition, Huang argued that imperial princes should be sent to school with more common members of society so that they would be "informed of real conditions among the people and be given some experience of difficult labor and hardship." Opening scholarly access to the emperor was precisely the goal that Liang had in mind for Guangxu. Therefore, more than two hundred years after it was initially banned, Liang revived Huang's old *Plan*, printing and circulating thousands of copies of the text from the safety of China's foreign concessions.[46]

At the same time, Liang did not limit himself to Chinese tradition to make the case for empowering Guangxu through education. Instead, he drew on a whole world of information and models of foreign leaders in search of a new syncretic system for Guangxu.[47] For example, Liang wrote, "I've heard that sages consider the times and act accordingly. Bringing Kangxi and Yongzheng into the present day, I know the speed and vigor of their reforms would certainly be no less than Peter the Great, Wilhelm, or Meiji."[48] The invocation of Wilhelm is particularly telling. Wilhelm's education had been revolutionary within the German imperial tradition. He was the first ruler to attend public schools, where he was sent to learn, as his tutor put it, "the thoughts and feelings" of the people he would one day rule.[49] Attending school with his subjects, the German ruler learned not just the technical knowledge of his predecessors but the social knowledge deemed necessary for modern rulership.[50] Upon taking power, Wilhelm then launched education reforms around the country, seeking to displace the classical curriculum with a stronger emphasis on German language, physical fitness, and sentiments of national identity.[51]

More than changes to traditional institutions such as the Classic Mat, therefore, Chinese scholars also began to propose radical measures to expose Guangxu to new fields of learning that he could then spread around the country in the hopes of building a new type of political community. One of the most common suggestions was that Guangxu should study abroad. For this idea, Peter the Great (1672–1725) was deployed as a powerful argument for the importance of a ruler willing to expand his education, learn from the world, and then provide strong centralized leadership.⁵² Kang Youwei, for example, wrote that "Peter the Great understood the times and undertook reforms that conformed with heaven ... he broke thousand-year-old customs of self-aggrandizing and self-imposed stupidity." In particular, Kang highlighted the new approach to education wherein Peter "studied the manufacturing of the Netherlands and England, traveled throughout the world, and was not ashamed to learn from others."⁵³ Kang also wrote about counterexamples to Peter's successful fight against conservative officials. In a not too subtle attack against Cixi, Kang described the conservative empress dowager of Poland whose imprisonment of the emperor (Kang claimed) led to Poland's downfall.

For Kang, an iconography of vigorous imperial leadership was essential to China's future, and in perhaps the strongest statement of his belief in the symbolic role of the emperor in the empire, Kang requested that Guangxu send copies of his portrait all around the country along with a message indicating his "affection for the people."⁵⁴ United behind the emperor and inspired by his example, Kang argued, the country would be spurred to reform.⁵⁵

Yan Fu similarly stressed the role Guangxu needed to play in China's development of a modern society and encouraged him to study abroad as a critical first step in a broader reform effort.⁵⁶ Yan described a perilous situation wherein battles between other countries threatened to destroy Asia. He said that only China could resolve the crisis, and "in China, there is only one person who can accomplish this, and that is His Majesty the Emperor."⁵⁷ Not surprisingly, Yan admired England for the strength of its navy, its commercial power, and its overseas colonies.⁵⁸ But Yan also lauded Peter the Great, favorably comparing Russia's strength on land to Britain's on sea. What China needed most, Yan argued, was for Guangxu to follow Peter's lead in traveling abroad and expanding his education to learn from the best practices of foreign countries. Yan thus devised a plan for the emperor. He said that Guangxu ought to have the empress dowager temporarily act as regent for the country while he sailed around the world in a small armada with an entourage of trusted advisors and a stockpile of money to learn from the West and hire advisors to serve at court.⁵⁹

Yan understood that his call for Guangxu to study abroad was an unprecedented suggestion, yet he said the times called for nothing less: "in this time of disaster, the likes of which no Chinese emperor in all of history has seen, Your Majesty must take the opportunity to act and undertake an enterprise unlike anything an emperor has ever done before."⁶⁰ By traveling abroad and hiring foreign tutors, Yan argued, Guangxu would learn about the differences and similarities in governance between the West and China and thus be able to select policies to help rescue the country from the brink of disaster. While Kang and Liang's advocacy of Guangxu expanding his learning is most often understood as part of their power struggle with Cixi, that Yan here called for Cixi to be granted greater powers while Guangxu went abroad suggests that it was not only Cixi's political opponents who fought to use court education for dynastic reconstruction.

Zhang Zhidong as well, in his famous work *Quanxue pian* (Exhortation to learn, 1898), linked the power of the throne to its ability to embrace new forms of education and set a model for the rest of the country to follow. Zhang said that all the illustrious rulers in the past were simultaneously sovereign and teacher and personally instructed the empire through their example. Although the work is considered a conservative alternative to the proposals of Kang and Liang, in this post Sino-Japanese war period, Zhang suggested that the emperor's education needed to include foreign studies. Although *Quanxue pian* does not contain an explicit call for Guangxu to study abroad, Zhang described how countries all around the world had benefited from the travels of their enlightened rulers. For example, he argued that Russia's strength in the current day was a direct result of Peter the Great's foreign tour. He also devoted a section of his work to the education of the king and prince of Siam. Noting that France had long desired to conquer the kingdom, Zhang said that Siam was saved only when the king decided to send his son to study in a British Naval Academy and then traveled to Europe himself. Extolling the virtue of these other imperial leaders studying abroad to strengthen their countries, Zhang thus asked, "How can China alone not take its place among such countries?"⁶¹ Zhang did not mention Guangxu by name, but the text nonetheless suggested that the power of the throne was tied to the monarch's personal embrace of new forms of learning. For China to flourish, therefore, Guangxu should study abroad.

In each of the calls, we see that in the post-Taiping emperorship, the emperor's education was not only a sanctioned forum for scholarly contestation but also—through writers' continual assertion of a direct link between the emperor's learning and the future of the country—a way of elevating the figure of the emperor to new levels of scrutiny and promise. As scholars such as Kang and Liang began to fuse this domestic tradition with new understandings of court-driven reforms and public displays of imperial power from countries such as Russia, Germany, and Japan, discussions of the emperor's education came more and more to be tied with the attempt to build a new type of political community. Chapters 4 and 5 will explore these efforts in more depth, but already in the 1890s we see early connections between proposed reforms to court education and the construction of an emperor-centered national community.

THE HUNDRED DAYS REFORM AND THE DANGEROUS PROMISE OF POWER

With these proposals, Kang, Liang, and other reformers joined the long line of writers over the previous decades who sought to use educational reforms to gain influence over the emperor and promote their visions of strength. Earlier chapters have discussed how officials such as Woren used the emperor's classroom to advance personal intellectual agendas by placing texts in the curriculum, as well as how papers such as *Shenbao* attempted to break their way into the planning and development of Guangxu's education. Kang and other advocates of reform now combined elements of both these earlier developments—printing their memorials in the Shanghai press and calling on friendship networks in Beijing to pass along their writings—to urge Guangxu to embrace education reforms, both for the throne and for the rest of the country, to ensure that the emperor would be connected to his people and inspire reform.[62]

In the first half of 1898, proposals for educational reform centered on bringing the Qing in line with global contemporaries gained purchase at court. On January 28, for example, Guangxu wrote approvingly of a suggestion to add shooting with modern rifles to the military examinations.[63] Then, on February 15, he ordered a special examination to identify members of the bureaucracy with knowledge of world affairs for promotion.[64] In these first few months of 1898, Guangxu and Cixi enacted reform measures cooperatively, and the court presented an image of harmonious imperial relations and power as they pursued a path of gradual reform. Many of the same observers in the foreign community who in 1891 had been enthralled with Guangxu's study of English now pointed to his purchasing of foreign books as proof that those earlier lessons were paying dividends and that the emperor was leading the country down a new path of engagement with the West.[65]

But behind the scenes, the emphasis on new forms of learning and the empowerment of new groups of scholars threatened the delicate power balance at court, and officials throughout the bureaucracy fought back against changes emanating from Guangxu's edicts. It was on June 11 that the emperor issued the edict now understood as the first in the "Hundred Days Reform." In a long decree, Guangxu chastised officials for being too conservative and argued that dramatic changes were needed to save the country from disaster. Guangxu looked to take charge in asserting the power of the throne in inspiring new fields of learning, reinvigorating the imperial family, and rejuvenating the empire. He wrote that to survive, people all around the country needed to study from the examples of other states across the globe.[66] Within this drive to learn from the world, Guangxu adopted his imperial predecessors' strategy of using the throne as patron of learning: the emperor promised imperial rewards for anyone who wrote books of useful knowledge.[67]

Guangxu also worked to assert himself as the lead pedagogue of the empire. A central component of the reform plans was the establishment of a university in Beijing. In that same June 11 edict, Guangxu wrote that "a great university should be built in the capital as a first example of our aims, and be made the model for the capitals of the provinces to copy."[68] The capital was to be a model for the empire, but more fundamentally, it was Guangxu who was the ultimate exemplar. When Guangxu decided to establish the new university in Beijing, he appointed one of his former tutors, Sun Jia'nai, as its head.[69] The emperor's classroom would thus be brought out from the confines of the Forbidden City and Qing imperial pedagogy put on display for all to see as the implicit calls from earlier generations for the emperor to serve as a model to the people were given an explicit and material form.

However, just as Sun had previously battled with colleagues in the classroom, he and Guangxu now faced stiff resistance to their ideas. Throughout the summer, as the pages of the national press were filled with Guangxu's calls for reform, they were also littered with signs that the bureaucracy was fighting the emperor's attempts to exercise unitary power. In edicts throughout June, Guangxu consistently reprimanded officials for dragging their feet.[70] This was perhaps to be expected. Many components of Guangxu's plans threatened the careers and livelihoods of an entire generation of officials. Not only was the emperor emphasizing the importance of knowledge these men did not have, but he was also ordering a streamlining of the government, eliminating "superfluous" departments and posts.

It is hardly surprising, then, that the emperor had a difficult time convincing officials to forward memorials whose suggested reforms included death sentences for their careers.[71]

This tension brings us to the most dramatic of all the reform measures of the summer of 1898, the one that ultimately ended the emperor's time on the throne. Furious that proposals for reform were not reaching him, on September 13 Guangxu issued an edict opening the road of speech not only to lower-ranking officials but to all commoners throughout the empire. The monopoly long held by high officials on advising the throne was broken, and their role in shaping the future of the country imperiled. Access to the emperor and the promise to guide his decision making was a foundational idea of the post-Taiping emperorship. When Guangxu, frustrated by the bureaucracy's unwillingness to heed his will, opened access to the throne to the country at large, he sent a wave of panic through the bureaucratic ranks. In an attempt to save their position within the emperorship and keep their dreams of power alive, these officials turned to Cixi. The empress dowager had proven before that she retained a critical mass of ritual and charismatic authority, and officials now called on her to prevent the emperor from upending the system.

Immediately after his September 13 decree, Guangxu's edicts demonstrated that he knew he had enraged many in the bureaucracy and was aware of the storm mounting against him. On September 16 he visited Cixi at the Summer Palace, and on September 17 he sent Kang Youwei out of Beijing, fearing for his ally's safety. Guangxu was scheduled to have an audience with Itō Hirobumi on September 20, and so on September 19 Cixi returned to the Forbidden City to attend the meeting. In the morning audience, Guangxu spoke with Itō as Cixi sat behind the screen, reattaching the "leading strings" to guide the throne.[72]

Then, on September 21, at the urging of all those threatened by the emperor's reforms, Cixi stepped out from behind the screen and retook her position center stage and at the core of imperial power. That day she issued an edict in Guangxu's name that described the Qing as beset by innumerable challenges, requiring wisdom and leadership beyond his abilities. "Guangxu" therefore asked that Cixi resume her "tutelage," the framework from 1886 after his assumption of personal power in which Cixi held final say over important affairs of state. The emperor told the country and the world that, for the safety of the empire, a period of regency would be restored to the emperorship, with Cixi firmly implanted as lead pedagogue:

The Empress Dowager Cixi, had since the reign of the late Emperor Tongzhi twice held the regency with much success, and that although the Empire was then also laboring under great difficulties she always issued triumphant and successful when grappling with critical questions. Now we consider the safety of the Empire handed down to us by our Imperial Ancestors above all things else; hence under the critical situation we have thrice petitioned her Majesty to graciously accede to our prayer and personally give us the benefit of her wise instructions in the government. She has, fortunately for the prosperity of the officials and inhabitants of the Empire, granted our request. Henceforth, her Majesty will conduct the affairs of State in the ordinary Throne Hall where the full Court etiquette is not observed, and where the sovereign may converse more freely with those having audience.[73]

Not only were the leading strings reattached, but all pretense of Guangxu's authority was now dropped. Cixi fully replaced the emperor as the lynchpin of the constitutional system.

Just as she had in 1861 and 1875, Cixi worried about rival factions using force to oust her. On September 22 she ordered security in the Forbidden City tightened, and a week later she canceled a planned trip outside Beijing to review military forces, instead sending the troops bonuses to ensure their loyalty.[74] As she had done in 1861 and 1875, as well, Cixi rewarded officials with posts in all levels of government, bringing back those who were earlier dismissed and granting them new rights and privileges.[75] Among those returned to positions of power were many who would play central roles in court education over the next decade. Xu Tong, one of Guangxu's former teachers, took Cixi's side in the dispute and thus saved his career. In addition, Lu Runxiang (1841-1915), future tutor to Xuantong, had been dismissed during the Hundred Days but was now reappointed as libationer of the Imperial Academy.[76]

More broadly, Cixi worked to refashion Guangxu's image from one of strong personal leadership (exemplified by his stewardship of reformed military examinations) to one of complete weakness. On September 25 she issued an edict in the emperor's name describing his prolonged illness, of being "weak and incapable," and begging for doctors to come to Beijing to try and help him.[77] In the aftermath of the Sino-Japanese War, reformers such as Kang and Liang argued that China needed a powerful emperor at the center of the national community to drive reforms around the country. But in the aftermath of the Hundred Days, Cixi worked to consolidate imperial charisma around herself.

As she sought to bring back those officials disaffected by the Hundred Days Reforms, Cixi also reached out to communities disappointed by their termination. In particular, she began to engage the foreign community—some of the most enthusiastic supporters of Guangxu's reforms—in an attempt to secure her power. The most visible of these early actions was a December 13, 1898, meeting between Cixi and the women of Beijing's foreign legation, the first of its kind. That morning, an elaborate parade of sedan chairs and horse-mounted escorts guided the women from the British Legation to the Imperial Winter Palace. Reaching the gate, the women dismounted from their chairs and entered the palace complex. As Sarah Conger, wife of the American minister in Beijing, described the scene:

> We were taken to another gate inside of which was standing a fine railroad coach presented to China by France. We entered this car, and eunuchs dressed in black pushed and hauled it to another stopping place, where we were received by many officials and served with tea. This railroad passed through a beautiful city, clean and imperial. After a little rest and tea-sipping, we were escorted by high officials to the throne-room. Our heavy garments were taken at the door, and we were ushered into the presence of the Emperor and Empress Dowager.

After exchanging formal greetings, each woman first bowed to Guangxu who then dutifully retreated from the event. Proceeding to greet Cixi, the foreign women "stepped before Her Majesty and bowed with a low courtesy. She offered both her hands and we stepped forward to her. With a few words of greeting, Her Majesty clasped our hands in hers, and placed on the finger of each lady a heavy, chased gold ring, set with a large pearl." Joining the women for a banquet after the formal audience, Cixi—seated in a "yellow throne chair"—appeared "bright and happy and her face glowed with good will. There was no trace of cruelty to be seen."[78]

As she had done for the past four decades with Chinese and Manchu officials, Cixi used the charisma of imperial gifts to try and forge relationships with her different political constituencies. For the moment, in the winter of 1898, it appeared to work: many of the foreign guests were seemingly in awe of the novelty of the event, the environs of the palace, as well as Cixi's personal touch. For Conger, despite Cixi's suppression of the Hundred Days Reforms, the audience signaled an openness and eagerness for reform. Although she had sidelined the emperor, Cixi was successfully bringing new allies and new forms of power to the emperorship.

Ironically, eight years after Guangxu had first sought to assert his imperial will through the study of English, the language was back at the center of court politics—at least in the Western imagination. "Think of this!" Conger wrote: "English was the first language spoken at Court to Their Majesties by foreign women. English, modified, is the commercial language of China, and in its purity has been carried to the very throne of China by a woman."[79] To the women of the foreign legations in 1898, it seemed—just as it had to others in 1891 with Guangxu's English lessons—that Western learning and ideals would triumph in China as the throne was exposed to new forms of learning. The only difference in 1899 was that it was Cixi, not Guangxu, who occupied the seat.

The 1890s were a dramatic time for the emperor's education. Guangxu's study of English early in the decade generated a feeling of delirious euphoria among many in the foreign community, convinced that Western civilization had won the day in China. For those same observers, it was easy to draw a straight line from Guangxu's study of English and interest in Western books to the reform decrees of the summer of 1898. For men such as Kang Youwei, Liang Qichao, and Yan Fu as well, Guangxu's early interest in topics outside the classical canon suggested a willingness to embrace the example of men such as Peter the Great and travel the world seeking knowledge to lead the country down a new path.

At the same time, the 1890s also demonstrated the very real constraints that Cixi and other members of the bureaucracy placed on Guangxu's ability to lead but which had long been fundamental to the Qing emperorship. Cixi's censure of Guangxu in 1894 (which ended his study of English) and her return to power in 1898 (which ended even nominal notions of his rule) were the latest examples of what Tongzhi had experienced in the previous generation. In their classrooms, Qing rulers read texts and listened to tutors that described emperors as moral exemplars for the people and as the intellectual and political leaders of the empire. But when Guangxu attempted to put this ideal into practice, he discovered that the rhetoric and reality of the emperor's education were separated by a wide chasm of fictional grandeur. The long-standing unwritten Qing constitution restrained the ability of the emperor to exercise autocratic power, even when in service of liberal reform. In this way, the Hundred Days Reform of 1898 was the continuation of a battle under way since the young Tongzhi took the throne in 1861 with different groups of scholars competing to win over the emperor in the hopes of advancing their cause.

This contest had long produced many victims. In 1898 one of the more prominent of those was the imperial tutor Weng Tonghe. Shortly into the reform program in June, Weng was dismissed from his posts. An edict accused him of trying to monopolize power at court and said that he was only being spared harsher punishment thanks to his many years of service in the emperor's classroom.[80] This accusation—monopolizing power over the emperor through his education—was deployed many times throughout the post-Taiping era, and Weng was only its latest victim. Though the edict dismissing him was issued in Guangxu's name, both the emperor and the empress dowager seemingly had cause to order his purge.[81] Weng was long a loyal servant of Cixi, preaching the importance of filial piety to both Tongzhi and Guangxu. Yet he was also a champion of his imperial students, working closely with Guangxu and encouraging his interests and bringing new texts—and people such as Kang Youwei—to the emperor's attention.

Whatever the cause of Weng's June dismissal, once the Hundred Days were over and Cixi returned to the center of power, he emerged as a prominent scapegoat in the empress dowager's narrative of the events. In an edict on December 4, Cixi stripped Weng of all his titles and confined him to house arrest. The edict was far harsher than that from six months earlier. Cixi—in Guangxu's name—now blamed Weng's pedagogy for all the problems, not only of that summer, but of the entire decade. The edict read in part that Weng

> never taught us in the orthodox way, nor did he ever explain to us the Classics or history to show us instances of heroism and patriotism among the ancients. He merely thought to procure the imperial favor by presenting us with light reading, famous water-colored paintings, and specimens of ancient art. In fact, by specious and crafty ways Weng Tonghe wormed himself into our confidence, catering to our wishes and anticipating them in many ways. Hence when our difficulties with Japan occurred it was he who decided for war, and then again for peace, while he had the cunning and craftiness to pass any blame therein upon others. By this and other noxious ways he has brought our empire to a point from which it will be hard to recover.[82]

In this narrative, Weng had failed in his task to transform the young Guangxu into a virtuous leader and thus brought the empire to the verge of collapse.

An unorthodox curriculum, however, was merely the prelude to Weng's truly unforgivable sin: introducing Kang Youwei to the emperor. Cixi wrote that Kang manipulated the throne to advance a treasonous agenda. In light of this more recent crime, Cixi, ventriloquizing Guangxu, said, "We feel angrier than ever, and have decided that the mere order for him to return home is an insufficient punishment for the baseness of his conduct. We therefore feel compelled to cashier and strip Weng Tonghe of all his rank and titles and to dismiss him forever from the public service."[83] Compared with Guangxu's treatment of Weng just a few years earlier when the emperor ordered his tutor's trip home be paid for by public expense for all the good he had done for the monarch and his empire, Cixi's words represent a striking reversal of fortune. For scholars such as Weng (as for those from centuries before such as Cheng Yi), court education suggested the promise to bring change, but it was also a dangerous political arena.

Despite these edicts and announcements, Cixi was unable to control the narrative of the 1898 Reforms, and her return to power was marked by a dramatic reversal of her own image. From 1861 to 1898 Cixi had worked to cultivate the persona of a classical ruler along the lines of the heroes of antiquity and her Qing predecessors. Though her time in power was indeed characterized in part by factional struggle and political violence, until the suppression of the Hundred Days Reform her image in China and around the world was more that of a "Yao or Shun among women" than of the archenemies of progress. Beginning in the fall of 1898, however, her enemies (at least those who escaped death), quickly launched a propaganda campaign establishing their vision of the empress dowager. Writing from exile, Kang Youwei and Liang Qichao founded newspapers, journals, study societies, and traveled the world giving interviews to sympathetic Western audiences. Papers described Kang and Liang as the emperor's tutors (positions they never held) and blamed Cixi for single-handedly preventing Guangxu from implementing the liberal visions of his teachers. Through new organizations such as the Protect the Emperor Society (Baohuanghui), Kang not only verbally derided Cixi's authority but also launched a failed uprising in an attempt to restore Guangxu (and thereby himself) to the center of power.[84]

In the next chapter, we see how, facing these threats as well as many others, Cixi embarked on a multifaceted campaign to remake the emperorship, stripping Guangxu of power and placing herself firmly at the center of the Qing polity. Cixi long used education and public displays of learning to argue for her legitimacy, and in the aftermath of the twin crises of the failed 1898 Reforms and the Boxer Uprising in 1900, she built on this foundation to construct a new regime of female-focused education. The first decade of the twentieth century was in many ways a new era for the Qing, defined by the establishment of the national school system and nascent (written) constitutionalism. In this context of changing social and political structures—and in seeking both domestic and international support for her rule—Cixi sought to infuse traditional imperial power with new images and the language of modern governance by providing a group of female nobles with a cosmopolitan education. The project drew on both Cixi's own history of education at court and foreign models of widespread female education. In this way, Cixi's advocacy of new forms of education was part of a larger attempt to remake the monarchy and bolster both her own power and the dynasty's international image.

4

CIXI'S PEDAGOGY

Female Education and Constitutional Governance, 1898–1908

"At dawn on the twenty first day of the fifth lunar month" of 1904, Shang Yanliu (1875–1963) arrived at the Hall of Preserving Harmony (Baohe dian) in the Forbidden City for the Palace Examination, the final stage of the Civil Service Examination system. As with millions of other aspiring scholars and officials across the country, Shang's life had been structured around the rhythm of the examination system, studying as a child and traveling to the exams as a young adult. Now, at the age of thirty-one, Shang was taking part in a ritual dating back at least a thousand years, the final step in entering the emperor's service. As he described the scene, "Kneeling at the bottom of the steps in Chung-ho Court, each candidate received a sheet, and returned to his seat. The floor of the court was completely covered with a yellow velvet carpet ... right in the center was an imperial throne situated on a three-tiered scarlet dais covered by a five-color dragon pattern brocade."[1] But when Shang arrived in 1904, the throne was empty. The Guangxu emperor, nominally the chief examiner of the empire, was nowhere to be seen.

This scene was emblematic of broader changes at court and around the country. The first decade of the twentieth century was a time of great experimentation in Qing governance, as officials and intellectuals searched for ways to combine domestic and foreign ideals to devise a new system that would save the country from the rising tide of both imperialist aggression and domestic unrest.[2] The Palace Examination described by Shang would turn out to be the last in Chinese history, as the Civil Examination System was replaced by a national school system. At the same time as these educational reforms, the Qing began a project to transform the basis of its political legitimacy: the adoption of a written constitution and the transformation into a constitutional monarchy. Both these projects drew on global movements of the late nineteenth and early twentieth centuries in which countries around the world invested in widespread state-sponsored education for their citizens while monarchs worked to build new ties between rulers and those they ruled through new forms of ritual and pageantry. The Qing actively participated in this process as well, not just creating a national school system but also using that system to host new celebrations that sought to link students with the imperial family and deepen connections between the court in Beijing and its subjects around the country to prepare for the coming constitutional monarchy.

Yet, as Shang's description of the empty throne suggests, Guangxu was not the primary focus of these efforts. Following the Sino-Japanese War, scholars had argued for Guangxu to take visible steps to embrace new forms of learning and leadership and publicly present himself as a model for the country. In the aftermath of the failed 1898 Reforms, however, Cixi instead emerged as the center of power, and over the next decade she worked not only to solidify her position but also to disseminate a new image of herself—and by association the Qing state—as a vibrant leader committed to reform. In placing herself at the center of these efforts, Cixi drew on both early dynastic history and the model of her fellow nineteenth-century female sovereigns to experiment with new gendered forms of statecraft. These projects sought to position Cixi as the mother of a nascent nation and the Qing as a sovereign member of the world community.[3]

In this era, learning to rule for the Qing court therefore now included studying European styles of monarchic leadership. This chapter explores one component of that vast project, Cixi's efforts to root her authority on two ideals of modern governance: female education and constitutional rule. The first step in that process was removing the emperor from power. More broadly, however, the project was focused on Cixi's personal diplomacy, the promotion of female education, and the creation of a new group of nobles who would take a more public-facing approach to present the Qing royal family as the center of a reforming monarchy.[4] By presenting the reeducation of the imperial family as a link between local classical traditions and shared global practices, Cixi and her allies attempted to root Qing rule not just in Chinese and Manchu traditions but also in an emerging discourse of shared global governance.[5]

The effort by the imperial family to present themselves as the center of the nation, however, was met with a strong countermovement: revolutionaries who increasingly depicted Cixi herself as the heart of the problem. In 1903, for example, Sun Yat-sen (1866–1925) argued that Cixi's meetings with foreigners were proof that she was unfit to lead, and in 1904 revolutionaries planned to stage a rebellion to coincide with public celebrations for her seventieth birthday.[6] Thus, simultaneous with the Qing reform efforts, attempts were well under way to present the imperial family as symbols—not of an emergent nation, but rather as the chief obstacle to national unity.

TOWARD AN EMPERORLESS EMPERORSHIP

In the aftermath of the 1898 Reforms, Cixi systematically worked to remove the emperor from the emperorship. She frequently issued edicts in Guangxu's name that described his poor health and inability to recover from illness, attempting to deprive him of any potential imperial charisma. Then, in January 1900, Cixi initiated plans to fully displace Guangxu. Under the guise of establishing an heir-apparent to the sick and childless emperor, she appointed Pujun (1885-1942), son of Zaiyi, Prince Duan (1856-1922), as adopted heir to Tongzhi. Prince Duan was a fierce opponent of the 1898 Reforms. In naming his son as heir, Cixi signaled to the members of the bureaucracy who had resisted Guangxu that they would play a central role in the country's future. In some ways then, Cixi was preparing to reestablish the framework of regency from 1861 and 1875. Pujun would assume the role that Tongzhi and Guangxu had in their youths: an empty vessel at the center of the emperorship that would attract the service and devotion of princes and scholar-officials.

In other important ways, however, the 1898 project was fundamentally different from the previous eras. Not only was Guangxu still alive, but Cixi made no promises and issued no timeline for a transition of power—either back to Guangxu or to Pujun. Moreover, unlike in 1861 or 1875, Cixi did not attempt to mollify her critics with an appointment as imperial tutor. Instead, she placed only her firm allies in charge of Pujun's curriculum. Chongqi, a veteran of both Tongzhi's and Guangxu's classrooms and critic of Kang Youwei, was named head teacher. Cixi also rewarded Xu Tong, Guangxu's former tutor who opposed the 1898 Reforms, placing him second in command of the heir apparent's education.[7]

Also unlike in previous eras, the announcement of an heir apparent, instead of helping to solidify Cixi's power, resulted in severe backlash. After reading the edicts that set the stage for Guangxu to be replaced, Jing Yuanshan—the advocate of female education who three years earlier had portrayed Cixi as the ideal of an educated woman and leader—organized over a thousand people to sign a telegram protesting the move. The message said that when news of the empress dowager's plans reached Jing and others in Shanghai, it "caused an uproar in the people's minds." Jing relayed rumors that foreign powers might even use military force to put Guangxu back on the throne if he was indeed deposed. Jing therefore wrote: "We appeal to you, for the sake of the country, to exercise your justice and loyalty, and to petition the Emperor to stay on the throne and not to consider stepping down. By doing so, we could allay the concerns of the Empress, on the one hand, and mitigate the shock both in China and abroad, on the other. This will be fortunate for the imperial family, as well as for all under heaven!" All around the country, people joined in Jing's call. In Sichuan, Shaanxi, Hubei, Guangxi, Guangdong, and Zhejiang, groups of scholars and merchants gathered to debate how to respond, and many sent their own petitions to Beijing in support of Guangxu. Some were even reported to be considering declaring independence if Cixi did not return power to Guangxu.[8]

This backlash seemed to surprise Cixi, and in the following days she sought both to punish people such as Jing and at the same time to allay some of their fears. Ten days after the initial announcement of Pujun's education, for example, Cixi issued an additional edict expanding the scope of the personnel and texts inside the emperor-in-waiting's classroom. While the initial teachers were her staunch allies, Cixi now said that in addition to the original appointments of Chongqi and Xu Tong, new tutors would be sought for Pujun's classroom. She declared the start of the heir's education as a crucial moment for him and the country and therefore ordered a search for men of good character and scholarship to guide his learning.[9] But now in 1900, Cixi found that reformer-officials had little interest in retaking their spot in the constitutional apparatus, and in the days following Cixi's call, Pujun entered the classroom with no additional teachers.[10] For months thereafter, the heir apparent's education receded from announcements from court. Pujun's classroom proved to be a far less useful tool than had Tongzhi's and Guangxu's. When it finally reemerged, the only news was that Xiangheng (1832–1904) would now serve as an additional Manchu-language instructor.[11] Xiangheng was a member of the imperial clan and had served in a variety of military and political posts during the Tongzhi and Guangxu eras. For the previous eighteen years, he had been the highest-ranking official in the Hubei

Banner Garrison.[12] Xiangheng was thus hardly the constituency Cixi had hoped to attract to her service by expanding the pool of Pujun's tutors, and she was forced to rely ever more on officials such as Chongqi—officials deeply opposed to engagement with, or learning from, foreign powers—both in court classrooms and throughout the larger structure of government.[13] Chongqi, for example, was now made both the heir apparent's tutor and president of the Board of Revenue.[14]

The first two months of 1900 were thus a tumultuous time for Cixi as she struggled to rebuild a ruling coalition. The situation, however, would get much worse before getting better. Having ruptured her relationship with many reform-minded officials, the empress dowager looked elsewhere to bolster her coalition and secure her place at the heart of court. A "Coalition United in Righteousness" (Yihequan), better known as the Boxers, battling against foreign influence in Shandong, emerged as a potential new ally. Prince Duan—father of the heir apparent—was one of the first members of court to actively support the Boxers, personally helping to guide their attacks on foreign institutions in Beijing.[15] When Cixi declared her support for the Boxers, Prince Duan was placed in charge of the court's war against the foreign powers. Yet powerful provincial leaders all around China refused to go along and promised foreign governments that they would protect expatriates in their regions.[16] The Qing court and Qing Empire were divided, and Cixi's authority had seemingly vanished.

After the court fled Beijing, as it had done under Xianfeng fifty years before, the heart of imperial authority became metonymic sites for the "pedagogy of imperialism." Public executions in squares next to posters advertising English-language classes and a grand memorial ceremony for Queen Victoria on the spot of Qianlong's military reviews served to denigrate the Qing. There were now even pictures of foreign troops sitting on the Qing throne.[17] Cixi's allies, as well, were punished. At the insistence of the foreign powers, Prince Duan was exiled to Xinjiang, while his son, the heir apparent, was stripped of his title, kicked out of the palace, and erased from public presentations of the emperorship.[18] Chongqi, meanwhile, committed suicide before he could be captured by the Allied troops.[19] Finally, as part of Cixi's punishment for supporting the Boxers, the foreign powers demanded that Guangxu be returned to power. They insisted on his physical presence at court, hoping that the emperor would be a more malleable figurehead for the changes they would impose and the effort to ensure that the Qing was just strong enough to uphold the imperialists' hard-won treaty privileges.[20]

CIXI'S GENDERED CHARM OFFENSIVE

Yet despite the nominal return of Guangxu to power, over the next few years Cixi worked to replace the emperor with herself and a new group of nobles at the heart of the Qing state. In the context of seeking both new domestic and international support for her power, she launched a protracted campaign to refashion the throne. She embraced new forms of technology and political theater from England, Japan, and the rest of the world to place herself at the center of the public image of a remade empire, one that drew its strength not only from the domestic intellectual traditions of the Manchu Way and Confucian Canon but also from a global language of modern governance.

The first strategy Cixi deployed in this mission was, just as after the end of the 1898 Reforms, to host the women of the international diplomatic corps inside the Forbidden City and at the Summer Palace. For the first time as well, Cixi also met with the men of the legations. In audiences and personal interaction with members of the diplomatic corps, Cixi attempted to convince the foreign community that her involvement with the Boxers had been an aberration and that she was committed to reform. She also demonstrated that she was intent on changing long-standing gender norms at court: at the audience held on January 27, 1902, in front of the entire diplomatic corps, the emperor and empress dowager sat side by side on the throne, Cixi having dropped completely the pretense of "ruling from behind the screen."[21]

Then, on February 1, Cixi held her first audience with the foreign women since returning from Xi'an. A palpable air of excitement washed over the women of the legations in preparation for the event. In a parade of twenty-nine green sedan chairs surrounded by mounted escorts, the women traveled from the legation into the Imperial City, and finally into the Forbidden City. Dismounting from their chairs, they boarded "red Imperial chairs, which were carried by black robed eunuchs to the court gate of the Palace, where we were received by high officials and escorted to a waiting room, where tea was served." Sarah Conger, having already been wooed once before by Cixi in 1898, now described the environs of the Forbidden City with a sense of wonder. The sea of marble, yellow roof tiles, and the lavish dress of all the court women lined up waiting to receive the foreign women created for her a fairytale atmosphere, "yet the bright sun was shining upon a living picture." The light and colors transfixed Conger: "I never saw its equal in artistic beauty," she wrote. "Would that the tip of my pen were clever

FIGURE 4.1 "The Official Audience of Their Majesties." Image from Katherine Carl, *With the Empress Dowager* (London: Century, 1907), 146.

enough, and that the daintiness and richness of my ink were so quality-blessed that they might tell this valuable story."[22] Inside the formal audience, Guangxu and Cixi shook hands with the women before the emperor receded into the background of the event.[23] Later, Cixi joined the women for a banquet, where, according to Conger, she was "thoughtful, serious in every way, and ever mindful of the comfort and pleasure of her guests. Her eyes are bright, keen, and watchful that nothing may escape her observation. Her face does not show marks of cruelty or severity; her voice is low, soft, and attractive; her touch is gentle and kind."[24] The empress dowager was eager to use the charisma of her imperial presence and gifts in the aftermath of the Boxers to reestablish her authority.

By stepping out from behind the screen, Cixi presented an image of female rulership that drew on both early dynastic history and the contemporary world. For centuries in the early imperial era, empress dowagers had met with officials and foreign envoys, seated in positions of authority next to young emperors. But beginning in the Eastern Jin (317–420) regulations emerged that placed a screen between powerful women and their officials.[25] Despite women playing important roles in imperial politics, religion, education, and art in the Song, Ming, and Qing, the barrier of the screen remained intact until the twentieth century.[26] But now, Cixi's new position suggested that the empress dowager would rule more in the mold of her pre-Jin predecessors and global contemporaries.

Queen Victoria (r. 1837–1901) in particular provided Cixi with a model to follow in the creation of this new image. Victoria had been a critical participant in the late nineteenth-century transformation of the British crown into a national symbol.[27] Not only did Victoria frequently communicate with her empire via the new technology of the telegraph, but she also allowed herself and the imperial family to be photographed, starting a process of "endless materialization" of the throne in the service of national identity.[28] Cixi apparently saw much of herself in Victoria, or at least wanted to convince her foreign guests that she ought to be treated as an equal member of a global club of female rulers. To this end, she hung steel engravings of the British queen in the palace, making sure her foreign guests could not miss the connection.[29]

As Victoria had done as well, Cixi began to use photographs and her own image to argue for Qing sovereignty. After Cixi received framed photographs of Nicholas II of Russia (r. 1894–1917) in 1902 as a gift from the ambassador's wife, she began to gift images of herself to foreign visitors in an attempt to place herself among a cohort of world leaders.[30] While Qing emperors were long painted by court artists in a variety of different settings, the portraits had a limited viewing audience.[31] Beginning in 1903, however, as Cixi sought to refashion the throne, she actively expanded the audience of imperial portraiture and used photography to position herself as the public ruler and face of the Qing on equal standing with other world leaders.[32] Over the next several years, Cixi presented photos of herself to rulers and diplomats of at least ten foreign powers. More dramatically, she also posed for photographs with the women of the foreign legation, going so far as to hold their hands as a sign of both personal friendship and diplomatic engagement.[33]

The photos were not snapshots of reality, but rather an attempt to create a new image for Cixi and the Qing. Painted elements, for example, were added to make Cixi look younger, and thus, in seeking a new image for China, Cixi started with herself.[34] Of course, Cixi was not always successful in her project, as the photographs simultaneously turned her into the embodiment of the Qing state to be honored and a "social celebrity" to be mocked.[35] Yet by placing herself publicly at the heart of a new Qing imperial iconography (flanked by the foreign women), Cixi suggested that she and her empire deserved to be treated as an equal participant in the world community of states.[36]

Cixi had a number of allies in this project, particularly the women of the foreign legation. At the suggestion of Sarah Conger, for example, Cixi commissioned a portrait to be displayed at the St. Louis World's Fair in 1904 to further disseminate her refurbished image. As Conger described her motivations, "For many months I had been indignant over the horrible, unjust caricatures of Her Imperial Majesty in illustrated papers, and with a growing desire that the world might see her more as she really is, I had conceived the idea of asking her Majesty's permission to speak with her upon the subject of having her portrait painted."[37] For almost a year, the American painter Katherine Carl lived in a complex at the Summer Palace, visiting nearly daily with Cixi and painting her portrait. In her writings, Carl praised Cixi for everything from her demeanor, her devotion to and mastery of the Classics, and her love and talent for language.[38] While Cixi had long sought to portray herself to the scholar-officials of the bureaucracy as a female sage ruler, she now applied that same strategy to potential allies in the international community. As with the photographs, Cixi ensured that when she was painted by foreign artists such as Herbert Vos, the portraits depicted the empress dowager (and by extension the Qing) in a positive and vibrant light.[39]

In this new era, Cixi also continued to adapt long-standing practices of cultural production and imperial gift giving to cultivate her authority. After returning to

FIGURE 4.2 "The Empress Dowager Writing a 'Great Character.'" Image from Katherine Carl, *With the Empress Dowager* (London: Century, 1907), 136.

Beijing from her Boxer exile, not only did Cixi continue the Kangxi era practice of publicly writing calligraphy as gifts, but she also expanded the audience of recipients to include members of the foreign diplomatic corps.[40] Like the image of Cixi as a devoted student of the Classics immortalized in her Tongzhi era court portrait, so too did the image of Cixi as calligrapher and bestower of imperial grace become inscribed into visual representations of the monarchy during the latter years of her reign. Katherine Carl, recounting her experience with the empress dowager, for example, included an illustration of officials gathered around Cixi as she performed calligraphy.

Finally, Cixi added a new international component to her personal education and public pedagogy. As described in earlier chapters, in the years following the 1861 coup, Cixi had studied the Classics and worked to present herself as a diligent steward of the domestic intellectual tradition. Returning to Beijing, she now began studying English in an attempt to present herself, and by extension the Qing, as a participant in the global community. Foreign observers were intrigued by the presence of English in the Forbidden City, and some began to believe that Cixi would lead the Qing on a project of Westernization.[41] For example, in 1902, in looking for "clear and unmistakable evidence of good faith from the Empress Dowager," the *North China Herald* described Cixi's efforts to learn English as proof that she was serious about reforms:

> It is commonly reported now that the Empress Dowager is learning English and that her little speech to the Legation ladies, "I hope we shall meet very often," was the first fruit of the new study. The wonderful old lady believes that international difficulties are chiefly due to mutual ignorance of each other's tongue on the part of those engaged in international politics in Peiking... it is becoming more evident that the Empress Dowager is inclining to the Reform Policy of the Emperor.[42]

Two years later, Cixi's study of English entered a more formal phase when she hired an American woman to serve as tutor. The empress dowager was now seen as leading a charge among women in the imperial family to embrace the teachings of the world to enter the community of nations.[43]

Whenever Cixi deployed her, albeit limited, English vocabulary, foreign friends made sure to include it in their accounts as evidence for their argument that Cixi, despite her support of the Boxers, was not in fact disdainful of the West.[44] In both

1876 and 1891, proponents of Guangxu's English lessons had stressed the benefits that would emerge from the monarch's ability to communicate directly with foreign leaders. Now, with hardly anyone pretending that Guangxu would ever return to power, it was Cixi's interest in the language that won praise and worked to create a new image of the Qing throne.[45]

FEMALE EDUCATION FOR THE CONSTITUTIONAL MONARCHY

From 1861 to 1900 Cixi had deployed a range of Chinese and Manchu cultural practices, adopting and adapting imperial tradition in the realms of scholarship and artistic production to argue for the legitimacy of her rule. Now in the twentieth century, Cixi's internationalism began to root her rule not only in the authority of her ancestors but by reference to global norms of modern governance. Cixi's personal image and education were important components in this project. So too, however, were attempts to promote widespread education for women in China. In personal interactions with foreign women, Cixi presented herself as dedicated to the cause of female education to bring China in line with global norms.[46] At the center of this effort was the attempt to create a new group, the cosmopolitan Qing noblewoman, as an embodiment of Cixi's new vision of rulership.

The establishment of new educational institutions for Qing women appeared in the context of the administrative and educational changes of the New Policy Reforms (*xinzheng bianfa*), including the construction of a national school system and plans for the adoption of a constitution.[47] Within these changes, however, the place of women and female education was uncertain. Regulations and plans for the school system issued in 1902 and 1904, for example, provided no space for the education of women. Despite growing movements around the world for universal female education, initial plans for the Qing system were for boys and men, and female education was left in the hands of private individuals. Many high officials and architects of the new school system, such as Zhang Zhidong, believed allowing girls to be educated outside the home was a danger to social stability.[48]

At the same time, however, there was a growing belief among the urban elite in China that female education was fundamental to strengthening the nation. All around the country, private groups of merchants, lineages, and other organizations began establishing schools for women.[49] The *World's Chinese Students' Journal*, for example, founded with the aim of uniting both domestic and overseas students behind the goal of promoting reform, captured the sentiment in the most explicit of terms. In the opening issue, the editors wrote that the "destiny of a nation is inextricably involved in the condition of the woman, and the country will be strong in proportion as the woman, as mother and wife, is strong physically, morally, and intellectually." The journal therefore concluded that "if we wish to keep abreast with the march of civilization and join the family of nations, we must give our women education. It is the only guarantee to our future greatness, the only hope of our national salvation."[50]

Paired with the belief that female education was critical to the strength of the nation, there was now also a growing conviction that constitutional countries were more powerful than autocratic ones.[51] The first issue of the *Journal*, for example, presented female education and a constitution as two foundational pillars for the construction of a strong Chinese nation.[52] Debates about constitutionalism had in fact been in the air in Chinese theories of the state for at least twenty-five years.[53] Chinese intellectuals had begun to study constitutions as part of a broader pattern of Western-oriented reforms in the second half of the nineteenth century.[54] Then, in their proposals to Guangxu in 1898, reformers had advocated creating a period of tutelage under the emperor's leadership as the education and political consciousness of the country were raised to a level high enough to participate in a constitutional system.[55] In 1898 these calls seemed radical, however, and the idea of the Qing adopting a written constitution remained on the fringe of political discourse.[56]

Yet in the context of the New Policy Reforms and Japan's defeat of Russia in the Russo-Japanese War of 1904-1905, many at court became convinced that adopting a written constitution was the key to uniting the population, encouraging feelings of patriotism, and thereby strengthening the country. In 1905 Cixi declared that "the reason for the wealth and power of countries around the world lies in their enactment of constitutions."[57] Thus the court declared its intention to investigate the best practices of the contemporary world and bring the Qing in line with global norms of governance by transforming into a constitutional monarchy.[58] This does not mean, however, that the Qing was enacting an "emancipatory political project," as around the world constitutions were often as much about control as they were liberty and in fact served as effective tools of empire.[59] The "unwritten Qing constitution" discussed in previous chapters was a delicate compromise between the throne and its domestic political constituencies, promising access to a diverse body of scholars and officials. While still struggling to solidify that domestic balance of power, the twentieth-century project of constitutional transformation added an international element as the Qing strove to regain its sovereignty by aligning its governance with contemporary foreign norms—not just in the sense of adopting a constitution but, as the *WCSJ* said, also in promoting education for women to build the foundation of a strong country.

It was the combination of these sentiments that appeared at the heart of the effort to train a cohort of noblewomen. Members of this group were to be given their own schools with specialized curricula to prepare them for new roles in the modern monarchy.[60] The first step in the creation of the female nobles came in 1904, a year before Cixi's public statement on the importance of constitutions. In that year Cixi proposed the establishment of an institution called the Society for the Education of Women (Yukun wenhui, also referred to as the Yukun hui and the Yukun zongxue hui).[61] Although the school would not come to fruition, the debate and discussion surrounding its proposal set the stage for later projects and speaks both to Cixi's effort to create new educational opportunities for women to augment the Qing's image and to the challenges the idea would face from other powerful forces around the country.

The school intended to enroll the wives and daughters of princes and high officials above the fifth rank. Critically, however, women of reputable gentry and merchant families, regardless of their educational background, were invited to sit in on the lectures.[62] By casting a wide net for potential students in the school, Cixi suggested an alteration to long-standing Qing conceptions of nobility. As implied by the inclusion not only of both Manchu and Chinese women but also of those from outside the bureaucracy entirely, this new group signaled a breakdown of the original Qing model of rule that differentiated between the hereditary Manchu military caste and Chinese civilian populations.[63] In this way, the Qing moved closer to the new Japanese definition of nobility, wherein military leaders and powerful businessmen were ennobled as barons and brought in to serve in the House of Peers.[64]

The curriculum as well indicated a new internationalist push. Initial news reported that the women would be given daily lessons in simple composition as well as foreign languages. Just as Cixi had impressed foreign visitors with her study of English, the students at her school would be trained to interact with the diplomatic community, presenting a new face of the Qing to the world. Some early reports suggested that, at least as a public relations campaign, plans for the development of the school were paying dividends. The Tianjin paper *Dagong bao*, for example, was enthusiastic about the prospect of such a school and suggested that its example would lead to the flourishing of female education.[65] The school also fit well with Cixi's other ventures around that time, namely, surrounding herself with Manchu women who had lived abroad and who spoke foreign languages as part of her engagement with the women of the diplomatic corps. In fact, one early description of the school explicitly described its purpose as training the wives and daughters of Manchu princes and high officials in the languages and practices of the West to prepare them to participate in diplomatic gatherings and serve as translators and cultural ambassadors.[66]

Soon after the initial proposals for the Yukun hui, the 1905 formal declaration of the intent to adopt a constitution and open a bicameral parliament led to a broader push to reeducate Qing nobles in the tools of modern governance. The court worked to open schools to train male members of the imperial family and Bannermen community in military affairs and constitutional arts.[67] Though they built on a long tradition of specialized education for Qing imperial elite, the schools were now explicitly modeled on institutions in foreign countries, particularly Japan, in seeking to build a new class of noble-experts to serve the constitutional monarchy.[68] In their foreign-inspired buildings, staffs, and curricula, the schools for male nobles worked to reeducate the imperial family while presenting the Qing as a modern nation, worthy of full sovereignty along the lines of constitutional monarchies such as England, Germany, and Japan.[69]

As plans for the male schools unfolded, so too did calls for the establishment of a companion school for the education of female nobles. In a December 1905 audience, Prince Qing (Yikuang, 1838–1917) argued that alongside the formation of a military school for male nobles, the government ought to create an additional school specifically for female nobles. Perhaps as proxy for Cixi or perhaps based on his own conviction, Prince Qing's proposal initiated a process that saw the effort to educate elite Qing women begin to transition from a private initiative of Cixi via the stalled Yukun hui to a formal component of the larger task of reeducating the imperial family for the constitutional era. Providing women access to education was coming to be understood as essential to modern governance, and so without a school for female nobles, the Qing's reform efforts would be incomplete.

Prince Qing proposed a two-pronged approach to educating the women in modern affairs that would result in both personal edification and the strengthening of the empire. First, he suggested the school should "employ first rate foreign female teachers to give lessons" to the daughters of princes and dukes. By employing foreign women, the prince reasoned, the school for female nobles would ensure that its students received the best classroom education available. At the same time, however, Prince Qing proposed that the women's education should not be limited to the confines of a schoolhouse, and that to best serve the country in the future they needed real-world experiences. He therefore also recommended that imperial women should be encouraged to accompany their brothers and fathers posted abroad in order to learn from the outside world and gain new skills.[70]

Despite these ambitious plans, the initial discussions about the establishment of a school for the education of female members of the imperial elite failed to strictly define the scope of who qualified as a noble. Although Cixi's efforts with the Yukun hui had apparently broken the barrier between Manchu and Chinese populations, Prince Qing's initial proposals for a school referred to the student population as "women of the imperial clan" (*huangzu nü*) and called for the establishment of a "School for Women of the Imperial Clan" (*huangzu nü xuetang*). While he did not attach ages or other qualifying factors to his description of the potential students, he seems to have eliminated merchant families from the possibility of ennoblement. In this way, Prince Qing's vision of Qing nobility might at first appear to have been narrower than Cixi's. Yet, the very name of the school suggests that, like Cixi, Prince Qing was inspired by Japan, and the efforts to create a Qing school for female nobles was built on the ideal of aligning the Qing with foreign models in the creation of a constitutional monarchy.

In 1885 Japan had established the Peeresses' School (Kazoku jogakkō) as a counterpart to the long-standing Japanese School for Nobles (Gakushūin). Although the Gakushūin had originally been for members of the imperial family only, when Japan passed the peerage act in 1884 the student body was expanded to include the children of those new peers. The creation of the Peeresses' School was also directly connected to the coming of the constitutional era and new international engagements. Early on, the school for female nobility served to train the peeresses in Western learning and aesthetics. In 1887, for example, the school issued regulations that required the students to wear Western-style clothes, and the curriculum included physical education, dancing, and English.

The Peeresses' School was also an avenue through which the Meiji government worked to present the empress as both matron and model for the country. The school was described as having been founded by Empress Haruko (posthumous title Empress Shōken, 1848-1914), wife of the Meiji emperor, and the empress would visit the school, offer gifts of imperial calligraphy, meet with students, and present herself as a model for the young women.[71] Reports in the Chinese press about the Japanese school in the first years of the twentieth century consistently emphasized the central role of the Japanese empress in its founding, participating in ceremonies with students, and encouraging the spread of education among noblewomen in Japan.[72] Thus both the school and Empress Haruko were presented as models for Cixi and the Qing as a way to augment the power of the throne by embracing international norms of both nobility and female education.[73]

By 1906, as reports of the Qing plan for the education of female nobles spread, the Japanese model was indeed dominant, both at court and in the press. One newspaper in Beijing noted: "Women's learning is the foundation of education and we must pay attention to it. We should copy the Japanese school for female nobles and establish a school for female nobles and select the daughters of high officials to enter the school and study."[74] As the newspaper made clear, part of copying the Japanese model implied admitting nonhereditary elites into the definition of Qing nobility. And in fact, by suggesting that the daughters of high officials should be included in the school, the paper argued to redefine the traditional Qing service nobility along Japanese lines. Cixi agreed that in establishing a school for female nobles, both the "curriculum and regulations should imitate Japan's Peeress School."[75] The Japanese connection was so strong, in fact, that Cixi apparently hoped to arrange a meeting with the female Japanese education reformer Shimoda Utako (1854-1936) to help establish a palace school.[76]

But opening the school proved to be a challenge. In the spring of 1906, Prince Qing lamented that many women in the imperial family had yet to start their educations, and he again requested the establishment of a school for the daughters of princes and Manchu high officials of the second and third rank.[77] The prince hoped that by studying in the new school, the young women would develop an understanding of decorum (*liyi*) while also cultivating a patriotic heart (*aiguo zhi xin*).[78] Prince Qing's dual invocation of the traditional ideas of ritual and propriety associated with *liyi* alongside the new value of "patriotism" suggests both the challenges and the opportunities involved in the project. While many high officials were concerned with a potential threat to social stability caused by newly educated women, others saw these same women as potential frontline soldiers in the battle to define the nation.

Those supportive of the idea of a school for female nobles—people such as the wife of Prince Qing—took up the cause directly with Cixi, urging the formation of such an institution.[79] These proposals and discussions were frequently reprinted in the domestic press, bringing both the ideals and obstacles of the project into full public view. In both private and public, advocates of the female nobles drew a direct link between female education, national salvation, and international respect. As *Dagong bao* reported, Cixi said that foreign countries emphasized female education, but China was lagging behind.[80] Opening a school for female nobles and creating a cohort of women who would present an image of the Qing as engaged with, and respected by, the world was thus seen as crucial to the court's project of nation building. The national press reported frequently that female education and the creation of a cosmopolitan cohort of female nobles was an "urgent task" for Cixi.[81] In the papers of Chinese communities around the world as well, Cixi's support for female education and the creation of specialized schools for female nobles were seen as part of the larger project of embracing elements of Western ideas of education and governance.[82]

The question of exactly who would be allowed to enter the school, however, continued to present a challenge in articulating the Qing noblewomen. Prince Qing's spring 1906 proposals envisioned a much narrower definition of nobility than had originally been discussed for the school. The proposals for the Yukun hui in 1904 suggested that wives and daughters of officials of above the fifth rank qualified for formal enrollment, while many others of nonhereditary status could attend lectures. Yet now, Prince Qing defined noble women as only those belonging to Manchu families of the second and third ranks. In September another report stated that the school would soon open, enrolling women from families above the third rank.[83] Thus, despite the desire to create a group of cosmopolitan women to serve the throne, the court grappled with the lingering question of how wide they ought to extend the right to contribute to governance. The creation of this group of female nobles was already a substantial change to the principles underlying Qing rule, and it seems that although Cixi and others at court sought to break the original mold and recast it along international, particularly Japanese, lines, they found the process fraught with stumbling blocks.

Nevertheless, at multiple points throughout 1907 there were signs that plans for the school were being finalized.[84] In March and April foreign papers reported on the imminent opening of the school, while the Chinese press published rumors regarding its personnel.[85] In all these reports, the school was presented as a hybrid institution of domestic and foreign traditions that would position its female students to become both stewards of classical knowledge and vanguards of the new constitutional Qing state. One report in May suggested that a female descendent of Confucius would be appointed as the school's director.[86] Another report in July described Cixi's plan to dispatch a female member of the imperial clan to study abroad in Europe and the United States and upon her return take up the reins at the school for female nobles. In this report, it was said that the school would proceed with a pedagogy that "completely imitated the Western style."[87] A school supported by the empress dowager, run by a descendant of Confucius and perhaps a woman with experience studying abroad, and filled with students from the imperial nobility learning skills of the modern world: the school for female nobles epitomized the divergent strands of authority Cixi sought to weave together in her refashioning of imperial power for the twentieth century.

Critically as well, the students themselves were not intended as the sole recipients of this new pedagogy. The court and press consistently referred to the school as "a model for the whole country."[88] The noble women were to serve the throne not only through their work at court but more broadly by modeling behavior for the rest of the population and by presenting a new, composite image of the emperorship and an ideal of the potential national community.[89] This ideal included fusing traditional elements of Confucian education with new subjects such as foreign languages to prepare the women to play a larger public role in the coming constitutional era. It also, however, was inherently tied to the idea of Cixi as the leader and face of the country. Although Prince Qing and others supported the creation of a school for noblewomen, at court and in the press, the school was presented as decidedly Cixi's vision. Reports consistently described Cixi as the main source of support for the school, frequently meeting with other high officials to urge them to hasten completion of the project, and even offering her personal money to support the effort.[90] Just as she had throughout the second half of the nineteenth century, Cixi used plans for the school for female nobles as a form of public pedagogy and propaganda, arguing for the legitimacy of her rule through the guise of devotion to learning.

Despite this, however, or perhaps because of the central role Cixi played, the school for female nobles gained as many detractors as supporters.[91] Amid a general angst about changing gender relations across the country, opponents of female education used supposed instances of misconduct at schools to argue against government sanctioned female education.[92] As Joan Judge has described, Zhang

Zhidong was among the many high officials who cautioned "against (unarticulated) dangers involved in allowing young girls to enter schools" in general.[93] Zhang also argued specifically against the opening of the school for noblewomen. His position was given national attention when *Dagong bao* printed a telegram he sent to the Ministry of Education in which he said that there were many corrupt practices in schools for women around the country, and since the entire country looked to the imperial family for inspiration, any mistakes in implementing such a school would cause great harm to the state. While he therefore argued that the founding of the school needed to be postponed until success was guaranteed, he also appeared to accept the notion that the imperial family in general, and the female nobles specifically, should be models for the people.[94]

The school for female nobles was in a permanent holding pattern for the rest of the Qing. Yet although the nobles' school never came to fruition, Cixi's desire to provide elite Qing women with a cosmopolitan education was manifest in the creation of a range of other schools for Manchu women in Beijing. For example, in 1906 the wife of the Manchu grand secretary and imperial household member Kungang (1836-1907) proposed the establishment of a "School for Female Interpreters" (Yiyi nüxue).[95] The curriculum included standard subjects such as ethics and Chinese, but it also provided for courses in medicine and foreign languages.[96] When the school opened in April 1906, it had seventy-eight students divided into two classes.[97] Although the exact composition of the student body is unclear, newspaper reports at the time described it as a school for princesses (*da gongzhu*), giving credence to the idea that the court and Manchu high officials were pursuing forms of female education not yet fully available to the general population.[98] In fact, one of the primary goals of the new school was to train interpreters for the court. The top students would then be eligible to serve in Cixi's personal retinue as she worked to lead the Qing into a new era of governance.[99]

CONNECTING COURT AND COUNTRY FOR THE CONSTITUTIONAL MONARCHY

Plans for the school for female nobles thus took place within the context of broader changes in China in which Cixi worked to position herself and the women around her as embodiments of a new Qing state, one whose authority was connected to global trends of female education and constitutional governance. In part, this meant working to educate members of the Qing nobility in the art of constitutional governance to prepare for their roles in new institutions such as the National Assembly.[100] Cixi therefore ordered the Imperial Clan Court to establish a "Constitutional Research Center" (Xianzheng yanjiu suo) where members of the imperial clan could study and train for the new era of governance. Imperial family members were also encouraged to study abroad to learn from the experiences of other constitutional monarchies.[101] In addition, Cixi ordered a group of scholars to take turns offering daily lectures on history, the Classics, and other subjects to members of court.[102] The content of these lectures reflected the changing times and educational needs of the imperial family, emphasizing Western learning and the history of foreign countries with books such as *Xiyang tongshi jiangyi* (Lessons on the comprehensive history of Western countries).[103]

Yet more than simply providing members of the imperial family with new types of knowledge, the lectures were part of a broader effort to present the imperial family as representatives of a new type of regime. An official named Xu Dingchao (1845-1917), for example, requested that the lectures on constitutions delivered to the court be published and distributed to schools around the country.[104] At the same time that the Qing was promulgating its first election laws to prepare for the constitution—laws that sought to "link the sentiments of the rulers and the ruled and reduce the harm caused by alienation"—the court was thus searching for ways to teach people around the country about the imperial family and deepen the connections between monarch and subject.[105] In arguing for compulsory education for the imperial family, for example, Prince Gong said they needed to "set an example to the people."[106]

In this context, the national school system offered an opportunity to build connections between ruler and ruled to begin the process of teaching people around the country about their place in the coming constitutional monarchy. In fact, building on the model of Japan, "loyalty to the monarch" was one of the guiding principles in founding the new school system, and textbooks upheld Confucius and the emperor as "twin symbols of continuity" in the development of the nation.[107] From the very start, the rhythms of the school year tied students all around the country to the imperial family: the birthdays of the emperor, empress dowager, and Confucius all came with mandated ritual celebrations at school.[108] Regulations for students at the Imperial University in Beijing as well included mandatory commemorations of Cixi's, Guangxu's, and Confucius's birthdays.[109]

Thus despite the removal of Guangxu from participation in the functional operation of the state, the constitutional monarchy placed a high value on the symbolic power of the emperor and the rest of the imperial family in constructing the political community.

In fact, beginning in 1905, imperial birthdays became major celebrations at schools around the country as a new set of ritual practices emerged that sought to bind young schoolchildren to the imperial family. In July 1905, for example, over five thousand students gathered to celebrate Guangxu's birthday. On that day, Yuan Shikai hosted foreign military and diplomatic officials as well as businessmen to celebrate together with the students in a newly constructed pavilion. Foreign commentators marveled not only at the festivities, which included music, plays, and acrobats, but also the supposed "growing spirit of patriotism" among the people evident in the celebration.[110] Similar events unfolded around the country. In Beijing in 1906, for instance, a school for girls organized gymnastics and other athletic competitions to celebrate Guangxu's birthday.[111] All across the country, imperial birthdays emerged as a pedagogical opportunity for the court to instruct students of their duties in the new political system, as "showy processions of uniformed school-children and students" were gathered together and lectured by high officials "on their duties to their country."[112]

In part, these events drew on a long history of connections between imperial birthdays and education. Kangxi famously performed his learned authority by publicly doing math on his birthday; students at the Palace School for Princes had the day off on the birthday of an emperor; and emperors frequently added extra examinations in the Civil Service Examination system in celebration of their own birthdays.[113] But these twentieth-century celebrations were additionally inspired by foreign models of public imperial ritual and pedagogy. In Japan, the emperor's birthday was celebrated as a national holiday, and around the British Empire, the queen's birthday was a school holiday.[114] As the Qing court worked toward implementing the constitution to join Japan and Britain as constitutional monarchies, celebrations of imperial birthdays thus became part of the articulation of an ideology of imperial citizenship that combined Qing traditions with a new language of cosmopolitan governance.

Inside the classroom as well, students were taught in history and geography lessons to "conflate" the Qing with China as the court worked to develop feelings of loyalty and nationalism among a restive population.[115] In many of these narratives, the imperial family was singled out for attention in an attempt to combine "loyalty to ruler and love of nation."[116] The 1904 curriculum, for example, stipulated that classes in Chinese history would discuss the "great and virtuous deeds of the sage rulers," and beginning in the fifth year of their education, students started to learn about sage rulers from the Qing.[117] Textbooks produced by a variety of publishing houses in the first years of the Qing national school system promoted emperor-centered narratives of the great events of history, from the unification of the country to the Southern Tours, pacification of border regions, and more. Yet at the same time, the textbooks made a seamless transition from discussions of the individual heroics of early Qing rulers to the problems facing "Our Country" in the current day and the need to unite behind reform efforts and the development of the constitution.[118] In some texts, Cixi appeared personally in the narrative, credited with the New Policy reforms, and sponsoring the adoption of the constitution. In an even more explicit link between the imperial family and students in the new constitutional system and the construction of a healthy nation, one textbook included an image of sporting events celebrating the empress dowager's birthday.[119]

Then in 1908, the court sought to teach students and the whole country that the imperial family represented timeless symbols of national unity: that year students were mobilized to adorn the funerals of both Cixi and Guangxu. Students from the Imperial University and other schools around Beijing were ordered to attend the events, and more than two hundred students from newly reformed Bannermen schools attended a memorial for Guangxu.[120] In fact, the funerals of Cixi and Guangxu were in some ways the most elaborate attempt by the Qing to link the monarchy with the nation and, in death, present the emperor and empress dowager as symbols of unity in the new constitutional era. The funerals were lavish and expensive affairs, commanding not only the attention of the country and the world but also financial contributions from leaders all around China.[121]

Guangxu's funeral was held on May 1, 1909. After weeks of preparation, the streets of Beijing were lined with onlookers, including many foreign dignitaries sent to Beijing specifically for the occasion.[122] The presence of foreigners and Chinese was both sanctioned and encouraged by an imperial decree, a stark contrast to the measures the court had taken to hide Tongzhi's wedding from public view years earlier.[123] In the early afternoon a parade of soldiers, religious representatives, and a host of other officials filled a specially constructed street in Beijing. Guangxu's hearse then emerged, carried by 128 men. Observing the sea of red, purple, and yellow sedan chairs and flags, one foreign observer was "overcome" by the "splendor," writing: "The colors of the procession yesterday were magnificent; they were worth going a hundred miles to see. Those canopies and flags, those chairs, that hearse, they were wonderful.... They bury the greatest of their dead with the greatest of earthly splendor, the colors of the sunset."[124] While scholars throughout Chinese history had stressed the importance of a frugal and private sovereign, the Qing project of constitutional transformation saw the production of newly public performances of rulership that sought to bind the imperial family with the people of the country.

In fact, the funeral procession was specifically intended to have an edifying effect on the Chinese student population of Beijing. Zhang Zhidong ordered all students to attend at least one portion of the long procession and pay respects to the deceased emperor.[125] Early in life, Guangxu had been a symbol of the promise of power to scholars. As an adult, the emperor was stripped of his imperial charisma and influence and had largely faded from view. Yet in death he became useful again in the service of constructing an imagined future based on an equally imagined past.

Cixi's funeral was held several months later, on November 9, 1909. In a weeklong procession from the Forbidden City to the Eastern Tombs (Dongling), hundreds of porters, soldiers, and other officials transported the body of the late empress dowager. *Times* correspondent G. E. Morrison described the initial part of the procession in nearly identical terms with Guangxu's funeral. And Morrison, like the unnamed admirer of Guangxu's funeral, found Cixi's "most impressive."[126] In some ways, however, Cixi's funeral lacked Cixi's charm. While the empress dowager had embraced photography as a tool of diplomacy, the court forbade photos of her funeral, and Duanfang (1861–1909) was dismissed in part for allowing his subordinates to record the event.[127]

In the end, the funerals would turn into powerful metaphors for the death of the dynasty itself. Yet, they were in many ways the prototypical performance that monarchies across the world were learning to stage in the attempt to argue for imperial families as emblems of national identity, and a more public performance of royal rituals was part of the broader project of adapting Qing traditions to global norms. Streets lined with students and soldiers representing both the reformed military and the national school system; foreign representatives paying respect to the deceased rulers; lavish processions of chariots and other symbols of state power: this description fits equally well the Qing imperial funerals and that of the Meiji emperor in Japan several years later.[128] Yet in the end, reforming rituals of rulership and attempting to construct memories of a shared national past did not win the Qing the same authority it did Japan, and the Qing project to elevate the imperial family in the national consciousness made them the subject for nearly as many assassination attempts as instances of praise or celebration.

By embracing new forms of education and public pedagogy, the imperial family and noble students were intended to become icons of the new constitutional monarchy, spreading the image of a reforming Qing state. Two elements of the reforming state were the ideals of female education and constitutional governance, embodied by Cixi and the abortive attempt to produce a cohort of cosmopolitan female nobles. Although the efforts sputtered, Cixi's work won her praise among many in the foreign community and contributed to a partial rehabilitation of her image after the calamitous Boxer experience.[129] As Beijing physician Marian Sinclair and her husband, acclaimed missionary and educator Isaac Taylor Headland, saw it, the "movement towards female education . . . must ever be placed to the credit of this great woman. From the time she came from behind the screen, and allowed her portrait to be painted, the freedom of woman was assured."[130] In their view, Cixi succeeded in using tools of cultural production to create a new imperial iconography that in turn created the necessary conditions to spur reform and reshape the image of the Qing in the world. After her death, as well, some Chinese writers continued to give Cixi credit for promoting and popularizing education among women. In a speech delivered in London in April 1911 (and reprinted after the 1911 Revolution), the influential journalist and legal educator Diao Minqian (Dr. T. Z. Tyau, 1888-1970), lauded Cixi's influence in promoting ideals of greater gender equality and spreading female education.[131]

These new educational opportunities for women were embedded within the broader context of the Qing attempt to position the imperial family as a link between local classical traditions and shared global practices as the court searched for new forms of authority in turbulent times. Yet just as the attempt to open a school for female nobles was met with stiff resistance, the broader effort to reeducate the imperial family for the coming constitutional era was fraught with speedbumps. Officials frequently lamented the paltry education level of members of the imperial family and foretold of dangers to the dynasty if the situation persisted.[132] Zhao Binglin (1876-1927) captured the sentiment in a memorial when, citing the

Daxue, he wrote that the monarch must take responsibility for the country like a family, embracing learning and choosing wise teachers for himself to enact sound policies. Zhao said that "if the imperial family is at peace then the whole county can receive its blessings ... if the imperial family is in danger, then the whole country suffers its misfortune." Highlighting the connection between education and reconstruction, he promised a bright future for the Qing if the court would ensure the "talents of the imperial family."[133]

But plans for the adoption of a constitution were met with violent resistance, and the project of female rulership was short lived. After the deaths of Guangxu and Cixi in 1908, a new era began with Empress Dowager Longyu (1868–1913) (Guangxu's widow) imbued with authority that Cixi had intended for herself. Longyu was presented as a conscientious ruler who sympathized with the plight of the common people and was dedicated to the education of the new young emperor.[134] However, Longyu had little of Cixi's accumulated cultural authority or political capital. In the weeks after Cixi died, Prince Regent Zaifeng (1883–1951), father to the new three-year-old emperor, therefore worked to consolidate the authority of the throne around himself and sideline the empress dowager.[135]

Just as they had for many years, observers looked to the new ruler's education for hints about the direction in which he would lead the country. For some, Zaifeng presented cause for hope. At the end of 1908, for example, the *World's Chinese Students' Journal* wrote of the regent: "The nation at the present juncture could not have chosen a more suitable man to take over the onerous responsibilities left by his predecessors.... Of all the princes he is considered to be the most enlightened and the most moral."[136] In particular, it was Zaifeng's experience abroad and his devotion to learning that convinced the students of his potential for personal leadership in the short term and stewardship of his son's education.[137] These sentiments were echoed by many in the foreign community who looked at Zaifeng as a "dignified" and "intelligent" ruler capable of bringing China further into the world community.[138]

As they had for decades, Chinese scholars also saw court education as tied to larger programs of reform around the country. In 1910, for example, Tang Shouqian (1856–1917), an influential leader of the constitutional movement, submitted a memorial about the multiple threats currently facing the Qing, what he described as a military war (*bingzhan*), a trade war (*shangzhan*), and a war of learning (*xuezhan*). To help solve all three, Tang presented an extended discourse on the prince regent's education. Tang argued that since the prince regent was acting as sovereign in the place of the young emperor, it was crucial that he adopt both the learning and the rituals of the emperor. Tang explicitly linked patriotism, fatherly love, and education, writing, "I personally say that if the prince regent loves the country, then it is appropriate to study; if he loves the emperor, then it is even more so appropriate to study."[139] Tang urged Zaifeng to follow the example of the Duke of Zhou, who, while acting as regent, was said to have continued to be diligent in his studies, reading over one hundred pages every night and holding audiences with up to seventy scholars. Just as officials had reminded Tongzhi and Guangxu after they assumed the throne that Kangxi never ceased to surround himself with scholars, Tang told Zaifeng that the fate of the constitutional project lay in the ruler's dedication to learning and embrace of scholarly participation in government.

Things, did not, however, operate smoothly under Zaifeng. Though he was widely praised for his learning, he also frequently clashed with the new constitutional institutions and was targeted for assassination by his enemies.[140] While battling the National Assembly over the future of the country, Zaifeng was simultaneously engaged in another project associated with the development of a constitutional monarchy and the formation of a new Qing nation: the education of his son, China's first constitutional monarch. Just as the court had sought to create new systems of education for nobles and devise rituals in the national school system to connect the imperial family with students around the country, plans for the young emperor's education emerged as a focal point in the project of constitutional transformation and the construction of a new Qing nation. That short-lived effort is the subject of the final chapter.

5

LEARNING TO BE A CONSTITUTIONAL MONARCH, 1908–1912

On September 10, 1911, the day the Imperial Astronomy Bureau had declared most auspicious, the three-year-old Xuantong emperor awoke early in the morning and traveled to the Butong Studio (Butong shuwu) in the imperial garden next to the Forbidden City in Beijing. Inside, he performed ceremonies to pay homage to the "first teacher" Confucius, as well as to tutors to the emperors of both classical antiquity and recent dynasties.[1] After completing these rites, Xuantong went to the Hanyuan Hall (Hanyuan dian) to receive his teachers and various high officials, including his father the prince regent and the presidents and vice presidents of all government ministries.[2] There, Xuantong clasped both hands in front of his body and bowed to his imperial tutors.[3] Thus began the first day of school for the final Qing emperor.

These ceremonies came exactly a month before the country was thrown into turmoil by the Wuchang Uprising and the first shots of the 1911 Revolution. Yet while images of revolutionaries plotting the overthrow of the dynasty dominate our picture of the final years of the Qing, they were not the only people seeking to remake the country. Inside the palace halls in Beijing and in the press around the world, others looked to the imperial family and the emperor to lead the way and teach the empire how to become a nation. For these groups, the emperor's education was critical to that process. As the high official and member of the Plain Yellow Banner Shixu (1853–1921) wrote, "In this current dangerous situation, it is more important than ever that the emperor prioritize his studies."[4] The emperor held important bureaucratic and symbolic roles in plans for the constitutional monarchy, and his childhood education served the dual purpose of preparing him to serve as the head of the government in the future while in the moment communicating an image to the world of a reformed Qing state.

This chapter examines debates surrounding plans for Xuantong's education, including the texts, teachers, and classmates that various groups argued would transform the young emperor into a uniting force for the country. These debates were the culmination of decades of battles between competing forces within the court, the bureaucracy, and reformist intellectuals outside of government. They reveal a new vision of the Qing state, one whose authority was simultaneously rooted in the Confucian intellectual tradition, the martial and linguistic heritage of the Manchu Way, and a global language of modern governance.

In a new era of constitutionalism, however, it was not just the curriculum but the emperor's relationship with people around the empire that was a central component of plans for his education. To bring the young monarch into the lives of people—particularly schoolchildren—throughout the country, the court created new rituals and celebrations for the start of Xuantong's education. These events sought to present the emperor as a site of loyalty, a model for the country's youth, and a link between all those around the empire learning what it meant to be part of a new type of political community.[5] That is to say, the emperor was by no means the only target of his education. On the eve of its collapse, the court mobilized a novel set of discourses and practices around Xuantong's education in an attempt to unite the people behind a new Qing nation.[6]

THE LEARNING OF A MODERN MONARCH

Xuantong was enthroned as the twelfth emperor of the Qing dynasty at the end of 1908, just a few months after the court issued its formal nine-year program of constitutional reform. In its plan, the court said that although constitutions differed from country to country, they were all based on the basic principle that the sovereign had absolute power, and, through the laws he established, the people had both rights and responsibilities. Applying this general conception to the specifics of China, the court articulated fourteen "powers of the sovereign" that would form the basis of the Qing constitutional monarchy. These included his right to reign for "a thousand generations," issue laws, open and close parliament, declare war, appoint officials and judges, and personally regulate the affairs of the imperial clan.[7] The fourteen points thus maintained the Qing emperor's long-standing role as chief arbiter of the rituals, laws, and military affairs of the country.

At the same time, the powers and responsibilities of the monarch in the Qing constitution drew heavily on a new global discourse of sovereignty and suggested that Xuantong's life on the throne would have more in common with his contemporaries in Japan and Germany than with his own ancestors such as Kangxi or Qianlong. After studying various forms of constitutional monarchies around the globe, the court deemed the Japanese model preferable to that of others such as Britain, as Japan's was the "only one that in no way infringed on imperial prerogatives, having been issued directly as a gift by the sovereign without prior public review or scrutiny."[8] As Xiaowei Zheng has recently described, a wide range of officials converged on the idea that constitutionalism was the key to national strength and the belief that the Japanese model offered the Qing the best way to "strengthen rather than weaken the authority of the emperor by deflecting to the cabinet and its prime minister political criticism that would otherwise be directed at the emperor himself."[9] In fact, the fourteen clauses in the Qing announcement encapsulated the same powers that the Meiji Constitution granted to the Japanese emperor, and some were little more than adaptations of the Japanese text.[10] In many ways, therefore, the place of the emperor in the Qing constitution was the product of over a decade of engagement with the Japanese model. In 1898 reformers such as Kang Youwei had urged Guangxu to learn from the example of the Meiji emperor, and in 1905, after Japan's victory in the Russo-Japanese War, Cixi had declared that constitutions were the source of national strength around the world. Now in 1908, these ideas converged around the need to reform court education to prepare the young Xuantong for his role in the world of constitutional monarchies.

As the editors of *Shenbao* wrote in January 1909, the ascension of the emperor marked the beginning of a new era in Chinese history, one in which the country had an opportunity to learn from the best examples in the world.[11] This was a constant theme over the next two years, and the day after Xuantong began his formal education in 1911, the editors outlined the importance of ensuring that the emperor's education was designed to prepare him to rule in a new era of history, explicitly linking the pedagogical project to the fate of the country: "The sovereign is responsible for the order and disorder of a state. The sovereign's childhood education is the foundation of his having virtue or not. As this is the year when His Majesty will begin his studies, the next several decades of China's order and disorder are closely tied in with the inauguration of his studies."[12] For thirty years the paper had been urging reforms to the emperors' curriculum, not the least of which was increased engagement between the emperor and the outside world, including the right of the press to participate in molding the imperial mind. Now in the constitutional era, the editors at *Shenbao* warned the imperial tutors to pay great attention to cultivating the spirit of the times in Xuantong's character. Not only would this prepare him to govern, but it would also send a signal to the country and the world that the Qing was on a path toward reform.

In fact, at a time when revolutionaries threatened to tear the empire apart, it was not just the court and *Shenbao* editors who looked to the emperor to maintain unity and order. Some in the international community—hoping to avoid the disruptions that might come from the fall of the Qing—argued that Xuantong was key to uniting the country. In a 1910 report, for example, the American diplomat in Beijing Henry Fletcher wrote to the secretary of state in Washington, suggesting that changes to the emperor's curriculum would maintain not only the security of the Qing but peace in the region. Fletcher said that while Xuantong's education might appear "at first blush to be a matter of purely domestic concern, it will, on consideration, be found to have direct and most important bearing on the foreign relations of China." Fletcher argued that if, in this time of great unrest, Xuantong's education took advantage of the growing popularity of new forms of learning, the emperor would be transformed into a powerful force of unity and leadership, and that the "foundations of his Dynasty may be re-laid on solid ground." While for many years the court had declared Manchu the "root of the dynasty," Fletcher argued that the United States should encourage Qing officials to add English to the emperor's studies. With a curriculum connected to the trends of the world, Fletcher said, the emperor would lead the Qing to a bright future and ensure the United States a privileged place in China.[13]

The project to transform Xuantong into a constitutional monarch and symbol of the nation thus had both domestic and international support as multiple groups sought to use the emperor's education to help shape the future of the country. Immediately after he took the throne in 1908, these groups began putting forth suggestions for the emperor's curriculum, highlighting the need to train Xuantong as a cultural hybrid, combining elements from his contemporaries around the world and the heroes of China's past. One suggestion was that before the emperor began his formal studies, the court should hang "portraits of Chinese and Foreign emperors and kings from ancient times and today" along with descriptions of their cultural and military achievements on the walls of the hall.[14] This way, Xuantong would be familiarized with other world leaders and historical models, and, so the argument went, the young emperor would be prepared to take his place among the world community of monarchs. Looking at a picture of Kangxi or Meiji hardly seems like an effective antidote to revolution, but in the eyes of many at the time, history and the contemporary world suggested monarchical leadership was key to national strength.

To build a curriculum that combined Qing traditions with those of global powers, officials called for a thorough investigation of books used in the Japanese imperial palace and those from early Qing history.[15] Newspapers and magazines from Shanghai to Sichuan reported that the prince regent would examine the texts used in Kangxi's early education as well as the literary, governmental, and military accomplishments of rulers throughout world history in preparation for Xuantong's studies.[16] In fusing the curriculum of early Qing rulers with that of other world leaders, the court laid the ground for a variety of writers who argued that the goals of Xuantong's education should not be to mold him into a Confucian scholar.[17] As the editors of the paper *Dagong bao* in Tianjin suggested, the situation surrounding the emperor's education was different from that in the early years of the dynasty, and thus while in those times it had been critical for the Manchu emperor to don the garb of Confucian scholar to consolidate his rule, in this new era the court needed to expand its repertoire in governing the empire.[18]

With the Civil Service Examination abolished in 1905, the emperor's traditional role as chief arbiter of classical knowledge was no longer seen as the foundation of imperial authority. Instead, as the Manchu Bannerman Jinliang (1878-1962) argued, rather than spending his time mastering every sentence in the classical canon, Xuantong should be exposed to both Chinese and Western learning (*xixue*). In this way, Jinliang said, Xuantong would lead the spread of new forms of learning and "comfort the wishes of the scholars and people under heaven."[19] At the dawn of this new era of governance, Xuantong's symbolic role in inspiring support in the regime and change around the country was just as important—or perhaps even more so—than his empirical role in the bureaucracy. And for many, the presence of Western learning in the emperor's curriculum was key to building confidence in the court and transforming Xuantong into a symbol of the new Qing state.

But in this first decade of the twentieth century, what was "Western learning," and how would it "bring comfort" to the people? Though hardly more specific than *xixue* itself, "science" (*kexue*) was the key term that represented both reform to the emperor's curriculum and China's engagement with the Western world.[20] In the minds of many Chinese intellectuals of the era, the wealth and power of Europe, America, and more recently Japan were fundamentally tied to their promotion of science and constitutional governments. "Science" was thus a rhetorical marker of solidarity and identification with the world community, and people throughout the country looked to Xuantong's curriculum, seeking evidence that those around the young monarch had embraced the principles of the modern world.

Early reports about Xuantong's education indeed indicated that science would be included in his education, and the court worked to spread its message that in this new constitutional era, *kexue* would be on par with *dianxue* (classical studies) in training the new monarch.[21] Throughout 1910, reports suggested that plans for the emperor's education were focused on three areas of learning: *guoxue* (national learning), *kexue*, and *junxue* (military studies), embodiments of the Confucian tradition of classical studies, Western learning, and the martial tradition of the Manchu Way.[22] The three subjects reflected a broader attempt to balance the multiple strands of authority imbedded in Qing conceptions of rulership.

THE TEXTS, TEACHERS, AND CONTROVERSIES IN XUANTONG'S TRAINING

As had been the case in previous decades, partisans for each discipline jockeyed for the primacy of their field, arguing for more time, texts, and teachers in the classroom. In addition, however, officials and the press now also called on the court to hire new, specialized teachers for fields of Western learning. In a dramatic expansion of the concept of scholarly participation in government imbedded in ceremonies such as the Daily Lectures and Classic Mat, calls emerged for the first time urging the court to employ teachers from outside officialdom. Pang Hongshu (1843–1911), for example, asked the court to search far and wide for the emperor's tutors, hiring men of broad learning regardless of their bureaucratic rank or even nationality.[23] For years, the court had rewarded members of key political constituencies and scholarly factions with posts in the emperor's classroom. Now in an era where many around the country were questioning the wisdom of the classical canon, these skeptics as well sought representation in the project of molding Xuantong into a constitutional monarch.

However, despite the widespread rhetorical commitment to the idea that national learning and science were equally important and promises that Xuantong would have specialized teachers for both, there was significant conflict over how broadly to expand the search for teachers and who was qualified to serve in the emperor's classroom.[24] Although for many in the press new subjects in the curriculum suggested new opportunities for access to the imperial student, high court officials were concerned about the implications of opening up access to the heart of the emperorship. In the 1890s, during Guangxu's brief study of English (discussed in chapter 3), Zhang Deyi and Shen Duo's presence in the emperor's classroom—unjustified by their official titles or bureaucratic ranks—had aroused the ire of many officials. Now, in searching for a science tutor for Xuantong, the court debated how to balance the demands of a new curriculum with long-standing questions of ritual propriety and scholarly competition in the emperor's education.

These debates produced many speedbumps in the development of Xuantong's curriculum. In the matter of selecting a science teacher, contrary to Pang's suggestion that the teacher need not be an official—or even Chinese—the court ultimately declared that while the teacher would be someone who had studied abroad in Europe or America, he would have to be an official with a rank above the second or third degree.[25] And although the court attempted to portray the emperor's classroom as a harmonious space, frequently trumpeting Xuantong's progress in learning to read, battles between different scholastic and political factions stymied the development of a formal curriculum.[26] Unable to find a balance between the competing forces, the court announced that the formal inauguration of Xuantong's studies, originally scheduled for early 1911, would have to be delayed.[27]

Finally, on July 11, 1911, the court announced the official plans for Xuantong's education, connecting the activities of the emperor's classroom to both the country's past and its future. In an edict published widely in the Chinese press and quickly translated in English-language papers, the court told the country and the world that "the Emperor has ascended the throne at a tender age. In order to form a link of succession to the sovereigns of our illustrious empire, and as his age at present is just the one most amenable to good impressions, his education should be pursued in haste so as to develop his sagely faculties and establish a base of good governance."[28] This was the same language used to describe the start of both Tongzhi's and Guangxu's education, drawing on the idea that the young emperor would devote himself to learning and lead the country on a path of rejuvenation. Yet just a few years into both the constitutional transition and the new national school system, the idea of youth took on additional connotations. It was not just the emperor who was young, but the Qing national community as well. "Establishing a base of good governance" meant learning new roles for the emperor and the people, and Xuantong's education was understood as an important element of, and progressing simultaneously with, the larger project of rebuilding the country's unity, sovereignty, and power.

In rhetoric tightly connected to the rest of the world but firmly rooted in Qing traditions, the court outlined a hybrid curriculum for the young ruler. The Confucian scholars Lu Runxiang and Chen Baochen were announced as the primary tutors. As with their predecessors, the pair was tasked with providing "expansive and clear expositions of the learning which an Emperor or a King should acquire, pointing out the factors causing peace and war in China and abroad." Yet for Lu and Chen, and unlike those that came before them, the "learning which an emperor should acquire" was now explicitly defined as including new knowledge discovered during the "present progressive competition in civilization" and the age of "constitutional government."[29] At the start of the twentieth century, the task of the imperial tutors was thus to connect the emperor not just to the dynastic past through lessons on the Classics but also to the contemporary world through new forms of learning.

At the same time, however, the aim was not to simply mimic the West in Xuantong's education. The edict closed by appointing the prince regent to supervise all matters of Xuantong's education, and noting that since Manchu is the "root of Our Dynasty," Yiketan (1862–1922), a member of the eminent Suwan Gūwalgiya clan and Plain Yellow Banner, would take charge of ensuring that Xuantong learned the language.[30] Until the very end, the Qing emphasized the importance of maintaining its distinctive linguistic and cultural markers in creating a model of modern imperial leadership. As the court had done in previous decades as well, it rewarded a wide range of high officials with nominal titles associated with the upbringing of the young emperor in the hope of creating a broad ruling coalition.[31]

Yet, rather than winning the support of its constituents, this rhetoric was hijacked and turned back against the court. Using the same phrases from the edict announcing Lu and Chen as imperial tutors, an editorial in *Shenbao* on July 12, 1911, said that the task assigned to the teachers was a grave responsibility but that "we don't know if Lu Runxiang and Chen Baochen can make clear the worldwide constitutional movement or the new developments in knowledge of the past decade."[32] The foreign press picked up on these reports and similarly lamented the choice of tutors for the young emperor. The *North China Herald*, for instance, characterized Lu and Chen as "erudite" but "without knowledge of Western things or modes of thought."[33]

In some ways, the press criticism of Lu and Chen as insufficiently versed in constitutionalism or world knowledge was a referendum on the entire project of transforming into a constitutional monarchy. Lu was president of the Bideyuan, a constitutional advisory commission.[34] But he was also deeply opposed to many of the changes to China's educational and governmental systems of the past decade, beginning with his opposition to the 1898 Reforms. Discussing plans for the new national school system, for example, Lu said that the teachers were unqualified and that the textbooks being used were worthless. Altogether, Lu saw the reforms as a "misfortune as great as the Qin burning of the books."[35] Yet at the same time, Lu was not wholly opposed to introducing new fields of learning into governance. In 1903 he edited a study guide with exemplary answers for the Civil Service Examination that referenced a wide range of world historical and political events and taught its users about many new fields of learning.[36]

For Lu, appointment to the emperor's classroom was both an honor and an opportunity to help shape the emperorship and the country at large, balancing his belief in the value of the Classics with new strands of learning.[37] But for many other observers, Lu represented China's past, not its future, and they bemoaned his presence in both the new constitutional halls of government and the emperor's classroom. Criticism of officials had long been a key feature of the late Qing press, and though they largely avoided attacking the emperor, journalists did not shy away from judging those around him for perceived deficiencies.[38] At the start of Xuantong's education, attacking Lu became proxy for attacking the Qing commitment to constitutional reform.

The criticism of Chen, on the other hand, was tied less to a perceived conservatism than to rivalries within the bureaucracy and factional infighting at court. Although in 1909 and 1910 he had been mentioned as a possible tutor, by the early part of 1911 he had fallen out of grace and was transferred out of the capital.[39] This downturn in his career was directly tied to conflicts with the prince regent, and Chen's appointment as imperial tutor shocked many around the country. Chen had previously been selected as one of the imperial appointees to the National Assembly under the quota for eminent scholars. During his time in the assembly, however, he joined many of his colleagues in fighting with Zaifeng for an imperial pardon for Kang Youwei and Liang Qichao.[40] When news first broke about Chen's appointment, therefore, everyone—including Chen himself—was caught off guard:

"On that day around noon Chen was gathered with friends talking about affairs in the capital. Suddenly a retainer came in carrying a letter. After opening the letter and reading it, Chen began beaming with pleasure. The guests all asked why, and it was from then that they knew that Chen again had the fate of being a tutor in the Yuqing Palace." Having alienated Zaifeng, how did Chen make his way back into high office? Chen's appointment seems to have come from special intervention from Empress Dowager Longyu and speaks to the competition for power at the heart of the emperorship.[41] Herself locked in a power struggle with Zaifeng, Longyu sought to place her ally Chen in the classroom to influence and control Xuantong.

But at the time, many commentators were perplexed as to why Chen had been chosen over other, equally qualified candidates, and the selection of imperial tutors left a trail of embittered officials. Li Dianlin (1842–1916), for example, was particularly enraged. On account of not being appointed the emperor's teacher as he expected, Li refused another job in government.[42] This was a black eye for the court, and commentators suggested that the questionable methods of appointment would do damage to the task at hand of educating the emperor.[43]

Not just the tutors but also the overall curriculum was called into question. In a lengthy article published two days after the court's July 11 edict, an anonymous author writing in the pages of *Shenbao* criticized the court's plans for Xuantong's education. As the court suggested with the transition to a constitutional monarchy, the article said that the goal shared by all was for the emperor to be able to lead China in "harmony with global norms." But it rejected Xuantong's curriculum as insufficiently connected with the rest of the world. To begin with, instead of starting the emperor's education with readings from the Classics, the author argued, the imperial tutors should bring the emperor's education in line with global pedagogical practices and use new-style textbooks in his studies. If this were done, "then on the one hand [the tutors] will be able to teach the principles of science, and on the other hand [the emperor] will be able to even more effectively learn the teachings of the Confucian Classics."[44]

The criticism went further, arguing that being emperor in the twentieth century required a variety of skills not mentioned in the court's plan for Xuantong. Most important in this new era, Xuantong needed to add study of foreign languages to his curriculum so that he could rule in the age of *datong* (Great Unity). Learning foreign languages would allow the emperor to serve as a symbol of China on the international stage, engage with leaders of other states, and represent the

FIGURE 5.1 The emperor's teachers report for duty. "Dianxue shu wen" 典學述聞 [News of the emperor's education], *Qianshuo huabao*, no. 992 (1911): 3.

country in the world community of constitutional monarchies. The reference to *datong* is particularly instructive in understanding the relationship the press sought to build between the young emperor and people around the country. Found in the *Liji* (*Book of Rites*), the phrase refers to a society in which little government is needed and people live in harmony. In the first decade of the twentieth century, Kang Youwei gave the idea new life. In his *Datong shu* (Book of Great Unity, 1901), Kang argued for the abolition of national boundaries, national languages, as well as offices such as king and emperor.[45] The anonymous author was not arguing for wiping away China's borders or abolishing the emperorship. Yet by drawing on the utopian ideal of *datong* in which people largely governed themselves, *Shenbao* suggested that Xuantong's key function in the future would be to serve as an icon of unity rather than actively regulating the lives of the people, much like his contemporaries in Britain and Japan. This was the continuation of a shift under way over the past several decades that had seen a growing emphasis on the emperor's symbolic role and power in the culture and away from his functional role in the bureaucracy. Yet it was not a vision shared by all, and many of the voices involved in planning Xuantong's education continued to believe that the strength of the country depended in part of the emperor's management of the emperorship and empirical tasks of governance.

IN SEARCH OF A NEW COURT CURRICULUM

Fundamentally, criticisms of the court's plan for the emperor's curriculum now argued that to be a symbol of the new regime and to inspire loyalty in changing times, Xuantong's education needed a deeper engagement with global trends. This included not only studying foreign languages but also adding modern military training, as well as hiring a nursemaid knowledgeable in Japanese practices to care for the emperor's health. In this way Lu and Chen, just like the Classics and traditional methods of pedagogy, were sidelined in the emperor's education to better prepare Xuantong as a modern monarch. As *Shenbao* put it, "over the past decade our country has been part of a time of many changes. In the future Our Majesty will come out into the world as emperor in extraordinary times," and his education therefore could not stick to the ways of the old world.[46]

Though unstated, what these critiques suggested was that Xuantong should have the same type of education that Japanese nobles—including Hirohito (1901-1989), the future Showa emperor, were at that very moment receiving at the Peers College in Tokyo. From the time he was born, a large group of doctors and servants had nurtured Hirohito, feeding him Western-style food and dressing him in custom French clothing. As a child, Hirohito and his brothers would often act out battles, with the heir apparent always practicing for the future by playing the winning role. This education continued when Hirohito entered the Peers School in 1908. General Nogi Maresuke (1849-1912), the newly appointed head of the school, believed that "devotion to duty and love of the military" were the most important qualities for a monarch, and he devised a strict military-style education for the young prince.[47] Exposed to both Western learning and Japanese traditions, the boy was taught to honor his ancestors and develop the physical and intellectual skills necessary to protect and expand his grandfather's empire. Moreover, Hirohito came of age in an era of dramatic growth in public rituals celebrating the monarchy in Japan. Thus at the same time Hirohito was learning to be an emperor in school, people all around Japan were receiving frequent and grand lessons in learning to be members of an emperor-centered national community.[48]

In 1911, then, both the Qing and Japanese empires were attempting to teach young rulers to lead imperial families, to sit atop constitutional monarchies, and to serve as symbols of national pride. In the aftermath of the Sino-Japanese (1894-1895) and Russo-Japanese (1904-1905) Wars, however, only Japanese pedagogy seemed to be effective in producing imperial leadership and loyalty. In announcing their plans for Xuantong's education, the Qing had sought to present the image of an emperor educated in the ways of the modern world. But instead of disseminating a convincing picture of cosmopolitanism and strength, the court was consistently attacked for falling short of its own promises.

Officials in charge of planning Xuantong's education were not immune to this outside pressure. Not long after they issued initial plans for Xuantong's curriculum—and the press criticized it—new reports surfaced indicating changes to the emperor's education. While never explicitly acknowledging articles such as those described earlier from July 13, the sudden emergence of the themes advocated in *Shenbao* suggests that the press had indeed influenced the development of Xuantong's curriculum, and new plans for Xuantong's education began more and more to resemble Hirohito's. In effect, the court sanctioned the right of the press to participate in molding the imperial mind.

In the wake of these criticisms, the three imperial tutors met on July 27 with Zaifeng to finalize the emperor's curriculum.[49] The tutors had spent the previous few days examining the records and precedents of court education, and they now determined that because of Xuantong's young age, it was best not to begin with a full load of schooling. They suggested that the emperor begin with half days and focus on learning to write characters by copying canonical texts.[50] Xuantong was apparently a quick study, and the court planned to present George V (r. 1910–1936) a sample of Xuantong's writing as a gift to celebrate the British king's recent coronation.[51] Just as with the images of world leaders in his classroom, the court imagined a future wherein Xuantong would represent the Qing in a global community of constitutional monarchs.

In the weeks following that July 27 meeting, the Chinese press carried detailed reports of the new plans for the emperor's education. On September 3, for example, it was reported that instead of starting with the *Great Learning*, Xuantong would first read the *Xiaojing* (*Classic of Filial Piety*). This represented a compromise at court, as the text was chosen because, as his tutor Chen Baochen argued, "its meanings are simple and clear and its chapter divisions are also very clear, not unlike the recently produced textbooks."[52] Just as *Shenbao* had suggested, the court was debating incorporating elements from the new national school system—textbooks—into the imperial curriculum. While the decision to start Xuantong's education with the *Classic of Filial Piety* instead of an elementary school textbook surely disappointed some, that Chen argued for its efficacy in large part based on similarities to textbooks suggests the degree to which the court grappled with the criticisms of Xuantong's initial curriculum.

The court more wholeheartedly embraced other elements of the critiques, in particular the study of foreign languages. By the first week of September, the prince regent said that it was as important for Xuantong to be trained in Western languages as it was for him to study the Classics, Chinese, and Manchu. For Zaifeng, studying foreign languages was in fact not just a symbolic gesture to changing norms in China but also a practical matter of Xuantong's engagement with other world leaders. The prince said that by studying Western languages, Xuantong would be able to "prepare for meetings with foreign guests and be able to communicate without an interpreter."[53] These discussions clearly harkened back to debates from the Tongzhi and Guangxu eras, where officials and the press described the emperor's linguistic skills as central to his ability to exercise functional power in the state. And now from Zaifeng's perspective, Xuantong's personal leadership and ability to assert his will over the bureaucracy by learning foreign languages was key to ensuring China's strength in the twentieth century.

Just as in those earlier eras, the inclusion of multiple languages in the emperor's curriculum suggested an opportunity for a range of scholars to serve at court. Now in 1911, *Shenbao* was heartened by the emphasis on foreign languages, not just for the ways in which it might connect the Qing with the world, but also for the new opportunities it provided scholars to participate in the emperor's education. The paper wrote approvingly of a report that Liang Dunyan (1858-1924) and Wu Tingfang (1842-1922) would train Xuantong in Western languages.[54] Both men represented a departure from the traditional career track of imperial tutors. Liang had studied abroad as a youth and was president of the Office of Foreign Affairs, while Wu was born in Malacca and educated in Hong Kong and London. Not only would they bring new forms of knowledge into Xuantong's curriculum, but they would also signal to those inside and outside the bureaucracy that the emperor's education was an open forum for new ideas. In this way, employing Liang and Wu capitalized on Pang Hongshu's earlier call to look for teachers across the globe, bringing a wide array of officials into the emperor's service and articulating a vision of Qing imperial citizenship not bound by place of birth. Although the court had disappointed in the hunt for a science tutor by restricting the search to the bureaucracy, *Shenbao* was again hopeful that the presence of foreign languages in the curriculum would provide opportunities for access and power to a broader spectrum of society.

Announcements regarding the emperor's education throughout the summer also showed a newfound belief that Xuantong's physical fitness was directly related to the overall health of the monarchy.[55] The prince regent had previously argued that an emphasis on military affairs was a core characteristic of modern leadership.[56] This was seemingly a lesson Zaifeng learned in 1901 while in Germany, where he was sent to offer an official apology to Kaiser Wilhelm II for the murder of Baron von Ketteler (1853-1900) during the Boxer Uprising. After meeting with Wilhelm, Zaifeng traveled around Germany and attended several military reviews, one of which was led by the kaiser and his brother. Wilhelm's personal role in leading the military left a large impact on Zaifeng's conception of the role of the emperor and imperial family in constitutional empires. As regent, for example, Zaifeng modeled himself on the kaiser by holding grand ceremonies and reviews of the Palace Guard.[57]

Now in 1911, Zaifeng's emphasis on military training for Xuantong gained support around the country, as many argued that all around the world, heads of state personally wore armor and trained the military, and for Xuantong—and therefore the Qing–to join the world community of nations, he needed to do the same.[58] To the delight of the press, a flurry of suggestions by the head of the Qing army and navy and several Manchu officials now emphasized martial matters in the emperor's curriculum.[59] This included adding the history of military affairs to the lessons delivered by Lu and Chen, ensuring that Xuantong had a classmate with experience in the military, and adding a daily calisthenics class to the emperor's routine.[60]

Yet these groups emphasized the need for Xuantong to be trained in military affairs in pursuit of contrasting models of the throne. The emperor's education sought to prepare him as both an active leader in the state and the symbol of the nation. But the various constituencies the Qing sought to draw together in service of this project had competing views of the relative weight of those roles. For many Manchu officials, the martial heritage of the Qing and patrimonial model of rule continued to loom large in understandings of imperial leadership. For these officials, a curriculum that stressed martial tactics harkened back to the early Qing where young emperors such as Kangxi were taught to take personal control of the army and subdue the dynasty's Inner Asian adversaries. Many other officials and writers in the press, meanwhile, fixated on countries such as Japan and Germany, where the monarch sat atop a professionalized military force as a symbol of national strength. For these writers, the aim was to combine the domestic bureaucratic tradition with global constitutional practices in producing a new mold for Xuantong.

These different strands of authority and conceptions of the emperor were manifest not only in debates around the curriculum and teachers but also in the physical structures of the classroom. In an attempt to combine domestic and global practices, the empress dowager ordered the construction of a hybrid space of learning for Xuantong, to be known as the Crystal Palace (Shuijinggong).[61] A three-story glass structure filled with electric lamps and lanterns illuminating the building throughout the night, the Crystal Palace was intended to be a sight like nothing ever seen before.[62] The building made heavy use of marble and iron, giving it a unique character among buildings in Beijing.[63] These construction materials played heavily on modernist architecture from Europe and stood in stark contrast to the timber-frame buildings of the rest of the Forbidden City, signaling an embrace of global forms for the new pedagogical regime of Xuantong's education.

The Crystal Palace was in fact the only Western-style building in the Forbidden City, and the name itself suggested an attempt at international engagement.

London's Crystal Palace, a grand iron and glass structure built for the Great Exhibition of 1851, amazed visitors at the fair and brought great acclaim to its hosts. The building—its name, image, and associated wonder—were well known to the late Qing reading public, having been frequently discussed and depicted in a range of periodicals and newspapers since its construction.[64] In writing about the Qing Crystal Palace, press reports frequently focused on the heavy use of iron and glass and the three-storied vertical façade.[65] These details suggested that the most critical aspect of the Crystal Palace was its difference, the very fact that it stood apart from other buildings in the Forbidden City. Yet in other ways, by building an imperial structure in this Western style, the court was continuing the long Qing tradition of incorporating the architectural forms and symbolic power of multiple traditions—be it the Potala Palace replica in Chengde or the Western Palaces of the Yuanming yuan—into its iconography of rulership and authority.[66]

In other ways as well, the building was Longyu's attempt to reclaim a classical heritage. The Crystal Palace was a modern version of the Ming tang (Hall of Light, Hall of Illumination), an ancient structure that articulated the cosmic position of the emperor and served as a center of political power and educational activities. From inside the secluded structure whose design was said to represent a microcosm of the universe, the ruler would perform state rituals and sacrifices. After the ancient Zhou dynasty, succeeding regimes debated the exact construction of the building, yet it remained a potent symbol of imperial power and legitimacy, meant to display "royal magic and virtue."[67] Perhaps its most opulent post-Zhou form came under the direction of Wu Zetian (r. 690–705), as those with the most to prove went to the greatest lengths to root their rule in the charisma of myth and ritual.

Now, with the inauguration of Xuantong's education amid a rising tide of revolutionary fervor and threats to the dynasty, the court drew on the domestic past and the global present to construct a new facade of imperial charisma. The sea of lights illuminating the Crystal Palace was a modern analogue to the royal magic and virtue of classical antiquity associated with buildings such as the Ming Tang, while the nomenclature and architecture of the building itself put the Qing in conversation with the day's great empire, Great Britain. Just as in days long past where the Ming Tang served as the "center of wisdom for the state" and a place where "the power of the Monarch was constantly revitalized," so too would the Crystal Palace provide a platform for the education and power of the emperor.[68] Yet of course, as with the grand imperial rituals in Britain, the construction of the

Crystal Palace did not reflect, so much as hope to inspire, power and unity.[69] Creating splendid spaces for the emperor's education, the court sought to communicate a message of power to many audiences—the emperor, the tutors, the domestic population, and the international community.

LINKING THE EMPEROR AND HIS PEOPLE: NEW ROLES AND RITUALS FOR THE NATION'S YOUTH

Around the start of Xuantong's schooling, the court issued an edict in the emperor's name that said there had never been a country in which ruler and ruled were united yet the country was not strong. The edict therefore emphasized the importance of building ties between the emperor and people as key to restoring peace.[70] Plans for Xuantong's education thus included efforts to bring the young ruler into closer contact with people around the country, particularly children in the new national school system. By introducing students to the emperor through rituals and celebrations, the court made learning loyalty a primary aim of the new educational system, and by introducing the emperor to students by opening his classroom, it suggested to both Xuantong and the country that building a constitutional monarch was a collaborative process.

As plans for Xuantong's education developed, many writers picked up on this idea and proposed models of court pedagogy to help link the emperor and his people. For example, in 1911 Gan Yonglong, writing in *Dongfang zazhi* (*Eastern Miscellany*), profiled the education of the young emperor of Persia, Ahmad Shah (1898-1930). Extolling the recent promulgation of a constitution and improving economic conditions around the country, the article argued that it was changes in education—and court education most fundamentally—that enabled Persia's dramatic transformation. Gan found in the description of the young Persian emperor's education a prescription for Xuantong and China:

> Inside the Persian emperor's palace there is one part that has already been converted into an education court. Here there are twelve youngsters, some of whom have graduated from Paris, some from London, and others from schools from capitals across Europe and America. These youngsters surround the Persian

Emperor, serving as retainers, but at the same time being responsible for instructing him. They teach the Persian emperor in every field of new studies. In this way in one body they are both servant and teacher. In addition, there are also a certain number of old and venerable teachers who pass on the essentials of traditional Persian national learning and instruct the emperor.[71]

By surrounding the emperor with young scholars who had studied abroad, but also by providing an older generation of teachers to pass on the cultural heritage, the Persians had devised a system in which the emperor was connected to his ancestors and the prestige associated with the imperial line, yet at the same time exposed to the newest teachings of the world and the people of his country. As Gan said, "national learning and new learning were brought together."[72]

Surrounding emperors and princes with classmates to help in their education was in fact a long-standing practice in China. Known as *bandu*, these students were selected from members of the imperial family of a similar age to the primary student. They worked alongside their more august classmate with their own teachers and were sometimes called on to suffer corporal punishment in place of a misbehaving prince.[73] In both Tongzhi's and Guangxu's classrooms, for example, Manchu princes sat alongside the young emperors as they worked in the classroom.[74]

But now in the Xuantong era, as the court worked to build new connections between the emperor and the country, there was widespread agreement that the emperor's classmates needed to be of a different sort. Zaifeng and the imperial tutors sought out candidates based on merit, not lineage. *Shenbao* reported that "whereas the matter of accompanying students in the Yuqing Palace is a matter of great importance, the prince regent wants to select people of meritorious conduct who have a solid foundation of the learning and ways of government of the past and present and of China and foreign countries." Lu Runxiang, Chen Baochen, and Zaifeng each had different ideas about who was best for the job, yet all their suggestions were accomplished members of officialdom, not simply children of the imperial clan. Perhaps most tellingly, Zaifeng proposed Zhang Jian (1853-1926) and Tang Shouqian, two of the three founders of the Association for Constitutional Preparation (Yubei lixian gonghui).[75] While many at the time and since were skeptical that the Qing truly intended to adopt a constitution, preparations for Xuantong's education suggest that the court was committed to training the young emperor for life as a constitutional monarch.

Significantly, Xuantong's education therefore meant building connections with people throughout the empire and engaging with his peers around the world. To help prepare Xuantong for those interactions, the empress dowager argued for an expansion of Xuantong's *bandu* in terms of both the applicant pool and the number in the classroom. First, to aid in his foreign-language training, Longyu urged the selection of students with good pronunciation of foreign languages for the job of imperial classmate.[76] Then, to connect the emperor with his vast empire, Longyu wanted to "select twenty or thirty bright students under the age of twelve from schools from every province to come in turns and accompany the emperor in his studies while practicing the dialects (*fangyan*) of all the provinces."[77] Multilingualism had long been seen as critical to the functioning of the throne and its simultaneous rulership of key political constituencies.[78] Now in the twentieth century, however, language was not only a tool to articulate the emperor's commitment to traditional power bases of Manchus and Mongolians. It was also a way to bring all the disparate people of the empire into the new national community, and the Qing into the global community of nations.

Not just there to take a beating, Xuantong's classmates were intended to play a formative role in his education, connecting him to all corners of his empire and the world at large. As with many things for the court in this era, however, plans did not go so smoothly. Yiketan pushed back against his colleagues and argued that the *bandu* ought to come from only the sons of high ministers and princes.[79] Continuing the fight of his *anda* predecessors, Yiketan sought to ensure that Manchu traditions and teachings maintained their central space in the emperorship. There was enough disagreement at court about appropriate classmates that Xuantong started his education alone, save photos of other world leaders on his walls.[80]

Although Xuantong was not joined in the classroom by any of his young countrymen at the start of his studies, the court found other ways to bring the emperor into the lives of schoolchildren around the empire. Beginning in the summer of 1911, the empress dowager and Ministry of Education began planning for ceremonies to be held at schools throughout the country to coincide with Xuantong's official first day of school on September 10.[81] This was a dramatic expansion of the project to transform students into model imperial citizens using celebrations of important court events to link the throne and people around the empire. As discussed in chapter 4, the project began in 1905 and 1906 at schools for nobles and at common schools around the country, as students were mobilized in both celebrations of imperial birthdays as well as services commemorating imperial deaths.

Now in 1911, the Ministry of Education ordered schools of all levels in every province to prepare celebrations, stopping their regular classes to hold special events coinciding with the emperor's first day of school.[82] The head of each school was to lead students and teachers in ceremonies to honor Xuantong, linking people around the country with the young monarch—as well as with each other— by performing the same prescribed set of rituals. The ministry ordered schools to raise the national flag, face the Forbidden City in Beijing, and join together to salute and offer congratulations to the emperor for beginning his studies.[83] Indeed, on September 10, 1911, students and teachers all around the country celebrated the inauguration of Xuantong's education and the start of his training as their constitutional monarch.[84]

Although students were the primary target for the celebrations surrounding Xuantong's education, the court sought to reach additional communities as well. To that end, the Ministry of Education "sent, to every district of the Empire, a large, square wooden tablet, with four characters engraved on it, which is to be suspended in the Hall of the Confucius Temple" to commemorate the emperor's first day of school.[85] The tablets were inscribed with the phrase "*tiandi wei yan*," drawn from *Zhongyong* (*Doctrine of the Mean*). This was the same passage at the heart of Xianfeng's final (and ultimately the last in history) Imperial Lecture in 1853. For "everything in the universe to take its proper place," as the phrase says, the emperor needed to be returned to the center of both the moral and the political order through the rituals of learning. Though Xuantong was of course too young to deliver an explication of a classical passage and thus assert his learned authority, the court nonetheless attempted to repurpose this component of imperial pedagogy: reports claimed that the young emperor himself wrote the calligraphy on the plaque. Even though at the time most assumed the writing was actually the work of Lu Runxiang, local magistrates handled the tablets with great care as though they were an extension of the imperial brush. In Shanghai, officials prepared to hang the tablet in the Education Hall on September 10 as part of celebrations of the "happy occasion" of Xuantong's first day of school.[86]

In an era filled by assassination attempts and revolutionary plots to overthrow the dynasty, there were of course many who did not see the start of Xuantong's education as a "happy occasion." A week before the ceremonies for Xuantong's first day of school, *Shenbao* speculated that for many people in Beijing, the event would be marked by little more than a perfunctory hanging of the dragon flag.[87] Yet, motivated by genuine emotion or simply following orders, the streets of

Beijing were covered in decorations on September 10. Schools and storefronts around the capital were bedecked with flags adorned with festoons, lanterns, and other signs of revelry. By many accounts, on September 10 the capital streets had a more festive atmosphere than during celebrations two years prior to honor Xuantong's ascension to the throne.[88] In Shanghai as well, civil and military officials wore ceremonial clothing for several days before the celebration, the city was decorated with ornate lanterns, and the Mixed Court closed for three days to honor the emperor's first day of school.[89]

All around the country, then, whether through ceremonies at schools, decorations in the streets, or donning ritual clothing, the emperor was manifest in the lives of people, and the start of his education was celebrated as a day of national unity. Images in the press showing a parade of young cadets celebrating Xuantong's first day of school further spread the ideal of the emperor's classroom as central site in the construction of the nation. Except for the Qing insignias and queues, the picture looks as if it came straight out of a Republican era textbook,

FIGURE 5.2 Celebrating the emperor's first day of school. "Dianxue zhi sheng" 典學志盛 [Resplendent record of the emperor's education], *Qianshuo huabao*, no. 988 (1911): 1.

where elementary education presented flags, military drills, and Western clothing as paramount symbols of the new nation-state.[90]

As described earlier, the Qing project of constitutional transformation also had support from the international community, weary of the destabilizing impact a revolution might have on their commercial interests around China. To aid the court's effort to link the young emperor with people around the country, therefore, public buildings within the foreign concessions in Shanghai flew dragon flags and hung double-sided red paper lanterns to celebrate the start of Xuantong's studies.[91] Moreover, at a school inside the French Concession, representatives from both the French government and Qing gathered to celebrate the event.[92] By participating in ceremonies surrounding Xuantong's education, the French lent their weight to the idea that China's future was tied to the health of the emperorship, and that the emperor ought to be the centerpiece of the new national identity. In a speech during the event, one French official made the link explicitly clear, saying that "in courageously tackling his studies his Majesty had given a grand example to all the children who were his subjects and to all the foreign children who lived on the soil of his empire."[93] This was precisely the court's goal for Xuantong's education: presenting him as the icon of a remodeled regime to rally domestic unity and international respect for the Qing.

As with the domestic community, however, not all foreign commentators bought into the Qing project. The *North China Herald*, for example, lamented the loss of the emperor's youth with his impending studies, wishing him more time to "play contently with the magnificent toy train, gifts of the Russian Tsar, or drill his playmates in the palace grounds."[94] In a separate article, the paper described the start of Xuantong's studies as a lonely affair. Contrasting the day with that of Black Monday (the start of a new semester in the old form British school calendar), the paper wrote that "the bustling of settling in, the interest of knowing who has come and who has left ... of these joys the youthful Emperor of China knows not, nor will he ever know." The paper concluded that, "as if to accentuate the contrast, the day on which he begins schooling is a holiday for every school in China. The Emperor works alone."[95]

But the *North China Herald* did not have it quite right. September 10, 1911, was in some sense a holiday for schoolchildren in China—they did not have to attend normal classes. Yet the aim was in fact to ensure that emperor was not alone. By joining together, facing the palace in Beijing, and hoisting flags and saluting, schoolchildren and their teachers were ritually linked with their peers around the country, the imperial tutors, and Xuantong himself. Chinese newspaper reports about the emperor's first day of school moved seamlessly from descriptions of the young Xuantong studying to students in schools across the country facing his classroom in celebration, drawing the two spaces together and connecting Beijing with the rest of the country.⁹⁶ *Dagong bao*, for example, printed a two-part article titled "Huangshang dianxue zhi lijie" (The ceremonies of His Majesty's education"). The first section described ceremonies Xuantong would perform in Beijing on his first day of school, while the second section previewed the celebrations to be held at schools across the country on the same day.⁹⁷ The descriptions of the scene in the Forbidden City, including details such as the incense to be burned, followed by explanations of the countrywide celebrations such as the songs to be sung, sought to close the conceptual gap between ruler and ruled and humanize the monarchy while at the same time signaling the emperor's unique status.⁹⁸

Along with their textbook lessons, these rituals and celebrations taught students that loyalty to the emperor was a central element of the new national identity. The ways in which the court sought to impart these lessons represented a new form of imperial pedagogy, one that drew lessons from both dynastic history and the contemporary world. Much like Japanese schoolchildren reading the Imperial Rescript on Education, for students around China, facing Beijing and saluting in the direction of the emperor's classroom inside the Forbidden City was a reminder of the duty owed to the Qing monarch. Synchronized across the empire and carried around the country in the pages of the press, these ceremonies argued for a national identity structured around loyalty to an emperor whose body and education were representative of both a unique domestic history and a shared global language of modern learning.

The court invested heavily in this project of educating a constitutional monarch. Even as the imperial treasury was depleted in the final months of the dynasty, Xuantong's three tutors received substantial raises upon assuming office.⁹⁹ Though some questioned the logic of spending so much money on a student to create a "single emperor" when the same money could be used to create "ten thousand common people," most simply reported the news without comment.¹⁰⁰ Drawing lessons from both its own history and the contemporary world, the Qing court argued that there was a direct link between the emperor's education and the future of the country, and that the emperor was key to national unity and strength.

Clearly, the court failed to convince many of this idea, and Han revolutionaries around the country believed their duty was to overthrow the Manchu regime, not salute its young emperor. For some, however, the Qing message resonated. As papers were filled with reports about the court's plans for the emperor's *bandu* and celebrations at schools to honor his first day, one family sought a place for their son inside the emperor's classroom and a chance to participate in the process of educating the monarch and strengthening the Qing.

Just weeks before the Wuchang Uprising in Hubei, Jiang Xizhang (1907–2004), a four-year-old from Shandong, made national headlines for his quest to serve in the emperor's classroom. Jiang was born into a well-educated family and displayed remarkable literary skills, earning the reputation of a prodigy. In the post-Civil Examination world, what was Jiang to do with his abilities? His father and local education officials thought that the best use of the child's skills was to "enter the palace and wait upon the emperor in his studies." With a letter of introduction from provincial officials in hand, Jiang's father traveled with the boy to the Ministry of Education in Beijing. When they arrived, "the staff at the ministry fought over each other to have a look at the promising and bright child."[101]

Officials at the ministry then put the young boy through a series of tests to determine his literary abilities. An official asked if Jiang was able to compose pairing lines of poetry. When the boy said that, yes, he could, the official started off with an opening line of "His Majesty Reads" (*huangshang dushu*), to which Jiang responded, "The Son of Heaven Studies" (*tianzi dianxue*). After a few more rounds, the group moved into a large hall within the ministry where a plaque bestowed by the emperor hung with the phrase "*Jing jiao quan xue*" (Respect teachers and encourage learning). The officials asked Jiang to explicate the phrase character by character, which the boy did without issue. Next, the minister of education took out a newspaper, which Jiang was able to punctuate on the fly and read with ease. The minister was indeed impressed, and he gifted Jiang a set of newly published textbooks.[102] For all those at the ministry that day, the young boy represented hope that the court's attempt to use Xuantong's education to unite the country around the constitutional monarchy was indeed paying dividends.

At the same time, there was great turmoil around the country, and both the solemn and celebratory rituals at court were in many ways disconnected from people's lives outside of Beijing. Here, too, some writers thought, the emperor's education might help heal the divisions. Two days after Jiang's story appeared in the Chinese press, the *North China Herald* echoed the sentiment of the *Shenbao* article quoted at the start of this chapter, linking the development of Xuantong's education with that of the nation at large. The British paper wrote that, although "it is far cry from a baby Emperor more or less painfully cunning Chinese characters in the Yuqing Palace to the perishing millions in the Yangtze Valley," the link "is, or will one day be, direct, and the best hope for His Majesty's schooling is that it will strengthen and vivify the chord of communication."[103] Like many Chinese and Manchu officials, the paper saw Xuantong's education as a chance to unite a fractious country behind the Qing.

What began as a debate about how to incorporate new forms of learning into the emperorship in the effort to restabilize the country in the 1860s thus ended in the first decade of the twentieth century as an effort to build a nation out of empire. The opening ceremonies of Xuantong's education, plans for his curriculum, classmates, and rituals were part of the larger Qing project of refashioning the throne for the twentieth century, combining elements of traditional Chinese statecraft, Manchu ideals of rulership, and the global trappings of constitutional monarchy. As it had for fifty years since Xianfeng's death, the court presented the emperor's education as an opportunity to shape the future of the country, and up until its final day, it actively worked to create more children like Jiang Xizhang, students devoted to learning and loyal to the emperor. With a curriculum meant to inspire and celebrations meant to unite, the court articulated a vision of the country's future wherein the emperor's education would help forge a new Qing nation.

But, of course, things did not turn out that way. Just three weeks after Jiang visited the Ministry of Education—and exactly one month since the opening ceremonies of Xuantong's schooling—the Wuchang Uprising threw the country into war. As Yuan Shikai led negotiations for the court's abdication, Lu Runxiang and Chen Baochen continued to hold class for Xuantong, hoping the new year might bring better fortune for the Qing.[104] But as 1911 turned into 1912 and Sun Yat-sen declared the founding of the Republic, Longyu ordered a stop to the emperor's lessons in what *Shenbao* now described as the "pathetic and laughable capital."[105] Finally, when the court issued its abdication edict on February 12, 1912 (just five days after Puyi's sixth birthday), the emperor's education had barely started, and he could not understand the words on the page that ended his reign, Qing rule, and dynastic history in China.

CONCLUSION

Emperor and Nation in Modern China

On February 15, 1912, just three days after the Qing abdicated, revolutionary leader and inaugural president of the Republic of China Sun Yat-sen made a surprising trip. Along with a large procession of officials, Sun visited the tomb of the first Ming emperor, Zhu Yuanzhang, but not to castigate him for the history of imperial rule, his notorious violence against scholars, or his infamous autocratic tendencies. Instead, calling Zhu "Our Great Emperor," Sun went to report the news that the revolutionaries had avenged the Ming's loss and reclaimed China for the Chinese people. In speeches at the tomb and in photographs in front of a portrait of Zhu, Sun presented the founding emperor of the Ming dynasty as a symbol of the new Chinese nation.

As scholars have previously noted, there is on the face of it a "contradiction inherent in announcing the formation of a republic to an imperial ancestor."[1] But in making his visit, Sun sought to claim the cultural charisma of the Ming for the Republic, placing the roots of the new state deep into Chinese history. As it was reported at the time, the parade of soldiers and symbols of the Republic was "enough to wake up the great warrior founder of the Ming."[2] In two speeches that day addressed to Zhu, Sun recounted how centuries earlier, "Our Emperor" had arisen in a time of great turmoil, vanquished his enemies, and cleared China of barbarian rulers.[3] While in some ways Sun thus equated himself to Zhu—both having rid China of a foreign regime—he also subordinated himself to the former emperor, elevating Zhu as the ultimate symbol of the Chinese people.

Despite the dynastic system having just been overthrown, the event celebrated the teachings and leaders of the past. The ceremony was described as honoring "the great virtues of our sage emperors of whom Confucius taught and of whose wisdom our national poets and historians have lavished their praises in successive ages."[4] Emperors and their teachers were thus nationalized, as Sun saw the visit to the Ming tombs as an opportunity to fortify his own power, creating a genealogy of Han nationalism that transcended political form.[5] And as Charles Musgrove has shown, in arguing for Nanjing as the ideal capital city for the new nation, Sun tied his project to the glories of the dynastic past, claiming that Nanjing had "a 'royal air' and impeccable capital credibility, having served as the capital of ten imperial kingdoms and dynasties."[6] In fact, Sun was not alone in drawing on the figure of the emperor in forging the nation. In the early days of the revolution, Li Yuanhong (1854-1928) had offered sacrifices to the Yellow Emperor, asking him to "assist the participants in the establishment of a republic."[7] Sun's successor, Chiang Kai-shek (1887-1975), similarly visited the Ming tombs and praised laudatory biographies of Zhu Yuanzhang.[8] When, under Chiang, the Republic buried Sun next to Zhu, they self-consciously positioned the Republic as heirs to the Ming, drawing on the inherited authority of the dynastic past and emperors of old to unite the modern nation.[9]

These projects suggest that the figure of the emperor played a larger role in the politics of post-Qing regimes than usually understood. Overthrowing thousands of years of dynastic rule yet taking power in a world in which republics as a form of government were not common, Sun and his allies searched for symbols of authority and unity, not just through modern political rituals but also in the cultural reservoir of imperial charisma. As one Chinese commentator wrote at the time, in honoring a "great national hero" and offering traditional sacrifices to the ancient ruler, "the new Republic will be no infant among the nations of today, but will take her place in due time, as the restoration in pristine vigour and excellence of one of the oldest civilizations of mankind." The new nation would thus be "sustained by the glory and heroism of a great past"—a past personified by the emperor.[10]

The "contradiction" of resting the authority of the Republic on the back of figures such as Zhu Yuanzhang might thus be indicative of a broader pattern of state building in the twentieth century wherein young and fragile regimes saw potential in the symbolism of the emperor—both dead and living—as a way to more deeply root claims to power. This postimperial use of the emperor is perhaps the clearest example of the transnational "cavalcade of impotence," wherein monarchs around the world were presented as symbols of unity and power without actually being invested with control over the state.[11] That is to say, suggesting that the figure of the emperor played a constructive role in postimperial politics is indicative not of a stagnant political culture in China, but rather that Chinese states were enmeshed in a transnational system in which modern political regimes worked to anchor themselves in dynastic traditions. In China in particular, the use of the royal was tied to the desire to combat federalism and the search for symbols that could transcend provincial loyalties.[12]

This project—transforming the autocratic son of heaven into symbol of the people and nation—was in many ways what the Qing had attempted in the final decade of its rule with the texts, rituals, and discourse associated with the creation of the national school system, plans for the constitution, and preparations for Puyi's education as the Xuantong emperor. In these new systems, the imperial family was frequently presented to the country as exemplars of learning and symbols of the nation. This was the last in a series of changes to the emperorship in the post-Taiping era, developments that provided fragments of a mold with which Sun and his allies could begin to form the new nation.

This process began in 1861 as a debate over how to bring new forms of learning into the emperorship in the hopes of stabilizing a country with rebellions raging and a child on the throne. Over the next several decades, as the challenges facing the Qing grew, so too did the debate over the nature of court education and the place of the imperial family in the political community. In the 1870s and 1880s an expanded group of writers sought changes to the emperors' curricula which they hoped would help drive reform around the country. Particularly in the aftermath of the Sino-Japanese War of 1894–1895, questions surrounding reforms to court education increasingly became tied to a broader effort to remake the Qing state into a constitutional monarchy and emperor-led national community. By the turn of the twentieth century, then, the emperor was only a small portion of the intended audience of his education, as his lessons (as well as those of the rest of the imperial family) were intended to present people around the country with a model of learning and leadership. The history of court education in the post-Taiping era, then, is one of a competition between multiple forms of learning and ideologies in the project of reconstruction, an expanding group of actors seeking to participate in governance, and of a fluid understanding of the relative importance of the emperors' empirical and symbolic roles in the state.

In this conclusion, I briefly retrace these relationships and metamorphoses, exploring how the figures covered in the book—scholars such as Weng Tonghe and Woren and imperial leaders such as Cixi and Guangxu—both inherited and reformed a dynamic tradition of learning and governance whose legacy could still be seen in the nation-building projects of the Republic. In fact, the story goes well beyond Sun Yat-sen and his use of Zhu Yuanzhang. The last Qing emperor, Puyi, was himself frequently the target of reeducation campaigns from postimperial states, as leaders of a variety of regimes saw in the ex-emperor a potentially potent evangelist for their causes. After reviewing the late-Qing narrative, therefore, I will return to the post-Qing world and the afterlife of the late imperial discourse of the learning of the emperor.

THE LEARNING OF THE EMPEROR IN LATE IMPERIAL AND MODERN CHINA

Emperors in late imperial China had long been described as both the lead student and teacher of the realm, tasked with educating themselves and the people in such a way as to unify and strengthen the country.[13] As Wm. Theodore de Bary has described, beginning in the Song, an "ancillary tradition" related to the developing orthodoxy of Way learning (*daoxue*) emerged dedicated to elucidating the "learning of the emperor" (*diwang zhi xue*). Zhu Xi and others described *diwang zhi xue* as the lessons that an emperor was obliged to study and scholars had a responsibility to impart to "perpetuate the Way of government practiced and transmitted in ancient times."[14] Scholars thus worked to place texts in the curricula that would advance their ideals of the healthy ordering of society, ensuring themselves a continued place of prominence at court while presenting the emperor as the ultimate symbol of the state.

This legacy could still be felt in the Qing. For example, on June 3, 1677, a decade after consolidating power at court and with his armies busy fighting rebellions on multiple fronts of the empire, the Kangxi emperor issued an edict explaining his own understanding of the meaning of *diwang zhi xue*. The learning of the emperor, Kangxi said, "takes as its first priority the illumination of principle, the investigation of things and extension of knowledge."[15] This task required constant study, and Kangxi frequently described himself as obsessed with learning, spending so much time reading as a child that he became sick from lack of sleep. Now on the throne, the emperor believed it was his responsibility to both continue his own education and serve as teacher to the people of his empire.[16] But Kangxi was not satisfied with the pedagogical methods inside the imperial palace. Having an official simply explicate a passage did not get to the essence of the Classics and histories. Rather, the emperor said that to benefit from the lessons, there must be a dialogue between scholar and monarch, a mutual discussion of texts that would lead to an understanding of the principles at stake.[17] For Kangxi, therefore, *diwang zhi xue* meant not just the "learning of the emperor" but the emperor's teachings as well.

Kangxi's pedagogical musings and his relationship to scholar-officials in the realm of court education speaks to one of the cornerstones of Qing rule and imperial power in the late dynastic state.[18] Throughout the Qing, groups of officials and the emperor negotiated within the confines of a vast "bureaucratic monarchy," a system governed in part by a corpus of texts whose varied interpretation afforded partisans on all sides ammunition for their arguments about power and responsibility in the state.[19] The relationship between ruler and scholar, alternating roles as teacher and pupil, was thus central to the ideal working of the Qing emperorship. As the Jiaqing emperor put it, emperors must first study to cultivate their virtue and then pass on these teachings to benefit the people of the realm.[20]

In the nineteenth century this tradition was joined by a wave of epochal changes, some outside the control of the Qing and some of their own making. Many of the problems facing Jiaqing and his successors were seemingly unrelated to the "learning of the emperor"— population growth and global silver shortages to name just two. But sometimes the crises had an accidental connection to court education that suggests an opportunity for a new lens through which we may explore the era. For example, when around noon on September 15, 1813, a small band of rebels attacked the Forbidden City in Beijing, the princes Mianning (1782-1850) and Miankai (1795-1838) heard the commotion from inside their classroom, jumped up from their studies, and ran out of the Palace School for Princes to lend a hand in suppressing the attack, successfully shooting rebels off the walls with firearms.[21] What were the books they left behind? How did their martial education balance traditional weaponry with new technologies? How were the princes being educated in this time of increasing pressure from both within and without?

When Mianning came to the throne a few years later as the Daoguang emperor (r. 1820-1850), he in fact linked many of the problems of the day in part to a decay in systems of court education. At the very beginning of his reign, Daoguang issued an edict describing the importance of youth education for members of the imperial family. The emperor said that while beginning education at a young age is important for the common man, it is even more so for rulers. If a common person does not learn the lessons of the Way, Daoguang said, he will bring harm to himself, but if a ruler does not, he will endanger the entire world.[22] Throughout his reign, Daoguang attempted to impart this lesson to his sons, sending them all to the Palace School and assigning eminent scholars as their personal tutors.[23] He also used traditional mechanisms such as the Imperial Lecture to convey the message. In 1823, shortly after taking the throne, he delivered an explication of an iconic passage from the *Daxue* (Great learning), stipulating that bringing peace to the empire started from personal cultivation.[24]

Despite what recent scholarship has shown to be the flexibility of Daoguang era governance, however, the challenges facing the Qing only grew during his reign as domestic rebellion was joined by aggressive imperialist encroachment.[25] The year 1850, then, with both Daoguang's death and the start of the Taiping Rebellion, is frequently seen as a critical turning point in the history of the Qing. With declining imperial revenues, increasing political activism by princes, long-term scholarly discontent, and rising regional interests, Daoguang's death is understood as effectively ending "the history of the Qing emperorship." Thus the effort to suppress the Taiping Rebellion and the subsequent reform efforts of the Tongzhi Restoration and Self-Strengthening Movement are seen as taking place "in an environment in which the emperorship no longer functioned."[26] From one perspective, an examination of court education would seem to confirm this perspective: Xianfeng would indeed be the final Qing emperor to attend the Palace School, as well as the last to deliver an Imperial Lecture or hold a Classic Mat.

This book has suggested, however, that by taking court education as our lens, we may in fact see the regencies of the post-Xianfeng era as the latest incarnation of an ever-flexible Qing emperorship.[27] The Tongzhi, Guangxu, and Xuantong emperors each ascended the throne at the same time they began their education in ruling the Qing Empire. In this era, Cixi and officials at court built on the legacy of the early Qing to argue that while the emperor was young, the empress dowagers would hold ultimate power while working to educate themselves in the ways of governance. This was an explicitly temporary situation, with the periods of regency and dowager power bound by the time frame of the emperors' childhood education. When Tongzhi came of age in 1873 and Guangxu in 1889, their marriage ceremonies in those years signified the end of their formal education, the assumption of personal power, and the opportunity to put childhood lessons into practice.[28]

The emperors' education was thus closely tied to broader questions of governance as the court and officials around the country tried to restabilize the Qing. In this era of growing crises, what were the texts, who were the teachers, and what were the lessons that were important for the young emperors to learn? Over the course of the era, these questions played out in the form of a competition between multiple scholarly and political factions, each hoping to mold the emperor in their image. As Weng Tonghe described the scene, work on this task began early each day before the rest of the Forbidden City awoke: "Sparse stars and faint moonlight surround the imperial palace; ministers and officials rise in the night to take their place in the palace halls; teachers diligently conduct their lessons; reading by the wick of oil lamps illuminates the court early in the morning."[29] The "ministers and officials rising in the night to take their place in the palace halls" and the "teachers diligently conducting their lessons" were thus two linked components of the larger matrix of officials and institutions of an emperorship seeking to navigate a new world.

In fact, the empress dowagers frequently described the emperors' education as one of the most important tasks of the emperorship. In 1866, for example, the adopted mother of one of Tongzhi's tutors, Li Hongzao, died, and Li requested the full twenty-seven months of mourning leave established by Confucian ritual standards. Yet this was contrary to Qing practices for high officials, and the empress dowagers rejected his request. They declared that Tongzhi's education took priority and said that Li could demonstrate his virtue by serving the emperor in the classroom. Li's rebuttal argued that his primary duty was to teach the young emperor the importance of filial devotion, and that he would only be an effective pedagogue if he put those values into practice himself. The empress dowagers again rejected Li's line of reasoning, saying that the importance of educating Tongzhi superseded strict adherence to ritual codes.[30]

In this new era, however, the content of that education was an open question. A decade earlier, when Tongzhi's father (the Xianfeng emperor) had taken the throne, scholars such as Zeng Guofan and Woren had told Xianfeng that the emperor's dedication to learning was an important part of the larger project of restabilizing the dynasty. Yet in urging Xianfeng to embrace his role as student, these scholars said that he need only study the Classics.[31] For the series of young emperors who came after Xianfeng, however, the fields of learning available to both country and court were greatly expanded, and discussions surrounding court education were quickly enmeshed in that changing world. In this time of increasing challenges, scholars and officials began to reimagine the emperor's personal education and work to redefine the learning—and teaching—of the emperor.

This process was possible in part because of changes happening outside of the Forbidden City, but also because the final three Qing emperors ascended the throne at the same time they were set to begin their education. The regencies of the Tongzhi, Guangxu, and Xuantong eras all defined the period of the emperors' youthful education as an opportunity for them to study "in order to form the foundation of governance" which they would put into practice when they came of age and assumed personal power.[32] Yet by not clearly defining what the emperor should study or what was involved in that "foundation," the post-Taiping emperorship deployed the idea of the emperors' youth to suggest to officials that his education was a space in which they could work to impart their own ideas and help chart the future course of the country by convincing the emperor to adopt their particular program of learning.

In the early days of the emperors' education, therefore, different visions about how best to reconstitute dynastic power, the place of Manchu versus Chinese ideals at court, the introduction of Western learning, and many other debates of the era were all present in the classroom. Court education was by no means the only avenue for these developments, as all around the country local and provincial leaders worked to construct new policies and institutions to protect their regions. As this book has shown, however, a focus on court education in the post-Taiping period provides a new lens into many of the key developments of the late Qing. As Weng Tonghe frequently argued, reforms to the emperors' education could not be divorced from the larger changes around the country. When accepting his post in Guangxu's classroom, he wrote that "the restoration (*weixin*) of the emperor's education is like the sun rising over the entire world."[33] Weng thus staked his claim that, like the rising sun illuminates the earth, reforms to court education would shine across the empire and illuminate the path forward. Of course, this was a self-serving description of the potential impact of the emperor's education, one that granted scholars such as Weng a leading role in shaping the future of the country.

Moreover, Weng had a particular conception of what that future should look like—one that was not shared by all his colleagues—and the emperors' classroom was in many ways a hostile work environment emblematic of larger debates taking place around the country. Not only did Weng battle for time in the classroom with the Manchu tutors, but he and his fellow scholars increasingly had to contend with new voices from outside the bureaucracy who sought to influence the emperors' curriculum. Writers in the domestic press frequently argued, for example, that new languages ought to be added to the emperor's education to prepare him to sidestep the bureaucracy and play a direct role in Qing foreign relations. These potential curriculum changes came with conflicts over class time, personnel, ritual, and ideology, each of which played out in debates at court and inside the emperors' classroom. While flexible, the post-Taiping emperorship was thus also fragile, as the range of voices seeking to mold the emperor each sought to monopolize power and influence in the classroom and around the country.

During the periods of regency, scholar-officials, the domestic press, and foreign observers in fact frequently looked to the emperor's performance in the classroom and engagement with their educational program to forecast his future behavior from the throne. In initial plans for Guangxu's education, for example, Prince Chun had laid out a timeline for the emperor's development in martial skills, progressing from learning to draw a bow to shooting live arrows and finally full-scale mounted archery.[34] In 1885, then, when Guangxu successfully made the transition from a wooden to live horse in his martial training, the teachers and officials gathered in attendance beamed with pride that the young boy was beginning to look like a Manchu monarch who might help restore the conquest-era martial prowess that Prince Chun thought was needed to reclaim the country's place in the world.[35]

Other groups, however, saw hope that Guangxu's education was providing him with a different understanding of the best path forward. Just two years later, for example, Zeng Jize (1839–1890), eldest son of Zeng Guofan and an important minister and diplomat in his own right, recounted in his diary an audience with Guangxu. On that day, the emperor peppered Zeng with questions about trains, ships, and other technologies, as well as events from England, Russia, France, and Germany.[36] For Zeng and his like-minded colleagues busy promoting the spread of new fields of learning around the country, Guangxu's interest in these questions suggested a future for the Qing wherein the emperor would lead a top-down reform effort to embrace Western learning throughout the empire.[37] This was an idea that many in the foreign community embraced. The *North China Herald*, for example, described both the emperor and the empress as "models to the people in virtue and knowledge," and the paper and international community kept close watch on court education for signs that the emperor might one day lead China into a new era of engagement with Western powers.[38]

Despite the steady rise of regional interests and powerful provincial leaders over the course of the nineteenth century, the emperor was thus understood as occupying a unique role in shaping the future of China. He could, it was thought, choose a set of teachings and then deploy both his empirical power in the bureaucracy and the power of his example around the country to reshape society. This was a belief held not just by high officials such as Zeng Jizi or Prince Chun but also by other more common Qing subjects, such as the Shanxi provincial degree holder Liu Dapeng (1857–1942). Liu agreed that the emperor should be a model for the people, but he hoped that Guangxu would embrace a very different set of teachings from those imagined by Zeng or Prince Chun, let alone the *North China Herald*: Liu dreamed of meeting with Guangxu and convincing the emperor to expel foreigners and execute any high officials who might stand in the way of Liu's vision of a revitalized, but strictly Confucian, society.[39]

Liu would see his vision washed away in the first decade of the twentieth century, as, in the words of his biographer Henrietta Harrison, "the state gradually abandoned its Confucian values in favor of a new emphasis on nationalism and a vision of modernity tied to international trade and large-scale urban industry."[40] It was in fact in the decades after Zeng Jize's meeting with Guangxu that the Qing increasingly studied the statecraft and educational policies of countries such as Japan, Great Britain, and Germany. In this new global context of nationalizing monarchies, debates about what was important for the emperor to study became a question not only of the balance among Chinese, Manchu, and Western texts, but also of how his education could be connected with the rest of the country and help to unite people behind the imperial center. As Zhang Zhidong said in his famous work *Exhortation to Learn* (1898), all the illustrious rulers of the past were simultaneously sovereign and teacher and personally instructed the empire through their example, and in this new era, the power of the throne would be tied to its ability to embrace new forms of education and set a model for the country.[41]

Zhang's text was written in the period when the end of Guangxu's formal education, the end of the regency, and his coming to personal power coincided with major changes and challenges across the country, particularly the loss to Japan in the Sino-Japanese War. That loss instigated a decade's long push toward Japanese- and German-style reforms to the army, the organization of the government, as well as the traditional institutions of court education. In this new era, reports in the domestic press argued more and more for Japanese-style education for the Qing emperor as part of the broader project of reform. On April 10, 1899, for example, *Shenbao* told its readers that the Japanese emperor and empress were convening high officials to lecture them on history and current affairs.⁴² And in 1903 *Shenbao* again wrote that "Japanese newspapers report that the Meiji emperor believes that national strength gradually comes from promoting cultural rather than military affairs, and therefore orders that beginning from the sixth day of the first month of this year, imperial clansmen will go to the Classic Mat to listen to Confucian ministers give lectures every day." The report noted that during the first lesson, the officials discussed topics ranging from Spain to ancient Japanese history, and the *Doctrine of the Mean*.⁴³

Shenbao thus presented readers with the image of a monarch who saw a broad education for himself and his family as an important step in helping to transform the country. Yet not only the persistence of terminology such as "Classic Mat" and "Confucian minister" (*ruchen*) but also the presence of traditional Chinese texts in the curriculum such as the *Doctrine of the Mean* and the *Book of Changes* provided an argument that China did not need to abandon the classical canon. Rather, the country was capable of Meiji-style success if Qing emperors would work to infuse their traditional curricula with new fields of learning. As Zhang Zhidong had said, in this new era of global competition and learning from the world, the emperor needed to be a model for the rest of the country, and nationwide change could flow from inside the Forbidden City.

Yet as the Qing embraced the idea that changes to court education should present the imperial family as models of a hybrid style of learning, Cixi sidelined the emperor and placed herself at the center of that project. Through both changes to her personal education—adding English lessons to her earlier studies of the Classics, for example—and the effort to create a school for female nobles, Cixi took command of court education in an effort to refashion the emperorship and remake the Qing. In particular, she hoped the new noblewomen would serve as the embodiment of her effort to fuse traditional imperial pedagogy with new global ideals of education and governance. The project drew on a language of power and legitimacy based in part on the principle of widespread female education, and Cixi's advocacy of the school for female nobles suggests some of the ways in which she sought to weave new strands of authority into a traditional ruling ideology. Like the students who lined the streets at the imperial funerals in 1908, the women at the school for female nobles were intended to be models of both patriotism and cosmopolitanism as the court sought to teach people how to participate in a new imperially sanctioned national community. Cixi herself, meanwhile, claimed to be a model for China along the lines of Victoria in England.[44]

So too in the abortive plans for Puyi's education did the court seek to infuse Chinese and Manchu traditions with global practices to create a model modern emperor. Learning to read by reciting passages ten to fifty times (or more), Puyi heard the sounds of both ancient sages and contemporary writers in his classroom as tutors began to teach him the hybrid curriculum of the Chinese Classics, Manchu Way, science, and constitutionalism, which the court hoped would prepare him for his future roles and help to unify the country behind the constitutional monarchy.[45] Moreover, in this new era the court also worked to bring Puyi's education outside of the Forbidden City, creating rituals and celebrations in the new national school system to celebrate the young monarch's first day of school, making pride in and loyalty to the imperial house a core lesson for millions of children around the country. Particularly in the final decade of Qing rule, therefore, discussions about court education became intimately connected with emergent ideals of constitutionalism, cosmopolitanism, and nationalism. Learning to rule meant not just what the emperor needed to study but, as Kangxi had suggested centuries earlier, what he needed to model and teach so that the people knew what it meant to be a member of the political community.

In this way, the focus on the emperor, his education, and particularly his presence in national culture were part of the process by which the Qing sought to transform dynastic sovereignty and create a national community. This was a model on which Republican leaders—wittingly or not—continued to build. As David Strand has shown, the politics of the Republic and beyond called for active and visible leaders, modeling behavior and speaking to the people.[46] And as Rudolf Wagner describes, the omnipresence of Sun Yat-sen's image in the Republican period as a tool of nation building itself emerged from the late Qing study of foreign leaders, their public images, and the growing conviction that China could be saved only by "someone with grand stature and charisma," not the hidden or private sovereign of eras past.[47] Much like calls for Tongzhi to model martial values, for Guangxu to study abroad and then tour the country, or students in the Qing national school system celebrating Puyi's first day of school, trips such as Sun Yat-sen's to the Ming tombs described at the opening of this conclusion were thus a form of public pedagogy that sought to use the figure of the emperor to help create notions of a shared past and common future in building the new nation.

THE MANY REEDUCATIONS OF PUYI

Surprisingly perhaps, the postimperial use of the emperor included not just leaders from the distant past, such as Zhu Yuanzhang, who could be easily wrapped in new mythologies to appeal to the modern nation. Puyi was himself often the focus of similar projects. In the post-Taiping era, the Qing court had actively developed a discourse that linked court education, dynastic reconstruction, and, in its final years, nation building. In the decades after the fall of the Qing, multiple actors appropriated that discourse by reeducating Puyi in the knowledge and ideals of their regimes to make him both an icon of and evangelist for new political and social structures. For decades after the 1911 Revolution, Puyi and his education therefore remained a part of national politics as successive regimes searched for symbols that could help to reunite a fractured political landscape. These regimes spanned the ideological spectrum, yet each fought to secure Puyi's participation to bolster their own authority.[48] In doing so, they bound the emperor, the people, and the nation in ways that can still be seen today.

To avoid a protracted war after the Wuchang Uprising in 1911, revolutionaries agreed to let Puyi and the imperial family remain in the Forbidden City and promised to protect their private property and to provide a stipend to support the court. The "Articles of Favorable Treatment" thus meant that the Qing emperor was not only spared death but allowed to live a life of considerable luxury. This was in stark contrast to the violence wrought on Bannermen communities around the country where revolutionaries carried out mass slaughter of Manchu populations.[49] While Sun's use of Zhu Yuanzhang might be explained in the context of ethnic nationalism, the continued use of Puyi during the twentieth century thus appears more complicated.

As Puyi himself later wrote, the former emperor lived the "most absurd childhood possible."[50] Particularly through the lens of his own memoir and Bernardo Bertolucci's camera, Puyi's childhood does tend to look detached from the realities of the times.[51] Yet for many around him and across the country, Puyi—not necessarily the individual, but rather the symbolism he embodied—held meaning and purpose. As Pamela Crossley has noted, "The inability of republican leaders to create a unified order permitted many forms of political mayhem to continue, one of which was persisting attempts to restore Puyi to power," and a wide range of groups "could not divest themselves of the idea that in Puyi there might, in fact, be the possibility of restoring peace to China with a constitutional monarchy."[52] As had been the case for Tongzhi and Guangxu in the past century, the education of a young emperor—this time without a throne—was still seen as an opportunity to shape the future of the country. The *New York Times* wrote in 1917 that the Republic was "none too firmly seated," and based on the "prestige of his birth... it may fall to his [Puyi's] lot to frame a government according to the ideas which, formed in boyhood, make the man who may make the nation." The *Times* thus paid particular attention to Puyi's childhood education because, although it doubted that he would be made emperor again, it nonetheless saw him as having a special role to play in uniting the country, and it wondered what type of political regime his education would convince him would be best able to bring order to the chaos of the post-Qing world.[53]

In the aftermath of the revolution, there were, however, many around Puyi who held out hopes that he and the Qing would be restored to power. This was particularly true of his tutors, and Puyi's education carried on as planned before the revolution.[54] Though often mocked by the national media, Lu Runxiang, Chen Baochen, and Yiketan held classes for Puyi every day, wore their Qing robes, and drew salaries from the imperial treasury.[55] At the same time, as the ranks of officials serving the former Qing thinned out, the tutors were given expansive duties, often serving to link the court with the Republic. In August 1912, for example, when Empress Dowager Longyu expressed a desire to meet with Sun Yat-sen at the Summer Palace, it was left to the tutors to try to arrange the event.[56] What's more, posts as imperial tutor were sometimes a bridge between service in the former Qing court and the Republic.[57]

In this and other ways in the early years after 1911, education helped to link the remnant Qing court and the Republican government. In her attempt to maintain good relations with the Republic, for example, Longyu presented herself and the court as patrons of education, donating books from the Imperial Library to the new National Library.[58] When Longyu died in 1913, the Republic closed schools all around the country and sent schoolchildren to join cabinet members to line the streets of Beijing for the funerary procession.[59] The scene was nearly identical to the funerals of Guangxu and Cixi five years earlier, as both the Qing court and the Republic upheld the notion that students and the imperial family were connected in the fabric of the national community. In fact, the Republic worked to elevate Longyu in the national consciousness, describing her as a "female Yao or Shun" and even going so far as to propose a statue be commissioned of her likeness. As Jia Feng has argued, the Republic's attempt to place Longyu "in the genealogy of the founding heroes of the republic," much like Sun Yat-sen's visit to the Ming tombs, "enabled the republican government to legitimate its dubious origins."[60]

The Republic's valorization of Longyu was one of the many ways in which the new regime drew on lingering imperial charisma to boost its authority. Puyi's continuing education played a role in that project as well. The Chinese press frequently reported on his lessons, presenting the Republic as guardians of a newly nationalized past embodied in the young boy.[61] The foreign press picked up on this idea, gushing at the benevolence displayed by the Republic in its treatment of Puyi. In 1914, for example, the *New York Times* wrote that "China, the land of contradictions, affords the unique spectacle of a republic caring for a deposed Emperor, and not only caring for him but taking a kindly interest in his studies and his welfare."[62]

At the same time, the presence of the emperor and the opportunity to shape his education also provided enemies of the Republic with a potential figurehead for their political ambitions.[63] These enemies sometimes included foreign countries, as one German official proposed sending Puyi to study abroad in Germany before returning to China, reclaiming his throne, and leading a German-Chinese imperial alliance.[64] As restorationist plots developed around the country, foreign audiences actively wondered about the role Puyi and his education might play in China's future. Writers asked, for example, if there would "come a time when loyal subjects will demand their real Emperor. And will the little boy be brought up in the wisdom of modern civilization, so that he can take charge of the governing of the oldest Nation in the world?"[65] When the Board of Rites decided to add English to Puyi's curriculum in 1915, then, some interpreted the change as evidence that monarchists were planning their assault on the Republic, preparing the boy with the new linguistic skills he would need to take over as the head of state. Most worrying to the Republic was that there were thousands of applicants for the job.[66]

Many of these projects seem far-fetched, yet as the Republic struggled to consolidate power, its leaders were concerned by the continuing appeal of Puyi as a figurehead for some variation of a constitutional monarchy. In 1917, therefore,

President Li Yuanhong approved a plan that sought to protect his government by depriving his enemies of Puyi as a symbol for a competing regime. But the Republic was not going to execute Puyi; instead, they were going to reeducate him. To that end in early 1917, the Republic agreed to send the ex-emperor to America. The United States was chosen because Li did not want Puyi to study in a place that might "prejudice him against Republican government."[67] A former emperor taught to dream of imperial restoration was dangerous, but a former emperor converted to the cause of Republicanism was potentially valuable.

At the same time, however, others sought to elevate Puyi as an alternative to the Republic. In the summer of 1917, before the deposed emperor could be sent abroad, Zhang Xun (1824-1923) took over Beijing and restored Puyi to the Qing throne. The day before the brief 1917 Restoration, Puyi was studying in the Nanshufang, reading from *Doctrine of the Mean* and discussing the nature of imperial rule with his tutor Chen Baochen.[68] Zhang had little interest in Puyi the person; instead, he sought the power he believed would follow from little more than the symbol of a reoccupied throne. Despite, or perhaps still because of, Puyi's youth, his allure as representative of an alternative to the Republic survived Zhang's short-lived plot. Many prominent Chinese cultural and intellectual figures, such as Luo Zhenyu (1866-1940), Wang Guowei (1877-1927), and Gu Hongming (1857-1928), remained loyal to the Manchu Qing, now understood as defenders of a classical tradition under attack by Republicanism and Western culture.[69] On his deathbed in 1918, for example, Guangxu's former English teacher, Zhang Deyi, wrote a memorial to Puyi lamenting the fall of the Qing and exhorting the deposed emperor to devote himself to studies so that he would develop into a sagely and benevolent ruler.[70]

The continuing appeal of Puyi to monarchists, cultural conservatives, and foreign powers suggested to leaders of the Republic that something needed to change if they were going to consolidate power and unite the country. In 1918, therefore, President Xu Shichang (1855-1939) again sought to reeducate Puyi, giving him lessons in English and constitutionalism. These classes were meant to convince Puyi to join the ranks of the Republic and deprive monarchists of their symbol.[71] Xu's plan, however, seems to have backfired. Reginald Johnston (1874-1938), the man tasked with reeducating the former emperor, had two years earlier joined the Confucian Society, and although he encouraged Puyi to cut off his queue and embrace some other markers of Western culture, Johnston was as much an evangelist for Confucianism and imperial power as he was for Western learning or constitutional thinking.[72]

It seems that in the 1920s, while under Johnston's tutelage, Puyi became more interested in power for himself. According to Puyi, "In my early teens I began to understand that my textbooks had something to do with me and grew interested in how to be a 'good emperor,' in why an emperor was an emperor, and in what heavenly significance there was in this."[73] His tutors pushed him toward this line of thinking. Chen Baochen in particular was a bitter enemy of the Republic and longed for a Qing restoration. For Chen, the best way to do this was to bide his time and wait for the Republic to collapse, keeping Puyi ready to retake his place at the center of the polity. He therefore taught Puyi stories of former emperors and officials who, deposed from power, quietly waited for the people to call them back to service.[74] Puyi, for his part, began to argue more and more that he needed to study abroad so that he could learn how to be a modern leader.[75]

For a decade after abdication, therefore, Puyi remained a player in postimperial politics, as representatives of multiple regimes not only kept the ex-emperor alive but actively sought to mold him into a symbol of their governing ideology. In part this was due to lingering loyalty to the Qing among certain communities and attempts at dynastic restoration. But the Republic as well saw use in Puyi, and successive iterations of that regime worked to incorporate the power of the dynastic past into the new state by reeducating him and transforming the former emperor into a proponent of new national values.

There were, of course, many who found the situation odd at best, dangerous at worst. In 1919 a young Mao Zedong (1893-1976) wrote that "no one who has been emperor does not want to be emperor again" and argued that the safest thing to do was to kill Puyi.[76] Five years later, with Puyi still very much alive, a young Chinese student recently returned from studying in France published an essay in which he wondered, "Why have we not killed Puyi?"[77]

Yet several decades later, with Mao the leader of the newly established People's Republic of China and Puyi once again dethroned (this time from his nominal position as the Kangde emperor of the Japanese puppet-state Manchukuo), Mao decided that rather than kill Puyi, he too would seek to reeducate the former emperor. For several years the Soviets had kept Puyi in "cold storage" in a Siberian prison, apparently not willing to "trust the Chinese Communists with such a priceless potential puppet."[78] But now handed over to Mao, Puyi was transferred to a North China prison for political reeducation.

In 1956, after several years of lessons, the PRC began to publicly use Puyi as evidence of the power of its ideology and the effectiveness of its pedagogy. He first testified against a group of Japanese defendants at a trial in China for their role in Manchukuo and then gave interviews to foreign journalists, dutifully describing how he deserved punishment for his crimes.[79] During this period of reeducation, the PRC demanded that Puyi reassess his role in Manchukuo. As a witness at the Tokyo trials, the Allied Powers had been happy for Puyi to describe himself as a hapless puppet, thus proving Japan's nefarious plans for Manchuria and East Asia as a whole.[80] The PRC, however, now required that Puyi admit his long-standing desire for power and full complicity in the crime of Manchukuo. The communist project sought to indict all of China's dynastic past, and Puyi was transformed into a symbol of both the oppression inherent in the imperial system and the liberational power of communist teachings.[81]

On December 4, 1959, Puyi's reeducation was deemed complete and he was released from jail. He returned to Beijing to live a quiet, yet purposeful, life.[82] Puyi was presented to both the domestic and international press as a star pupil of communist teachings. Upon his release, he told the world that "Puyi, who was once emperor, is now dead. As the last emperor of the Manchu dynasty... I was rubbish of society. During my imprisonment, I have learned new techniques and have asked to take part in production."[83] In that moment he was referring to his work in the botanical garden, but Puyi would soon embark on a larger project of historical production and pedagogy that sought to contribute to the development of a new national narrative.

In 1961, for example, he wrote a lengthy account in *Renmin ribao* (People's daily), about Japan's aggression in the Mukden Incident in 1931. In the article, Puyi recounted his complicity with the Japanese, and he urged the people to embrace Mao's teachings to resist the continued threat of imperialism. With the article, the party transformed Puyi into an evangelist for the regime and mobilized him to rally national sentiment. Puyi said, "I want to thank the Chinese Communist Party, the People's Government, and the People of the Motherland for dealing with me so magnanimously, for my transformation through education, and for setting me on the path to rebirth."[84]

The next year the party sought to provide Puyi an expanded stage on which he could perform his "reeducation and rebirth." It was thus in 1962 that Puyi began work on his memoirs, what we might consider to be a confessional autobiography.[85] Just as his previous declarations had, the book charged the entirety of China's past with the crimes of a feudal mindset and an autocratic political system, perfectly embodied—Puyi said—in his childhood education and the ways in which he was trapped by pageantry and cut off from the people of the country.[86] Although Mao had written in 1919 that Puyi needed to die, the chairman now found that the ex-emperor could be of use in constructing the new nation. As he worked on the memoirs, Puyi told the press that, "when I was released from custody and became a free citizen, I became an emperor for the fourth time—one of 650 million emperors and empresses who together rule China under the glorious leadership of the Communist Party and its Chairman, Mao Zedong."[87]

The final lines of Puyi's book credited Mao with completing the former emperor's education, an education that had begun half a century earlier on the eve of revolution as the Qing sought to train a constitutional monarch: "'Man,'" Puyi now wrote, "was the very first word I learned to read in my first reader, the *Three Character Classic*, but I had never understood its meaning before. Only today, with the Communist Party and the policy of remolding criminals, have I learned the significance of this magnificent word and become a real man."[88] Mao justified his place atop the political system in part by virtue of the power of his teachings.[89] Puyi's reeducation and participation in the communist project was therefore a cogent expression of Mao's pedagogical power and symbolic of the potential for the new nation and all its citizens. It was, perhaps, the final transformation of the learning and teaching of the emperor.

CHARACTER GLOSSARY OF SELECT CHINESE AND JAPANESE NAMES AND TERMS IN TEXT

aiguo zhi xin 愛國之心
Airen 愛仁
anda 諳達
bandu 伴讀
Baohe Dian 保和殿
Baohuanghui 保皇會
Bideyuan 弼德院
bingzhan 兵戰
Butong shuwu 補桐書屋
Chen Baochen 陳寶琛
Cheng Yi 程頤
Chongqi 崇綺
Ci'an 慈安
Cixi 慈禧
Da gongzhu 大公主
Dagong bao 大公報
Daoguang 道光
daoxue 道學
datong 大同
Datong shu 大同書
Daxue 大學
dianxue 典學
Diao Minqian 刁敏謙
dide 帝德
Dijian tushuo 帝鑒圖說

Ding Weiliang 丁韙良
Diwang cheng gui 帝王盛軌
diwang zhi xue 帝王之學
Dong Yuanchun 董元醇
Dongling 東陵
Du Shoutian 杜受田
Duanfang 端方
Duanhua 端華
Empress Shōken 昭憲皇后
fangyan 方言
Feng Guifen 馮桂芬
feng san wu si 奉三無私
Fubi jiamo 輔弼嘉謨
Gakushūin 學習院
Gan Yonglong 甘永龍
Gao Xieceng 高燮曾
Guangxu 光緒
Gu Hongming 辜鴻銘
Gu Yanwu 顧炎武
guoxue 國學
guoyu 國語
Guozijian 國子監
Haiguo Tuzhi 海國圖志
Hanlinyuan 翰林院
Hanyuan dian 涵元殿

Hirohito 裕仁
Hong Xiuquan 洪秀全
Hongde dian 弘德殿
Hongde dian xingzou 弘德殿行走
Huang Zongxi 黃宗羲
Huang Zunxian 黃遵憲
huangzu nü 皇族女
Huangzu nü xuetang 皇族女學堂
Huanqiu Zhongguo xuesheng bao 環球中國學生報
Itō Hirobumi 伊藤博文
Jiang Xizhang 江希張
Jiaqing 嘉慶
jing jiao quan xue 敬教勸學
Jing Yuanshan 經元善
Jingyan 經筵
Jinliang 金梁
jinshi 進士
junxue 軍學
juren 舉人
Kang Youwei 康有為
Kangde emperor 康德皇帝
Kangxi 康熙
Kazoku jogakkō 華族女學校
kexue 科學
Kungang 崑岡
Libu 禮部
Li Ciming 李慈銘
Li Dianlin 李殿林
Li Hongzao 李鴻藻
Li Hongzhang 李鴻章
Li Timotai 李提摩太
Li Wentian 李文田
Li Yuanhong 黎元洪
Liang Dunyan 梁敦彥
Liang Qichao 梁啟超

Liji 禮記
Lin Yuezhi 林樂知
Linyong jiangxue 臨雍講學
Liu Dapeng 劉大鵬
liyi 禮儀
Longyu 隆裕
Lun nüxue 論女學
Lu Runxiang 陸潤庠
Lu Shenpei 陸莘培
Luo Zhenyu 羅振玉
Manchukuo 滿洲國
Meiji emperor 明治天皇
Menggu yuyan wenzi 蒙古語言文字
Miankai 綿愷
Mianning 綿寧
Ming Tang 明堂
mingshi 名士
Mingyi daifang lu 明夷待訪錄
Nanshu fang 南書房
Neixing lu 內省錄
Ningshou gong 寧壽宮
Nogi Maresuke 乃木希典
Nü Xuebao 女學報
Pan Qinglan 潘慶瀾
Pang Hongshu 龐鴻書
Prince Chun, Yihuan 醇郡王奕譞
Prince Duan, Zaiyi 端郡王載漪
Prince Dun, Yicong 惇親王奕誴
Prince Gong, Yixin 恭親王奕訢
Prince Qing, Yikuang 慶親王奕劻
Prince Saionji 西園寺公望
Pujun 溥儁
Puyi 溥儀
Qi Junzao 祁寯藻
qiangang duduan 乾綱獨斷
Qianlong 乾隆

Qianqing gong 乾清宮	Tongwen guan 同文館
Qin 秦	Tongzhi 同治
Qin xin jin jian 啟心金鑒	Wang Guowei 王國維
Qing 清	*Wan'guo gongbao* 萬國公報
Qingyi 清議	Wei Yuan 魏源
Qintianjian 欽天監	Wei Zhongxian 魏忠賢
Qixiang 祺祥	*weixin* 維新
Quanxue pian 勸學篇	Weng Tonghe 翁同龢
Rijiang 日講	Weng Xincun 翁心存
Ruchen 儒臣	Wenhua Dian 文華殿
Shang Yanliu 商衍鎏	Wenyu 文郁
Shanghai shangwu yinshuguan 上海商務印書館	Woren 倭仁
	Woshenhunbu 倭什琿布
Shangshu 尚書	Wu Kedu 吳可讀
Shangshufang 上書房	Wu Tingfang 伍廷芳
shangzhan 商戰	Wu Zetian 武則天
Shen Duo 沈鐸	Xia Tongshan 夏同善
Shengyu 聖諭	Xianfeng 咸豐
Shengzu Ren huangdi tingxun geyan 聖祖仁皇帝庭訓格言	Xiangheng 祥亨
	Xianzheng yanjiu suo 憲政研究所
Shiduo 世鐸	*Xiaojing* 孝經
Shimoda Utako 下田歌子	Xiaozhuang 孝莊
Shixu 世續	Xinyou 辛酉
Showa emperor 昭和天皇	Xinzheng bianfa 新政變法
Shuijinggong 水晶宮	Xixue 西學
Shun 舜	*Xiyang tongshi jiangyi* 西洋通史講義
Shunzhi 順治	Xu Shichang 徐世昌
Songgui 松溎	Xu Dingchao 徐定超
Sun Jia'nai 孫家鼐	Xu Tong 徐桐
Sun Yijing 孫詒經	Xuantong 宣統
Sushun 肅順	*xuezhan* 學戰
Taizong 太宗	*xunzheng* 訓政
Tang Shouqian 湯壽潛	Yan Fu 嚴復
tiandi wei yan 天地位焉	Yan Yongjing 颜永京
tianxia taiping 天下太平	Yangxin dian 養心殿
tianzi dianxue 天子典學	Yao 堯

Yihequan 義和團
Yijinga 伊精阿
Yiketan 伊克坦
Yishan 奕山
Yiyi nüxue 譯藝女學
Yomiuri shimbun 読売新聞
Yuan Chang 袁昶
Yuan Shikai 袁世凱
Yuanming yuan 圓明園
Yubei lixian gonghui 預備立憲公會
Yukun hui 毓坤會
Yukun wenhui 毓坤文會
Yukun zongxue hui 毓坤總學會
yulun 御論
Yupi lidai tongjian jilan 御批歷代通鑑輯覽
Yuqing gong 毓慶宮
Yuzhi quanshan yaoyan 御製勸善要言
Yuzhi wuti qingwen jian 御製五體清文鑑
Zaichun 載淳
Zaifeng 載灃
Zaitian 載湉
Zeng Guofan 曾國藩
Zeng Jize 曾紀澤
Zhang Deyi 張德彝
Zhang Jian 張謇
Zhang Jiaxiang 張家驤
Zhang Xun 張勳
Zhang Zhidong 張之洞
Zhao Binglin 趙炳麟
zhengda guangming 正大光明
Zhiping baojian 治平寶鑑
Zhongyong 中庸
Zhu Xi 朱熹
Zhu Yuanzhang 朱元璋
Ziguang ge 紫光閣
Zongli yamen 總理衙門
zhuangyuan 狀元
Zhuangzi 莊子
Zuozhuan 左傳

NOTES

INTRODUCTION

1. Weng Tonghe 翁同龢, *Weng Tonghe riji* 翁同龢日記, 8 vols. (Shanghai: Zhongxi shuju, 2012), 1:157.
2. William Rowe, *China's Last Empire: The Great Qing* (Cambridge, Mass.: Belknap Press of Harvard University Press, 2009), 149-56. See also Susan Mann Jones and Philip Kuhn, "Dynastic Decline and the Roots of Rebellion," in *The Cambridge History of China*, vol. 10, ed. John K. Fairbank (Cambridge: Cambridge University Press, 1978), 108-10; Lillian Li, *Fighting Famine in North China: State, Market, and Environmental Decline, 1690s–1900s* (Stanford, Calif.: Stanford University Press, 2007), 72–73; Tobie Meyer-Fong, *What Remains: Coming to Terms with Civil War in 19th Century China* (Stanford, Calif.: Stanford University Press, 2013), 7-8.
3. Rowe, *China's Last Empire*, 156. In a recent study on the White Lotus Rebellion, Yingcong Dai has intriguingly suggested that the rebels were not as potent a force as we have long thought, and that it was the "unwillingness, rather than incapacity" of the Qing military that prevented a rapid suppression of the rebellion. See Yingcong Dai, *The White Lotus War: Rebellion and Suppression in Late Imperial China* (Seattle: University of Washington Press, 2019), 10.
4. A variety of historians have explored this idea, most often with a focus on the Qianlong era scholars Hong Liangji 洪亮吉 (1746-1809) and Zhuang Cunyu 莊存與 (1719-1788) as examples of growing alienation between throne and bureaucracy. For notable works, see Phillip Kuhn, *Origins of the Modern Chinese State* (Stanford, Calif.: Stanford University Press, 2002), 114-16; Benjamin Elman, *Classicism, Politics, and Kinship: The Ch'ang-chou School of New Text Confucianism in Late Imperial China* (Berkeley: University of California Press, 1990), xxxiii, 112. Also see the seminal essay on the image of Heshen, David S. Nivison, "Ho-Shen and His Accusers: Ideology and Political Behavior in the Eighteenth Century," in *Confucianism in Action*, ed. David S. Nivison and Arthur F. Wright (Stanford, Calif.: Stanford University Press, 1960), 209-43.
5. For a lively new encapsulation of these themes, see Stephen Platt, *Imperial Twilight: The Opium War and the End of China's Last Golden Age* (New York: Knopf, 2018).
6. Weng Xincun 翁心存, *Weng Xincun riji* 翁心存日記, 5 vols. (Beijing: Zhonghua shuju, 2011), 4:1705.
7. *Qing shilu* 清實錄 (Qing veritable records), 21st day of 4th month of 2nd year of the Tongzhi era (Beijing: Zhonghua shuju, 1986), 283-2, accessed online through Scripta Sinica database,

Hanji quanwen ziliao ku 漢籍全文資料庫, http://hanchi.ihp.sinica.edu.tw/ihp/hanji.htm. Hereafter cited as *QSL*. The Palace Examination was the final stage of the Civil Service Examination System. Beginning in 973, the emperor himself was supposed to administer the exam, cementing ties between the throne and the bureaucracy. See Benjamin Elman, *A Cultural History of Civil Examinations in Late Imperial China* (Berkeley: University of California Press, 2000), 14, 134. For more examples of this type of exam question, see *QSL*, 21st day of 4th month of 4th year of the Tongzhi era, 207-2; *QSL*, 21st day of 4th month of 7th year of the Tongzhi era, 167-1.

8. Pierre-Étienne Will, "Views of the Realm in Crisis: Testimonies on Imperial Audiences in the Nineteenth Century," *Late Imperial China* 29, no. 1s (2008): 125.

9. For recent examinations of Qing responses to the challenges of the era and their implications for later regimes, see Stephen R. Halsey, *Quest for Power: European Imperialism and the Making of Chinese Statecraft* (Cambridge, Mass.: Harvard University Press, 2015); and Hans van de Ven, *Breaking with the Past: The Maritime Customs Service and the Global Origins of Modernity in China* (New York: Columbia University Press, 2014). Much work on the relationship between late Qing state-making efforts and later regimes is based on insights provided by R. Bin Wong, *China Transformed: Historical Change and the Limits of European Experience* (Ithaca, N.Y.: Cornell University Press, 1997), 153–58. A wide range of scholars have explored education reforms in the period, both government sponsored and privately initiated. Some important works in these areas include Hiroshi Abe, "Borrowing from Japan: China's First Modern Educational System," in *China's Education and the Industrialized World*, ed. Ruth Hayhoe and Marianne Bastid (Armonk: M. E. Sharpe, 1987), 57–80; Knight Biggerstaff, *The Earliest Modern Government Schools in China* (Ithaca, N.Y.: Cornell University Press, 1961); and Edward J. M. Rhoads, *Stepping Forth Into the World: the Chinese Educational Mission to the United States, 1872–81* (Hong Kong: Hong Kong University Press, 2011).

10. Pamela Kyle Crossley, *A Translucent Mirror: History and Identity in Qing Imperial Ideology* (Berkeley: University of California Press, 1999), 2, 28–29.

11. Pamela Kyle Crossley, "The Rulerships of China," *The American Historical Review* 97, no. 5 (December 1992): 1471.

12. Harold Kahn, *Monarchy in the Emperor's Eyes: Image and Reality in the Chien-lung Reign* (Cambridge, Mass.: Harvard University Press, 1971). Catherine Jami has explored another side of this dynamic, the ways in which the Kangxi emperor used new forms of learning to increase his own power at court. See Catherine Jami, *The Emperor's New Mathematics: Western Learning and Imperial Authority During the Kangxi Reign (1662–1722)* (Oxford: Oxford University Press, 2012).

13. Kahn, *Monarchy in the Emperor's Eyes*, 115–67.

14. Later chapters will discuss variations in the form of the regencies in these different eras, but they can generally be said to have lasted from 1861 to 1873 for Tongzhi, from 1875 to 1889 for Guangxu, and for the duration of Xuantong's short reign from 1908 to 1912. In both the Tongzhi and Guangxu eras, the formal end of the regencies corresponded with the emperors' weddings, in 1873 when Tongzhi was seventeen *sui* and 1889 when Guangxu was nineteen *sui*. During the periods of regency, the empress dowagers held the imperial seal and thus final authority on matters of state. For the process by which they took possession of the seals, see Luke S. K.

Kwong, "Imperial Authority in Crisis: An Interpretation of the Coup d'État of 1861," *Modern Asian Studies* 17, no. 2 (1983): 228–30. While I do not explore the detailed history of control of the seal and its relationship to sanctioning reforms, I hope that my broader attention to the court in this period might inspire others to take up this important matter.

15. Marianne Bastid, "Official Conceptions of Imperial Authority at the End of the Qing Dynasty," in *Foundations and Limits of State Power in China*, ed. S. R. Schram (Hong Kong: Chinese University Press, 1987), 147.
16. Exemplary scholarship around these issues includes Denis Twitchett, "How to Be an Emperor: T'ang T'ai-tsung's Vision of His Role," *Asia Major* 9, no. 1/2 (1996): 1–102; Wm. Theodore de Bary, *Neo-Confucian Orthodoxy and the Learning of the Mind-and-Heart* (New York: Columbia University Press, 1981), 28, 83–117; Peter Bol, *Neo-Confucianism in History* (Cambridge: Harvard University Press, 2010), 115–52; and Julia Murray, "Didactic Picturebooks for Late Ming Emperors and Princes," in *Culture, Courtiers, and Competition: The Ming Court, 1368–1644*, ed. David Robison (Cambridge, Mass.: Harvard University Press, 2008), 231–68.
17. Jack Chen, *The Poetics of Sovereignty: On Emperor Taizong of the Tang Dynasty* (Cambridge, Mass.: Harvard University Asia Center, 2011), 81–105.
18. Kahn, *Monarchy in the Emperor's Eyes*, 4–5.
19. Marie Guarino, "Learning and Imperial Authority in Northern Sung China (960-1126): The Classics Mat Lectures" (Ph.D. diss., Columbia University, 1994), 7–9. Also see Jiang Peng 姜鵬, *Beisong jingyan yu songxue de xingqi* 北宋經筵與宋學的興起 (Shanghai: Shanghai guji chubanshe, 2013).
20. Guarino, "Learning and Imperial Authority," 7–9, 143–44, 147–65.
21. Guarino, "Learning and Imperial Authority," 23.
22. Hung-lam Chu, "The Jiajing Emperor's Interaction with His Lecturers," in *Culture, Courtiers, and Competition: The Ming Court, 1368–1644*, ed. David Robison (Cambridge, Mass.: Harvard University Press, 2008), 202, 198. A similar dynamic played out in Korea. See Jahyun Kim Haboush, "Confucian Rhetoric and Ritual as Techniques of Political Dominance: Yŏngjo's Use of the Royal Lecture," *Journal of Korean Studies* 5, no. 1 (1984): 39–62.
23. Xu Jing 許靜, "Mingqing jingyan zhidu tedian yanjiu" 明清經筵制度特點研究, *Liaocheng daxue xuebao*, no. 2 (2013): 78–87.
24. Chen Dong 陳東, "Qingdai jingyan zhidu" 清代經筵制度, *Kongzi yanjiu*, no. 3 (2009): 97.
25. John W. Dardess, *Confucianism and Autocracy: Professional Elites in the Founding of the Ming Dynasty* (Berkeley: University of California Press, 1983), 224.
26. Kongmiao he Guozijian Bowuguan 孔廟和國子監博物館, ed., *Mingqing huangdi jiangxue lu* 明清皇帝講學錄 (Beijing: Gugong chubanshe, 2016), 17–22.
27. Kongmiao he Guozijian Bowuguan 孔廟和國子監博物館, ed., *Mingqing huangdi jiangxue lu*, 19, 89–93.
28. Scholarship that has introduced this concept includes Kuhn, *Origins of the Modern Chinese State*; William Rowe, *Speaking of Profit: Bao Shichen and Reform in Nineteenth Century China* (Cambridge, Mass.: Harvard University Asia Center, 2018); Pierre-Étienne Will, "Checking Abuses of Power Under the Ming Dynasty," in *China, Democracy, and Law: A Historical and Contemporary Approach*, ed. Mireille Delmas-Marty and Pierre-Étienne Will (Leiden: Brill, 2012), 117–67; and David Schaberg, "The Zhouli as Constitutional Text," in *Statecraft and*

Classical Learning: The Rituals of Zhou in East Asian History, ed. Benjamin Elman and Martin Kern (Leiden: Brill, 2009), 33–63.

29. Phillip Kuhn, "Political Crime and Bureaucratic Monarchy: A Chinese Case of 1768," *Late Imperial China* 8, no. 1 (1987): 80–104. Beatrice Bartlett famously explored a similar dynamic in her study of the Grand Council, arguing that it was precisely the "joint monarchical-councilor administration" that "enabled the dynasty to rise to greatness in its middle years and at the end prolong its life." Bartlett, *Monarchs and Ministers: The Grand Council in Mid-Ch'ing China, 1723–1820* (Berkeley: University of California Press, 1994), 1. While late Qing emperors did not leave the same type of records as Yongzheng or Qianlong, and thus this book does not deal with the same type of deep administrative history as Bartlett, the tension of shifting power balances between monarch and minister remained very much alive in the post-Taiping era.

30. De Bary, *Neo-Confucian Orthodoxy*, 28, 97.

31. Seunghyun Han, *After the Prosperous Age: State and Elites in Early Nineteenth-Century Suzhou* (Cambridge, Mass.: Harvard University Asia Center, 2016), 2–5; Wensheng Wang, *White Lotus Rebels and South China Pirates: Crisis and Reform in the Qing Empire* (Cambridge, Mass.: Harvard University Press, 2014), 5–6; William Rowe, "Rewriting the Qing Constitution: Bao Shichen's 'On Wealth' (Shuochu)," *T'oung Pao* 98 (2012): 178.

32. Much scholarship in this mold builds on the seminal volume edited by Paul Cohen and John Schrecker, *Reform in Nineteenth Century China* (Cambridge, Mass.: Harvard East Asian Research Center, 1976).

33. Kahn, *Monarchy in the Emperor's Eyes*, 44.

34. Rowe, "Rewriting the Qing Constitution," 189–90; Phillip Kuhn, "Ideas Behind China's Modern State," *Harvard Journal of Asiatic Studies* 55, no. 2 (1995): 302; Will, "Views of the Realm in Crisis," 125–59.

35. "Peking Gazette, 21st April, 1850: Memorial of Wang King-yun (Chinese), Vice-President (Chinese) of the Tung-ching Sx, or Court for Transmission of Dispatches from the Province to the Cabinet," in *Decree of the Emperor of China, Asking for Counsel, and the Replies of the Administration, 1850–51, with Other Papers*, trans. Thomas Wade (London: Harrison, 1878), 4; "Peking Gazette, 15th May, 1850: Memorial of Tsang Kwoh-fan, Junior Vice President (Chinese) of the Board of Ceremonies," in Wade, *Decree*, 10, 79; "Peking Gazette, April 1850: Memorial of Wojin, a Mongolian," in Wade, *Decree*, 27.

36. "Peking Gazette, 1st June, 1850: Subsequent Memorial of Tsang Kwoh-fan," in Wade, *Decree*, 79.

37. Xu Liting 徐立亭, *Xianfeng tongzhi di* 咸豐同治皇 (Changchun: Jilin wen shi chuban she, 1993), 15–16.

38. "Peking Gazette, 17th April, 1850: The Emperor's Reply to Tsang Kwoh-fan," in Wade, *Decree*, 14.

39. QSL, 8th day of 2nd month of 3rd year of Xianfeng era, 87-2.

40. Pamela Crossley, "Nationality and Difference in China: The Post-Imperial Dilemma," in *The Teleology of the Nation State: Japan and China*, ed. Joshua Fogel (Philadelphia: University of Pennsylvania Press, 2005), 142.

41. QSL, 15th day of 10th month of 11th year of Xianfeng era, 185-1, 185-2, 186-1.

42. *QSL*, 15th day of 10th month of 11th year of Xianfeng era, 185-1, 185-2, 186-1.
43. Kathryn Edgerton-Tarpley, *Tears from Iron: Cultural Responses to Famine in Nineteenth-Century China* (Berkeley: University of California Press, 2008), 101, 112–13.
44. Mark Elliott, *The Manchu Way: The Eight Banners and Ethnic Identity in Late Imperial China* (Stanford, Calif.: Stanford University Press, 2001), 11.
45. See his discussion of the "reimperialization" of government beginning in 1861 in Edward J. M. Rhoads, *Manchus and Han: Ethnic Relations and Political Power in Late Qing and Early Republican China, 1861–1928* (Seattle: University of Washington Press, 2000), 286–88.
46. Pamela Kyle Crossley, *Orphan Warriors: Three Manchu Generations and the End of the Qing World* (Princeton, N.J.: Princeton University Press, 1990), 223–28; Elliott, *The Manchu Way*, 345–46; Evelyn Rawski, *The Last Emperors: A Social History of Qing Imperial Institutions* (Berkeley: University of California Press, 1998), 3–4.
47. Mary Clabaugh Wright, *The Last Stand of Chinese Conservatism: The T'ung-Chih Restoration, 1862–1874* (Stanford, Calif.: Stanford University Press, 1962), 51–56.
48. Stephen R. Mackinnon, *Power and Politics in Late Imperial China: Yuan Shi-Kai in Beijing and Tianjin, 1901–1908* (Berkeley: University of California Press, 1980), 30–36.
49. In his study on ethnicity and the late Qing court, Rhoads similarly notes this lacuna, tying it to the larger body of scholarship on the nineteenth century that has long assumed an irrevocably weak court. Rhoads, *Manchus and Han*, 6-7.
50. Bastid, "Official Conceptions," 147.
51. Bastid, "Official Conceptions," 183.
52. Ho-fung Hung, *Protest with Chinese Characteristics: Demonstrations, Riots, and Petitions in the Mid-Qing Dynasty* (New York: Columbia University Press, 2011), 18, 134, 137, 158; Edgerton-Tarpley, *Tears from Iron*, 81–89; Meyer-Fong, *What Remains*, 21–32.
53. For classic takes on regionalism, see Franz Michael, "Regionalism in Nineteenth-Century China," introduction to *Li Hung-chang and the Huai Army: A Study in Nineteenth-Century Chinese Regionalism*, by Stanley Spector (Seattle: University of Washington Press, 1964), xxi-xliii; and Kwang-ching Liu, "The Limits of Regional Power in the Late Ch'ing Period: A Reappraisal," *Tsing Hua Journal of Chinese Studies*, 10, no. 2 (July 1974): 176-223. For more recent perspectives, see Elisabeth Kaske, "Fund-Raising Wars: Office Selling and Interprovincial Finance in Nineteenth-Century China," *Harvard Journal of Asiatic Studies* 71, no. 1 (2011): 69–141; and Zhang Xiaowei, "Loyalty, Anxiety, and Opportunism: Local Elite Activism During the Taiping Rebellion in Eastern Zhejiang, 1851-1864," *Late Imperial China* 30, no. 2 (2009): 39-83.
54. Wright, *Last Stand*, 7.
55. Wright, *Last Stand*, 50, 7.
56. These are vast bodies of scholarship. Key examples of the perspectives and contributions include, but are by no means limited to, William Ayers, *Chang Chih-tung and Educational Reform in China* (Cambridge, Mass.: Harvard University Press, 1971); Ja Ian Chong, "Breaking Up Is Hard to Do: Foreign Intervention and the Limiting of Fragmentation in the Late Qing and Early Republic, 1893-1922," *Twentieth-Century China* 35, no. 1 (November 2009): 75-98; Samuel C. Chu and Kwag-Ching Liu, eds., *Li Hung-Chang and China's Early Modernization* (New York: M.E. Sharpe, 1994); Kwang-ching Liu, "The Ch'ing Restoration," in *The Cambridge History of*

China, vol. 10, ed. John Fairbank (Cambridge: Cambridge University Press 1978), 409–90; Jonathan Porter, *Tseng Kuo-fan's Private Bureaucracy* (Berkeley: University of California Press, 1972); Peter Zarrow, "The New Schools and National Identity: Chinese History Textbooks in the Late Qing," in *The Politics of Historical Production in Late Qing and Republican China*, ed. Tze-Ki Hon and Robert Culp (Boston: Brill, 2007), 21–54; Gang Zhao, "Reinventing China: Imperial Qing Ideology and the Rise of Modern Chinese National Identity in the Early Twentieth Century," *Modern China* 32, no. 1 (2006): 3–30.

57. Pamela Kyle Crossley, *The Wobbling Pivot, China Since 1800: An Interpretive History* (Oxford: Wiley-Blackwell, 2010), 118, 133–54.
58. Crossley, *Wobbling Pivot*, 118.
59. Stephen Platt, *Provincial Patriots: The Hunanese and Modern China* (Cambridge, Mass.: Harvard University Press, 2007); Mary Rankin, *Elite Activism and Political Transformation in Zhejiang, 1865–1911* (Stanford, Calif.: Stanford University Press, 1986).
60. Also see the important work of Edward McCord on this issue, both "Militia and Local Militarization in Late Qing and Republican China: The Case of Hunan," *Modern China* 14, no. 2 (1988), 156–87, and *The Power of the Gun: The Emergence of Modern Chinese Warlordism* (Berkeley: University of California Press, 1993). The late nineteenth-century process was itself the outgrowth of earlier eras, as famously shown by Phillip Kuhn, *Rebellion and Its Enemies in Late Imperial China, Militarization and Social Structure, 1796–1864* (Cambridge, Mass.: Harvard University Press, 1970).
61. Prasenjit Duara, *Culture, Power, and the State: Rural North China, 1900–1942* (Stanford, Calif.: Stanford University Press, 1988), 5, 25, 59.
62. Peter Zarrow, *After Empire: The Conceptual Transformation of the Chinese State, 1885–1924* (Stanford, Calif.: Stanford University Press, 2012), 24–118.
63. Paul Bailey, *Reform the People: Changing Attitudes Towards Popular Education in Early Twentieth Century China* (Cambridge, Mass.: Harvard University Press, 1971).
64. Bailey, *Reform the People*, 31–40; Tze-ki Hon, "Educating the Citizens: Visions of China in Late Qing History Textbooks," *The Politics of Historical Production in Late Qing and Republican China*, ed. Tze-ki Hon and Robert Culp (Leiden: Brill, 2007), 79–105; Peter Zarrow, *Educating China: Knowledge, Society, and Textbooks in a Modernizing World, 1902–1937* (Cambridge: Cambridge University Press, 2015), 11.
65. Roger R. Thompson, *China's Local Councils in the Age of Constitutional Reform, 1898–1911* (Cambridge, Mass.: Harvard University Press, 1995), 3.
66. Robert Culp, *Articulating Citizenship: Civic Education and Student Politics in Southeastern China, 1912–1940* (Cambridge, Mass.: Harvard University Asia Center, 2007), 1–4; Henrietta Harrison, *The Making of the Republican Citizen: Political Ceremonies and Symbols in China, 1911–1929* (Oxford: Oxford University Press, 2000), 60–63.
67. For an exemplary study of local education in the post-Taiping era and its ramifications for modern schools, see Barry Keenan, *Imperial China's Last Classical Academies: Social Change in the Lower Yangzi, 1864–1911* (Berkeley: University of California Press, 1994).
68. Wen-Hsin Yeh, *The Alienated Academy: Culture and Politics in Republican China, 1919–1937* (Cambridge, Mass.: Harvard University Press, 1990), 8.
69. Yeh, *The Alienated Academy*, 9.

70. Wright, *Last Stand*, 73–77.
71. Donald Keene, *Emperor of Japan: Meiji and His World, 1852–1912* (New York: Columbia University Press, 2002), 31.
72. Critiquing the despotism of the late-Ming state and motivated by anti-Manchu sentiment, Gu Yanwu argued that while the emperor should play a leading role in promoting and rewarding study, governance should be almost entirely left to local communities. See Ku Wei-ying, "Ku Yen-wu's Ideal of the Emperor: A Cultural Giant and Political Dwarf," in *Imperial Rulership and Cultural Change in Traditional China*, ed. Frederick P. Brandauer and Chun-Chieh Huang (Seattle: University of Washington Press, 1994), 230–47.
73. The idea of modern political forms as incompatible with the monarchy is expressed in a range of influential writings. Joseph Levenson, for instance, in analyzing Yuan Shikai, framed the discussion around the "draining of monarchical mystique." See "The Suggestiveness of Vestiges: Confucianism and Monarchy at the Last," in Levenson, *Confucian China and Its Modern Fate: A Trilogy* (Berkeley: University of California Press, 1968), 2:3–24. More recently, Peter Zarrow has thoughtfully explored the connection in more depth in "The Reform Movement, the Monarchy, and Political Modernity," in *Rethinking the 1898 Reform Period: Political and Cultural Change in Late Qing China*, ed. Rebecca Karl and Peter Zarrow (Cambridge, Mass.: Harvard University Press, 2002), 17–47.
74. James Hevia, *English Lessons: The Pedagogy of Imperialism in Nineteenth Century China* (Durham, N.C.: Duke University Press, 2003), 4.
75. "Editorial Selections," *North China Herald*, February 27, 1873.
76. "Readings for the Week," *North China Herald*, June 13, 1898.
77. W. M. Spellman, *Monarchies 1000–2000* (London: Reaktion, 2001), 11; Charlotte Backeraa, Milinda Banerjee, and Cathleen Sarti, "The Royal Nation in Global Perspective," in *Transnational Histories of the 'Royal Nation,'* ed. Milinda Banerjee (Cham, Switz.: Palgrave Macmillan, 2017), 1–17; Stefan Berger and Alexi Miller, eds., *Nationalizing Empires* (Budapest: Central European University Press, 2015).
78. David Cannadine, "The Context, Performance, and Meaning of Ritual: The British Monarchy and the Invention of Tradition, 1820–1977," in *The Invention of Tradition*, ed. Eric Hobsbawm and Terence Ranger (Cambridge: Cambridge University Press, 1983), 120; Takashi Fujitani, *Splendid Monarchy: Power and Pageantry in Modern Japan* (Berkeley: University of California Press, 1996); Milinda Banerjee, "The Royal Nation and Global Intellectual History: Monarchic Routes to Conceptualizing National Unity," in *Transnational Histories of the 'Royal Nation,'* ed. Milinda Banerjee (Cham, Switz.: Palgrave Macmillan, 2017), 21–43.
79. Jeroen Duindam, *Dynasties: A Global History of Power, 1300–1800* (Cambridge: Cambridge University Press, 2016), 312.
80. Fujitani, *Splendid Monarchy*, 26; Lilia Moritz Schwarcz, *The Emperor's Beard: Dom Pedro II and the Tropical Monarchy of Brazil* (New York: Hill and Wang, 2004), xix.
81. Eugen Weber, *Peasants Into Frenchmen: The Modernization of Rural France, 1870–1914* (Stanford, Calif.: Stanford University Press, 1976), 303–38.
82. Richard Wortman, *Scenarios of Power Myth and Ceremony in Russian Monarchy from Peter the Great to the Abdication of Nicholas II* (Princeton, N.J.: Princeton University Press, 2006), 25, 230.

83. James C. Albisetti, *Secondary School Reform in Imperial Germany* (Princeton, N.J.: Princeton University Press, 1983), 173.
84. Keene, *Emperor of Japan*, 171.
85. Maurizio Peleggi, *Lords of Things: The Fashioning of the Siamese Monarchy's Modern Image* (Honolulu: University of Hawaii Press, 2002), 3-7, 164-65.
86. Elisabeth Kaske, "The Pitfalls of Transnational Distinction: A Royal Exchange of Honors and Contested Sovereignty in Late Qing China," in *China and the World, the World and China: A Transcultural Perspective: Essays in Honor of Rudolf G. Wagner*, ed. Barbara Mittler (Gossenberg, Ger.: Ostasien, 2019), 2:137-69.
87. Michael Chang, *A Court on Horseback: Imperial Touring and the Construction of Qing Rule, 1680–1785* (Cambridge, Mass.: Harvard University Asia Center, 2007), 9-18.
88. Zhang Zhidong 張之洞, *Quanxue pian* 勸學篇 (1898) (Guilin: Guangxi Normal University Press, 2008), 17-18.
89. Zhang, *Quanxue pian*, 24-25.
90. Fujitani, *Splendid Monarchy*, 11, 109.
91. Fujitani, *Splendid Monarchy*, 109, 120.
92. "Rest in the Highest," *World's Chinese Students' Journal* 4, no. 3 (November-December 1909): 150-51.
93. "Rest in the Highest," 152.
94. Emily Mokros, "Reconstructing the Imperial Retreat: Politics, Communications, and the Yuanming Yuan Under the Tongzhi Emperor, 1873-4," *Late Imperial China* 33, no. 2 (December 2012): 80.
95. Li Wenjun 李文君, *Zijincheng babai yinglian bian'e tongjie* 紫禁城八百楹联匾额通解 (Beijing: Zijincheng chuban she, 2011), 61.
96. Phillip Kuhn, *Soulstealers: The Chinese Sorcery Scare of 1768* (Cambridge, Mass.: Harvard University Press, 1990), 187-222, 225.

1. NEW FORMS OF LEARNING FOR A NEW AGE OF IMPERIAL RULE, 1861–1874

1. Woren 倭仁, *Wo Wenduan gong yi shu* 倭文端公遺書 (Taibei: Cheng wen chuban she, 1968), 132-33.
2. Arthur W. Hummel, ed., *Eminent Chinese of the Ch'ing period (1644–1912)* (Washington, D.C.: U.S. Government Printing Office, 1944), 861-63.
3. Wu Xiangxiang 吳相湘, *Wanqing gongting shiji* 晚清宮庭實紀 (Taibei: Zheng zhong shu ju, 1952), 45-46; Weng, *Weng Tonghe riji* 翁同龢日記, 8 vols. (Shanghai: Zhongxi shuju, 2012), 1:94-95; Tony Teng, "Prince Kung and the Survival of the Ch'ing Rule, 1858-1898" (Ph.D. diss., University of Wisconsin, 1972), 47, 67-68; Jason Holloman Parker, "The Rise and Decline of I-Hsin Prince Kung, 1858-1865: A Study of the Interaction of Politics and Ideology in Late Imperial China" (Ph.D. diss., Princeton University, 1979), 52-55, 63.
4. It is unclear what ailed Xianfeng, though many accounts point to tuberculosis. At the time of his death, and often since, however, the death was blamed on a supposed penchant for drinking,

gambling, and other signs of immorality. The Taipings seized on this narrative and celebrated Xianfeng's demise as a victory for the rebel cause. See Stephen Platt, *Autumn in the Heavenly Kingdom: China, the West, and the Epic Story of the Taiping Civil War* (New York: Knopf, 2012), 217–18.

5. For an overview, see Ting-yee Kuo, "Self-Strengthening: The Pursuit of Western Technology," in *The Cambridge History of China*, vol. 10, ed. John Fairbank (Cambridge: Cambridge University Press 1978), 491–542. For a more focused study of the scientific and military projects of the era, see Benjamin Elman, "Naval Warfare and the Refraction of China's Self-Strengthening Reforms Into Scientific and Technological Failure, 1865–1895," *Modern Asian Studies* 38, no. 2 (May 2004): 283–326. For a case study on the new types of institutions that emerged as part of these efforts, see Jenifer Rudolph, *Negotiated Power in Late Imperial China: The Zongli Yamen and the Politics of Reform* (Ithaca, N.Y.: Cornell University Press, 2008).

6. Weng, *Weng Tonghe riji*, 1:157.

7. Luke S. K. Kwong, *A Mosaic of the Hundred Days: Personalities, Politics, and Ideas of 1898* (Cambridge, Mass.: Harvard University Press, 1984), 20.

8. Teng, "Prince Kung," 70–71.

9. Quoted in Teng, "Prince Kung," 89–91.

10. Patricia Ebrey, "Imperial Filial Piety as a Political Problem," in *Filial Piety in Chinese Thought and History*, ed. Alan Chan and Sor-hoon Tan (New York: Routledge Curzon, 2004), 122–24; Harold Kahn, "The Politics of Filiality: Justification for Imperial Action in Eighteenth Century China," *Journal of Asian Studies* 26, no. 2 (February 1967): 197–203.

11. Zhao Erxun 趙爾巽 ed., *Qing shigao* 清史稿 (Taibei: Hong shi chubanshe, 1981), 390:11727.

12. Evelyn Rawski, *The Last Emperors: A Social History of Qing Imperial Institutions* (Berkeley: University of California Press, 1998), 135.

13. Robert Oxnam, *Ruling from Horseback: Manchu Politics in the Oboi Regency, 1661–1669* (Chicago: University of Chicago Press, 1975), 201; Rawski, *The Last Emperors*, 135–36, 188.

14. Marianne Bastid, "Official Conceptions of Imperial Authority at the End of the Qing Dynasty," in *Foundations and Limits of State Power in China*, ed. S. R. Schram (Hong Kong: Chinese University Press, 1987), 152–53.

15. Liu Jinzao 劉錦藻, *Qingchao xu wenxian tongkao* 清朝續文獻通考 (Shanghai: Commercial Press, 1936), 174:9233-1.

16. Liu, *Qingchao xu wenxian tongkao*, 174:9233-1. The memorial was also published in the *Peking Gazette* (Jingbao 京報), and then in the *North China Herald* on November 16, 1861.

17. Wu, *Wanqing gongting shiji*, 67–69.

18. Wu, *Wanqing gongting shiji*, 71–72

19. David S. Nivison, "Ho-Shen and His Accusers: Ideology and Political Behavior in the Eighteenth Century," in *Confucianism in Action*, ed. David S. Nivison and Arthur F. Wright (Stanford, Calif.: Stanford University Press, 1960), 209–43.

20. *QSL*, 7th day of 10th month of 11th year of Xianfeng era, 160-2.

21. *QSL*, 15th day of 10th month of 11th year of Xianfeng era, 185-1, 185-2, 186-1.

22. *QSL*, 21st day of 4th month of 7th year of Tongzhi era, 167-1, 167-2.

23. Mary C Wright, "What's in a Reign Name: The Uses of History and Philology," *Journal of Asian Studies* 18, no. 1 (1958): 103.

24. Bastid, "Official Conceptions," 160.
25. See, for example, the memorial by Jia Zhen 賈楨 (1798-1874) and Zhou Zupei 周祖培 (1793-1867), reproduced in Zhao Erxun, *Qing shigao*, 390:11727.
26. See, for example, Isaac Taylor Headland, *Court Life in China: The Capital, Its Officials and People* (New York: Revell, 1909), 26; Philip Sergeant, *The Great Empress Dowager of China* (New York: Dodd, Mead, 1911), 23.
27. In his early twentieth-century work *Shengde jilüe* 聖德紀略 (Taibei: Wenhai Press, 1970), 10-11, Qu Hongji 瞿鴻禨 (1850-1918) recounts a conversation with Cixi in which she described to him how Xianfeng had tutored her in document classification.
28. Wu Qingchi 吳慶坻, *Jiaolang cuolu* 蕉廊脞錄 (Taibei: Wenhai Press, 1969), 1:6; "Huangdi juxing dahun dianli zhi qing" 皇帝舉行大婚典禮誌慶, *Shenbao*, May 15, 1872; "Shou lian xulu" 壽聯續錄, *Shenbao*, November 20, 1894; "Daqingguo cixi taihou bixia" 大清國慈禧太后陛下, *Datong bao* 7, no. 1 (1907): 1; "Dahang huangdi aici" 大行皇帝哀辭, *Shenbao*, December 27, 1908.
29. Kwong, *Mosaic of the Hundred Days*, 22.
30. *QSL*, 25th day of 3rd month of inaugural year of Tongzhi era, 623-2, 624-1.
31. Ying-Kit Chan, "A Precious Mirror for Governing the Peace: A Primer for Empress Dowager Cixi," *Nan Nü* 17, no. 2 (2015): 214-44.
32. Weng, *Weng tonghe riji*, 2:476, 493-94; *QSL*, 24th day of 5th month of 3rd year of Tongzhi era, 288-1, 288-2. See also Kwong, *Mosaic of the Hundred Days*, 22.
33. Weng, *Weng tonghe riji*, 2:517.
34. Li Yuhang and Harriet T. Zurndorfer, "Rethinking Empress Dowager Cixi Through the Production of Art," *Nan Nü*, 14, no. 1 (2012): 17-18; Ying-chen Peng, "Staging Sovereignty: Empress Dowager Cixi (1835-1908) and Late Qing Court Art Production" (Ph.D. diss., University of California, Los Angeles, 2014), 171; Kwong, *Mosaic of the Hundred Days*, 32.
35. Peng, "Staging Sovereignty," 35-36.
36. *QSL*, 26th day of 10th month of 11th year of Xianfeng era, 225-2, 226-1, 226-2.
37. Quoted in Parker, "The Rise and Decline of I-Hsin Prince Kung," 283.
38. *QSL*, 2nd day of 2nd month of inaugural year of Tongzhi era, 491-2, 492-1.
39. Wan Yi 萬依, *Qingdai gongting shi* 清代宮廷史 (Shenyang: Liaoning renmin chuban she, 1990), 117. I have examined these issues in more depth in Daniel Barish, "Han Chinese, Manchu, and Western Spaces: The Changing Facade of Imperial Education in Qing Beijing," *Frontiers of History in China* 14, no. 2 (2019): 212-42.
40. The phrase comes from the "Kongzi xianju" (Confucius dwelt in leisure) chapter of the Book of Rites (*Liji*). For the full analysis, see Matthias L. Richter, *The Embodied Text: Establishing Textual Identity in Early Chinese Manuscripts* (Leiden: Brill, 2013), 166.
41. Li, *Zijincheng babai yinglian bian'e tongjie*, 74-81.
42. *QSL*, 2nd day of 2nd month of inaugural year of Tongzhi era, 491-2, 492-1, 492-2.
43. James Polachek, *The Inner Opium War* (Cambridge, Mass.: Harvard University Press, 1992), 222-23, 275-76.
44. Hummel, *Eminent Chinese*, 125.
45. Polachek, *The Inner Opium War*, 179, 217-18.
46. Wright, *Last Stand*, 52, 87-89, 174.

47. Kwang Ching-Liu, "Politics, Intellectual Outlook, and Reform: The T'ung-wen kuan Controversy of 1867," in *Reform in Nineteenth Century China*, ed. Paul Cohen and John Schrecker (Cambridge, Mass.: Harvard University Press, 1976), 89–90.
48. Hummel, *Eminent Chinese*, 858; Kwong, *Mosaic of the Hundred Days*, 50.
49. Polachek, *The Inner Opium War*, 275–76. As Polachek shows, Qi was widely known as a patron of Han Learning (222–23). Yet, as Kwang-Ching Liu suggests, Qi also symbolized "the new trend of amalgamating the introspective moral emphasis of the Sung Learning with the Han learning's emphasis on accurate knowledge of the ancient classics." See Liu, "Politics, Intellectual Outlook, and Reform," 89–90. See also Hummel, *Eminent Chinese*, 125.
50. *QSL*, 2nd day of 2nd month of inaugural year of Tongzhi era, 492-1.
51. Zheng Zhongxuan 鄭仲烜, "Qingchao huangzi jiaoyu yanjiu" 清朝皇子教育研究 (Ph.D. diss., Taiwan National Central University, 2011), 211.
52. Mark Elliott, *The Manchu Way: The Eight Banners and Ethnic Identity in Late Imperial China* (Stanford, Calif.: Stanford University Press, 2001), 11.
53. Edward J. M. Rhoads, *Manchus and Han: Ethnic Relations and Political Power in Late Qing and Early Republican China, 1861–1928* (Seattle: University of Washington Press, 2000), 143-45.
54. Zheng, "Qingchao huangzi jiaoyu yanjiu," 211.
55. Weng, *Weng Tonghe riji*, 1:215. This information in Weng's diary must have come from his father, who was then tutor to the Tongzhi emperor. The entry from the same day in the Veritable Records corroborates the scene.
56. *QSL*, 12th day of 2nd month of inaugural year of Tongzhi era, 516-1.
57. Weng, *Weng Tonghe riji*, 1:215.
58. This was a marked contrast to their interactions with other officials, wherein it was the officials' responsibility to kneel in front of the prince. See Wang Shuang 王霜, *Zhongguo diwang gongting shenghuo* 中國帝王宮廷生活 (Beijing: Guoji wenhua chuban gongsi, 1992). Harold Kahn vividly describes the scene of princes bowing to their teachers in *Monarchy in the Emperor's Eyes: Image and Reality in the Ch'ien-lung Reign* (Cambridge, Mass.: Harvard University Press, 1971), 118.
59. Weng, *Weng Tonghe riji*, 1:215.
60. Weng, *Weng Tonghe riji*, 1:462–63.
61. Weng, *Weng Tonghe riji*, 1:462–63.
62. See, for example, memorial by Yihuan 奕譞, "Zou wei huangshang dushu ying yan junchen zhi fen" 奏為皇上讀書應嚴君臣之分, Tongzhi 4.3.18 (First Historical Archives, Series of Documents from Various Palace Depositories [宮中全總] doc. no. 04-01-14-0071-025). Hereafter documents from this portion of the archives are cited as FHA-GZQZ. See also memorial by Yihuan 奕譞, "Zou wei meng huangtaihou xun jiao huangshang ruxue dushu qing chi xiashou du zhi yuan reng zhao jiu zhang qiyu bude shan zuo shi" 奏為蒙皇太后訓教皇上入學讀書請飭下授讀之員仍照舊章其餘不得擅坐事, Tongzhi 11.9.29 (FHA-GZQZ doc. no. 04-01-14-0074-061).
63. Weng, *Weng Tonghe riji*, 2:791.
64. Weng, *Weng Tonghe riji*, 2:589.
65. Weng, *Weng Tonghe riji*, 2:589.
66. Weng, *Weng Tonghe riji*, 2:708.
67. Weng, *Weng Tonghe riji*, 2:791.

68. Weng, *Weng Tonghe riji*, 2:795-96. This seems have settled things for a few years. But in the tenth year of the Tongzhi reign, Weng, by now completely exasperated, again complained about the Chinese lessons starting late, blaming the *anda* for exceeding their allotted time. *Weng Tonghe riji*, 2:911.
69. For an overview of this process of transmission and dissemination, see Xiong Yuezhi 熊月之, *Xixuedongjian yu wanqing shehui* 西學東漸與晚清社會 (Shanghai: People's Press, 1994).
70. Memorial by Yixin 奕訢, "Zou yin zongsi jicha huangshang dushu kecheng ji hongde dian yiqie shiwu xie'en zhe" 奏因總司稽查皇上讀書課程及弘德殿一切事物謝恩折, Tongzhi 0.2.3 (First Historical Archives, Grand Council Series [軍機處全總] doc. no. 03-0208-4463-062. Hereafter documents from this portion of the archives are cited as FHA-JJC.
71. Weng, *Weng Tonghe riji*, 1:408-9.
72. Grady Lolan Wang, "The Career of I-Hsin, Prince Kung, 1858-1880: A Case Study in the Limits of Reform in the Late Ch'ing" (Ph.D. diss., University of Toronto, 1980), 260. Cixi also considered dismissing Prince Gong to be part of Tongzhi's education, teaching the young boy not only the importance of ritual etiquette but also the dangers of challenging her. See Xiao Yishan 蕭一山, *Qingdai tongshi* 清代通史 (Taibei: Taiwan shang wu yin shu guan, 1963), 3:654-55.
73. *QSL*, 12th day of 3rd month of 4th year of Tongzhi era, 131-2.
74. Kuo, "Self-Strengthening," 505.
75. Hummel, *Eminent Chinese*, 862.
76. Liu, "Politics, Intellectual Outlook, and Reform," 93-100.
77. Modified translation from Hummel, *Eminent Chinese*, 861-62. See also Tonio Andrade, *The Gunpowder Age* (Princeton, N.J.: Princeton University Press, 2016), 293-94. Ting-yee Kuo translates the sentiment as "the way to uphold the foundation of the state is to emphasize propriety and righteousness but not expedient schemes. The basic policy of the state is to cultivate man's mind and not techniques." See Kuo, "Self-Strengthening," 529.
78. Roberta Lion Long, "Metaphysics and East-West Philosophy: Applying the Chinese T'i-yung Paradigm," *Philosophy East and West* 29, no. 1 (January 1979): 49. See also Joseph Levenson, "Rejection of T'i-yung and Rejection of Innovation: Wo-jen," in his *Confucian China and Its Modern Fate: A Trilogy* (Berkeley: University of California Press, 1968), 1:69-75.
79. Li Xizhu 李細珠, *Wan qing baoshou sixiang de yuanxing: woren yanjiu* 晚清保守思想的原型: 倭仁研究 (Beijing: Shehui kexue wenxian chubanshe, 2000), 147.
80. Hummel, *Eminent Chinese*, 862-63.
81. *QSL*, 11th day of 2nd month of inaugural year of Tongzhi era, 515-1.
82. Li, *Wan qing baoshou sixiang de yuanxing*, 137-39.
83. Parker, "The Rise and Decline of I-Hsin Prince Kung," 11-12.
84. Memorial by Yihuan 奕譞, "Zou wei feng taihou yizhi zongsi huangdi dushu kecheng deng shiwu shi nan shengren qing huangtaihou ling xuan tuo yuan shi" 奏為奉太后懿旨總司皇帝讀書課程等事務實難勝任請皇太后另選妥員, Tongzhi era, precise date unclear (FHA-JJC doc. no. 03-4700-058).
85. Catherine Jami, *The Emperor's New Mathematics: Western Learning and Imperial Authority During the Kangxi Reign (1662–1722)* (Oxford: Oxford University Press, 2012), 57-81, 139-59.

1. NEW FORMS OF LEARNING FOR A NEW AGE OF IMPERIAL RULE 199

86. These appeals were translated and published in "The New College at Pekin," *North China Herald*, March 16, 1867.
87. Memorial by Yihuan 奕譞, "Zou wei gong ni huangshang xuexi menggu yuyan wenzi bing qishe deng zhangcheng shi" 奏為恭擬皇上學習蒙古語言文字并騎射等章程事," Tongzhi 0.2.4 (FHA-GZQZ doc. no. 04-01-38-0186-001).
88. Mao Xianmin 毛憲民, "Lun qingdi wugong liang ju yu qishe shangwu jingshen" 論清帝武功良具與騎射尚武精神, in *Qingdai gongshi tanxi* 清代宮史探析, ed. Qingdai gongshi yanjiu hui 清代宮史研究會 (Beijing: Forbidden City, 2007), 69–84; Weng, *Weng Tonghe riji*, 2:829–30.
89. Memorial by Yihuan 奕譞, "Zou wei gong ni huangshang xuexi menggu yuyan wenzi bing qishe deng zhangcheng shi" 奏為恭擬皇上學習蒙古語言文字并騎射等章程事," Tongzhi 0.2.4 (FHA-GZQZ doc. no. 04-01-38-0186-001).
90. Weng, *Weng Tonghe riji*, 2:745.
91. Weng, *Weng Tonghe riji*, 2:479, 481.
92. See, for example, Zou Ailian 鄒愛蓮, "Cong gongke dang yu weng tonghe riji tan tongzhi huangdi de dianxue jiaoyu" 從功課檔與翁同龢日記談同治皇帝的典學教育, in *Qingdai gongshi tanxi* 清代宮史探析, ed. Qingdai gongshi yanjiu hui (Beijing: Forbidden City, 2007), 604–21.
93. Wu, *Wanqing gongting shiji*, 170–71.
94. This is a common theme in Weng's writing. For one example, see Weng, *Weng Tonghe riji*, 2:579. Weng had a similar complaint when trying to teach Tongzhi using *Dijian tushuo*. Weng, *Weng Tonghe Riji*, 2:701, 724.
95. Liu, "Politics, Intellectual Outlook, and Reform," 96.
96. Eunuchs played important roles at court throughout Chinese history, often serving as alternative power bases from scholar-officials. This competition goes a long way toward explaining the image in historical sources of eunuch power or influence as a common cause of dynastic decline. For a more nuanced study of the bureaucratization of eunuchs and their important role in the political and military successes of a dynasty, see Lu Yang, "Dynastic Revival and Political Transformation in late T'ang China: A Study of Emperor Hsien-Tsung (805–820) and His Reign" (Ph.D. diss., Princeton University, 1999). For the Qing, see Norman Kutcher, *Eunuch and Emperor in the Great Age of Qing Rule* (Berkeley: University of California Press, 2018).
97. *QSL*, 22nd day of 7th month of 5th year of Tongzhi era, 253-1, 253-2.
98. Weng, *Weng Tonghe riji*, 2:795.
99. Weng, *Weng Tonghe riji*, 2:779–80.
100. Weng, *Weng Tonghe riji*, 2:866–67.
101. *QSL*, 20th day of 9th month of 11th year of Tongzhi era, 492-1; "Shiyue shi'yi ri jingbao quanlu" 十月十一日京報全錄, *Shenbao*, December 4, 1872; "Zhongwai zhengshi jinwen" 中外政事近聞, *Jiaohui xinbao*, 1873 (230): 7–8.
102. *QSL*, 20th day of 9th month of 11th year of Tongzhi era (p. 492-1). Modified translation from *North China Herald*, ed., *Translation of the Peking Gazette for 1872* (Shanghai: North China Herald, 1873), 108.
103. "Editorial Selections: The Accession of the Emperor," *North China Herald*, February 27, 1873.
104. "Xin zhengyue ershi liu ri jingbao quanlu" 新正月二十六日京報全錄, *Shenbao*, March 20, 1873.

105. *QSL*, 3rd day of 2nd month of 11th year of Tongzhi era, 343-1, 343-2. Modified translation from *North China Herald*, ed. *Translation of the Peking Gazette for 1872*, 23.
106. Yuanchong Wang, *Remaking the Chinese Empire: Manchu-Korean Relations, 1616–1911* (Ithaca, N.Y.: Cornell University Press, 2018), 165-66; Hummel, *Eminent Chinese*, 209.
107. "Eryue shi ri jingbao quanlu" 二月十二日報全錄, *Shenbao*, April 3, 1873.
108. Memorial by Yihuan 奕譞, "Zou qing huangshang jiaotong kecheng zhuan jiu jing shi aozhi yi ji zhi zhi bing jishi jian yi wubei shi" 奏請皇上交通課程專究經史奧旨以基邹治并及時兼肄武備事, Tongzhi 11.9.29 (FHA-GZQZ doc. no. 04-01-01-0914-027).
109. "Peking Gazettes," *North China Herald*, March 10, 1873.
110. Kwong, *Mosaic of the Hundred Days*, 43.
111. *North China Herald*, ed., *Translation the Peking Gazette for 1873* (Shanghai: North China Herald, 1874), 20-21.
112. Emily Mokros, "Reconstructing the Imperial Retreat: Politics, Communications, and the Yuanming Yuan Under the Tongzhi Emperor, 1873-4," *Late Imperial China* 33, no. 2 (December 2012): 76-118.
113. Mokros, "Reconstructing the Imperial Retreat," 83, 104.
114. Zhongguo diyi lishi dang'an guan, ed., *Yuanming yuan* 圓明園 (Shanghai: Shanghai guji chubanshe, 1991), 1:720-22, 724-26.
115. Wu, *Wanqing gongting shiji*, 221-24.
116. Quoted in Teng, "Prince Kung and the Survival of the Ch'ing Rule," 176-79.
117. Zhongguo diyi lishi dang'an guan, *Yuanming yuan*, 745.
118. Wu, *Wanqing gongting shiji*, 226.
119. *North China Herald*, ed., *Translation of Peking Gazette for 1875* (Shanghai: North China Herald and Supreme Court Consular Gazette, 1876), 7-8.
120. *QSL*, "Preface to Veritable Records of Tongzhi era" (*Muzong yi huangdi shilu shoujuan yi xu* 穆宗毅皇帝實錄首卷一 序), 1-1.
121. "The Past and Future of China," *North China Herald*, October 10, 1863.

2. THE MALLEABILITY OF YOUTH

1. Luke S. K. Kwong, *Mosaic of the Hundred Days: Personalities, Politics, and Ideas of 1898* (Cambridge, Mass.: Harvard University Press, 1984), 44-45.
2. *North China Herald*, ed., *Translation of Peking Gazette for 1875* (Shanghai: North China Herald and Supreme Court Consular Gazette, 1876), 7-8, January 13, 1875.
3. Weng Tonghe, *Weng tonghe riji*, 8 vols. (Shanghai: Zhongxi shuju, 2012), 3:1123. See also, Kwong, *Mosaic of the Hundred Days*, 42, 44-45.
4. Ying-kit Chan, "Corpse Admonition: Wu Kedu and Bureaucratic Protest in Late Qing China," *Journal of Chinese History* 2, no. 1 (2018): 109-43; Marianne Bastid, "Official Conceptions of Imperial Authority at the End of the Qing Dynasty," in *Foundations and Limits of State Power in China*, ed. S. R. Schram (Hong Kong: Chinese University Press, 1987), 160-71. Kathryn Edgerton-Tarpley has also suggested that the controversy negatively affected the state's ability to respond to famine in the 1870s as the throne was unable to galvanize support for its policies. See

2. THE MALLEABILITY OF YOUTH 201

Edgerton-Tarpley, *Tears from Iron: Cultural Responses to Famine in Nineteenth-Century China* (Berkeley: University of California Press, 2008), 33–35.
5. *North China Herald, Translation of Peking Gazette for 1875*, 11, January 15, 1875. Modified translation.
6. *North China Herald, Translation of Peking Gazette for 1875*, 8, January 13, 1875.
7. *North China Herald, Translation of Peking Gazette for 1875*, 7, January 13, 1875.
8. *North China Herald, Translation of Peking Gazette for 1875*, 17, January 26–27, 1875.
9. *North China Herald, Translation of Peking Gazette for 1875*, 10, January 15, 1875. Modified translation.
10. *Qing shilu* 清實錄 (Beijing: Zhonghua shuju, 1986), 7th day of 12th month of 13th year of Tongzhi era, 77-1. Hereafter *QSL*.
11. Bastid, "Official Conceptions," 169.
12. "Gonglu yuxing" 恭錄諭行, *Shenbao*, January 31, 1876.
13. Memorial by Yihuan 奕譞, "Zou wei jian ming zhaoliao huangdi kecheng mianyu zhuoding qing han kecheng deng shi 奏為簡命照料皇帝課程面諭酌定清漢課程等事," Guangxu 2.1.29 (First Historical Archives, Series of Documents from Various Palace Depositories [宮中全總], doc. no. 04-01-02-0152-007). Documents from this portion of archives hereafter referred to as FHA-GZQZ.
14. I have examined these issues in more depth in Daniel Barish, "Han Chinese, Manchu, and Western Spaces: The Changing Facade of Imperial Education in Qing Beijing," *Frontiers of History in China* 14, no. 2 (2019): 212–42.
15. Wang Zilin 王子林, "Qing taizi gong" 清太子宮," *Zijincheng*, no. Z1 (2006): 114.
16. Reginald Johnston, *Twilight in the Forbidden City* (Mattituck, N.Y.: Amereon House, 1995), 226–27.
17. Li Wenjun 李文君, *Zijincheng babai yinglian bian'e tongjie* 紫禁城八百楹联匾额通解 (Beijing: Zijincheng chuban she, 2011), 124, 125.
18. Edgerton-Tarpley, *Tears from Iron*, 94–101.
19. Zhao Erxun ed., *Qing Shigao* 清史稿 (Taibei: Hong shi chubanshe, 1981), 441:12419.
20. Zhao, *Qing Shigao*, 441:12417–19. Also see his biographical information compiled by the National Palace Museum (Taiwan), http://npmhost.npm.gov.tw/ttscgi2/ttsquery?0:0:npmauac:TM%3D%AE%5D%DB%DF%B8g. Sun Yijing does not appear to be related to the more famous scholar of the era, Sun Yirang 孫詒讓 (1848–1908).
21. *QSL*, 12th day of the 12th month of the inaugural year of the Guangxu era, 351-2.
22. Memorial by Yicong 奕誴, "Zou wei qin zun yizhi xuanze huangshang ruxue ji qi shi" 奏為欽遵懿旨選擇皇上入學吉期其事, Guangxu 0.12.15 (First Historical Archives, Grand Council series [軍機處全總], doc. no. 03-7208-016). Documents from this portion of the archives hereafter cited as FHA-JJC.
23. Iwo Amelung, "The *Complete Compilation of New Knowledge*, Xinxue beizuan 新學備纂 (1902): Its Classification Scheme and Its Sources," in *Chinese Encyclopedias of New Global Knowledge (1870–1930)*, ed. Melina Dolezelova-Velingerova and Rudpolf Wagner (Heidelberg: Springer, 2014), 92, n. 31; Timothy Weston, *The Power of Position: Beijing University, Intellectuals, and Chinese Political Culture, 1898–1929* (Berkeley: University of California Press, 2004), 22–23, 27–31.

24. Michael G. Chang, *A Court on Horseback: Imperial Touring & the Construction of Qing Rule, 1680–1785* (Cambridge, Mass.: Harvard University Asia Center, 2007), 11–18.
25. Press participation in the politics of court education in the 1870s is tied with what Joan Judge has described as an attempt by new groups of writers and intellectuals to "expand popular power" in later decades. See Judge, *Print and Politics 'Shibao' and the Culture of Reform in Late Qing China* (Stanford, Calif.: Stanford University Press, 1997), 3–9, 68.
26. "Lun huan si yi yi dushu" 論宦寺亦宜讀書, *Shenbao*, February 26, 1876.
27. Norman Kutcher notes that some of Guangxu's tutors warned him about the danger of empowering eunuchs. See Kutcher, *Eunuch and Emperor in the Great Age of Qing Rule* (Berkeley: University of California Press, 2018), 4.
28. Xie Junmei 謝俊美, "Guangxu huangdi de dushu suiyue" 光緒皇帝的讀書歲月, *Wenshi bolan*, no. 03 (2006): 46.
29. Weng, *Weng Tonghe riji*, 3:1226. The phrase *zhengda guangming* appears in many forms around the Forbidden City and in Qing discussions of governance—for example, inscribed on a large plaque that hangs in the Qianqing gong. Scholars have variously translated the phrase as "Rectitude and Honor," as I have adopted here, as well as "Justice and Honor," "Upright and Pure in Thought," "Upright Governance and Pervasive Clarity," or, as Yong-tsu Wong explains the full meaning of the phrase, "open-mindedness and magnanimous appropriate to a great ruler." See Yong-tsu Wong, *A Paradise Lost, The Imperial Garden Yuanming Yuan* (Honolulu: University of Hawai'i Press, 2001), 27.
30. Kwong, *Mosaic of the Hundred Days*, 53.
31. Weng, *Weng Tonghe riji*, 3:1226.
32. Wenshi ziliao yanjiu weiyuanhui 文史資料研究委員會, ed., *Wanqing gongting shenghuo jianwen* 晚清宮廷生活見聞 (Beijing: Wenshi ziliao chubanshe, 1982), 6.
33. Xie, "Guangxu huangdi de dushu suiyue," 46.
34. Weng, *Weng Tonghe riji*, 3:1226.
35. For more on the book, see Julia Murray, "Didactic Picturebooks for Late Ming Emperors and Princes," in *Culture, Courtiers, and Competition: The Ming Court, 1368–1644*, ed. David Robison (Cambridge, Mass.: Harvard University Press, 2008), 231–68.
36. Weng, *Weng Tonghe riji*, 3:1226.
37. Weng, *Weng Tonghe riji*, 3:1226.
38. Zheng Zhongxuan, "Qingchao huangzi jiaoyu yanjiu" 清朝皇子教育研究, Ph.D diss., Taiwan National Central University, 2011, 215–16.
39. Weng, *Weng Tonghe riji*, 3:1240.
40. Weng, *Weng Tonghe riji*, 3:1299. For more examples, as well as a few instances of less rave reviews, see 2:1310–16.
41. Weng, *Weng Tonghe riji*, 3:1248, 1255.
42. Xie Junmei 謝俊美, *Weng Tonghe* 翁同龢 (Shanghai: Shanghai renmin chuban she, 1987), 25.
43. Weng, *Weng Tonghe riji*, 3:1244.
44. See, for example, Michael Lackner and Natascha Vittinghoff, eds., *Mapping Meanings: The Field of New Learning in Late Qing China* (Leiden: Brill, 2004); Meng Yue, "Hybrid Science versus Modernity: The Practice of the Jiangnan Arsenal, 1867–1904," *East Asian Science, Technology and Medicine* 16 (1999): 13–52; and Edward J. M. Rhoads, *Stepping Forth Into the World: The Chinese Educational Mission to the United States, 1872–81* (Hong Kong: Hong Kong University Press, 2011).

45. "Dixue lun" 帝學論, *Shenbao*, February 4, 1876.
46. For example, Memorial by Gao Xieceng 高燮曾, "Zou qing juxing rijiang shi" 奏請舉行日講事, Guangxu 17.2.10 (FHA-JJC doc. no. 03-5553-005); Memorial by Pan Qinglan 潘慶瀾, "Zou wei qing fu jingyan yi chong shengxue er yushi bian shi" 奏為請復經筵以崇聖學而御世變事, Guangxu 29.7.16 (FHA-JJC doc. no. 03-5420-005); Memorial by Pan Qinglan 潘慶瀾, "Zou wei qing fu jingyan yi chong shengxue wei ziqiang zhi ben zonghe rencai deng jingchen guanjian shi" 奏為請復經筵以崇聖學為自強之本綜核人才等敬陳管見事, Guangxu 22.9.13 (FHA-JJC doc. no. 03-5614-021); Memorial by Wenyu 文郁, "Zou wei qing zhi juxing jingyan dadian shi" 奏為請旨舉行經筵大典事, Guangxu 15.3.30 (FHA-JJC doc. no. 03-5551-011).
47. Xu Jing, "Mingqing jingyan zhidu tedian yanjiu" 明清經筵制度特點研究, *Liaocheng daxue zuebao*, no. 2 (2013): 87.
48. "The Recuperation of China," *Chinese Recorder and Missionary Journal*, November 1, 1881.
49. "The Recuperation of China."
50. "Lun renjun yitong taguo yuyan wenzi shi" 論人君宜通他國語言文字事, *Shenbao*, February 15, 1876. The linguistic capabilities of the emperor had long played a role in Qing politics. In the seventeenth century, for example, early Qing rulers focused on learning Chinese to consolidate their rule. The Shunzhi emperor, for one, could not speak or read Chinese at the time he ascended the throne. He therefore worked to educate himself in the language to aid his rule. See Xiang Si 向斯, *Qingdai huangdi dushu shenghuo* 清代皇帝讀書生活 (Beijing: Zhongguo Shudian, 2008), 3.
51. "Lun renjun yitong taguo yuyan wenzi shi."
52. This is a long-standing trope in East Asia. See Sixiang Wang, "The Sounds of Our Country: Interpreters, Linguistic Knowledge, and the Politics of Language in Early Chosŏn Korea," in *Rethinking East Asian Languages, Vernaculars, and Literacies, 1000–1919*, ed. Benjamin Elman (Leiden: Brill, 2014), 58–95.
53. In some ways this remained true for much of the rest of the dynasty, as writers in venues such as *Shibao* frequently attacked officials but suggested that if the emperor himself were allowed to make decisions, the country would be set on the correct path of reform. See Judge, *Print and Politics*, 65, 147.
54. Yicong, "Zou wei qin zun yizhi xuanze huangshang ruxue ji qi shi."
55. "Jinghua suoshi" 京華瑣事, *Shenbao*, October 14, 1884.
56. "Jingyou zashu" 京友雜述, *Shenbao*, November 4, 1884.
57. "Rixia jiwen" 日下紀聞, *Shenbao*, February 21, 1885.
58. Yihuan, "Zou wei jian ming zhaoliao huangdi kecheng mianyu zhuoding qing han kecheng deng shi."
59. Murata Yujiro, "The Late Qing 'National Language' Issue and Monolingual Systems: Focusing on Political Diplomacy," *Chinese Studies in History* 49, no. 3 (May 2016): 112–15.
60. For a description of this scene in the Tongzhi era (1873), see "Correspondence Respecting the Audience Granted to Her Majesty's Minister and Other Representatives at Pekin by the Emperor of China," in *British Parliamentary Papers: China 5* (Shannon: Irish University Press, 1971), 31–33. For the Guangxu era, see Mrs. Archibald Little, *Intimate China: The Chinese as I Have Seen Them* (London: Hutchinson, 1899), 523–31.
61. "Guangxu ba'nian liuyue ershi liu ri jingbao quanlu" 光緒八年六月二十六日京報全錄, *Shenbao*, August 20, 1882.

62. Ying-chen Peng, "Staging Sovereignty: Empress Dowager Cixi (1835-1908) and Late Qing Court Art Production," Ph.D. diss., University of California, Los Angeles, 2014, 139-40.
63. Lloyd E. Eastman, *Throne and Mandarins: China's Search for a Policy During the Sino-French Controversy, 1880–1885* (Cambridge, Mass.: Harvard University Press, 1967), 102-3.
64. North China Herald, ed., *Translation of Peking Gazette for 1884* (Shanghai: North China Herald and Supreme Court Consular Gazette, 1885), appenda, 2, April 8, 1884.
65. Mary Backus Rankin, "'Public Opinion' and Political Power: Qingyi in Late Nineteenth Century China," *Journal of Asian Studies* 41, no. 3 (1982): 465-66.
66. Quoted in Eastman, *Throne and Mandarins*, 105.
67. Eastman, *Throne and Mandarins*, 214-20.
68. North China Herald, *Translation of Peking Gazette for 1884*, 47, April 9, 1884; 51, April 14, 1884.
69. Hongxing Zhang, "Studies in Late Qing Dynasty Battle Paintings," *Artibus Asiae* 60, no. 2 (2000): 265-96.
70. "Dicheng chunjing" 帝城春景, *Shenbao*, March 7, 1885.
71. *QSL*, 14th day of 6th month of 12th year of Guangxu era, 90-1.
72. *QSL*, 10th day of 6th month of 12th year of Guangxu era, 87-1, 87-2.
73. "Peking Gazettes," *North China Herald*, October 13, 1886.
74. "Benguan jiefeng dianyin" 本館接奉電音, *Shenbao*, July 14, 1886.
75. Robert Oxnam, *Ruling from Horseback: Manchu Politics in the Oboi Regency, 1661–1669* (Chicago: University of Chicago Press, 1975), 186.
76. Li Yuhang, "Oneself as a Female Deity: Representations of Empress Dowager Cixi as Guanyin," *Nan Nü* 14, no. 1 (2012): 101-3.
77. Peng, "Staging Sovereignty," 149.
78. Li, "Oneself as a Female Deity," 113.
79. Peng, "Staging Sovereignty," 150, 156, 180. See also Ka Bo Tsang, "In Her Majesty's Service: Women Painters in China at the Court of the Empress Dowager Cixi," in *Local/Global: Women Artists in the Nineteenth Century*, ed. Deborah Cherry and Janice Helland (Burlington, Ver.: Ashgate, 2006), 35-58.
80. North China Herald, ed., *Translation of Peking Gazette for 1889* (Shanghai: North China Herald and Supreme Court Consular Gazette, 1890), 82-83, June 20, 1889.
81. North China Herald, *Translation of Peking Gazette for 1889*, 111-12, August 12, 1889; 148, October 19, 1889.
82. North China Herald, *Translation of Peking Gazette for 1889*, 5, January 9, 1889; 10-11, January 19, 1889.
83. North China Herald, *Translation of Peking Gazette for 1889*, 69, May 26, 1889.
84. North China Herald, *Translation of Peking Gazette for 1890* (Shanghai: North China Herald and Supreme Court Consular Gazette, 1891), 143, August 9, 1890; 200, October 29, 1890.
85. North China Herald, *Translation of Peking Gazette for 1889*, 153, October 28, 1889.
86. North China Herald, *Translation of Peking Gazette for 1890*, 44, March 25, 1, 1890; 153, August 21, 1890; 211-12, November 13, 1890.
87. North China Herald, ed., *Translation of Peking Gazette for 1891* (Shanghai: North China Herald and Supreme Court Consular Gazette, 1892), 125-26, September 10, 1891.
88. Tobie Meyer-Fong, *What Remains: Coming to Terms with Civil War in 19th Century China* (Stanford, Calif.: Stanford University Press, 2013), 21-32.

89. North China Herald, ed., *Translation of Peking Gazette for 1891*, 125–26, September 10, 1891; 167, November 24, 1891.
90. Memorial by Wenyu, "Zou wei qing zhi juxing jingyan dadian shi."
91. Wenyu, "Zou wei qing zhi juxing jingyan dadian shi."
92. Memorial by Gao Xieceng, "Zou qing juxing rijiang shi."
93. Gao, "Zou qing juxing rijiang shi."
94. *QSL*, 11th day of 2nd month of 17th year of Guangxu era, 910-2.
95. North China Herald, *Translation of Peking Gazette for 1891*, 40, March 20, 1891.
96. Memorial by Chen Baochen 陳寶琛, "Zou wei shengxue bu yi jiu kuang qing xuanzhao ruchen zhaocheng jin jiang shi" 奏為聖學不宜久曠請宣召儒臣照常進講事, Guangxu 7.4.16 (FHA-GZQZ doc. no. 04-01-12-101-0468).
97. Huang Zunxian 黃遵憲, "Ba Meiguo liuxuesheng ganfu" 罷美國留學生感賦, in *Huang Zunxian quanji* 黃遵憲全集 (Beijing: Zhonghua shuju, 2005), 1:103. Modified translation from William Hung, "Huang Tsun-Hsien's Poem 'The Closure of The Educational Mission in America,'" *Harvard Journal of Asiatic Studies* 18, no. 1/2 (June 1, 1955): 50–73.
98. For the poem in the context of Huang's diplomatic career, see Douglas R. Reynolds, *East Meets East: Chinese Discover the Modern World in Japan, 1854–1898: A Window on the Intellectual and Social Transformation of Modern Japan* (Ann Arbor, Mich.: Association for Asian Studies, 2014), 148. My translation is indebted to those of both Hung and Reynolds.
99. Japanese statesman Fukuzawa Yukichi 福澤諭吉 (1835–1901), for example, argued that it was the responsibility of the Imperial Household to encourage learning. See his 1882 work "On The Imperial Household" (Teishitsuron 帝室論) and his 1883 "The Independence of Learning" (Gakumon-no Dokuritsu 学問の独立), in Eiichi Kiyooka, *Fukuzawa Yukichi on Education: Selected Works* (Tokyo: University of Tokyo Press, 1985), 137, 177. The "Imperial Rescript on Education" (1890) crystallized the connection between education and the emperor. Read out loud and memorized by students across Japan, the rescript urged them to "pursue learning and cultivate arts, and thereby develop intellectual faculties and perfect moral powers" to "guard and maintain the prosperity of Our Imperial Throne." This is not to say that the era in Japan was characterized by total reverence to the throne or the "emperor system." See Carol Gluck, *Japan's Modern Myths: Ideology in the Late Meiji Period* (Princeton, NJ: Princeton University Press, 1985), 26, 103, 123–49.

3. PUTTING LESSONS INTO PRACTICE

1. Weng Tonghe 翁同龢, *Weng Tonghe riji* 翁同龢日記, 8 vols. (Shanghai: Zhongxi shuju, 2012), 6:525.
2. Zhang, a Han Bannerman, was a member of both the first class of Tongwen guan students and first Qing first mission abroad. Shen remains more obscure. For Zhang, see Jenny Huangfu Day, *Qing Travelers to the Far West: Diplomacy and the Information Order in Late Imperial China* (Cambridge: Cambridge University Press, 2018), chap. 3. See also Douglas R. Reynolds, *East Meets East: Chinese Discover the Modern World in Japan, 1854–1898: A Window on the Intellectual and Social Transformation of Modern Japan* (Ann Arbor, Mich.: Association for Asian Studies, 2014), chap. 2.
3. William Alexander Parsons Martin, *A Cycle of Cathay: Or, China, South and North, with Personal Reminiscences* (New York: Revell, 1900), 316.

4. Zou Zhenhuan 鄒振環, "Guangxu huangdi de yingyu xuexi yu jinru qingmo gongting de yingyu duben" 光緒皇帝的英語學習與進入清末宮廷的英語讀本, *Qingshi yanjiu*, no. 03 (2009): 107-15.
5. Weng, *Weng Tonghe riji*, 6:2524.
6. Martin, *A Cycle of Cathay*, 317.
7. Pamela Kyle Crossley, *A Translucent Mirror: History and Identity in Qing Imperial Ideology* (Berkeley: University of California Press, 1999), 11-12.
8. Mårten Söderblom Saarela, "Manchu and the Study of Language in China (1607-1911)" (Ph.D. diss., Princeton University, 2015), 163-64.
9. For example, see Charles Denby writing to Walter W Gresham on March 22, 1895, in Yan Guangyao 閻廣耀, *Meiguo dui hua zhengce wenjian xuanbian: cong yapian zhanzheng dao di'yi ci shijie dazhan* 美國對華政策文件選編: 从鸦片战争到第一次世界大戰, 1842-1918 (Beijing: People's Publishing, 1990), 364.
10. "China Waking Up: That Is the Meaning of the Emperor Learning English," *New York Times*, February 4, 1892. For an interesting alternative perspective on the role of shared language in international relations from the same era, see the *New York Daily Graphic*, November 3, 1879. There, an article prophesized the imminent spread of the Chinese language to the United States and noted that "it looks a trifle off to be sending missionaries to a country which seems to be at least as intelligent and quite as moral as our own, and it remains to be demonstrated whether China does not have it in her power to confer quite as great benefits upon us as we shall be able in any way to counter upon her." Quoted in Guoqi Xu, *Chinese and Americans: A Shared History* (Cambridge, Mass.: Harvard University Press, 2014), 105.
11. James Hevia, *English Lessons: The Pedagogy of Imperialism in Nineteenth Century China* (Durham, N.C.: Duke University Press, 2003).
12. Weng, *Weng Tonghe riji*, 6:2524.
13. Guo Jing 郭晶 and Yi Fan 易帆, *Zijincheng de xuetang: yibu mingqing huangzi jiaoyu jingdian zhi zuo* 紫禁城的學堂一部明清皇子教育經典之作 (Beijing: China Customs, 2006). For more on new books introduced into Guangxu's curriculum, see Chen Lin 陳琳, "Guangxu huangdi de duiwai guannian yanjiu" 光緒皇帝的對外觀念研究 (M.A. thesis, Hunan Normal University, 2012), 15-16.
14. Min Tu-ki, *National Polity and Local Power: The Transformation of Late Imperial China* (Cambridge, Mass.: Harvard University Asia Center, 1990), 123.
15. Stacey Bieler, "'Yan Yongjing,' in the Biographical Dictionary of Chinese Christianity," http://bdcconline.net/en/stories/yan-yongjing, accessed April 10, 2019.
16. Xu Yihua 徐以驊, "Yan Yongjing yu shenggonghui" 顏永京與聖公會, *Jindai Zhongguo*, no. 10 (2000): 193-215; Yan Huiqing 顏惠慶 and Yao Songling 姚崧齡, *Yan Huiqing zizhuan* 顏惠慶自傳 (Taibei: Biographical Literature Publishing, 1973).
17. Zou Zhenhuan, "Guangxu huangdi xue yingyu" 光緒帝學英語, *Wanbao wencui*, no. 17 (2010): 51.
18. Zou, "Guangxu huangdi de yingyu xuexi yu jinru qingmo gongting de yingyu duben," 107-15.
19. Martin, *A Cycle of Cathay*, 317.
20. Zou, "Guangxu huangdi xue yingyu," 51.
21. Timothy Richard, "Daqing da huangdi xuexi yingwen shi" 大清大皇帝學習英文事, *Wan'guo gongbao*, 4, no. 37 (February 1892): 2-3.

22. Richard, "Daqing da huangdi xuexi yingwen shi," 3-4.
23. Martin, *A Cycle of Cathay*, 317.
24. Ji Yaxi 季壓西 and Chen Weimin 陳偉民, *Cong 'tongwen san guan' qibu* 從同文三館'起步 (Beijing: Xueyuan, 2007), 289-96.
25. Zou, "Guangxu huangdi de yingyu xuexi yu jinru qingmo gongting de yingyu duben," 107-15. Guangxu was certainly the best customer. Even in the final years of his life, he sent frequent requests for books covering a wide range of topics related to foreign affairs. In the months before his death, he ordered over fifty books. See Ye Xiaoqing 葉曉青, "Guangxudi zuihou de yuedu shumu" 光緒帝最後的閱讀書目, *Lishi yanjiu*, no. 02 (2007): 180-83.
26. Isaac Taylor Headland, *Court Life in China: The Capital, Its Officials and People* (New York: Revell, 1909), 126-28. The translation of European knowledge into Chinese was of course not an invention of these nineteenth-century Protestant missionaries. They built on the strong foundation and legacy of many others, notably the Jesuits who came before them. See Benjamin Elman, *On Their Own Terms: Science in China, 1550–1900* (Cambridge, Mass.: Harvard University Press, 2005), chaps. 2–5.
27. Robert Ellsworth Lewis, *The Educational Conquest of the Far East* (New York: Revell, 1903), 206.
28. Life and Light, "The Emperor Studying English," *Woman's Missionary Advocate*, August 1893.
29. "Pengshan xiaose" 蓬山曉色, *Shenbao*, January 21, 1893.
30. See, for example, Frank Carpenter, "The Emperor of Japan: A Busy Man Imbued with the Spirit of Progress," *Detroit Free Press*, December 2, 1894.
31. Zhong Dexiang 鍾德祥, "Zou wei jinlai gong wen wo huangshang mao qin dianxue" 奏為近來恭聞我皇上懋勤典學, Guangxu 20.7.16 (Taiwan Digital Archives, Grand Council Archives, doc. no. 133895), http://catalog.digitalarchives.tw/item/00/16/8a/d7.html.
32. Memorial by Yikuang 奕劻, "Zou wei chaming yuan bao fanyi guan shenduo di xian shanxie cuowu qing zhi gengzheng shi" 奏為查明原保翻譯官沈鐸底銜繕寫錯誤請旨更正事, Guangxu 19.12.25 (First Historical Archives, Series of Documents from Various Palace Depositories [宮中全總] [(FHA-GZQZ], doc. no. 04-01-01-0990-009); memorial by unclear author, "Zou wei yingwen zheng fanyi guan houxuan zhang deyi deng yuan qi man qing jiang shi" 奏為英文正翻譯官候選張德彝等員期滿請獎事, Guangxu 19.8.4 (FHA-GZQZ, doc. no. 04-01-12-0560-142).
33. Luke S. K. Kwong, *Mosaic of the Hundred Days: Personalities, Politics, and Ideas of 1898* (Cambridge, Mass.: Harvard University Press, 1984), 60.
34. Weng, *Weng Tonghe riji*, 6:2801-03.
35. "Kiyokuni kōtei no eigo kenkyū" 清國皇帝の英語研究, *Yomiuri shimbun*, July 13, 1895.
36. Alexis Dudden, *Japan's Colonization of Korea: Discourse and Power* (Honolulu: University of Hawaii Press, 2006), 4.
37. Dudden, *Japan's Colonization of Korea*, 59.
38. Nanxiu Qian, "Revitalizing the Xianyuan (Worthy Ladies) Tradition: Women in the 1898 Reforms," *Modern China* 29, no. 4 (October 1, 2003): 405-7.
39. Qian, "Revitalizing the Xianyuan," 418.
40. Paul Bailey, *Gender and Education in China: Gender Discourses and Women's Schooling in the Early Twentieth Century* (New York: Routledge, 2007), 22-23, 162n.66.

41. *Qing shilu* 清實錄 (Beijing: Zhonghua shuju, 1986), 2nd day of 2nd month of 52nd year of Kangxi era, 504-2, hereafter *QSL*; 22nd day of 2th month of 5th year of Yongzheng era, 389-2; 29th day of 8th month of 13th year of Qianlong era, 334-2; 20th day of 12th month of 35th year of Qianlong era, 782-2.
42. Kwong, *Mosaic of the Hundred Days*, 75.
43. Memorial by Pan Qinglan 潘慶瀾, "Zou wei qing fu jingyan yi chong shengxue wei ziqiang zhi ben zonghe rencai deng jingchen guanjian shi" 奏為請復經筵以崇聖學為自強之本綜核人才等敬陳管見事, Guangxu 22.9.13 (First Historical Archives, Grand Council series [軍機處全總] [FHA-JJC], doc. no. 03-5614-021).
44. Peter Zarrow, "Late-Qing Reformism and the Meiji Model: Kang Youwei, Liang Qichao, and the Japanese Emperor," in *The Role of Japan in Liang Qichao's Introduction of Modern Western Civilization to China*, ed. Joshua Fogel (Berkeley: Institute of East Asian Studies, 2004), 40-67.
45. Liang Qichao 梁启超, "Bianfa tongyi" 變法通議, in *Liang Qichao quanji* 梁启超全集 (Beijing: Beijing Publishing, 1999), 12.
46. Huang Zongxi and Wm. Theodore de Bary, *Waiting for the Dawn: A Plan for the Prince* (New York: Columbia University Press, 1993), 4-8, 33-34, 71-73.
47. Zarrow, "Late-Qing Reformism and the Meiji Model," 40-67.
48. Liang Qichao, "Bianfa tongyi," 12.
49. James C. Albisetti, *Secondary School Reform in Imperial Germany* (Princeton, N.J.: Princeton University Press, 1983), 173-74.
50. Foreign commentators had earlier made favorable comparisons between Guangxu and Wilhelm—for example, in 1894, when Guangxu personally supervised a military examination. See Mrs. Archibald Little, *Intimate China: The Chinese as I Have Seen Them* (London: Hutchinson, 1899), 566.
51. Albisetti, *Secondary School Reform*, 3-4.
52. For an in-depth discussion of the late Qing understanding and use of Peter the Great, see Don C. Price, *Russia and the Roots of the Chinese Revolution, 1896–1911* (Cambridge, Mass.: Harvard University Press, 1974), 29-62.
53. Kang Youwei, "Jincheng Eluosi Da bide bianzheng ji xu" 進呈俄羅斯大彼得變政記序, in *Kang Youwei wuxu zhen zouyi* 康有為戊戌真奏議, ed. Huang Zhangjian 黃彰健 (Taibei: Zhongyang yanjiuyaun lishi yuyan yanjiu suo, 1974), 82.
54. Kung-ch'üan Hsiao, "The Case for Constitutional Monarchy: K'ang Yu-Wei's Plan for the Democratization of China," *Monumenta Serica* 24 (January 1, 1965): 27.
55. This theme is found frequently in Kang's writings; see, for example, his Seventh Memorial to the Throne (*shang qingdi di'qi shu* 上清帝第七書), in *Wuxu Bianfa* 戊戌變法, ed. Zhongguo Shixue hui 中國史學會 (Shanghai: Shenzhou guoguang she, 1953), 2:203-6.
56. Yan Fu 嚴復, "Zhong'e jiaoyi lun" 中俄交誼論, in *Wanqing wenxun* 晚清文選, ed. Zheng Zhenduo 鄭振鐸 (Shanghai: Shanghai Shenghuo shudian, 1937), 682-83.
57. Yan Fu, "Shang jin shang huangdi wanyeshu"上今上皇帝萬言書, in Zhongguo Shixue hui, *Wuxu Bianfa*, 2:322.
58. For a comprehensive study on Yan, see Benjamin Schwartz, *In Search of Wealth and Power: Yen Fu and the West* (Cambridge, Mass.: Harvard University Press, 1964).

3. PUTTING LESSONS INTO PRACTICE   209

59. Yan, "Shang jin shang huangdi wanyeshu," 320-21.
60. Yan, "Shang jin shang huangdi wanyeshu," 320-21.
61. Zhang, Quanxue pian, 12, 72.
62. Kwong, Mosaic of the Hundred Days, 130-31; Kang Youwei, Riben bianzheng kao 日本變政考 (Beijing: Forbidden City, 1998), preface 2a.
63. North China Herald, ed., The Emperor Kuang Hsü's Reform Decrees, 1898 (Shanghai: North China Herald, 1900), 4 (January 28, 1898)
64. North China Herald, The Emperor Kuang Hsü's Reform Decrees, 6, February 15, 1898.
65. Society for the Diffusion of Christian and General Knowledge Among the Chinese, Eleventh Annual Report for the Year Ending 31st October 1898 (Shanghai: North China Herald, 1898), 15, 32-35.
66. North China Herald, The Emperor Kuang Hsü's Reform Decrees, 10-11, June 11, 1898.
67. North China Herald, The Emperor Kuang Hsü's Reform Decrees, 14, July 7, 1898.
68. North China Herald, The Emperor Kuang Hsü's Reform Decrees, 10-11 (June 11, 1898.
69. Even before the 1898 reforms, Sun believed that a vibrant university in the capital was crucial to the projection of Qing authority. In 1896, responding to initial calls to form such a school, Sun urged the construction of an expansive campus, arguing that foreign powers would judge the sincerity of Qing reforms based on the construction of the new school. Education reforms were thus directly linked to the ever-present threat of imperialism. Should the Qing be judged sincere in their reform efforts, Sun argued, foreign powers would embrace China into the world community of nations. If the school was not impressive, however, Sun warned it could be used as pretext for more violent pedagogy. Timothy Weston, The Power of Position: Beijing University, Intellectuals, and Chinese Political Culture, 1898–1929 (Berkeley: University of California Press, 2004), 29.
70. North China Herald, The Emperor Kuang Hsü's Reform Decrees, 12-13, June 20, 1898.
71. North China Herald, The Emperor Kuang Hsü's Reform Decrees, 36-37, September 12, 1898.
72. Part of the meeting is reproduced in Ssu-yu Teng and John Fairbank, eds., China's Response to the West, a Documentary Survey, 1839–1923 (Cambridge, Mass.: Harvard University Press, 1954), 179-80. For an account generous to Cixi in its interpretation, see Sue Fawn Chung, "The Much Maligned Empress Dowager: A Revisionist Study of the Empress Dowager Tzǔ-Hsi in the Period 1898-1900" (Ph.D. diss., University of California, Berkeley, 1975), 69-70.
73. North China Herald, The Emperor Kuang Hsü's Reform Decrees, 44, September 21, 1898.
74. North China Herald, The Emperor Kuang Hsü's Reform Decrees, 45 (September 22, 1898); 47-48 (September 29, 1898).
75. North China Herald, The Emperor Kuang Hsü's Reform Decrees, 53-54, October 14, 1898; 54-55, November 1, 1898.
76. North China Herald, The Emperor Kuang Hsü's Reform Decrees, 57 (November 12, 1898).
77. North China Herald, The Emperor Kuang Hsü's Reform Decrees, 45, September 25, 1898; 59, December 1, 1898.
78. Sarah Pike Conger, Letters from China: With Particular Reference to the Empress Dowager and the Women of China (Chicago: McClurg, 1909), 39-41.
79. Conger, Letters from China, 42-43.

80. *QSL*, 27th day of 4th month of 24th year of Guangxu era, 484-1, 484-2.
81. There is debate over who ordered the initial firing of Weng in June. For the two perspectives, see Kwong, *Mosaic of the Hundred Days*, 160–65, 241–42, and Tang Zhijun and Benjamin Elamn, "The 1898 Reforms Revisited: A Review of Luke S. K. Kwong's *A Mosaic of the Hundred Days: Personalities, Politics, and Ideas of 1898*," *Late Imperial China* 8, no. 1 (June 1987): 211–12.
82. *QSL*, 21st day of 10th month of 24th year of Guangxu era, 674-1, 674-2. Modified translation from version published in North China Herald, *The Emperor Kuang Hsü's Reform Decrees*, 59, December 4, 1898.
83. *North China Herald*, *The Emperor Kuang Hsü's Reform Decrees*, 59, December 4, 1898. Modified translation.
84. For a study of the ways in which Kang, and to a lesser extent Liang, used the press and groups such as the Baohuanghui to became more influential in creating the narrative of 1898 than they were in the actual reform efforts, see Sang Bing 桑兵, *Gengzi qinwang yu wan qing zhengju* 庚子勤王與晚清政局 (Beijing: Beijing daxue chubanshe, 2004).

4. CIXI'S PEDAGOGY

1. Ellen Klempner, "Memories of the Chinese Imperial Civil Service Examination by Shang Yen-Liu," *American Asian Review* 3, no. 1 (Spring 1985): 73.
2. Joshua Hill, *Voting as a Rite: A History of Elections in Modern China* (Cambridge, Mass.: Harvard University Asia Center, 2019), 55, 65.
3. In some ways, this project built on earlier efforts both by Cixi and the international community to use gender and gift exchange to rethink the sovereignty of the Qing. See Lydia Liu, *The Clash of Empires: The Invention of China in Modern World Making* (Cambridge, Mass.: Harvard University Press, 2004), 140–80. The project also shares much with Maurizio Peleggi's analysis of the Siam monarchy in which he argues that their "consumer behavior" was a key factor in presenting themselves both as distinctly national leaders while also members of the world aristocratic community. Peleggi, *Lord of Things: The Fashioning of the Siamese Monarchy's Modern Image* (Honolulu: University of Hawaii Press, 2002), 20.
4. I have previously examined some of these issues in Daniel Barish, "Empress Dowager Cixi's Imperial Pedagogy: The School for Female Nobles and New Visions of Authority in Early Twentieth Century China," *Nan Nü: Men, Women, and Gender in China* 20, no. 2 (2018): 256–84.
5. Elisabeth Kaske has recently examined similar dynamics through the lens of the exchange of orders and medals in her study of the "transnational history of monarchic nation-building" and the "development of a common visual imagery of rulership" around the turn of the twentieth century. See Kaske, "The Pitfalls of Transnational Distinction: A Royal Exchange of Honors and Contested Sovereignty in Late Qing China," in *China and the World, the World and China: A Transcultural Perspective: Essays in Honor of Rudolf G. Wagner*, ed. Barbara Mittler et al. (Gossenberg, Ger.: Ostasien, 2019), 2:137–69.
6. Sun Yat-sen, "A Refutation of an Article in the *Pao-huang Pao*," in *Prescriptions for Saving China, Selected Writings of Sun Yat-sen*, ed. Julie Lee Wai (Stanford, Calif.: Stanford University Press, 1994), 31.

7. *Qing shilu* 清實錄 (Beijing: Zhonghua shuju, 1986), 24th day of 12th month of 25th year of Guangxu era, 1026-1, 1026-2. Hereafter cited as *QSL*.
8. Yongming Zhou, *Historicizing Online Politics: Telegraphy, the Internet, and Political Participation in China* (Stanford, Calif.: Stanford University Press, 2006), 59-60, 64-65.
9. *QSL*, 5th day of 1st month of 26th year of Guangxu era, 3-2.
10. *QSL*, 7th day of 1st month of 26th year of Guangxu era, 5-1.
11. *QSL*, 6th day of 4th month of 26th year of Guangxu era, 54-2.
12. *Zhongyang yanjiuyuan lishi yuyan yanjiu suo* 中央研究院歷史語言研究所 (Institute of History and Philology, Academia Sinica), Grand Secretariat Archives Project, Biographical Packet no. 004453, accessed at http://archive.ihp.sinica.edu.tw/ttscgi/ttsquery?0:18721130:mctauac:TM%3D%B2%BB%A6%EB, March 22, 2017.
13. This is not to say that the divide was Chinese versus Manchu/Mongolian. Pamela Kyle Crossley deftly shows the nuanced and varied Manchu positions in *Orphan Warriors: Three Manchu Generations and the End of the Qing World* (Princeton, N.J.: Princeton University Press, 1990), 173-79.
14. Arthur W. Hummel, ed., *Eminent Chinese of the Ch'ing Period (1644–1912)* (Washington, D.C.: U.S. Government Printing Office, 1944), 209.
15. Hummel, *Eminent Chinese*, 174.
16. Joseph Esherick, *The Origins of the Boxer Uprising* (Berkeley: University of California Press, 1987), 285-90.
17. James Hevia, *English Lessons: The Pedagogy of Imperialism in Nineteenth Century China* (Durham, N.C.: Duke University Press, 2003), 197-202, 229.
18. Edward J. M. Rhoads, *Manchus and Han: Ethnic Relations and Political Power in Late Qing and Early Republican China, 1861–1928* (Seattle: University of Washington Press, 2000), 72-73; Aixinjueluo Zaifeng 愛新覺羅載灃, *Chun qin wang Zaifeng riji* 醇親王載灃日記 (Beijing: Qunzhong chuban she, 2014), 70.
19. Hummel, *Eminent Chinese*, 209.
20. Hevia, *English Lessons*, 250-53.
21. Sarah Pike Conger, *Letters from China: With Particular Reference to the Empress Dowager and the Women of China* (Chicago: McClurg, 1909), 217.
22. Conger, *Letters from China*, 218.
23. Susan Mary Keppel Townley, *My Chinese Note Book* (New York: Methuen, 1904), 267.
24. Conger, *Letters from China*, 221.
25. Lien-sheng Yang, "Female Rulers in Imperial China," *Harvard Journal of Asiatic Studies* 23 (1960-1961): 47-61.
26. Huishu Lee, *Empresses, Art, & Agency in Song Dynasty China* (Seattle: University of Washington Press, 2010); Shuo Wang, "Qing Imperial Women: Empresses, Concubines, and Aisin Gioro Daughters," in *Servants of the Dynasty: Palace Women in World History*, ed. Anne Walthall (Berkeley: University of California Press, 2008), 137-71.
27. David Cannadine, "The Context, Performance, and Meaning of Ritual: The British Monarchy and the Invention of Tradition, 1820-1977," in *The Invention of Tradition*, ed. Eric Hobsbawm and Terence Ranger (Cambridge: Cambridge University Press, 1983), 120.

28. John Plunkett, *Queen Victoria: First Media Monarch* (Oxford: Oxford University Press, 2003), 7, 240. Photography was also central to imagining the emperor in Japan and creating an emperor-centered nation. See Morris Low, *Japan on Display: Photography and the Emperor* (New York: Routledge, 2006).
29. Katherine Carl, *With the Empress Dowager of China* (New York: Century, 1907), 206-7. Cixi was not alone in seeing a connection between herself and Victoria. During the Boxer Uprising, Gu Hongming (1857-1928) had argued that "the only solution to the Anglo-Chinese conflict is to let the female heads of state speak directly to each other," and Gu saw Cixi and Victoria as equals, each the mother of the counties. See Liu, *Clash of Empires*, 176-77.
30. Conger, *Letters from China*, 217-18; Townley, *My Chinese Note Book*, 267. See also Peng, "Staging Sovereignty," 64.
31. Wu Hong, "Emperor's Masquerade: 'Costume Portraits' of Yongzheng and Qianlong," *Orientations* 26, no. 7 (1995): 25-41. There are, however, a few examples of Ming/Qing imperial portraits being used in diplomatic exchange. See Jan Stuart and Evelyn Rawski, *Worshipping Ancestors: Chinese Commemorative Portraits* (Washington, D.C.: Freer Gallery of Art, 2001), 140.
32. Cheng-hua Wang, "Going Public: Portraits of the Empress Dowager Cixi, Circa 1904," *Nan Nü* 14, no. 1 (2012): 119-76.
33. Wang, "Going Public," 138; David Hogge, "Empress Dowager and the Camera," MIT Visualizing Cultures, http://ocw.mit.edu/ans7870/21f/21f.027/empress_dowager.
34. Hogge, "Empress Dowager and the Camera"; Ying-chen Peng, "Lingering Between Tradition and Innovation: Photographic Portraits of Empress Dowager Cixi," *Ars Orientalis* 43 (2013): 157.
35. Wang, "Going Public," 175.
36. Hogge, "Empress Dowager and the Camera"; Peng, "Lingering Between Tradition and Innovation," 157-74; Carl, *With the Empress Dowager*, 206-20; Claire Roberts, "The Empress Dowager's Birthday: The Photographs of Cixi's Long Life Without End," *Ars Orientalis* 43 (2013): 176-95.
37. Conger, *Letters from China*, 247-48.
38. Carl, *With the Empress Dowager*, 12, 131-32. See also Katharine A. Carl, "A Personal Estimate of the Character of the Late Empress Dowager, Tze-Hsi," *Journal of Race Development* 4, no. 1 (1913): 58-71. Interestingly, Carl notes that Cixi encouraged her to learn Manchu instead of Chinese, as the empress dowager thought it would be easier for a foreigner to grasp.
39. "Painting an Empress," *New York Times*, December 17, 1905; Luke S. K. Kwong, "No Shadows," *History Today* (September 2000): 42-43.
40. Conger, *Letters from China*, 352. For an analysis of the practice from the Kangxi era, see Jonathan Hay, "The Kangxi Emperor's Brush-Traces: Calligraphy, Writing, and the Art of Imperial Authority," in *Body and Face in Chinese Visual Culture*, ed. Wu Hong (Cambridge, Mass.: Harvard University Press, 2005), 311-33.
41. "Peking: Imperial Audiences Sir Robert Hart Next to Be Received," *North China Herald*, March 12, 1902.
42. "Miscellaneous Articles," *North China Herald*, March 19, 1902.
43. "Benguo xueshi" 本國學事, *Jiaoyu shijie* 教育世界 85 (1904): 1. Another component of the court's efforts to engage with the international community was the increase in members of the imperial family sent to study abroad. See Wang Xiuli 王秀麗, "Wanqing guizhou liuxue xingqi

yuanyin tansuo" 晚清貴冑留學興起原因探索, *Qingdao daxue shifan xueyuan xuebao* 25, no. 1 (2008): 57-61.
44. "Painting and Empress," *New York Times*, December 17, 1905.
45. "Miscellaneous Articles," *North China Herald*, March 19, 1902.
46. Margaret Ernestine Burton, *The Education of Women in China* (New York: Revell, 1911), 114-17.
47. Peter Zarrow, *Educating China: Knowledge, Society, and Textbooks in a Modernizing World, 1902–1937* (Cambridge: Cambridge University Press, 2015), 11-18.
48. Paul Bailey, *Gender and Education in China: Gender Discourses and Women's Schooling in the Early Twentieth Century* (New York: Routledge, 2007), 27-28.
49. Xiaoping Cong, *Teachers' Schools and the Making of the Modern Chinese Nation-State, 1897–1937* (Vancouver: University of British Columbia Press, 2007), 35, 53; Bailey, *Gender and Education*, 26.
50. "Female Education," *World's Chinese Students' Journal* 1, no. 1 (1906): 3.
51. For an insightful exploration of the development of constitutional thinking, see Xiaowei Zheng, *The Politics of Rights and the 1911 Revolution in China* (Stanford, Calif.: Stanford University Press, 2018), particularly 61-75, 109-19. In addition to notions such as patriotism and representation that others have explored in connection with the development of constitutional thinking, Elisabeth Kaske has shown how many Chinese intellectuals saw constitutions as a powerful way to extract additional tax revenue from the population. See her "Taxation, Trust, and Government Debt: State-Elite Relations in Sichuan, 1850–1911," *Modern China* 45, no. 3 (2019): 278.
52. "Our Travelling Commissioners," *World's Chinese Students' Journal* 1, no. 1 (1906): 2.
53. Peter Zarrow, "Constitutionalism and the Imagination of the State: Official Views of Political Reform in the Late Qing," *Creating Chinese Modernity: Knowledge and Everyday Life, 1900–1940*, ed. Zarrow (New York: P. Lang, 2006), 51-82.
54. Wei Qingyuan 韋慶遠, Gao Fang 高放, and Liu Wenyuan 劉文源, *Qing mo xianzheng shi* 清末憲政史 (Beijing: Zhongguo renmin daxue chuban she, 1993), 49-84.
55. See, for example, Kang Youwei's "Seventh Memorial to the Throne" (*Shang qingdi di'qi shu* 上清帝第七書), in *Wuxu Bianfa*, ed. Zhongguo Shixue hui, 2:203-6.
56. Zarrow, "Constitutionalism and the Imagination of the State," 51.
57. "Xuanshi yubei lixian xianxing liding guanzhi yu" 宣示預備立憲先行釐定官制諭, in *Qing mo chou bei li xian dang'an shi liao* 清末籌備立憲檔案史料, ed. Gugong bowuyuan Ming-Qing dang'an bu 故宮博物院明清檔案部 (Beijing: Zhonghua shu ju, 1979), 43.
58. Norbert Meienberger, *The Emergence of Constitutional Government in China (1905–1908): The Concept Sanctioned by the Empress Dowager Tzu-Hsi* (Bern, Switz.: P. Lang, 1980), 44.
59. Linda Colley, "Writing Constitutions and Writing World History," in *The Prospect of Global History*, ed. James Belich (Oxford: Oxford University Press, 2016), 160-77. The Qing, as Japan had done, was developing a constitution and promoting itself as constitutionally legitimated state to gain equal footing in the international community. For more on Japan's process, see Takii Kazuhiro, *The Meiji Constitution: The Japanese Experience of the West and the Shaping of the Modern State* (Tokyo: International House, 2007).
60. "A School for Noble Ladies," *World's Chinese Students' Journal* 1, no. 3 (1906): 45.
61. The name of the school defies simple translation. *Yu* 毓 carries connotations of both giving birth and education, while *kun* 坤, one of the eight trigrams, may be said to represent female

principles of nature and earth. The name also conjures associations with the Yikun gong 翊坤宮 (Palace of Earthly Honor), one of Cixi's palaces in the Forbidden City.

62. Huang Xiangjin 黃湘金, "Guizhou nü xuetang kaolun" 貴冑女學堂考論, *Beijing Shehui Kexue* 3 (2009): 59-67.
63. Although individual Chinese officials had been rewarded for meritorious service with noble titles in the past, these were isolated cases. As Edward Rhoads has demonstrated, differentiated treatment of Manchus and Han remained a tenet of Qing governance throughout the second half of the nineteenth century. Rhoads describes a gradual easing of barriers and restrictions between the groups in the twentieth century, but he argues that it was not until 1907 that Cixi embraced the idea. Already in 1904, however, we see that in the realm of female education, Cixi appeared ready to expand the conception of nobility to include both Manchu and Chinese women. See Rhoads, *Manchus and Han*, 7, 35, 120.
64. Junji Banno, *The Establishment of the Japanese Constitutional System* (New York: Routledge, 1992), 2-3.
65. "Shishi yaowen" 時事要聞, *Dagong bao*, October 11, 1905.
66. Liu Jinzao, *Qingchao xu wenxian tongkao*, 114:8730-31.
67. Feng Yueran 馮月然, "Lujun guizhou xuetang yanjiu" 陸軍貴冑學堂研究 (M.A. thesis, Zhongyang Minzu University, 2010); Sun Yanjing 孫燕京, "Guizhou xuetang yu qingmo guizu" 貴冑學堂與清末貴族 (M.A. thesis, Beijing Normal University, 2005).
68. For background on the variety of schools created for members of the Qing imperial elite, see Pamela Kyle Crossley, "Manchu Education," in *Education and Society in Late Imperial China*, ed. Benjamin Elman and Alexander Woodside (Berkeley: University of California Press, 1994), 340-78.
69. Wang Dongliang 王棟亮, "Qingmo lujun guizhou xuetang shulüe" 清末陸軍貴冑學堂述略, *Lishi dang'an* 4 (2008): 60-64.
70. "Yu ni sheli huangzu nü xuetang" 諭擬設立皇族女學堂, *Shenbao*, December 1, 1905.
71. For a brief history of the school, see Joshi Gakushūin, ed., *Joshi Gakushūin gojunenshi* 女子學習院五十年史 (Tokyo: Joshi Gakushuin, 1935). For more on Empress Haruko's ventures in education, see Mamiko C. Suzuki, *Gendered Power: Educated Women of the Meiji Empress' Court* (Ann Arbor: University of Michigan Press), 13-37.
72. "Yi jian" 譯件, *Dagong bao*, July 30, 1902.
73. As early as 1897, the Qing minister to Japan published the complete regulations and curriculum for the school as part of the court's broader project of seeking models of educational reform. See "Riben huazu nü xuexiao guize" 日本華族女學校規則, in *Lingjiange congshu* 靈鶼閣叢書, ed. Jiang Biao 江標 (Taipei: Yiwen yinshuguan, 1964), vol. 81, np. In 1903 Zaizhen 載振 (1876-1947) visited the Peeresses' School as part of a larger project of investigating educational practices across the globe. For an account of the visit, see Timothy Richard, *Forty-Five Years in China: Reminiscences* (New York: Stokes, 1916), 319-20. For Zaichen's trip and his notes on schools, see Zaizhen 載振, *Yingyao riji* 英軺日記 (Taipei: Wenhai chubanshe, 1972), 120, 196, 223, 281, 360.
74. Huang Xiangjin, "Guizhou nü xuetang kaolun," 61.
75. "Tie dachen changtan yaozheng" 鐵大臣暢談要政, *Dagong bao*, October 25, 1906.

76. Joan Judge, "The Culturally Contested Student Body: Nü Xuesheng at the Turn of the Twentieth Century," in *Performing "Nation:" Gender Politics in Literature, Theater, and the Visual Arts of China and Japan, 1880–1940*, ed. Doris Croissant, Catherine Vance Yeh, and Joshua S. Mostow (Leiden: Brill, 2008), 122.
77. "Yi she guizhou nü xuetang" 議設貴冑女學堂, *Huanqiu Zhongguo xuesheng bao* 1, no. 2 (1906), 72; "Yi she guizhou nü xuetang" 議設貴冑女學堂, *Guangyi congbao* 4, no. 22 (1906): 22.
78. "Qing di ni juan lian chang she guizhou nü xuetang" 慶邸擬捐廉倡設貴冑女學堂, *Shenbao*, July 26, 1906.
79. "Sheli guizhou nü xuetang xuwen" 設立貴冑女學堂續聞, *Jiaoyu zazhi* 22 (1906): 60.
80. "Shengong zhuzhong nü xue" 深宮注重女學, *Dagong bao*, January 14, 1906; "Liang gong chuixun xuewu" 兩宮垂詢學務, *Dagong bao*, February 19, 1906.
81. "Tie dachen changtan yaozheng" 鐵大臣暢談要政, *Dagong bao*, October 25, 1906.
82. "To Promote Female Education," *Chinese Students' Bulletin* (U.S.) 2, no. 3 (1907): 54; "A School for the Nobility," *Chinese Students' Bulletin* (U.S.) 2, no. 4 (1907): 80.
83. "Qing she biaoben chenliesuo" 請設標本陳列所, *Dagong bao*, September 18, 1906.
84. "Yi she guizhou nü xuetang" 議設貴冑女學堂, *Huanqiu Zhongguo xuesheng bao* 1, nos. 5–6 (1907): 93.
85. "Article 1: No Title," *North China Herald*, March 15, 1907; "Zhi du mi bao guizhou nü xuetang zongban" 直督密保貴冑女學堂總辦, *Shenbao*, April 14, 1907.
86. "Lun bian guizhou nü xuetang zhangcheng" 諭編貴冑女學堂草程, *Shenbao*, May 3, 1907.
87. "Yi bao" 譯報, *Dagong bao*, July 30, 1907.
88. "Xian she guizhou nü xuetang yu Nanhai" 先設貴冑女學堂於南海, *Da tongbao* 8, no. 14 (1907): 29.
89. "Chang li guizhou nü xuetang" 倡立貴冑女學堂, *Zhili jiaoyu zazhi*, no. 17 (1907): 107.
90. "The Daughters of Nobles School," *North China Herald*, November 8, 1907.
91. "Guizhou nü xuetang you sheng zuli" 貴冑女學又生阻力, *Shenbao*, April 19, 1907.
92. Cong, *Teachers' Schools*, 52–57.
93. Joan Judge, "Talent, Virtue, and the Nation: Chinese Nationalisms and Female Subjectivities in the Early Twentieth Century," *American Historical Review* 106, no. 3 (2001): 777.
94. Huang Xiangjin, "Guizhou nü xuetang kaolun, 6n.24.
95. Huang Xiangjin 黃湘金, "Wanqing Beijing nüzi jiaoyu lan yao" 晚清北京女子教育攬要, *Jindai Zhongguo funü shi yanjiu* 25 (June 2015): 203.
96. "Qian chushi Riben Fa De suiyuan xie zuyuan zi ban yiyi nü xuetang" 前出使日本法德隨員謝祖沅自辦譯藝女學堂, *Xuebu guanbao* 10 (1906): np.
97. Huang, "Wanqing beijing nüzi jiaoyu lan yao," 203.
98. Xia Xiaohong 夏曉虹, "Wanqing nüxue zhong de Man Han maodun: huxing zisha shijian jiedu" 晚清女學中的滿漢矛盾: 惠興自殺事件解讀, *Ershiyi shijie shuangyue kan* 36 (December 2012): 113.
99. Weikun Cheng, "Going Public Through Education: Female Reformers and Girls' Schools in Late Qing Beijing," *Late Imperial China* 21, no. 1 (2000): 121–28.
100. The planned National Assembly had two hundred seats, one hundred of which the emperor would personally select. Of the eight categories of people eligible for membership, four were explicitly reserved for members of the imperial family and the hereditary service nobility. See

Zhang Pengyuan 張朋園, *Lixian pai yu xinhai geming* 立憲派與辛亥革命 (Taibei: Zhongyang yanjiuyuan jindai shi yanjiusuo, 1969), 313–20.

101. "Yu chi huangzu jiangqiu xianzheng" 諭飭皇族講求憲政, *Datong bao* 10, no. 3 (1908): 28; "Duo peiyang huangshi yingcai" 多培養皇室英才, *Datong bao* 10, no. 20 (1908): 29.
102. Chen Dong 陳東, "Qingdai jingyan zhidu yanjiu" 清代經筵制度研究 (Ph.D. dissertation, Shandong University, 2006), 32, 64.
103. Zhang Yijun 張毅君 "Wei guangxu di jinjiang 'geguo zhenglue gao'" 為光緒帝進講各國政略稿, in *Jindai shi ziliao zong 104 hao* 近代史資料總104 號, ed. Li Xuetong 李學通 (Beijing: Zhongguo shehui kexue chubanshe, 2002), 1–50.
104. "Jingshi jinxin" 京師近信, *Shenbao*, May 13, 1908.
105. Hill, *Voting as a Rite*, 70
106. "Chinese News," *North China Herald*, May 1, 1909.
107. Hiroshi Abe, "Borrowing from Japan: China's First Modern Educational System," in *China's Education and the Industrialized World*, ed. Ruth Hayhoe and Marianne Bastid (Armonk, N.Y.: M. E. Sharpe, 1987), 61–65; Paul Bailey, *Reform the People: Changing Attitudes Towards Popular Education in Early Twentieth Century China* (Cambridge, Mass.: Harvard University Press, 1971), 32; 59; Zarrow, *Educating China*, 21.
108. Ya-pei Kuo, "'The Emperor and the People in One Body': The Worship of Confucius and Ritual Planning in the Xinzheng Reforms, 1902–1911," *Modern China* 35, no. 2 (March 1, 2009), 139–40.
109. Timothy Weston, *The Power of Position: Beijing University, Intellectuals, and Chinese Political Culture, 1898–1929* (Berkeley: University of California Press, 2004), 53.
110. "Emperor's Birthday," *North China Herald*, August 11, 1905.
111. Bailey, *Gender and Education*, 72.
112. Arthur Henderson Smith, *China and America to-Day; a Study of Conditions and Relations* (New York: Revell, 1907), 118.
113. Catherine Jami, *The Emperor's New Mathematics: Western Learning and Imperial Authority During the Kangxi Reign (1662–1722)* (Oxford: Oxford University Press, 2012), 236; Fuge 福格, *Ting yu cong tan* 聽雨叢談 (Beijing: Zhonghua shuju, 1984), 218–19; Benjamin Elman, *A Cultural History of Civil Examinations in Late Imperial China* (Berkeley: University of California Press, 2000), 129.
114. Stefan Tanaka, *New Times in Modern Japan* (Princeton, N.J.: Princeton University Press, 2004), 16; Véronique Bénéï, *Manufacturing Citizenship: Education and Nationalism in Europe, South Asia and China* (London: Routledge, 2005), 244.
115. Peter Zarrow, "The New Schools and National Identity: Chinese History Textbooks in the Late Qing," in *The Politics of Historical Production in Late Qing and Republican China*, ed. Tze-Ki Hon and Robert Culp (Boston: Brill, 2007), 51.
116. Brian Moloughney and Peter Zarrow, "Making History Modern: The Transformation of Chinese Historiography, 1895–1937," in *Transforming History: The Making of a Modern Academic Discipline in Twentieth-Century China*, ed. Brian Moloughney and Peter Zarrow (Hong Kong: Chinese University Press, 2011), 12–13.
117. Zarrow, *Educating China*, 150.

118. For examples of these narratives, see Shanghai Commercial Press, ed., *Gaodeng xiaoxue zhongguo lishi jiaokeshu* (高等小學中國歷史教科書) (Shanghai: Shanghai Commercial Press, 1903 [1910]); Chen Maozhi 陳懋治, *Gaodeng xiaoxue zhongguo lishi jiaokeshu* (高等小學中國歷史教科書) (Shanghai: Shanghai wenming shuju, 1904); Yao Zuyi 姚祖義, *Zuixin zhongguo lishi jiaoke shu* 最新中國歷史教科書 (Shanghai: Shanghai Commercial Press, 1908); Jiang Weixiang 蔣維香, *Chudeng xiaoxue jianming zhongguo lishi jiaokeshu* 初等小學簡明中國歷史教科書 (Shanghai: Shanghai Commercial Press, 1908 [1911]); Guomin jiaoyu she, ed., *Xinti gaodeng xiaoxue zhongguo lishi* 新體高等小學中國歷史 (Shanghai: Wenming shuju, 1910).
119. Sally Bothwick, *Education and Social Change in China: The Beginning of the Modern Era* (Stanford, Calif.: Hoover Institute Press, 1983), 139.
120. "Chinese News," *North China Herald*, April 10, 1909; "Dezong jing huangdi jinian dahui" 德宗景皇帝紀念大會, *Shenbao*, August 16, 1909.
121. "Imperial Funeral Expenses," *North China Herald*, December 5, 1908.
122. "Funeral of the Late Emperor of China," *North China Herald*, April 24, 1909," "The Month," *Chinese Recorder and Missionary Journal*, June 1, 1909.
123. Tseng-Tsai Wang, "The Audience Question—Foreign Representatives and the Emperor of China, 1858-1873," *Historical Journal* 14, no. 3 (September 1971): 622.
124. "The Emperor's Funeral," *North China Herald*, May 8, 1909.
125. "Chinese News," *North China Herald*, April 10, 1909.
126. Quoted in Margareta T. J. Grießler, "The Last Dynastic Funeral: Ritual Sequence at the Demise of the Empress Dowager Cixi," *Oriens Extremus* 34, no. 1/2 (1991): 23.
127. Jun Zhang, "Spider Manchu: Duanfang as Networker and Spindoctor of the Late Qing New Policies, 1901-1911" (Ph.D. diss., University of California, San Diego, 2008), 221.
128. Takashi Fujitani, *Splendid Monarchy: Power and Pageantry in Modern Japan* (Berkeley: University of California Press, 1996), 146-54.
129. Burton, *The Education of Women in China*, 22.
130. Isaac Taylor Headland, *Court Life in China: The Capital, Its Officials and People* (New York: Revell, 1909), 72-73.
131. Diao Minqian 刁敏謙 (M. T. Z. Tyau 刁德仁), "The Educational Reform of China," *World's Chinese Students' Journal* 7 (1912): 53.
132. "Ni she huangzu xuetang" 擬設皇族學堂, *Zhili jiaoyu zazhi*, no. 16 (1906):1; "Ni she huangzu xuetang" 擬設皇族學堂, *Shenbao*, August 25, 1906.
133. Memorial by Zhao Binglin 趙炳麟, "Zou wei peizhi huangshi rencai qing ban zhao chongkai shangshufang ze xue zhengpin duan su fu ziwang dachen wei zong shifu jing chen guanjian shi" 奏為培植皇室人才請頒詔重開上書房擇學正品端夙負望大臣總師傅敬陳管見事, Guangxu 34.10.14 (First Historical Archives, FHA-GZQZ, doc. no. 04-01-11-0014-002).
134. "Huangtaihou zhuzhong quanye hui" 皇太后注重勸業會, *Tongwen bao*, no. 410 (1910): 6; "Huangshang dianxue jinwen" 皇上典學近聞, *Dagong bao* (Tianjin), August 15, 1910.
135. Rhoads, *Manchus and Han*, 132.
136. "Editorials, Prince Ch'un the Regent," *World's Chinese Students' Journal* 3 (November-December 1908), 133.
137. Editorials, "Prince Ch'un the Regent," 134.

138. Headland, *Court Life in China*, 171–82.
139. "Tang Shouqian zouchen cunwang daji" 湯壽潛奏陳存亡大計, *Shenbao*, March 24, 1910.
140. Rhoads, *Manchus and Han*, 154–56.

5. LEARNING TO BE A CONSTITUTIONAL MONARCH, 1908–1912

1. Liu Jinzao 劉錦藻, *Qingchao xu wenxian tongkao* 清朝續文獻通考 (Shanghai: Commercial Press, 1936), 176:9251.
2. "Chinese News," *North China Herald*, September 16, 1911.
3. *Qing shilu xuantong zhengji* 清實錄宣統政紀 (Beijing: Zhonghua shuju, 1986), 18th day of 7th month of 3rd year of Xuantong era, 1050-2, 1051-1.
4. "Shi taibao liqing huangshang quanxue" 世太保力請皇上勤學, *Dagong bao*, January 31, 1912.
5. "Huangshang dianxue zhi wen" 皇上典學誌聞, *Dagong bao*, February 12, 1909.
6. This was true in a variety of other venues as well. Joshua Hill, for example, has recently shown how a key purpose of elections and related activities in the late Qing was to provide space for the government to "inculcate the people with the attitudes and ideas deemed necessary for the recreation of China as a modern nation-state" and reinforce the relationship between ruler and ruled. Hill, *Voting as a Rite: A History of Elections in Modern China* (Cambridge, Mass.: Harvard University Press, 2019), 8–9, 70.
7. Liu, *Qingchao xu wenxian tongkao*, 394:11444.
8. Douglas Reynolds, *China, 1898–1912: The Xinzheng Revolution and Japan* (Honolulu: University of Hawaii Press, 2002), 189.
9. Xiaowei Zheng, *The Politics of Rights and the 1911 Revolution in China* (Stanford, Calif.: Stanford University Press, 2018), 114.
10. Lin Mingde 林明德, "Qingmo minchu riben zhengzhi dui zhongguo de yingxiang" 清末民初日本政制對中國的影響, in *Sino-Japanese Cultural Interchange: The Economic and Intellectual Aspects*, ed. Yue him Tam (Hong Kong: Institute of Chinese Studies, 1985), 195–96.
11. "Zhongguo lixian zhi mibao" 中國立憲之秘寶, *Shenbao*, January 26, 1909.
12. "Jinhuang dianxue" 今皇典學, *Shenbao*, September 11, 1911.
13. Henry Fletcher, "Education of the Young Emperor of China," *U.S. Department of State Pamphlets*, vol. 13 (Department of State, Division of Information, Series "D," no. 25, China, no. 4), 1, 2.
14. "Huangshang dianxue jiwen" 皇上典學紀聞, *Shenbao*, May 15, 1909.
15. "Huangshang dianxue jiwen."
16. "Huangshang dianxue gong ni banfa" 皇上典學恭擬辦法, *Jiaoyu zazhi* 1, no. 6 (1909): 37; "Huangshang dianxue gong ni banfa jiwen" 皇上典學恭擬辦法紀聞, *Sichuan jiaoyu guanbao*, no. 6 (1909): 1.
17. Tang Shouqian 湯壽潛, "Tang Shouqian zou chen cunwang daji" 湯壽潛奏陳存亡大計, *Shenbao*, March 23, 1910.
18. "Huangshang dianxue zhangzhi" 皇上典學章制, *Dagong bao* (Tianjin), May 7, 1910.
19. Jinliang 金梁, "Jinliang chengqing daizou jingchen huangshang dianxue shiyi shu" 金梁呈請代奏敬陳皇上典學事宜書, *Shenbao*, May 31, 1911.

20. For the process by which the term *kexue* 科學 replaced the earlier notion of *gezhi xue* 格致學, thus hiding a rich tradition of scientific inquiry, see Benjamin A. Elman, "From Pre-Modern Chinese Natural Studies to Modern Science in China," in Mapping *Meanings: The Field of New Learning in Late Qing China*, ed. Michael Lackner and Natascha Vittinghoff (Leiden: Brill, 2004), 25–73.
21. "Huangshang dianxue shiyi" 皇上典學事宜, *Datong bao* 10, no. 21 (1908): 32–33; "Jishi benguo zhi bu huangshang dianxue zhi yubei" 記事本國之部皇上典學之預備, *Jiaoyu zazhi* 1, no. 10 (1909): 71.
22. "Gongni dianxue zhangcheng zhi shenzhong" 恭擬典學章程之慎重, *Dagong bao*, June 4, 1910.
23. Memorial by Pang Hongshu 龐鴻書, "Zou wei huangshang dianxue zhi nian shen xuan shizi bo fang xuexing jiao xiu zhongwai jiantong zhi ru bu juguan jie zhuanru shijiang jingchen guanjian shi" 奏為皇上典學之年慎選師資博訪學行交修中外兼通之儒不拘管階准入侍講敬陳管見事, Xuantong 1.2.10 (First Historical Archives, GZQZ, doc. no. 04-01-12-0672-006).
24. "Jianguo yi xuan kexue dishi" 監國議選科學帝師, *Dagong bao*, February 27, 1910; "Jishi benguo zhi bu huangshang dianxue zhi choubei" 記事本國之部皇上典學之籌備, *Jiaoyu zazhi* 1, no. 2 (1910):11.
25. "Huangshang dianxue xuanze dishi jinzi" 皇上典學選擇帝師謹志, *Guangyi congbao*, no. 231 (1910): 1.
26. "Huangshang dianxue jinwen" 皇上典學近聞, *Dagong bao*, August 15, 1910.
27. "Huangshang dianxue shangke conghuan" 皇上典學尚可從緩, *Dagong bao*, November 22, 1910; "Huangshang dianxue zhi conghuan" 皇上典學之從緩, *Dagong bao*, February 9, 1911.
28. "Shangyu" 上諭, *Shenbao*, July 11, 1911. Modified translation from "Imperial Decrees," *North China Herald*, July 15, 1911.
29. "Imperial Decrees," July 15, 1911.
30. "Imperial Decrees," July 15, 1911.
31. Aixinjueluo Zaifeng 愛新覺羅載灃, *Chun qin wang Zaifeng riji* 醇親王載灃日記 (Beijing: Qunzhong chuban she, 2014), 307–10, 337.
32. "Shiping" 時評, *Shenbao*, July 12, 1911.
33. "Black Monday," *North China Herald*, September 16, 1911.
34. "Bideyuan zhi rencai yu dizhi" 弼德院之人才與地址, *Shenbao*, May 26, 1911.
35. Lu goes on to lament the fact that charging tuition of "100 times" what it used to be will lead to the impoverishment of students. See Zhao Erxun 趙爾巽, ed., *Qing shigao* 清史稿 (Taibei: Hong shi chubanshe, 1981), 259:12815–19.
36. Lu Runxiang 陸潤庠, ed., *Zhongwai cewen daguan* 中外策問大觀 (Shanghai: Yangeng shanzhuang, 1903).
37. "Lu shifu yinggai zuo deyi yu" 陸師傅應該作得意語, *Shenbao*, July 17, 1911.
38. Juan Wang, *Merry Laughter and Angry Curses: The Shanghai Tabloid Press, 1897–1911* (Vancouver: University of British Columbia Press, 2012), 22–23, 54; Joan Judge, *Print and Politics: "Shibao" and the Culture of Reform in Late Qing China* (Stanford, Calif.: Stanford University Press, 1996), 147.
39. "Guonei jinyao xinwen: Chen Baochen jiang wei dishi" 國內緊要新聞陳寶琛將為帝師, *Datong bao* 13, no. 13 (1910): 28.
40. Edward J. M. Rhoads, *Manchus and Han: Ethnic Relations and Political Power in Late Qing and Early Republican China, 1861–1928* (Seattle: University of Washington Press, 2000), 162.
41. "Chen shilang gai jian dishi yuanyin" 陳侍郎改簡帝師原因, *Shenbao*, July 16, 1911.

42. "Li dianlin buyuan wei jiyan dachen" 李殿林不願為禁烟大臣, *Shenbao*, July 19, 1911.
43. "Tingchen zheng bu guo baochen" 廷琛爭不過寶琛, *Shenbao*, July 17, 1911.
44. "Huangshang dianxue gongyan" 皇上典學貢言, *Shenbao*, July 13, 1911.
45. Kang Youwei 康有為, *Datong shu* 大同書 (1901) (Beijing: Zhonghua shuju, 1959).
46. "Huangshang dianxue gongyan."
47. Herbert Bix, *Hirohito and the Making of Modern Japan* (New York: Harper, 2001), 21–25, 32–37.
48. Takashi Fujitani, *Splendid Monarchy: Power and Pageantry in Modern Japan* (Berkeley: University of California Press, 1996), 121–45.
49. "Chinese News," *North China Herald*, August 5, 1911.
50. Memorial by Lu Runxiang, "Zou wei zun zhang zhuo ni yuqinggong gongke shike zhangcheng shi 奏為遵章酌擬毓慶宮功課時刻章程事," Xuantong 3.r6.4 (First Historical Archives, Grand Council series, FHA-JJC, doc. no. 03-7575-001).
51. "Huangshang dianxue yubei xiang" 皇上典學預備詳, *Shenbao*, July 21, 1911.
52. "Huangshang dianxue zhi yubei" 皇上典學之預備, *Shenbao*, September 3, 1911.
53. "Huangshang dianxue zhi yubei."
54. "Huangshang dianxue zhi yubei."
55. For changing notions of martial ideals and masculinity in the late Qing, see Nicolas Schillinger, *The Body and Military Masculinity in Late Qing and Early Republican China: The Art of Governing Soldiers* (London: Lexington Books, 2016), 49–94.
56. "Guomin gongbao ting ban zhi yuanyin" 國民公報停版之原因, *Dagong bao*, December 14, 1910.
57. Rhoads, *Manchus and Han*, 73, 144, 149. Zaifeng also sought to arrange a visit to Beijing by members of the German royal family. See Aixinjueluo Zaifeng, *Chun qin wang Zaifeng riji*, 366.
58. "Huangshang dianxue yubei xiang."
59. "Chinese News," *North China Herald*, July 22, 1911.
60. "Huangshang dianxue yubei xiang."
61. "Notes on Native Affairs: The Polytechnical College," *North China Herald*, August 26, 1911. I have examined this and other imperial classrooms in more depth in Daniel Barish, "Han Chinese, Manchu, and Western Spaces: The Changing Facade of Imperial Education in Qing Beijing," *Frontiers of History in China* 14, no. 2 (2019): 212–42.
62. "Cihou yu cui shuijinggong gongcheng" 慈后諭催水晶宮工程, *Shenbao*, August 21, 1911.
63. "Shuijinggong neirong ji wen," 水晶宮內容紀聞 *Shenbao*, August 15, 1911.
64. "Yingguo shuijing gong" 英國水晶宮 *Huatu xinbao* 2, no. 1 (1881): 5–6; "Jian shuijing gong" 建水晶宮, *Wanguo gongbao* 688 (1882):13; "Yingguo lundun shuijing gong"英國倫敦水晶宮, *Xinmin congbao* 27 (1903): 14.
65. As Cole Roskam has described in the context of Shanghai, in the second half of the nineteenth century there was a "growing awareness on the part of Chinese officials to the cross-cultural power of verticality, itself a Western-orientated signifier of spatial and, by extension, political authority." Roskam, "The Architecture of Risk: Urban Space and Uncertainty in Shanghai, 1843–74," in *Harbin to Hanoi: The Colonial Built Environment in Asia, 1840 to 1940*, ed. Laura Victoir and Victor Zatsepine (Hong Kong: Hong Kong University Press, 2013), 139.
66. Phillipe Forêt, *Mapping Chengde: The Qing Landscape Enterprise* (Honolulu: University of Hawaii Press, 2000), 51; Young-tsu Wong, *A Paradise Lost: The Imperial Garden Yuanming Yuan* (Honolulu:

University of Hawaii Press, 2001); Evelyn Rawski, *The Last Emperors: A Social History of Qing Imperial Institutions* (Berkeley: University of California Press, 1998), 19-23.
67. William Soothill, *The Hall of Light: A Study of Early Chinese Kingship* (London: Lutterworth Press, 1951), 72.
68. Soothill, *The Hall of Light*, 126. For more on the Ming Tang, see Hwang Ming-chorng, "Ming-Tang: Cosmology, Political Order, and Monuments in Early China" (Ph.D. dissertation, Harvard University, 1996); and Piero Corradini, "Ancient China's Ming Tang: Between Reality and Legend," *Rivista degli studi orientali* 69, no. 1/2 (1995): 173-206.
69. David Cannadine, "The Context, Performance, and Meaning of Ritual: The British Monarchy and the Invention of Tradition, 1820-1977," in *The Invention of Tradition*, ed. Eric Hobsbawm and Terence Ranger (Cambridge: Cambridge University Press, 1983), 101-64.
70. Zaifeng, *Chun qin wang Zaifeng riji*, 393.
71. Gan Yonglong 甘永龍, "Bosi huangdi dianxue jilüe" 波斯皇帝典學記略, *Dongfang zazhi* 8, no. 6 (1911): 1-2.
72. Gan, "Bosi huangdi dianxue jilüe," 1-2.
73. Zhang Naiwei 章乃煒, *Qinggong shuwen* 清宮述聞 (Beijing: Forbidden City, 1990), 378.
74. *Qing shilu* 清實錄 (Beijing: Zhonghua shuju, 1986), 2nd day of 2nd month of inaugural year of Tongzhi era, 491-2, 492-1; "Chun ming tan xie" 春明談屑, *Shenbao*, March 15, 1886.
75. "Huangshang dianxue yubei xiang," Zhang Jian, the 1894 *Zhuangyuan*, is perhaps most famous for his promotion of education reforms and for founding what many consider to be the country's first museum. He was also the head of the Jiangsu Provincial Parliament and one of the authors of Puyi's abdication edict. For more on Zhang, see Samuel C. Chu, *Reformer in Modern China, Chang Chien, 1853-1926* (New York: Columbia University Press, 1965); and Qin Shao, *Culturing Modernity: The Nantong Model, 1890-1930* (Stanford, Calif.: Stanford University Press, 2004). Tang Shouqian was an 1892 *jinshi*. In the first decade of the twentieth century, Tang was head of the Zhejiang Railway Company, and after the revolution, he was governor of Zhejiang province. For more on Tang, see Robert Keith Schoppa, "Power, Legitimacy, and Symbol: Local Elites and the Jute Creek Embankment Case," in *Chinese Local Elites and Patterns of Dominance*, ed. Joseph Esherick and Mary Backus Rankin (Berkeley: University of California Press, 1990), 140-61.
76. "Chinese News," *North China Herald*, July 22, 1911.
77. "Zhuandian" 專電, *Shenbao*, September 3, 1911.
78. Pamela Kyle Crossley, *A Translucent Mirror: History and Identity in Qing Imperial Ideology* (Berkeley: University of California Press, 1999), 11.
79. Yiketan 伊克坦, "Dai chen dianxue shiyi" 代陳典學事宜, in *Qing shigao liezhuan* 清史稿列傳, ed. Zhao Erxun 趙爾巽 (Taibei: Hongshi chuban she, 1981), 472, no. 259, 12820-12821.
80. "Notes on Native Affairs," *North China Herald*, June 3, 1910; September 2, 1911.
81. "Chinese News," *North China Herald*, July 22, 1911; "Huangshang dianxue zhudian yu zhi" 皇上典學祝典預誌, *Shenbao*, September 1, 1911.
82. "Zhuandian" 專電, *Shenbao*, July 21, 1911. See also "Chinese News," *North China Herald*, September 2, 1911; "Huangshang dianxue you xuejie tingke yi biao gonghe" 皇上典學由學界停課以表恭賀, *Longmen zazhi*, no. 5 (1911): 3.

83. "Qi yue shi'ba ri wei huangshang dianxue zhi qi ge xuetang jun xu wang que xingli wen" 七月十八日為皇上典學之期各學堂均須望闕行禮文, *Zhejiang jiaoyu guanbao*, no. 89 (1911); "Zhuandian" 專電, *Shenbao*, August 29, 1911.
84. "Qinghe dianxue hui zhi" 慶賀典學彙誌, *Shenbao*, September 11, 1911.
85. "Notes on Native Affairs," *North China Herald*, September 16, 1911; "The Emperor's Education," *North China Herald*, September 9, 1911.
86. "Notes on Native Affairs," *North China Herald*, September 16, 1911.
87. "Huangshang dianxue zhudian yu zhi" 皇上典學祝典預誌, *Shenbao*, September 1, 1911.
88. "Zhuandian" 專電, *Shenbao*, September 11, 1911. See also "The Emperor at School," *North China Herald*, September 16, 1911; "Huangshang dianxue di'yi ri" 皇上典學第一日, *Xiehe bao*, no. 48 (1911): 14.
89. "Qinghe dianxue hui zhi" 慶賀典學彙誌, *Shenbao*, September 11, 1911; "Huangshang dianxue zhi qingdian" 皇上典學之慶典, *Shenbao*, September 8, 1911.
90. Henrietta Harrison, *The Making of the Republican Citizen: Political Ceremonies and Symbols in China, 1911–1929* (Oxford: Oxford University Press, 1999), chaps. 2–3.
91. "Qinghe dianxue hui zhi" 慶賀典學彙誌, *Shenbao*, September 11, 1911.
92. "Faguan yangchengsuo kaihui ji" 法官養成所開會記, *Shenbao*, September 12, 1911.
93. "The French School," *North China Herald*, September 30, 1911.
94. "The Emperor at School," *North China Herald*, July 15, 1911.
95. "Black Monday," *The North China Herald*, September 16, 1911.
96. "Zhongguo dashi ji xuantong san'nian qi'yue shi'ba ri huangshang dianxue" 中國大事記宣統三年七月十八日皇上典學, *Dongfang zazhi*, no. 8 (1911): 8.
97. "Huangshang dianxue zhi lijie" 皇上典學時之禮節, *Dagong bao*, August 30, 1911.
98. In some ways these celebrations built on other ritual efforts to link the emperor and people, such as the reforms to the worship of Confucius in 1906 that synchronized the emperor's sacrifices with those of commoners around the empire. Yet whereas those reforms have been interpreted as desacralizing the emperor and preparing "the ground for his merging into the collectivity of the nation," the ceremonies at the start of his education explicitly elevated him above the crowd. See Ya-pei Kuo, "'The Emperor and the People in One Body': The Worship of Confucius and Ritual Planning in the Xinzheng Reforms, 1902–1911," *Modern China* 35, no. 2 (March 2009): 124.
99. "Jiao zhi" 交旨, *Shenbao*, July 17, 1911.
100. "Shiping" 時評, *Shenbao*, August 11, 1911; "Yuzhi daxueshi lu runxiang deng xianzai yuqing gong xingzou ci wu zhongyao zhe jia en" 諭旨大學士陸潤庠等現在毓慶宮行走差務重要着加恩, *Zhejiang guanbao* 3, no. 34 (1911): 5.
101. "Licheng xian hu you wu sui shentong chuxian" 歷城縣忽有五歲神童出現, *Shenbao*, September 14, 1911.
102. "Licheng xian hu you wu sui shentong chuxian."
103. "Black Monday."
104. Yan Chongnian 閻崇年, *Qing gong yi'an zhengjie* 清宮疑案正解 (Beijing: Zhonghua shuju, 2007), 176.
105. "Kelian kexiao zhi jingshi" 可憐可笑之京師, *Shenbao*, January 6, 1912.

CONCLUSION

1. Rebecca Nedostup, "Two Tombs: Thoughts on Zhu Yuanzhang, the Kuomintang, and the Meanings of National Heroes," in *Long Live the Emperor! The Uses of the Ming Founder Across Six Centuries of East Asian History*, ed. Sarah K. Schneewind (Minneapolis: Ming Studies, 2008), 360.
2. Lim Boon-Keng (Lin Wenqing), "President at the Ming Tombs, A Historic Ceremony," *North China Herald*, February 24, 1912.
3. The two speeches appear with slightly different titles in various editions of Sun's collected works, but usually as "Ye Mingtaizu ling wen" 謁明太祖陵文 and "Ye Ming Taizu ling zhugao guangfu chenggong minguo tongyi wen" 謁明太祖陵祝告光復成功民國統一文. See the digitized versions in the online collection of his works in the Sun Yat-Sen Studies Database, http://sunology.culture.tw/cgi-bin/gs32/gsweb.cgi/ccd=Oqb7nb/record?r1=6&h1=0 and http://sunology.culture.tw/cgi-bin/gs32/gsweb.cgi/ccd=Oqb7nb/record?r1=5&h1=0
4. Lim, "President at the Ming Tombs."
5. Nedostup, "Two Tombs."
6. Charles Musgrove, *China's Contested Capital: Architecture, Ritual, and Response in Nanjing* (Honolulu: University of Hawai'i Press, 2013), 34.
7. Henrietta Harrison, *The Making of the Republican Citizen: Political Ceremonies and Symbols in China, 1911–1929* (Oxford: Oxford University Press, 1999), 16–17.
8. Nedostup, "Two Tombs," 356; Q. Edward Wong, "Victor or Villain? The Varying Images of Zhu Yuanzhang in Twentieth Century Chinese Historiography," in *Long Live the Emperor! The Uses of the Ming Founder Across Six Centuries of East Asian History*, ed. Sarah K. Schneewind (Minneapolis: Ming Studies, 2008), 393.
9. Rudolf Wagner, "Ritual, Architecture, Politics and Publicity During the Republic: Enshrining Sun Yat-sen," in *Chinese Architecture and the Beaux-Arts*, ed. Jeffrey Cody, Nancy S. Steinhardt, and Tony Atkin (Honolulu: University of Hawai'i Press, 2011), 223–78.
10. Lim, "President at the Ming Tombs."
11. David Cannadine, "The Context, Performance, and Meaning of Ritual: The British Monarchy and the Invention of Tradition, 1820–1977," in *The Invention of Tradition*, ed. Eric Hobsbawm and Terence Ranger (Cambridge: Cambridge University Press, 1983), 120.
12. Prasenjit Duara, *Rescuing History from the Nation: Questioning Narratives of Modern China* (Chicago: University of Chicago Press, 1995), 177–86; Steven Phillips, "The Demonization of Federalism in Republican China," in *Defunct Federalisms: Critical Perspectives on Federal Failure*, ed. Emilian Kavalski and Magdalena Zolkos (Hampshire: Ashgate, 2008), 87–102.
13. John W. Dardess, *Confucianism and Autocracy: Professional Elites in the Founding of the Ming Dynasty* (Berkeley: University of California Press, 1983), 224.
14. Wm. Theodore de Bary, *Neo-Confucian Orthodoxy and the Learning of the Mind-and-Heart* (New York: Columbia University Press, 1981), 28, 97.
15. *Qing shilu* 清實錄 (Beijing: Zhonghua shuju, 1986), 4th day of 5th month of 16th year of Kangxi era, 857-1, 857-2. Hereafter cited as *QSL*.
16. Huang Chin-shing, *The Price of Having a Sage Emperor: The Unity of Politics and Culture* (Singapore: Institute of East Asian Philosophies, 1987), 9–11.

17. *QSL*, 4th day of 5th month of 16th year of Kangxi era, 857-1, 857-2.
18. The focus on education is not meant to diminish the importance of other aspects of the dynasty's power, particularly martial elements. For an examination of that dynamic, see Joanna Waley-Cohen, *The Culture of War in China: Empire and the Military Under the Qing Dynasty* (New York: Tauris, 2006). Scholarship has also highlighted the important role that other forms of ritual played in the construction of Qing power. See, for example, Macabe Keliher, *The Board of Rites and the Making of Qing China* (Berkeley: University of California Press, 2019); and Angela Zito, *Of Body & Brush: Grand Sacrifice as Text/Performance in Eighteenth-Century China* (Chicago: University of Chicago Press, 1997).
19. Phillip Kuhn, "Political Crime and Bureaucratic Monarchy: A Chinese Case of 1768," *Late Imperial China* 8, no. 1 (1987): 80–104. As Thomas Metzger has argued, power in the late imperial state existed as a "triangular" structure, wherein both scholars and the emperor were subjugated to the authority of the Classics. See Metzger, *Escape from Predicament: Neo-Confucianism and China's Evolving Political Culture* (New York: Columbia University Press, 1977), 179. For more on the texts within the system, see Benjamin Elman and Martin Kern, eds., *Statecraft and Classical Learning: The Rituals of Zhou in East Asian History* (Leiden: Brill, 2010). Of particular interest for the late Qing context is Rudolf Wagner's chapter, "The Zhouli as Late Qing Path to the Future," 359–87.
20. *QSL*, 12th day of 2nd month of 23rd year of Jiaqing era, 476-2.
21. Susan Naquin, *Millenarian Rebellion in China: the Eight Trigrams Uprising of 1813* (New Haven, Conn.: Yale University Press, 1976), 176–84.
22. *QSL*, 8th day of 11th month of inaugural year of Daoguang era, 457-2.
23. *QSL*, 27th day of 1st month of 16th year of Daoguang era, 277-1; 9th day of 1st month of 17th year of Daoguang era, 537-1; 12th day of 2nd month of 29th year of Daoguang era, 858-1. Daoguang's supposed rigorous personal education became a part of his international image as well. See Karl Friedrich Gützlaff, *The Life of Taou-Kwang, Late Emperor of China* (London: Smith, Elder, 1852), 8–9.
24. Kongmiao he Guozijian Bowuguan 孔廟和國子監博物館, *Mingqing huangdi jiangxue lu* 明清皇帝講學錄 (Beijing: Gugong chubanshe, 2016), 103.
25. For the flexibility of the Daoguang state, see Seunghyun Han, *After the Prosperous Age: State and Elites in Early Nineteenth-Century Suzhou* (Cambridge, Mass.: Harvard University Asia Center, 2016), 4–5; and Jane Kate Leopold, *Stretching the Qing Bureaucracy in the 1826 Sea-Transport Experiment* (Leiden: Brill, 2019), 39–63.
26. Pamela Kyle Crossley, "Nationality and Difference in China: The Post-Imperial Dilemma," in *The Teleology of the Nation State: Japan and China*, ed. Joshua Fogel (Philadelphia: University of Pennsylvania Press, 2005), 142.
27. Peter Zarrow has similarly noted the malleable nature of the emperorship and the importance of the emperor to late Qing society and culture. See Zarrow, *After Empire: The Conceptual Transformation of the Chinese State, 1885–1924* (Stanford, Calif.: Stanford University Press, 2012), 9–10.
28. These "Grand Weddings" (*dahun* 大婚) were in fact two of only four times in the Qing that an emperor was married while on the throne. See Evelyn Rawski, "Ch'ing Imperial Marriage and Problems of Rulership," in *Marriage and Inequality in Chinese Society*, ed. Rubie Watson and Patricia Ebrey (Berkeley: University of California Press, 1991), 190–93.

29. Weng Tonghe, *Ping lu cong gao* 瓶廬叢稿 (Taibei: Wenhai, 1967), juan 3, n.p. Also cited in Xie Junmei, *Weng Tonghe* 翁同龢 (Shanghai: Shanghai renmin chuban she, 1987), 46.
30. Ying-kit Chan, "Mourning During the Tongzhi Regency," *Monumenta Serica* 64, no. 2 (December 2016): 399-403.
31. Thomas Wade, *Decree of the Emperor of China, Asking for Counsel, and the Replies of the Administration, 1850–51, with Other Papers* (London: Harrison, 1878), 3-4, 10, 27, 46, 79.
32. *QSL*, 12th day of 2nd month of inaugural year of Guangxu era, 351-2.
33. "Guangxu er nian zheng yue chu qi ri jingbao quanlu" 光緒二年正月初七日京報全錄, *Shenbao*, February 21, 1876.
34. Memorial by Yihuan 奕譞, "Zou wei jian ming zhaoliao huangdi kecheng mianyu zhuoding qing han kecheng deng shi" 奏為簡命照料皇帝課程面諭酌定清漢課程等事, Guangxu 2.1.29 (First Historical Archives, FHA-GZQZ, doc. no. 04-01-02-0152-007).
35. Xie, *Weng Tonghe*, 60.
36. Zeng Jize 曾紀澤, *Zeng Jize riji* 曾紀澤日記 (Changsha: Yuelu, 1998), 3:1565.
37. Zeng himself spoke excellent English. See Timothy Richard, *Forty-Five Years in China: Reminiscences* (New York: Frederick A. Stokes, 1916), 208-9.
38. "Chinese Education," *North China Herald*, April 17, 1886.
39. Henrietta Harrison, *The Man Awakened from Dreams: One Man's Life in a North China Village, 1857–1942* (Stanford, Calif.: Stanford University Press, 2005), 83-84.
40. Harrison, *The Man Awakened from Dreams*, 4-5.
41. Zhang Zhidong, *Quanxue pian* 勸學篇 (Guilin: Guangxi Normal University Press, 2008), 12.
42. "Rihuang tingjiang" 日皇聽講, *Shenbao*, April 10, 1899.
43. "Rihuang tingjiang" 日皇聽講, *Shenbao*, January 16, 1903.
44. "Qing di ni juan lian chang she guizhou nü xuetang" 慶邸擬捐廉倡設貴冑女學堂, *Shenbao*, July 26, 1906.
45. In previous eras, Kangxi had required princes to recite all their texts 120 times. Evidence suggests that Tongzhi only did so 10–20 times, while Guangxu is said to have recited passages 20–50 times, depending on the material. See Zou Ailian 鄒愛蓮, "Cong gongke dang yu weng tonghe riji tan tongzhi huangdi de dianxue jiaoyu" 從功課檔與翁同龢日記談同治皇帝的典學教育 (An examination of the Tongzhi emperor's education from the schoolwork archive and Weng Tonghe's diary), in *Qingdai gongshi tanxi* 清代宮史探析 (Inquiries into palace history during the Qing), ed. Qingdai gongshi yanjiu hui 清代宮史研究會 (Beijing: Forbidden City, 2007), 604-21.
46. David Strand, *An Unfinished Republic: Leading by Word and Deed in Modern China* (Berkeley: University of California Press, 2011), 282.
47. Rudolf Wagner, "Living Up to the Image of the Ideal Public Leader: George Washington's Image in China," *Journal of Transcultural Studies* 10, no. 2 (Winter 2019): 75, 21.
48. In part, this is an extension of what Peter Zarrow observed regarding the Republic, that the legitimacy of the regime was based "simultaneously on the evils of the Qing and on claims to inheritance from the Qing." Zarrow, "Discipline and Narrative: Chinese History Textbooks in the Early Twentieth Century," in *Transforming History: The Making of a Modern Academic Discipline in Twentieth-Century China*, ed. Brian Moloughney and Peter Zarrow (Hong Kong: Chinese University Press, 2011), 175.

49. Edward J. M. Rhoads, *Manchus and Han: Ethnic Relations and Political Power in Late Qing and Early Republican China, 1861–1928* (Seattle: University of Washington Press, 2000), 187-205.
50. Aisin Gioro Puyi, *From Emperor to Citizen*, trans. W. J. F. Jenner (Beijing: Foreign Language Press, 1964), 38.
51. Bernardo Bertolucci, *The Last Emperor* (film), Columbia Pictures, 1987.
52. Pamela Kyle Crossley, *The Manchus* (Cambridge: Blackwell, 1997), 196.
53. "An Ex-Emperor's Education," *New York Times*, March 9, 1917.
54. "Shang lianlian zhuanzhi yuwei ye" 尚戀戀專制餘威耶, *Shenbao*, February 24, 1912.
55. "Shang lianlian zhuanzhi yuwei ye"; "Zhuandian" 專電, *Shenbao*, August 28, 1912; "Zhuandian," *Shenbao*, April 20, 1912.
56. "Zhuandian" 專電, *Shenbao*, August 27, 1912; "Sun jun dashou huangzu zhi huanying" 孫君大受皇族之歡迎, *Xiehe bao* 2, no. 48 (1912): 11-1.
57. Xu Shichang, for example, held several related posts before serving the Republic. See "Yidian" 譯電, *Shenbao*, March 1, 1913; "Xujun fuwei qing di shi" 徐君復為清帝師," *Xiehe bao* 3, no. 23 (1913): 13; "Jingzhong suowen" 京中瑣聞," *Shenbao*, June 4, 1914. Other officials, such as Zhao Erxun, expressed a desire to be appointed to the emperor's classroom but were never given the post. See "Zhuandian" 專電, *Shenbao*, October 8, 1915.
58. "Zhuandian" 專電, *Shenbao*, February 24, 1913.
59. "China," *North China Herald*, March 18, 1913; "The Ex-Emperor," *North China Herald*, March 15, 1913. For more on the funeral, see Jia Feng, "The Dragon Flag in the Republican Nation: The Dowager Empress Longyu's Death Ritual in 1913 and Contested Political Legitimacy in Early Republican China," in *Transnational Histories of the 'Royal Nation,'* ed. Milinda Banerjee (Cham, Switz.: Palgrave Macmillan, 2017), esp. 234-36.
60. Jia Feng, "The Dragon Flag in the Republican Nation," 235.
61. "Qing ting jinzhuang suo ji" 清廷近狀瑣記, *Shenbao*, June 11, 1912. Pamela Crossley has discussed a similar idea of the Republic claiming the emperor as property. See Crossley, *Translucent Mirror*, 337.
62. "The Chinese Ex-Emperor," *New York Times*, August 2, 1914.
63. For an examination of restorationist groups, see Lin Zhihong 林志宏 *Mingguo nai diguo ye: zhengzhi wenhua zhuanxing xia de qing yimin* 民國乃敵國也：政治文化轉型下的清遺民 (Taibei: Lian jing, 2009).
64. Hu Pingsheng 胡平生, *Minguo chu qi de fu bi pai* 民國初期的復辟派 (Taibei: Taiwan xuesheng shuju, 1985), 180.
65. "Little Pu Yi," *Boston Daily Globe*, April 12, 1914.
66. "Ex-Emperor's Education," *Peking Daily News*, March 18, 1914; "English Royal Tongue: Deposed Chinese Ruler to Be Taught by Special Teacher," *Washington Post*, March 21, 1915.
67. "No Title," *North China Herald*, April 21, 1917.
68. Wenyi bianyi she 文藝編譯社, ed., *Qi ri huang di yi wen* 七日皇帝軼事 (Jiulong: Zhongshan tushu gongsi, 1973), 10, 23-24.
69. For more on Luo, see Yang Chia-ling and Roderick Whitfield, eds., *Lost Generation: Luo Zhenyu, Qing Loyalists and the Formation of Modern Chinese Culture* (London: Saffron, 2012). For Gu, see

Chunmei Du, *Gu Hongming's Eccentric Chinese Odyssey* (Philadelphia: University of Pennsylvania Press, 2019).

70. Wang Qingxiang 王慶祥, *Puyi jiaowang lu* 溥儀交往錄 (Beijing: Dongfang chuban she, 1999), 324-25. Also see Jenny Huangfu Day, *Qing Travelers to the Far West: Diplomacy and the Information Order in Late Imperial China* (Cambridge: Cambridge University Press, 2018), 93.
71. Reginald Johnston, *Twilight in the Forbidden City* (Mattituck, N.Y.: Amereon House, 1995), 163.
72. "Zhuangshidun jun lun kongjiao" 庄士敦君論孔教, *Zongsheng xuebao* 2, no. 6 (1917): 17-18; Reginald Johnston, "Confucianism and Modern China," *Qinghua xuebao* 10, no. 4 (1935): 951-54.
73. Puyi, *From Emperor to Citizen*, 55.
74. Puyi, *From Emperor to Citizen*, 60.
75. "Puyi xiang chuyang liuxue," 溥儀想出洋留學, *Shenbao*, July 6, 1922.
76. Mao Zedong, "Karl and Puyi" (July 21, 1919), in *Mao's Road to Power: Revolutionary Writings, 1912–1949*, ed. Stuart Schram (Armonk, N.Y.: M. E. Sharpe, 1992), 1:368.
77. Hui Qi 會琦, "Puyi bu sha he wei" 溥儀不殺何為, *Xingshi zhoubao*, November, 1924. Cited in Hu Pingsheng, *Minguo chu qi de fu bi pai* 民國初期的復辟派 (Taibei: Taiwan xuesheng shuju, 1985), 414.
78. L. H. Lamb to A. L. Scott, August 24, 1948, British Foreign Office Archives, FO 371-69539, p. 3.
79. "Wo guo zuigao renmin fayuan tebie junshi fating shenpan er shi ba ming riben zhanzheng fanzui fenzi" 我國最高人民法院特別軍事法庭審判二十八名日本戰爭犯罪分子, *Renmin ribao*, July 21, 1956; "Pu-Yi Bobs Up in News, 1st Time in Six Years," *Chicago Daily Tribune*, July 21, 1956; "Pu Yi Re-Emerges as Key Witness When Reds Convict 28 Japanese," *New York Times*, July 21, 1956; "Pu Yi Tells Story of Disappearance," *New York Times*, August 10, 1956; "Henry Pu Yi Now Red China's Prisoner," *South China Morning Post*, August 10, 1956.
80. John Pritchard, ed., *The Tokyo Major War Crimes Trial: The Records of the International Military Tribunal for the Far East* (Lewiston, N.Y.: Edwin Mellen Press, 1998), 10:3917-4369.
81. Edward Behr, *The Last Emperor* (Toronto: Futura, 1987), 285. Fei Xiaotong 費孝通 (1910-2005) made a related observation about the ways in which older notions of a benevolent emperor became embodied in the Communist Party. See Peter Zarrow's discussion of Fei and this idea in *After Empire*, 295-96.
82. "Pu Yi Labors for Reds in Workshop," *New York Times*, April 10, 1960.
83. "The Oft Reformed Mr. Puyi," *Chicago Daily Tribune*, May 6, 1960.
84. Aixinjueluo Puyi 愛新覺羅溥儀, "Cong wo de jingli jielu riben junguozhuyi de zuixing: jinian 'jiu yi ba' shibian san shi zhounian" 從我的經歷揭露日本軍國注意的罪行:紀念九一八事變三十週年, *Renmin ribao*, September 17, 1961.
85. "Last of Manchu Emperors Writing His Memoirs," *South China Morning Post*, October 25, 1962. For a textual history and interpretation of the work in the history of imperial writing, see Olivia Anna Rovsing Milburn, "Imperial Writings: Rereading the Autobiography of Aisin Gioro Puyi," *Sungkyun Journal of East Asian Studies* 12, no.2 (2012): 101-22.
86. Puyi, *From Emperor to Citizen*, 46.

87. Quoted in "Pu Yi Dead at 61: Last of the Manchus," *Jerusalem Post*, October 27, 1967.
88. Puyi, *From Emperor to Citizen*, 483.
89. See Elizabeth Perry's discussion of Mao as "teacher-cum-revolutionary" and his desire to be known above all else as the "Great Teacher," in Perry, *Anyuan: Mining China's Revolutionary Tradition* (Berkeley: University of California Press, 2012), 4, 234.

BIBLIOGRAPHY

ARCHIVAL COLLECTIONS AND STATE DOCUMENTS

British National Archives, Foreign Office Archives.
British Parliamentary Papers: China 5. Shannon: Irish University Press, 1971.
Gugong bowuyuan ming qing dang'an bu 故宮博物院明清檔案部, ed. *Qingmo choubei lixian dang'an shi liao* 清末籌備立憲檔案史料 [Historical documents relating to establishment of a constitution at the end of the Qing]. Beijing: Zhonghua shuju, 1979.
Liu Jinzao 劉錦藻. *Qingchao xu wenxian tongkao* 清朝續文獻通考 [Continued comprehensive examination of Qing dynasty documents]. Shanghai: Commercial Press, 1936.
Neige daku 內閣大庫 [Grand Secretariat archives project]. *Zhongyang yanjiuyuan lishi yuyan yanjiu suo* 中央研究院歷史語言研究所 [Institute of History and Philology, Academia Sinica]. http://archive.ihp.sinica.edu.tw/mctkm2/index.html.
North China Herald, ed. *The Emperor Kuang Hsü's Reform Decrees, 1898*. Shanghai: North China Herald, 1900.
Qingdai gongzhongdang zouzhe ji junjichu dang zhe jian 清代宮中檔奏摺及軍機處檔摺件 [Qing dynasty palace memorials and Grand Council archives]. Taipei: National Palace Museum.
Qing shilu 清實錄 [Qing veritable records]. Beijing: Zhonghua shuju, 1986. Academia Sinica Scripta Sinica, *Hanji quanwen ziliaoku* 漢籍全文資料庫 database. http://hanchi.ihp.sinica.edu.tw/ihp/hanji.htm.
Wade, Thomas, trans. *Decree of the Emperor of China, Asking for Counsel, and the Replies of the Administration, 1850–51, with Other Papers*. London: Harrison, 1878.
Zhao Erxun 趙爾巽, ed. *Qing shigao* 清史稿 [Draft of Qing history]. Taibei: Hong shi chubanshe, 1981.
Zhongguo diyi lishi dang'an guan 中國第一歷史檔案館 [First historical archives of China]. Beijing.
Zhongguo diyi lishi dang'an guan 中國第一歷史檔案館, ed. *Yuanming Yuan* 圓明園 [Garden of Perfect Brightness]. Shanghai: Shanghai guji chubanshe, 1991.
Zhongshan xueshu ziliao ku 中山學術資料庫 [Sun Yat-sen studies database]. National Dr. Sun Yat-sen Memorial Hall. Taipei, Taiwan. http://sunology.culture.tw.

NEWSPAPERS AND JOURNALS

Beijing qianshuo huabao 北京淺說畫報
Beiyang huabao 北洋畫報
Boston Daily Globe
Chicago Daily Tribune
China News Agency English Service
Chinese Recorder and Missionary Journal
Dagong bao (Tianjin) 大公報
Datong bao (Shanghai) 大同報
Dianbao 電報
Detroit Free Press
Dongfang zazhi 東方雜誌
Fasheng 法聲
Guangyi congbao 廣義叢報
Gugong wupin diancha baogao 故宮物品點查報告
Guoji gongbao 國際公報
Huanqiu Zhongguo xuesheng bao 環球中國學生報
Huashang lianhe bao 華商聯合報
Hubei xuebao 湖北學報
Jiaoyu shijie 教育世界
Jiaoyu zazhi (Shanghai) 教育雜誌 (上海報)
Jiaoyu zazhi (Tianjin) 教育雜誌 (天津報)
Jing bao 京報
Lingtong 靈通
Longmen zazhi 龍門雜誌
Los Angeles Times
New York Times
North China Herald
Peking Daily News
Peking Gazette (*North China Herald* translations and collections)
Qianshuo huabao 淺說畫報
Qiaosheng 橋聖
Renmin ribao 人民日報
Shenbao 申報
Sichuan jiaoyu guanbao 四川教育館報
South China Morning Post
South China Morning Post and the Hongkong Telegraph
Tianjin shangbao tuhua zhoukan 天津商報圖畫週刊
Tongwen bao 通聞報
Waijiao bao 外交報
Wan'guo gongbao 萬國公報

Washington Post
Woman's Missionary Advocate
World's Chinese Students' Journal
Xiehe bao 協和報
Xuebu guanbao 學部館報
Yi wen lu 益聞錄
Yomiuri shimbun 読売新聞 (Tokyo)
Zhenguang bao 真光報
Zhejiang guanbao 浙江館報
Zhejiang jiaoyu guanbao 浙江教育館報
Zhengyi tongbao 政藝通報
Zhengzong aiguo bao 正宗愛國報
Zhili jiaoyu zazhi 直隸教育雜誌
Zhongguo huabao 中國畫報
Zhongxi jiaohui bao 中西教會報
Zhu Jiang bao 珠江報
Zongsheng xuebao 宗聖學報
Zuguo wenming bao 祖國文明報

ARTICLES, BOOKS, AND COLLECTED WRITINGS

Abe, Hiroshi. "Borrowing from Japan: China's First Modern Educational System." In *China's Education and the Industrialized World*, ed. Ruth Hayhoe and Marianne Bastid, 57–80. Armonk, N.Y.: M. E. Sharpe, 1987.

Aisin Gioro Puyi. *From Emperor to Citizen*. Trans. W. J. F. Jenner. Beijing: Foreign Language Press, 1964.

Aixinjueluo Puyi 愛新覺羅溥儀. *Wo de qian ban sheng* 我的前半生 [The first half of my life]. Beijing: Qunzhong chuban she, 1964.

Aixinjueluo Zaifeng 愛新覺羅載灃. *Chun qin wang Zaifeng riji* 醇親王載灃日記 [The diary of Prince Zaifeng]. Beijing: Qunzhong chuban she, 2014.

Albisetti, James C. *Secondary School Reform in Imperial Germany*. Princeton, N.J.: Princeton University Press, 1983.

Amelung, Iwo. "The *Complete Compilation of New Knowledge*, Xinxue beizuan 新學備纂 (1902): Its Classification Scheme and Its Sources." In *Chinese Encyclopedias of New Global Knowledge (1870–1930)*, ed. Melina Dolezelova-Velingerova and Rudpolf Wagner, 85–102. Heidelberg: Springer, 2014.

Andrade, Tonio. *The Gunpowder Age*. Princeton, N.J.: Princeton University Press, 2016.

Ayers, William. *Chang Chih-tung and Educational Reform in China*. Cambridge, Mass.: Harvard University Press, 1971.

Backeraa, Charlotte, Milinda Banerjee, and Cathleen Sarti. "The Royal Nation in Global Perspective." In *Transnational Histories of the 'Royal Nation,'* ed. Milinda Banerjee et al., 1–17. Cham, Switz.: Palgrave Macmillan, 2017.

Bailey, Paul. *Gender and Education in China: Gender Discourses and Women's Schooling in the Early Twentieth Century*. New York: Routledge, 2007.
—. *Reform the People: Changing Attitudes Towards Popular Education in Early Twentieth Century China*. Cambridge, Mass.: Harvard University Press, 1971.
Banerjee, Milinda. "The Royal Nation and Global Intellectual History: Monarchic Routes to Conceptualizing National Unity." In *Transnational Histories of the 'Royal Nation,'* ed. Milinda Banerjee et al., 21-44. Cham, Switz.: Palgrave Macmillan, 2017.
Banerjee, Milinda, et al, eds. *Transnational Histories of the 'Royal Nation.'* Cham, Switz.: Palgrave Macmillan, 2017.
Banno, Junji. *The Establishment of the Japanese Constitutional System*. New York: Routledge, 1992.
Barish, Daniel. "Empress Dowager Cixi's Imperial Pedagogy: The School for Female Nobles and New Visions of Authority in Early Twentieth Century China." *Nan Nü: Men, Women, and Gender in China* 20, no. 2 (2018): 256-84.
—. "Han Chinese, Manchu, and Western Spaces: The Changing Facade of Imperial Education in Qing Beijing." *Frontiers of History in China* 14, no. 2 (2019): 212-42.
Bartlett, Beatrice. *Monarchs and Ministers: The Grand Council in Mid-Ch'ing China, 1723-1820*. Berkeley: University of California Press, 1991.
Bastid, Marianne. "Official Conceptions of Imperial Authority at the End of the Qing Dynasty." In *Foundations and Limits of State Power in China*, ed. S. R. Schram, 147-86. Hong Kong: Chinese University Press, 1987.
Bénéï, Véronique. *Manufacturing Citizenship: Education and Nationalism in Europe, South Asia and China*. New York: Routledge, 2005.
Behr, Edward. *The Last Emperor*. Toronto: Futura, 1987.
Berger, Stefan, and Alexi Miller, eds. *Nationalizing Empires*. Budapest: Central European University Press, 2015.
Bertolucci, Bernardo. *The Last Emperor* (film). Columbia Pictures, 1987.
Bieler, Stacey. "Yan Yongjing." In *Biographical Dictionary of Chinese Christianity*. http://www.bdcconline.net/en/stories/y/yan-yongjing-1.php.
Biggerstaff, Knight. *The Earliest Modern Government Schools in China*. Ithaca, N.Y.: Cornell University Press, 1961.
Bix, Herbert. *Hirohito and the Making of Modern Japan*. New York: Harper, 2001.
Bol, Peter. *Neo-Confucianism in History*. Cambridge, Mass.: Harvard University Press, 2010.
Bothwick, Sally. *Education and Social Change in China: The Beginning of the Modern Era*. Stanford, Calif.: Hoover Institute Press, 1983.
Brunnert, H. S., et al. *Present Day Political Organization of China*. Shanghai: Kelly and Walsh, 1912.
Burton, Margaret Ernestine. *The Education of Women in China*. New York: Revell, 1911.
Cameron, Meribeth. *The Reform Movement in China, 1898-1912*. Stanford, Calif.: Stanford University Press, 1931.
Cannadine, David. "The Context, Performance, and Meaning of Ritual: The British Monarchy and the Invention of Tradition, 1820-1977." In *The Invention of Tradition*, ed. Eric Hobsbawm and Terence Ranger, 101-64. Cambridge: Cambridge University Press, 1983.

Carl, Katherine. "A Personal Estimate of the Character of the Late Empress Dowager, Tze-Hsi." *Journal of Race Development* 4, no. 1 (1913): 58–71.
———. *With the Empress Dowager of China*. New York: Century, 1907.
Chan, Ying-Kit. "Corpse Admonition: Wu Kedu and Bureaucratic Protest in Late Qing China." *Journal of Chinese History* 2, no. 1 (2018): 109–43.
———. "Mourning During the Tongzhi Regency." *Monumenta Serica* 64, no. 2 (December 2016): 389–410.
———. "A Precious Mirror for Governing the Peace: A Primer for Empress Dowager Cixi." *Nan Nü* 17, no. 2 (2015): 214–44.
Chang, Michael G. *A Court on Horseback: Imperial Touring & the Construction of Qing Rule, 1680–1785*. Cambridge, Mass.: Harvard University Asia Center, 2007.
Chen Dong 陳東. "Qingdai jingyan zhidu" 清代經筵制度 [The Qing system of classic mats]. *Kongzi yanjiu*, no. 3 (2009): 96–104.
———. "Qingdai jingyan zhidu yanjiu" 清代經筵制度研究 [Research on the Qing system of classic mats]. Ph.D. dissertation, Shandong University, 2006.
Chen, Jack. *The Poetics of Sovereignty: On Emperor Taizong of the Tang Dynasty*. Cambridge, Mass.: Harvard University Asia Center, 2011.
Chen Lin 陳琳. "Guangxu huangdi de duiwai guannian yanjiu" 光緒皇帝的對外觀念研究 [Research on the Guangxu emperor's views on the outside world]. M.A. thesis, Hunan Normal University, 2012.
Chen Maozhi 陳懋治. *Gaodeng xiaoxue zhongguo lishi jiaokeshu* 高等小學中國歷史 科書 [Common school Chinese history textbook]. Shanghai: Shanghai wenming shuju, 1904.
Cheng, Weikun. "Going Public Through Education: Female Reformers and Girls' Schools in Late Qing Beijing." *Late Imperial China* 21, no. 1 (June 2000): 107–44.
Chong, Ja Ian. "Breaking Up Is Hard to Do: Foreign Intervention and the Limiting of Fragmentation in the Late Qing and Early Republic, 1893–1922." *Twentieth-Century China* 35, no. 1 (November 2009): 75–98.
Chu, Hung-lam. "The Jiajing Emperor's Interaction with His Lecturers." In *Culture, Courtiers, and Competition: The Ming Court, 1368–1644*, ed. David Robinson, 186–230. Cambridge, Mass.: Harvard University Press, 2008.
Chu, Samuel C. *Reformer in Modern China, Chang Chien, 1853–1926*. New York: Columbia University Press, 1965.
Chu, Samuel, and Kwang-Ching Liu, eds. *Li Hung-Chang and China's Early Modernization*. New York: M. E. Sharpe, 1994.
Chung, Sue Fawn. "The Much Maligned Empress Dowager: A Revisionist Study of the Empress Dowager Tzŭ-Hsi in the Period 1898–1900." Ph.D. dissertation, University of California, Berkeley, 1975.
Cohen, Paul, and John Schrecker, eds. *Reform in Nineteenth Century China*. Cambridge, Mass.: Harvard East Asian Research Center, 1976.
Colley, Linda. "Writing Constitutions and Writing World History." In *The Prospect of Global History*, ed. James Belich, 160–77. Oxford: Oxford University Press, 2016.
Cong, Xiaoping. *Teachers' Schools and the Making of the Modern Chinese Nation-State, 1897–1937*. Vancouver: University of British Columbia Press, 2007.

Conger, Sarah Pike. *Letters from China: With Particular Reference to the Empress Dowager and the Women of China*. Chicago: McClurg, 1909.

Corradini, Piero. "Ancient China's Ming Tang: Between Reality and Legend." *Rivista degli studi orientali* 69, no. 1/2 (1995): 173-206.

Crossley, Pamela Kyle. "Manchu Education." In *Education and Society in Late Imperial China*, ed. Benjamin Elman and Alexander Woodside, 340-78. Berkeley: University of California Press, 1994.

——. *The Manchus*. Cambridge: Blackwell, 1997.

——. "Nationality and Difference in China: The Post-Imperial Dilemma." In *The Teleology of the Nation State: Japan and China*, ed. Joshua Fogel, 138-58. Philadelphia: University of Pennsylvania Press, 2005.

——. *Orphan Warriors: Three Manchu Generations and the End of the Qing World*. Princeton, N.J.: Princeton University Press, 1990.

——. "The Rulerships of China." *American Historical Review* 97, no. 5 (December 1992): 1468-83.

——. *A Translucent Mirror: History and Identity in Qing Imperial Ideology*. Berkeley: University of California Press, 1999.

——. *The Wobbling Pivot, China Since 1800: An Interpretive History*. Oxford: Wiley Blackwell, 2010.

Dai, Yingcong. *The White Lotus War: Rebellion and Suppression in Late Imperial China*. Seattle: University of Washington Press, 2019.

Dardess, John W. *Confucianism and Autocracy: Professional Elites in the Founding of the Ming Dynasty*. Berkeley: University of California Press, 1983.

Day, Jenny Huangfu. *Qing Travelers to the Far West: Diplomacy and the Information Order in Late Imperial China*. Cambridge: Cambridge University Press, 2018.

De Bary, Wm. Theodore. *Neo-Confucian Orthodoxy and the Learning of the Mind-and-Heart*. New York: Columbia University Press, 1981.

Du, Chunmei. *Gu Hongming's Eccentric Chinese Odyssey*. Philadelphia: University of Pennsylvania Press, 2019.

Duara, Prasenjit. *Culture, Power, and the State: Rural North China, 1900–1942*. Stanford, Calif.: Stanford University Press, 1988.

——. *Rescuing History from the Nation: Questioning Narratives of Modern China*. Chicago: University of Chicago Press, 1995.

Dudden, Alexis. *Japan's Colonization of Korea: Discourse and Power*. Honolulu: University of Hawaii Press, 2006.

Duindam, Jeroen. *Dynasties: A Global History of Power, 1300–1800*. Cambridge: Cambridge University Press, 2016.

Eastman, Lloyd. *Throne and Mandarins: China's Search for a Policy During the Sino-French Controversy, 1880–1885*. Cambridge, Mass.: Harvard University Press, 1967.

Ebrey, Patricia. "Imperial Filial Piety as a Political Problem." In *Filial Piety in Chinese Thought and History*, ed. Alan Chan and Sor-hoon Tan, 122-40. New York: Routledge Curzon, 2004.

Edgerton-Tarpley, Kathryn. *Tears from Iron: Cultural Responses to Famine in Nineteenth-Century China*. Berkeley: University of California Press, 2008.

Elliott, Mark. *The Manchu Way: The Eight Banners and Ethnic Identity in Late Imperial China*. Stanford, Calif.: Stanford University Press, 2001.

Elman, Benjamin. *Classicism, Politics, and Kinship: The Ch'ang-chou School of New Text Confucianism in Late Imperial China*. Berkeley: University of California Press, 1990.
—. *A Cultural History of Civil Examinations in Late Imperial China*. Berkeley: University of California Press, 2000.
—. "From Pre-Modern Chinese Natural Studies to Modern Science in China." In *Mapping Meanings: The Field of New Learning in Late Qing China*, ed. Michael Lackner and Natascha Vittinghoff, 25-73. Leiden: Brill, 2004.
—. "Naval Warfare and the Refraction of China's Self-Strengthening Reforms Into Scientific and Technological Failure, 1865-1895." *Modern Asian Studies* 38, no. 2 (May 2004): 283-326.
—. *On Their Own Terms: Science in China, 1550-1900*. Cambridge, Mass.: Harvard University Press, 2005.
Elman, Benjamin, and Martin Kern, eds. *Statecraft and Classical learning: The Rituals of Zhou in East Asian History*. Leiden: Brill, 2010.
Esherick, Joseph. *The Origins of the Boxer Uprising*. Berkeley: University of California Press, 1987.
Feng, Jia. "The Dragon Flag in the Republican Nation: The Dowager Empress Longyu's Death Ritual in 1913 and Contested Political Legitimacy in Early Republican China." In *Transnational History of the 'Royal Nation,'* ed. Milinda Banerjee et al., 223-42. Cham, Switz.: Palgrave Macmillan, 2017.
Feng Yuankui 馮元魁. *Guangxu di* 光緒帝 [The Guangxu emperor]. Changchun: Jilin wenshi chuban she, 1993.
Feng Yueran 馮月然. "Lujun guizhou xuetang yanjiu" 陸軍貴冑學堂研究 [Research on the Military School for Nobles]. M.A. thesis, Zhongyang Minzu University, 2010.
Fletcher, Henry. "Education of the Young Emperor of China." *U.S. Department of State Pamphlets*, vol. 13. Beijing, 1910.
Fogel, Joshua, ed. *The Role of Japan in Liang Qichao's Introduction of Modern Western Civilization to China*. Berkeley: Institute of East Asian Studies, 2004.
—. *The Teleology of the Nation State: Japan and China*. Philadelphia: University of Pennsylvania Press, 2005.
Forêt, Phillipe. *Mapping Chengde: The Qing Landscape Enterprise*. Honolulu: University of Hawaii Press, 2000.
Fuge 福格. *Ting yu cong tan* 聽雨叢談 [Conversations collected listening to the rain]. Beijing: Zhonghua shuju, 1984.
Fujitani, Takashi. *Splendid Monarchy: Power and Pageantry in Modern Japan*. Berkeley: University of California Press, 1996.
Gluck, Carol. *Japan's Modern Myths: Ideology in the Late Meiji Period*. Princeton, N.J.: Princeton University Press, 1985.
Grießler, Margareta. "The Last Dynastic Funeral: Ritual Sequence at the Demise of the Empress Dowager Cixi." *Oriens Extremus* 34, no. 1/2 (1991): 7-35.
Guarino, Marie. "Learning and Imperial Authority in Northern Sung China (960-1126): The Classics Mat Lectures." Ph.D. dissertation, Columbia University, 1994.
Guo Jing 郭晶 and Yi Fan 易帆. *Zijincheng de xuetang: yibu mingqing huangzi jiaoyu jingdian zhi zuo* 紫禁城的學堂：一部明清皇子教育經典之作 [Schools of the Forbidden City: On the education of princes during the Ming and Qing]. Beijing: China Customs, 2006.

Guomin jiaoyu she 國民教育社, ed. *Xinti gaodeng xiaoxue zhongguo lishi* 新體高等小學中歷史 [New-style common school Chinese history]. Shanghai: Wenming shuju, 1910.

Gützlaff, Karl Friedrich. *The Life of Taou-Kwang, Late Emperor of China*. London: Smith, Elder, 1852.

Haboush, Jahyun Kim. "Confucian Rhetoric and Ritual as Techniques of Political Dominance: Yŏngjo's Use of the Royal Lecture." *Journal of Korean Studies* 5, no. 1 (1984): 39–62.

Halsey, Stephen R. *Quest for Power: European Imperialism and the Making of Chinese Statecraft*. Cambridge, Mass.: Harvard University Press, 2015.

Han, Seunghyun. *After the Prosperous Age: State and Elites in Early Nineteenth-Century Suzhou*. Cambridge, Mass.: Harvard University Asia Center, 2016.

Harrison, Henrietta. *The Making of the Republican Citizen: Political Ceremonies and Symbols in China, 1911–1929*. Oxford: Oxford University Press, 1999.

——. *The Man Awakened from Dreams: One Man's Life in a North China Village, 1857–1942*. Stanford, Calif.: Stanford University Press, 2005.

Hay, Jonathan. "The Kangxi Emperor's Brush-Traces: Calligraphy, Writing, and the Art of Imperial Authority." In *Body and Face in Chinese Visual Culture*, ed. Wu Hong, 311–34. Cambridge, Mass.: Harvard University Press, 2005.

Headland, Isaac Taylor. *Court Life in China: The Capital, Its Officials and People*. New York: Revell, 1909.

Hevia, James. *English Lessons: The Pedagogy of Imperialism in Nineteenth Century China*. Durham, N.C.: Duke University Press, 2003.

Hill, Joshua. *Voting as a Rite: A History of Elections in Modern China*. Cambridge, Mass.: Harvard University Press, 2019.

Hogge, David. "Empress Dowager and the Camera." *MIT Visualizing Cultures*. http://ocw.mit.edu/ans7870/21f/21f.027/empress_dowager/.

Hon, Tze-ki. "Educating the Citizens: Visions of China in Late Qing History Textbooks." In *The Politics of Historical Production in Late Qing and Republican China*, ed. Tze-ki Hon and Robert Culp, 79–105. Leiden: Brill, 2007.

Hong, Wu. "Emperor's Masquerade: 'Costume Portraits' of Yongzheng and Qianlong." *Orientations* 26, no. 7 (July/August 1995): 25–41.

Hsiao, Kung-ch'üan. "The Case for Constitutional Monarchy: K'ang Yu-Wei's Plan for the Democratization of China." *Monumenta Serica* 24, no. 1 (January 1, 1965): 1–83.

Hu Pingsheng 胡平生. *Minguo chu qi de fu bi pai* 民國初期的復辟派 [The Restorationist Clique in early Republican China]. Taibei: Taiwan xuesheng shuju, 1985.

Huang, Chin-shing. *The Price of Having a Sage Emperor: The Unity of Politics and Culture*. Singapore: Institute of East Asian Philosophies, 1987.

Huang Xiangjin 黃湘金. "Guizhou nü xuetang kaolun" 貴冑女學堂考論 [Examination of the School for Female Nobles]. *Beijing shehui kexue* 3 (2009): 59–67.

——. "Wanqing beijing nüzi jiaoyu lan yao" 晚清北京女子教育攬要 [Overview of female education in late Qing Beijing]. *Jindai zhongguo fuü yanjiu* 25 (June 2015): 193–232.

Huang Zhangjian 黃彰健, ed. *Kang Youwei wuxu zhen zou yi* 康有戊戌真奏議 [Kang Youwei's 1898 memorials]. Taibei: Zhongyang yanjiuyaun lishi yuyan yanjiu suo, 1974.

Huang Zongxi and Wm. Theodore de Bary. *Waiting for the Dawn: A Plan for the Prince*. New York: Columbia University Press, 1993.

Huang Zunxian 黃遵憲. *Huang Zunxian quanji* 黃遵憲全集 [Complete works of Huang Zunxian]. Beijing: Zhonghua shuju, 2005.

Hummel, Arthur W., ed. *Eminent Chinese of the Ch'ing Period (1644–1912)*. Washington, D.C.: U.S. Government Printing Office, 1944.

Hung, Ho-fung. *Protest with Chinese Characteristics: Demonstrations, Riots, and Petitions in the Mid-Qing Dynasty*. New York: Columbia University Press, 2011.

Hung, William. "Huang Tsun-Hsien's Poem 'The Closure of the Educational Mission in America.'" *Harvard Journal of Asiatic Studies* 18, no. 1/2 (June 1955): 50–73.

Hwang, Ming-chorng. "Ming-Tang: Cosmology, Political Order, and Monuments in Early China." Ph.D. dissertation, Harvard University, 1996.

Jami, Catherine. *The Emperor's New Mathematics: Western Learning and Imperial Authority During the Kangxi Reign (1662–1722)*. Oxford: Oxford University Press, 2012.

Ji Yaxi 季壓西 and Chen Weimin 陳偉民. *Cong 'tongwen san guan' qibu* 從'同文三館'起步 [Starting from the Three Schools of Foreign Languages]. Beijing: Xueyuan, 2007.

Jiang Biao 江標. "Riben huazu nü xuexiao guize" 日本華族女學校規則 [Regulations for the Japanese School for Imperial Women]. In *Lingjian ge congshu* 靈鶼閣叢書 [Compendium from Lingjian Pavilion], ed. Jiang Biao 江標, vol. 81. Taipei: Yiwen yinshuguan, 1964.

Jiang Peng 姜鵬. *Beisong jingyan yu songxue de xingqi* 北宋經筵與宋學的興起 [Classic mat lectures in the Northern Song and the rise of Songxue]. Shanghai: Shanghai guji chubanshe, 2013.

Jiang Weixiang 蔣維喬. *Chudeng xiaoxue jianming zhongguo lishi jiaokeshu* 初等小學簡明中國歷史教科書 [Primary school simplified Chinese historical lessons textbook]. Shanghai: Shanghai Commercial Press, 1908 [1911].

Johnston, Reginald. "Confucianism and Modern China." *Qinghua xuebao* 10, no. 4 (1935): 951–54.

——. *Twilight in the Forbidden City*. Mattituck, N.Y.: Amereon House, 1995.

Joshi Gakushūin 女子學習院, ed. *Joshi Gakushūin gojunenshi* 女子學習院五十年史 [History of fifty years of the School for Japanese Noblewomen]. Tokyo: Joshi Gakushuin, 1935.

Judge, Joan. "The Culturally Contested Student Body: Nü Xuesheng at the Turn of the Twentieth Century." In *Performing "Nation:" Gender Politics in Literature, Theater, and the Visual Arts of China and Japan, 1880–1940*, ed. Doris Croissant, Catherine Vance Yeh, and Joshua S. Mostow, 105-32. Leiden: Brill, 2008.

——. *Print and Politics: "Shibao" and the Culture of Reform in Late Qing China*. Stanford, Calif.: Stanford University Press, 1996.

——. "Talent, Virtue, and the Nation: Chinese Nationalisms and Female Subjectivities in the Early Twentieth Century." *American Historical Review* 106, No. 3 (2001): 765–803.

Kahn, Harold. *Monarchy in the Emperor's Eyes: Image and Reality in the Ch'ien-lung Reign*. Cambridge, Mass.: Harvard University Press, 1971.

——. "The Politics of Filiality: Justification for Imperial Action in Eighteenth Century China." *Journal of Asian Studies* 26, no. 2 (February 1967): 197–203.

Kang Youwei 康有為. *Datong shu* 大同書 [Book of great unity]. Beijing: Zhonghua shuju, 1959 (1901).

——. *Kang nanhai xiansheng yizhu huikan* 康南海先生遺著彙刊 [A collection of Mr. Kang Nanhai's posthumous writings]. Taibei: Hongye Shuju, 1976.

———. *Riben bianzheng kao* 日本變政考 [A study of the institutional reforms in Japan]. Beijing: Forbidden City, 1998.
Karl, Rebecca E., and Peter Zarrow, eds. *Rethinking the 1898 Reform Period: Political and Cultural Change in Late Qing China*. Cambridge, Mass.: Harvard University Press, 2002.
Kaske, Elisabeth. "Fund-Raising Wars: Office Selling and Interprovincial Finance in Nineteenth-Century China." *Harvard Journal of Asiatic Studies* 71, no. 1 (2011): 69-141.
———. "The Pitfalls of Transnational Distinction: A Royal Exchange of Honors and Contested Sovereignty in Late Qing China." In *China and the World, the World and China: A Transcultural Perspective: Essays in Honor of Rudolf G. Wagner*, ed. Barbara Mittler et al., vol. 2, 137-69. Gossenberg, Ger.: Ostasien, 2019.
———. Taxation, Trust, and Government Debt: State-Elite Relations in Sichuan, 1850-1911." *Modern China* 45, no. 3 (2019): 239-94.
Kazuhiro, Takii. *The Meiji Constitution: The Japanese Experience of the West and the Shaping of the Modern State*. Tokyo: International House, 2007.
Keenan, Barry. *Imperial China's Last Classical Academies: Social Change in the Lower Yangzi, 1864–1911*. Berkeley: University of California Press, 1994.
Keene, Donald. *Emperor of Japan: Meiji and His World, 1852–1912*. New York: Columbia University Press, 2002.
Keliher, Macabe. *The Board of Rites and the Making of Qing China*. Berkeley: University of California Press, 2019.
Kiyooka, Eiichi. *Fukuzawa Yukichi on Education: Selected Works*. Tokyo: University of Tokyo Press, 1985.
Klempner, Ellen. "Memories of the Chinese Imperial Civil Service Examination System by Shang Yen-Liu." *American Asian Review* 3, no. 1 (Spring 1985): 48-83.
Kongmiao he Guozijian Bowuguan 孔廟和國子監博物館, ed. *Mingqing huangdi jiangxue lu* 明清皇帝講學錄 [Record of Ming-Qing imperial lectures]. Beijing: Gugong chubanshe, 2016.
Ku, Wei-ying. "Ku Yen-wu's Ideal of the Emperor: A Cultural Giant and Political Dwarf." In *Imperial Rulership and Cultural Change in Traditional China*, ed. Frederick P. Brandauer and Chun-Chieh Huang, 230-47. Seattle: University of Washington Press, 1994.
Kuhn, Phillip. "Ideas Behind China's Modern State." *Harvard Journal of Asiatic Studies* 55, no. 2 (1995): 295-337.
———. *Origins of the Modern Chinese State*. Stanford, Calif.: Stanford University Press, 2002.
———. "Political Crime and Bureaucratic Monarchy: A Chinese Case of 1768." *Late Imperial China* 8, no. 1 (1987): 80-104.
———. *Rebellion and Its Enemies in Late Imperial China, Militarization and Social Structure, 1796–1864*. Cambridge, Mass.: Harvard University Press, 1970.
———. *Soulstealers: The Chinese Sorcery Scare of 1768*. Cambridge, Mass.: Harvard University Press, 1990.
Kuo, Ting-yee. "Self-Strengthening: The Pursuit of Western Technology." In *The Cambridge History of China*, vol. 10, ed. John K. Fairbank, 491-542. Cambridge: Cambridge University Press, 1978.
Kuo, Ya-pei. "'The Emperor and the People in One Body': The Worship of Confucius and Ritual Planning in the Xinzheng Reforms, 1902-1911." *Modern China* 35, no. 2 (March 2009): 123-54.
Kutcher, Norman. *Eunuch and Emperor in the Great Age of Qing Rule*. Berkeley: University of California Press, 2018.

Kwong, Luke S. K. "Imperial Authority in Crisis: An Interpretation of the Coup d'État of 1861." *Modern Asian Studies* 17, no. 2 (1983): 221-38.

—. *A Mosaic of the Hundred Days: Personalities, Politics, and Ideas of 1898*. Cambridge, Mass.: Harvard University Press, 1984.

—. "No Shadows." *History Today* (September 2000): 42-43.

Lackner, Michael, and Natascha Vittinghoff, eds. *Mapping Meanings: The Field of New Learning in Late Qing China*. Leiden: Brill, 2004.

Langlois, John. "Chin-Hua Confucianism Under the Mongols." Ph.D. dissertation, Princeton University, 1973.

Leopold, Jane Kate. *Stretching the Qing Bureaucracy in the 1826 Sea-Transport Experiment*. Leiden: Brill, 2019.

Levenson, Joseph. *Confucian China and Its Modern Fate: A Trilogy*. Berkeley: University of California Press, 1968.

Lewis, Robert Ellsworth. *The Educational Conquest of the Far East*. New York: Revell, 1903.

Li, Lillian. *Fighting Famine in North China: State, Market, and Environmental Decline, 1690s–1900s*. Stanford, Calif.: Stanford University Press, 2007.

Li Wenjun 李文君. *Zijincheng babai yinglian bian'e tongjie* 紫禁城八百楹联匾額通解 [Explication of eight hundred hanging couplets in the Forbidden City]. Beijing: Zijincheng chuban she, 2011.

Li Xizhu 李細珠. *Wan qing baoshou sixiang de yuanxing: woren yanjiu* 晚清保守思想的原型: 倭仁研究. Beijing: Shehui kexue wenxian chubanshe, 2000.

Li, Yuhang. "Oneself as a Female Deity: Representations of Empress Dowager Cixi as Guanyin." *Nan Nü* 14, no. 1 (2012): 75-118.

Li, Yuhang, and Harriet T. Zurndorfer. "Rethinking Empress Dowager Cixi Through the Production of Art." *Nan Nü* 14, no. 1 (2012): 1-20.

Liang Qichao 梁启超. *Liang Qichao quanji* 梁启超全集 [Collected writings of Liang Qichao]. Beijing: Beijing Publishing, 1999.

Lin Mingde 林明德. "Qingmo minchu riben zhengzhi dui zhongguo de yingxiang" 清末民初日本政制對中國的影響 [The influence Japan's political system had on China in the late Qing and early Republican eras]. In *Sino-Japanese Cultural Interchange: The Economic and Intellectual Aspects*, ed. Yue him Tam, 187-214. Hong Kong: Institute of Chinese Studies, 1985.

Lin Zhihong 林志宏. *Mingguo nai diguo ye: zhengzhi wenhua zhuanxing xia de qing yimin* 民國乃敵國也: 政治文化轉型下的清遺民 [The republic as enemy: Qing loyalists in a shifting political culture]. Taibei: Lian jing, 2009.

Little, Mrs. Archibald. *Intimate China: The Chinese as I Have Seen Them*. London: Hutchinson, 1899.

Liu, Kwang-Ching. "The Ch'ing Restoration." In *The Cambridge History of China*, vol. 10, ed. John K. Fairbank, 409-90. Cambridge: Cambridge University Press, 1978.

—. "The Limits of Regional Power in the Late Ch'ing Period: A Reappraisal." *Tsing Hua Journal of Chinese Studies* 10, no. 2 (July 1974): 176-223.

—. "Politics, Intellectual Outlook and Reform: The T'ung-Wen Kuan Controversy of 1867." In *Reform in Nineteenth Century China*, ed. Paul Cohen and John Schrecker, 87-100. Cambridge, Mass.: Harvard University Press, 1976.

Liu, Lydia. *The Clash of Empires: The Invention of China in Modern World Making*. Cambridge, Mass.: Harvard University Press, 2004.

Long, Roberta Lion. "Metaphysics and East-West Philosophy: Applying the Chinese T'i-yung Paradigm." *Philosophy East and West* 29, no. 1 (January 1979): 49-57.

Lu Runxiang 陸潤庠, ed. *Zhongwai cewen daguan* 中外策問大觀 [Grand view of policy questions on Chinese and foreign affairs]. Shanghai: Yangeng Shanzhuang, 1903.

Mackinnon, Stephen R. *Power and Politics in Late Imperial China: Yuan Shi-Kai in Beijing and Tianjin, 1901–1908*. Berkeley: University of California Press, 1980.

Mann Jones, Susan, and Philip Kuhn. "Dynastic Decline and the Roots of Rebellion." In *The Cambridge History of China*, vol. 10, ed. John K. Fairbank, 107-62. Cambridge: Cambridge University Press, 1978.

Mao Xianmin 毛憲民. "Lun qingdi wugong liang ju yu qishe shangwu jingshen" 論清帝武功良具與騎射尚武精神 [On the martial tools and martial spirit of Qing emperors]. In *Qingdai gongshi tanxi* 清代宮史探析 [Research on palace history during the Qing], ed. Qingdai gongshi yanjiu hui, 69-84. Beijing: Forbidden City, 2007.

Martin, William Alexander Parsons. *A Cycle of Cathay: Or, China, South and North, with Personal Reminiscences*. New York: Revell, 1900.

McCord, Edward. "Militia and Local Militarization in Late Qing and Republican China: The Case of Hunan." *Modern China* 14, no. 2 (1988): 156-87.

———. *The Power of the Gun: The Emergence of Modern Chinese Warlordism*. Berkeley: University of California Press, 1993.

Meienberger, Norbert. *The Emergence of Constitutional Government in China (1905–1908): The Concept Sanctioned by the Empress Dowager Tzu-Hsi*. Bern, Switz.: P. Lang, 1980.

Metzger, Thomas. *Escape from Predicament: Neo-Confucianism and China's Evolving Political Culture*. New York: Columbia University Press, 1977.

Meyer-Fong, Tobie. *What Remains: Coming to Terms with Civil War in 19th Century China*. Stanford, Calif.: Stanford University Press, 2013.

Michael, Franz. "Regionalism in Nineteenth-Century China." Introduction to *Li Hung-chang and the Huai Army: A Study in Nineteenth-Century Chinese Regionalism*, by Stanley Spector, xxi-xliii. Seattle: University of Washington Press, 1964.

Milburn, Olivia Anna Rovsing. "Imperial Writings: Rereading the Autobiography of Aisin Gioro Puyi." *Sungkyun Journal of East Asian Studies* 12, no. 2 (2012): 101–22.

Min, Tu-ki, *National Policy and Local Power: The Transformation of Late Imperial China*. Cambridge, Mass.: Harvard University Asia Center, 1990.

Mokros, Emily. "Reconstructing the Imperial Retreat: Politics, Communications, and the Yuanming Yuan Under the Tongzhi Emperor, 1873-4." *Late Imperial China* 33, no. 2 (December 2012): 76–118.

Moloughney, Brian, and Peter Zarrow. "Making History Modern: The Transformation of Chinese Historiography, 1895–1937." In *Transforming History: The Making of a Modern Academic Discipline in Twentieth-Century China*, ed. Brian Moloughney and Peter Zarrow, 1–46. Hong Kong: Chinese University Press, 2011.

Murata Yujiro. "The Late Qing 'National Language' Issue and Monolingual Systems: Focusing on Political Diplomacy." *Chinese Studies in History* 49, no. 3 (May 2016): 108-25.

Murray, Julia. "Didactic Picturebooks for Late Ming Emperors and Princes." In *Culture, Courtiers, and Competition: The Ming Court, 1368–1644*, ed. David Robison, 231-68. Cambridge, Mass.: Harvard University Press, 2008.

Musgrove, Charles. *China's Contested Capital: Architecture, Ritual, and Response in Nanjing*. Honolulu: University of Hawai'i Press, 2013.

Naquin, Susan. *Millenarian Rebellion in China: The Eight Trigrams Uprising of 1813*. New Haven, Conn.: Yale University Press, 1976.

Nedostup, Rebecca "Two Tombs: Thoughts on Zhu Yuanzhang, the Kuomintang, and the Meanings of National Heroes." In *Long Live the Emperor! The Uses of the Ming Founder Across Six Centuries of East Asian History*, ed. Sarah K. Schneewind, 355-90. Minneapolis: Society for Ming Studies, 2008.

Nivison, David S. "Ho-Shen and His Accusers: Ideology and Political Behavior in the Eighteenth Century." In *Confucianism in Action*, ed. David S. Nivison and Arthur F. Wright, 209-43. Stanford, Calif.: Stanford University Press, 1960.

Oxnam, Robert. *Ruling from Horseback: Manchu Politics in the Oboi Regency, 1661–1669*. Chicago: University of Chicago Press, 1975.

Parker, Jason Holloman. "The Rise and Decline of I-Hsin Prince Kung, 1858-1865: A Study of the Interaction of Politics and Ideology in Late Imperial China." Ph.D. dissertation, Princeton University, 1979.

Peleggi, Maurizio. *Lords of Things: The Fashioning of the Siamese Monarchy's Modern Image*. Honolulu: University of Hawaii Press, 2002.

Peng, Ying-chen. "Lingering Between Tradition and Innovation: Photographic Portraits of Empress Dowager Cixi." *Ars Orientalis* 43 (2013): 157-74.

—. "Staging Sovereignty: Empress Dowager Cixi (1835-1908) and Late Qing Court Art Production." Ph.D. dissertation, University of California, Los Angeles, 2014.

Perry, Elizabeth. *Anyuan: Mining China's Revolutionary Tradition*. Berkeley: University of California Press, 2012.

Phillips, Steven. "The Demonization of Federalism in Republican China." In *Defunct Federalisms: Critical Perspectives on Federal Failure*, ed. Emilian Kavalski and Magdalena Zolkos, 87-102. Hampshire, UK: Ashgate, 2008.

Platt, Stephen. *Autumn in the Heavenly Kingdom: China, the West, and the Epic Story of the Taiping Civil War*. New York: Knopf, 2012.

—. *Imperial Twilight: The Opium War and the End of China's Last Golden Age*. New York: Knopf, 2018.

—. *Provincial Patriots: The Hunanese and Modern China*. Cambridge, Mass.: Harvard University Press, 2007.

Plunkett, John. *Queen Victoria: First Media Monarch*. Oxford: Oxford University Press, 2003.

Polachek, James. *The Inner Opium War*. Cambridge, Mass.: Harvard University Press, 1992.

Porter, Jonathan. *Tseng Kuo-fan's Private Bureaucracy*. Berkeley: University of California Press, 1972.

Price, Don C. *Russia and the Roots of the Chinese Revolution, 1896–1911*. Cambridge, Mass.: Harvard University Press, 1974.

Pritchard, John, ed. *The Tokyo Major War Crimes Trial: The Records of the International Military Tribunal for the Far East*. Lewiston, N.Y.: Edwin Mellen Press, 1998.

Qian, Nanxiu. "Revitalizing the Xianyuan (Worthy Ladies) Tradition: Women in the 1898 Reforms." *Modern China* 29, no. 4 (October 2003): 399-454.

Qu Hongji 瞿鴻襪. *Shengde jilüe* 聖德紀略 (Records of Sagely Virtue). Taibei: Wenhai Press, 1970.

Rankin, Mary Backus. *Elite Activism and Political Transformation in China: Zhejiang Province, 1865–1911.* Stanford, Calif.: Stanford University Press, 1986.

——. "'Public Opinion' and Political Power: Qingyi in Late Nineteenth Century China." *Journal of Asian Studies*, 41, no. 3 (May 1982): 453-84.

Rawski, Evelyn. "Ch'ing Imperial Marriage and Problems of Rulership." In *Marriage and Inequality in Chinese Society*, ed. Rubie Watson and Patricia Ebrey, 170-203. Berkeley: University of California Press, 1991.

——. *The Last Emperors: A Social History of Qing Imperial Institutions*. Berkeley: University of California Press, 1998.

Reynolds, Douglas R. *China, 1898–1912: The Xinzheng Revolution and Japan*. Cambridge, Mass.: Harvard University Press, 1993.

——. *East Meets East: Chinese Discover the Modern World in Japan, 1854–1898: A Window on the Intellectual and Social Transformation of Modern Japan*. Ann Arbor, Mich.: Association for Asian Studies, 2014.

Rhoads, Edward J. M. *Manchus and Han: Ethnic Relations and Political Power in Late Qing and Early Republican China, 1861–1928*. Seattle: University of Washington Press, 2000.

——. *Stepping Forth Into the World: The Chinese Educational Mission to the United States, 1872–81*. Hong Kong: Hong Kong University Press, 2011.

Richard, Timothy. *Forty-Five Years in China: Reminiscences*. New York: Frederick A. Stokes, 1916.

Richter, Matthias L. *The Embodied Text: Establishing Textual Identity in Early Chinese Manuscripts*. Leiden: Brill, 2013.

Roberts, Claire. "The Empress Dowager's Birthday: The Photographs of Cixi's Long Life Without End." *Ars Orientalis* 43 (2013): 176-95.

Roskam, Cole. "The Architecture of Risk: Urban Space and Uncertainty in Shanghai, 1843-74." In *Harbin to Hanoi: The Colonial Built Environment in Asia, 1840 to 1940*, ed. Laura Victoir, and Victor Zatsepine, 129-50. Hong Kong: Hong Kong University Press, 2013.

Rowe, William. *China's Last Empire: The Great Qing*. Cambridge, Mass.: Belknap Press of Harvard University Press, 2009.

——. "Rewriting the Qing Constitution: Bao Shichen's 'On Wealth' (Shuochu)." *T'oung Pao* 98 (2012): 178-216.

——. "The Significance of the Qianlong-Jiaqing Transition in Qing History." *Late Imperial China* 32, no. 2 (2011): 74-88.

——. *Speaking of Profit: Bao Shichen and Reform in Nineteenth Century China*. Cambridge, Mass.: Harvard University Asia Center, 2018.

Rudolph, Jennifer M. *Negotiated Power in Late Imperial China: the Zongli Yamen and the Politics of Reform*. Ithaca, N.Y.: Cornell University Press, 2008.

Saarela, Mårten Söderblom. "Manchu and the Study of Language in China (1607-1911)." Ph.D. dissertation, Princeton University, 2015.

Sang Bing 桑兵. *Gengzi qinwang yu wan qing zhengju* 庚子勤王與晚清政局 [The 1900 loyalist movement and late Qing politics]. Beijing: Beijing daxue chubanshe, 2004.

Schaberg, David. "The Zhouli as Constitutional Text." In *Statecraft and Classical Learning: The Rituals of Zhou in East Asian History*, ed. Benjamin Elman and Martin Kern, 33-63. Leiden: Brill, 2009.

Schram, Stuart, ed. *Mao's Road to Power: Revolutionary Writings, 1912–1949*. Armonk, N.Y.: M. E. Sharpe, 1992.

Schillinger, Nicolas. *The Body and Military Masculinity in Late Qing and Early Republican China: The Art of Governing Soldiers*. London: Lexington, 2016.

Schoppa, Robert Keith. "Power, Legitimacy, and Symbol: Local Elites and the Jute Creek Embankment Case." In *Chinese Local Elites and Patterns of Dominance*, ed. Joseph Esherick and Mary Backus Rankin, 140-61. Berkeley: University of California Press, 1990.

Schwarcz, Lilia Moritz. *The Emperor's Beard: Dom Pedro II and the Tropical Monarchy of Brazil*. New York: Hill and Wang, 2004.

Schwartz, Benjamin. *In Search of Wealth and Power: Yen Fu and the West*. Cambridge, Mass.: Harvard University Press, 1964.

Sergeant, Philip. *The Great Empress Dowager of China*. New York: Dodd, Mead, 1911.

Shanghai Commercial Press, ed. *Gaodeng xiaoxue zhongguo lishi jiaokeshu* 高等小學中國歷史教科書 [Common school Chinese history textbook]. Shanghai: Shanghai Commercial Press, 1903 [1910].

Shao, Qin. *Culturing Modernity: The Nantong Model, 1890–1930*. Stanford, Calif.: Stanford University Press, 2004.

Society for the Diffusion of Christian and General Knowledge Among the Chinese. *Eleventh Annual Report for the Year Ending 31st October, 1898*. Shanghai: North China Herald, 1898.

Soothill, William. *The Hall of Light: A Study of Early Chinese Kingship*. London: Lutterworth Press, 1951.

Spellman, W. M. *Monarchies 1000–2000*. London: Reaktion, 2001.

Strand, David. *An Unfinished Republic: Leading by Word and Deed in Modern China*. Berkeley: University of California Press, 2011.

Stuart, Jan, and Evelyn Rawski. *Worshipping Ancestors: Chinese Commemorative Portraits*. Washington, D.C.: Freer Gallery of Art, 2001.

Sun Yanjing 孫燕京. "Guizhou xuetang yu qingmo guizu" 貴冑學堂與清末貴族 [The School for Nobles and nobles at the end of the Qing). M.A. thesis, Beijing Normal University, 2005.

Sun Yat-sen. "A Refutation of an Article in the *Pao-huang Pao*." In *Prescriptions for Saving China, Selected Writings of Sun Yat-sen*, ed. Julie Lee Wai. Stanford, Calif.: Stanford University Press, 1994.

Suzuki, Mamiko C. *Gendered Power: Educated Women of the Meiji Empress' Court*. Ann Arbor: University of Michigan Press.

Tanaka, Stefan. *New Times in Modern Japan*. Princeton, N.J.: Princeton University Press, 2004.

Tang Zhijun and Benjamin Elman. "The 1898 Reforms Revisited: A Review of Luke S. K. Kwong's *A Mosaic of the Hundred Days: Personalities, Politics, and Ideas of 1898*." *Late Imperial China* 8, no. 1 (June 1987): 205-13.

Teng Ssu-yu and John Fairbank, eds. *China's Response to the West, a Documentary Survey, 1839–1923*. Cambridge, Mass.: Harvard University Press, 1954.

Teng, Tony. "Prince Kung and the Survival of the Ch'ing Rule, 1858-1898." Ph.D. dissertation, University of Wisconsin, 1972.

Thompson, Roger R. *China's Local Councils in the Age of Constitutional Reform, 1898–1911*. Cambridge, Mass.: Harvard University Press, 1995.

Townley, Susan Mary Keppel. *My Chinese Note Book*. New York: Methuen, 1904.
Tsang, Ka Bo. "In Her Majesty's Service: Women Painters in China at the Court of the Empress Dowager Cixi." In *Local/Global: Women Artists in the Nineteenth Century*, ed. Deborah Cherry and Janice Helland, 35-58. Burlington, Vt.: Ashgate, 2006.
Twitchett, Denis. "How to Be an Emperor: T'ang T'ai-tsung's Vision of His Role." *Asia Major* third series 9, no. 1/2 (1996): 1-102.
Van de Ven, Hans. *Breaking with the Past: The Maritime Customs Service and the Global Origins of Modernity in China*. New York: Columbia University Press, 2014.
Wagner, Rudolf. "Living Up to the Image of the Ideal Public Leader: George Washington's Image in China." *Journal of Transcultural Studies* 10, no. 2 (Winter 2019): 18-77.
——. "Ritual, Architecture, Politics and Publicity During the Republic: Enshrining Sun Yat-sen." In *Chinese Architecture and the Beaux-Arts*, ed. Jeffrey Cody, Nancy S. Steinhardt, and Tony Atkin, 223-78. Honolulu: University of Hawai'i Press, 2011.
——. "The Zhouli as Late Qing Path to the Future." In *Statecraft and Classical Learning: The Rituals of Zhou in East Asian History*, ed. Benjamin Elman and Martin Kern, 359-87. Leiden: Brill, 2010.
Waley-Cohen, Joanna. *The Culture of War in China: Empire and the Military Under the Qing Dynasty*. New York: Tauris, 2006.
Wan Yi 萬依. *Qingdai gongting shi* 清代宮廷史 [History of the court during the Qing dynasty]. Shenyang: Liaoning renmin chuban she, 1990.
Wang, Cheng-hua. "Going Public: Portraits of the Empress Dowager Cixi, Circa 1904." *Nan Nü* 14, no. 1 (2012): 119-76.
Wang Dongliang 王棟亮. "Qingmo lujun guizhou xuetang shulüe" 清末陸軍貴冑學堂述略 [Notes on the Military School for Nobles at the end of the Qing]. *Lishi dang'an* 4 (2008): 60-64.
Wang, Grady Lolan. "The Career of I-Hsin, Prince Kung, 1858-1880: A Case Study in the Limits of Reform in the Late Ch'ing." Ph.D. dissertation, University of Toronto, 1980.
Wang, Juan. *Merry Laughter and Angry Curses: The Shanghai Tabloid Press, 1897-1911*. Vancouver: University of British Columbia Press, 2012.
Wang Qingxiang 王慶祥. *Puyi jiaowang lu* 溥儀交往錄 [Records of Puyi's interactions]. Beijing: Dongfang chuban she, 1999.
Wang Shuang 王霜. *Zhongguo diwang gongting shenghuo* 中國帝王宮廷生活 (Palace life of Chinese emperors]. Beijing: Guoji wenhua chuban gongsi, 1992.
Wang, Shuo. "Qing Imperial Women: Empresses, Concubines, and Aisin Gioro Daughters." In *Servants of the Dynasty: Palace Women in World History*, ed. Anne Walthall, 137-71. Berkeley: University of California Press, 2008.
Wang, Sixiang. "The Sounds of Our Country: Interpreters, Linguistic Knowledge, and the Politics of Language in Early Chosŏn Korea." In *Rethinking East Asian Languages, Vernaculars, and Literacies, 1000-1919*, ed. Benjamin Elman, 58-95. Leiden: Brill, 2014.
Wang, Tseng-Tsai. "The Audience Question—Foreign Representatives and the Emperor of China, 1858-1873." *Historical Journal* 14, no. 3 (September 1971): 617-26.
Wang, Wensheng. *White Lotus Rebels and South China Pirates: Crisis and Reform in the Qing Empire*. Cambridge, Mass.: Harvard University Press, 2014.

Wang Xiuli 王秀麗. "Wanqing guizhou liuxue xingqi yuanyin tansuo" 晚清貴冑留學興起原因探索 [Exploration of reasons for the rise in studying abroad among nobles in the late Qing]. *Qingdao daxue shifan xueyuan xuebao* 25, no. 1 (March 2008): 57-61.

Wang, Yuanchong. *Remaking the Chinese Empire: Manchu-Korean Relations, 1616–1911.* Ithaca, N.Y.: Cornell University Press, 2018.

Wang Zilin 王子林. "Qing taizi gong" 清太子宮 [Palace of Qing princes]. *Zijincheng*, no. Z1 (2006): 112-17.

Weber, Eugen. *Peasants Into Frenchmen: The Modernization of Rural France, 1870–1914.* Stanford, Calif.: Stanford University Press, 1976.

Wei, Julie Lee, ed. *Prescriptions for Saving China: Selected Writings of Sun Yat-sen.* Stanford, Calif.: Stanford University Press, 1994.

Wei Qingyuan 韋慶遠, Gao Fang 高放, and Liu Wenyuan 劉文源. *Qing mo xianzheng shi* 清末憲政史 [A history of late Qing constitutional development]. Beijing: Zhongguo renmin daxue chuban she, 1993.

Weng Tonghe 翁同龢. *Ping lu cong gao* 瓶廬叢稿. Taibei: Wenhai, 1967.

———. *Weng Tonghe riji* 翁同龢日記 [The diary of Weng Tonghe]. 8 vols. Shanghai: Zhongxi shuju, 2012.

Weng Xincun 翁心存. *Weng Xincun riji* 翁心存日記 [The diary of Wengxincun]. 5 vols. Beijing: Zhonghua shuju, 2011.

Wenshi ziliao yanjiu weiyuanhui 文史資料研究委員會, ed. *Wanqing gongting shenghuo jianwen* 晚清宮廷生活見聞 [Palace life during the Late Qing]. Beijing: Wenshi ziliao chubanshe, 1982.

Wenyi bianyi she 文藝編譯社, ed. *Qi ri huang di yi wen* 七日皇帝軼事 [Anecdotes from seven days as emperor]. Jiulong: Zhongshan tushu gongsi, 1973.

Weston, Timothy. *The Power of Position: Beijing University, Intellectuals, and Chinese Political Culture, 1898–1929.* Berkeley: University of California Press, 2004.

Will, Pierre-Étienne. "Checking Abuses of Power Under the Ming Dynasty." In *China, Democracy, and Law: A Historical and Contemporary Approach*, ed. Mireille Delmas-Marty and Pierre-Étienne Will, 117-68. Leiden: Brill, 2012.

———. "Views of the Realm in Crisis: Testimonies on Imperial Audiences in the Nineteenth Century." *Late Imperial China* 29, no. 1s (2008): 125-59.

Wong, Edward. "Victor or Villain? The Varying Images of Zhu Yuanzhang in Twentieth Century Chinese Historiography." In *Long Live the Emperor! The Uses of the Ming Founder Across Six Centuries of East Asian History*, ed. Sarah K. Schneewind, 391-412. Minneapolis: Society for Ming Studies, 2008.

Wong, R. Bin. *China Transformed: Historical Change and the Limits of European Experience.* Ithaca, N.Y.: Cornell University Press, 1997.

Wong, Young-tsu. *A Paradise Lost: The Imperial Garden Yuanming Yuan.* Honolulu: University of Hawaii Press, 2001.

Wooldridge, William Charles. "Building and State Building in Nanjing After the Taiping Rebellion." *Late Imperial China* 30, no. 2 (2009): 84-126.

———. *City of Virtues: Nanjing in an Age of Utopian Visions.* Seattle: University of Washington Press, 2015.

Woren 倭仁. *Wo Wenduan gong yi shu* 倭文端公遺書 [The collected writings of Woren]. Taibei: Cheng wen chuban she, 1968.

Wortman, Richard. *Scenarios of Power: Myth and Ceremony in Russian Monarchy from Peter the Great to the Abdication of Nicholas II*. Princeton, N.J.: Princeton University Press, 2006.

Wright, Mary Clabaugh. *The Last Stand of Chinese Conservatism: The T'ung-Chih Restoration, 1862–1874*. Stanford, Calif.: Stanford University Press, 1962.

——. "What's in a Reign Name: The Uses of History and Philology." *Journal of Asian Studies* 18, no. 1 (1958): 103–6.

Wu Qiaozi 吳樵子, ed. *Zhiping baojian* 治平寶鑑 [Precious mirror for governance and peace]. Beijing: Zhongguo yanshi chubanshe, 1998.

Wu Qingchi 吳慶坻. *Jiaolang cuolu* 蕉廊脞錄 [Trifles from the Plantain Gallery]. Taibei: Wenhai Press, 1969.

Wu Xiangxiang 吳相湘. *Wanqing gongting shiji* 晚清宮庭實紀 [Record of the late Qing court]. Taibei: Zheng zhong shu ju, 1952.

Xia Xiaohong 夏曉虹. "Wanqing nüxue zhong de man han maodun: huxing zisha shijian jiedu" 晚清女學中的滿漢矛盾：惠興自殺事件解讀 [The Manchu-Chinese contradiction in late Qing female education: Exploration of the case of Hui Xiang's suicide]. *Ershiyi shijie shuangye kan* 36 (December 2012): 108–16.

Xiang Si 向斯. *Qingdai huangdi dushu shenghuo* 清代皇帝讀書生活 [The reading activities of Qing dynasty emperors]. Beijing: Zhongguo shudian, 2008.

Xiao Yishan 蕭一山. *Qingdai tongshi* 清代通史 [Comprehensive history of the Qing dynasty]. Taibei: Taiwan shang wu yin shu guan, 1963.

Xie Junmei 謝俊美. "Guangxu huangdi de dushu suiyue" 光緒皇帝的讀書歲月 [The Guangxu emperor's years of study]. *Wenshi bolan*, no. 03 (2006): 46–48.

——. *Weng Tonghe* 翁同龢 [Weng Tonghe]. Shanghai: Shanghai renmin chuban she, 1987.

Xiong Yuezhi 熊月之. *Xixuedongjian yu wanqing shehui* 西學東漸與晚清社會 [The eastward spread of Western learning and late Qing society]. Shanghai: People's Press, 1994.

Xu Jing 許靜. "Mingqing jingyan zhidu tedian yanjiu" 明清經筵制度特點研究 [Research on the special features of Ming-Qing classic mats]. *Liaocheng daxue xuebao*, no. 2 (2013): 78–87.

Xu Liting 徐立亭. *Xianfeng tongzhi di* 咸豐同治帝 [The Xianfeng and Tongzhi emperors]. Changchun: Jilin wenshi chuban she, 1993.

Xu Yihua 徐以驊. "Yan Yongjing yu shenggonghui" 顏永京與聖公會 [Yan Yonjing and the Anglican Church]. *Jindai zhongguo*, no. 10 (2000): 193–215.

Yan Chongnian 閻崇年. *Qing gong yi'an zhengjie* 清宮疑案正解 [Explaining the mysteries of the Qing palace]. Beijing: Zhonghua shuju, 2007.

Yan Fu 嚴復. "Zhong'e jiaoyi lun" 中俄交誼論 [On the friendship between China and Russia]. In *Wanqing wenxun* 晚清文選 [Selected writings from the late Qing], ed. Zheng Zhenduo 鄭振鐸, 682–83. Shanghai: Shenghuo shudian, 1937.

Yan Guangyao 閻廣耀. *Meiguo dui hua zhengce wenjian xuanbian: cong yapian zhanzheng dao di'yi ci shijie dazhan* 美國對華政策文件選編：从鴉片戰爭到第一次世界大戰 1842–1918 [Selection of American policy documents related to China, from the Opium War to the First World War]. Beijing: People's Publishing, 1990.

Yan Huiqing 顏惠慶 and Yao Songling 姚崧齡. *Yan Huiqing zizhuan* 顏惠慶自傳 [Autobiography of Yan Huiqing]. Taibei: Biographical Literature, 1973.

Yang, Chia-ling, and Roderick Whitfield, eds. *Lost Generation: Lu Zhenyu, Qing Loyalists and the Formation of Modern Chinese Culture*. London: Saffron, 2012.

Yang, Lu. "Dynastic Revival and Political Transformation in Late T'ang China: A Study of Emperor Hsien-Tsung (805–820) and His Reign." Ph.D. dissertation, Princeton University, 1999.

Yao Zuyi 姚祖義. *Zuixin zhongguo lishi jiaoke shu* 最新中國歷史教科書 [Most recent Chinese history textbook]. Shanghai: Shanghai Commercial Press, 1908.

Ye Xiaoqing 葉曉青. "Guangxudi zuihou de yuedu shumu" 光緒帝最後的閱讀書目 [The Guangxu emperor's final reading list]. *Lishi yanjiu*, no. 02 (2007): 180–83.

Ye Zhiru 葉志如. "Qingmo chouban guizhou fazheng xuetang shiliao xuan zai" 清末籌辦貴冑法政學堂史料選載 [Documents related to the establishment of the School for Study of Law and Administration for Nobles at the end of the Qing]. *Lishi dang'an*, no. 04 (1987): 43–55.

Yeh, Wen-Hsin. *The Alienated Academy: Culture and Politics in Republican China, 1919–1937*. Cambridge, Mass.: Harvard University Press, 1990.

Yue, Meng. "Hybrid Science versus Modernity: The Practice of the Jiangnan Arsenal, 1864 1897." *East Asian Science, Technology, and Medicine*, no. 16 (January 1999): 13–52.

Zaizhen 載振. *Yingyao riji* 英軺日記 [Diary of a voyage to England]. Taipei: Wenhai chubanshe, 1972.

Zarrow, Peter. *After Empire: The Conceptual Transformation of the Chinese State, 1885–1924*. Stanford, Calif.: Stanford University Press, 2012.

——. "Constitutionalism and the Imagination of the State: Official Views of Political Reform in the Late Qing." In *Creating Chinese Modernity: Knowledge and Everyday Life, 1900–1940*, ed. Peter Zarrow, 51–82. New York: Peter Lang, 2006.

——. "Discipline and Narrative: Chinese History Textbooks in the Early Twentieth Century." In *Transforming History: The Making of a Modern Academic Discipline in Twentieth-Century China*, ed. Brian Moloughney and Peter Zarrow, 169–208. Hong Kong: Chinese University Press, 2011.

——. *Educating China: Knowledge, Society, and Textbooks in a Modernizing World, 1902–1937*. Cambridge: Cambridge University Press, 2015.

——. "Late-Qing Reformism and the Meiji Model: Kang Youwei, Liang Qichao, and the Japanese Emperor." In *The Role of Japan in Liang Qichao's Introduction of Modern Western Civilization to China*, ed. Joshua Fogel, 40–67. Berkeley: Institute of East Asian Studies, 2004.

——. "The New Schools and National Identity: Chinese History Textbooks in the Late Qing." In *The Politics of Historical Production in Late Qing and Republican China*, ed. Tze-Ki Hon and Robert Culp, 21–54. Boston: Brill, 2007.

——. "The Reform Movement, the Monarchy, and Political Modernity." In *Rethinking the 1898 Reform Period: Political and Cultural Change in Late Qing China*, ed. Rebecca Karl and Peter Zarrow, 17–47. Cambridge, Mass.: Harvard University Press, 2002.

Zeng Jize 曾紀澤. *Zeng Jize riji* 曾紀澤日記 (Diary of Zeng Jize). Changsha: Yuelu, 1998.

Zhang, Hongxing. "Studies in Late Qing Dynasty Battle Paintings." *Artibus Asiae* 60, no. 2 (2000): 265–96.

Zhang, Jun. "Spider Manchu: Duanfang as Networker and Spindoctor of the Late Qing New Policies, 1901–1911." Ph.D. dissertation, University of California, San Diego, 2008.

Zhang Naiwei 章乃煒. *Qinggong shuwen* 清宮述聞 [Detailed account of Qing palace]. Beijing: Forbidden City, 2009.

Zhang Pengyuan 張朋園. *Lixian pai yu xinhai geming* 立憲派與辛亥革命 [The constitutionalists and the 1911 Revolution]. Taibei: Zhongyang yanjiuyuan jindai shi yanjiusuo, 1969.

Zhang, Xiaowei. "Loyalty, Anxiety, and Opportunism: Local Elite Activism During the Taiping Rebellion in Eastern Zhejiang, 1851-1864." *Late Imperial China* 30, no. 2 (2009): 39-83.

Zhang Yijun 張毅君. "Wei guangxu di jinjiang geguo zhenglue gao" 為光緒帝進講各國政略稿 [Draft lecture of world politics presented to the Guangxu emperor]. In *Jindai shi ziliao zong 104 hao* 近代史資料總104號 [Modern history documents, no. 104], ed. Li Xuetong 李學通, 1-50. Beijing: Zhongguo shehui kexue chubanshe, 2002.

Zhang Zhidong 張之洞. *Quanxue pian* 勸學篇 [Exhortation to learn]. Guilin: Guangxi Normal University Press, 2008 (1898).

Zhao, Gang. "Reinventing China: Imperial Qing Ideology and the Rise of Modern Chinese National Identity in the Early Twentieth Century." *Modern China* 32, no.1 (January 2006): 3-30.

Zheng, Xiaowei. *The Politics of Rights and the 1911 Revolution in China*. Stanford, Calif.: Stanford University Press, 2018.

Zheng Zhongxuan 鄭仲烜. "Qingchao huangzi jiaoyu yanjiu" 清朝皇子教育研究 [Research on the education of princes during the Qing dynasty]. Ph.D dissertation, Taiwan National Central University, 2011.

Zhongguo shixue hui 中國史學會, ed. *Wuxu Bianfa* 戊戌變法 [The Wuxu reforms]. Shanghai: Shenzhou guoguang she, 1953.

Zhou, Yongming. *Historicizing Online Politics: Telegraphy, the Internet, and Political Participation in China*. Stanford, Calif.: Stanford University Press, 2006.

Zito, Angela. *Of Body & Brush: Grand Sacrifice as Text/Performance in Eighteenth-Century China*. Chicago: University of Chicago Press, 1997.

Zou Ailian 鄒愛蓮. "Cong gongke dang yu weng tonghe riji tan tongzhi huangdi de dianxue jiaoyu" 從功課檔與翁同龢日記談同治皇帝的典學教育 [An examination of the Tongzhi emperor's education from the schoolwork archive and Weng Tonghe's diary]. In *Qingdai gongshi tanxi* 清代宮史探析 [Inquiries into palace history during the Qing], ed. Qingdai gongshi yanjiu hui 清代宮史研究會, 604-21. Beijing: Forbidden City, 2007.

Zou Zhenhuan 鄒振環. "Guangxu huangdi de yingyu xuexi yu jinru qingmo gongting de yingyu duben" 光緒皇帝的英語學習與進入清末宮廷的英語讀本 [The Guangxu emperor's English lessons and the English readers in the imperial court at the end of the Qing]. *Qingshi yanjiu*, no. 03 (2009): 107-15.

———. "Guangxu huangdi xue yingyu" 光緒皇帝學英語 [The Guangxu emperor's study of English]. *Wanbao wencui*, no. 17 (2010): 51.

INDEX

Page numbers in *italics* refer to figures.

Ahmad Shah (1898-1930), 154-55
Airen (1794-1863), 38
Allen, Young John (Ch. Lin Yuezhi, 1836-1907), 88, 94
Analects, 38, 49
anda (Manchu instructors): conflicts with Chinese colleagues, 40-41; Guangxu's education and, 63; place in ruling coalition of, 38; separate rituals for, 39-40; Tongzhi's education and, 38, 39-41, 46. *See also* Manchu Way; *specific instructors*
archery: Guangxu's education and, 58, 61, 64, 68, 69, 171; Manchu Way and, 11; Tongzhi's education and, 15-16, 38, 44-45, 48
Association for Constitutional Preparation (Yubei lixian gonghui), 155
Avatamsaka Sutra, 36

bandu (classmates), 155-56, 161-62
Baohe dian (Hall of Preserving Harmony), 109
Bastid, Marianne, 13-14
Beiyang Intendancy, 14-15
Bideyuan, 145
Board of Civil Appointments, 37-38
Board of Revenue, 37-38, 60
Board of Rites, 53, 60, 177

Board of Works, 42
Boxer Uprising (1900), 48, 61, 106-7, 113-14, 151
British Empire, 130
Buddhism, 36
Butong Studio (Butong shuwu), 137

calligraphy: Cixi and, 34; as gifts, 76, 117-19; Guangxu's education and, 59; Tongzhi's education and, 35-36; Xuantong's education and, 157
Cannadine, David, 19
Carl, Katherine, *115*, 117, *118*, *119*
Chang, Michael, 20
Chen, Jack, 6
Chen Baochen (1848-1935): Guangxu's education and, 81; Puyi's education and, 176, 178-79; Xuantong's education and, 144-46, 148, 150, 152, 155, 162
Cheng Yi (1033-1107), 7, 106
Chiang Kai-shek (1887-1975), 164
Chinese and Japanese Repository (newspaper), 53
Chinese Education Mission to the United States (1872-1881), 81
Chinese press: on Cixi's education, 119; on female education, 121-23, 125, 126, 128; on Guangxu's education, 62, 65, 67-70, 89, 90,

Chinese press (*continued*)
99; Guangxu's education and, 62, 65, 67-70, 87-89, 90-91, 99; on Japan, 125, 173; Puyi and, 180; on Xuantong's education, 139-40, 141, 143-44, 146-49, 150-51, 155, 157, 160-62; on Zaifeng, 134

Chinese Recorder and Missionary Journal (newspaper), 66-67

Chongqi (1829-1900), 48, 61, 111-13

Christianity, 89-90

Chu, Hung-lam, 7

Ci'an (1837-1881): death of, 81; education of, 33-34; Guangxu's education and, 57-58, 64-65, 67-68, 74, 81; Guangxu's enthronement and, 56-58; role and power of, 53; Tongzhi's education and, 37-39, 41-42, 47-48, 50, 53; Tongzhi's power and, 51-52; Xinyou Coup (1861) and, 29-32

Civil Service Examination system: abolition of, 141; imperial birthdays and, 130; *jinshi* degree and, 27, 59-60, 76; Lu Runxiang and, 145; Palace Examination and, 3, 76, 109, 187n7

Cixi (1835-1908): artistic production by, 70, 72-73, 75, 117-19; constitutional rule and, 128-33, 139; education of, 12-13, 32-34, 93-94, 119-20, 173; female education and, 93-94, 110, 120-29, 133, 173-74; female rulership and, 116-20; foreign policy and, 70-72; funeral of, 131-33; gift giving by, 70, 75, 103-4, 117-19; Guangxu's education and, 57-58, 64-65, 67-70, 73-74, 91-93, 98, 168-69; Guangxu's enthronement and, 56-58; Guangxu's tutelage and, 70-76, 101-7, 111-17; Hundred Days Reform and, 99, 110; opposition to, 110-12; photographs and portraits of, 116-17; Pujun's education and, 111, 112-13; role and power of, 3, 4, 6, 11, 12-13, 51-52, 53; succession crisis (1875) and, 55-56; Tongzhi's education and, 37-39, 41-42, 46, 47-48, 50, 53, 168-69; Tongzhi's power and, 51-52; Xinyou Coup (1861) and, 29-32; Xuantong's education and, 168-69

Classic Mat (*jingyan*): fusion of education and politics in, 6-7; Guangxu's education and, 66, 77-80, 95, 96; scholarly participation and, 142; Tongzhi's education and, 35-36; Xianfeng and, 9-10

Classic of Filial Piety, 38, 50

Classic of History, 36

classical studies (*dianxue*), 142

Confucian Classics: Cixi and, 12-13; Guangxu's education and, 59-61, 77, 80-81, 172; in Japan, 19-20; Kangxi's example and, 43-45; Puyi's education and, 174, 178-79; Tongzhi's education and, 35-41, 43-45, 46, 49, 52-53; Xuantong's education and, 137, 141-42, 144-48

Confucian Society, 178

Confucius, 7, 129

Conger, Sarah, 103-4, 114-16, 117

Constitutional Research Center (Xianzheng yanjiu suo), 129

constitutional rule: education reforms and, 109-10, 121-22, 128-33; in Japan, 139; powers and responsibilities of monarch in, 138-39; Puyi's education and, 174, 178; resistance to, 134; Xuantong's education and, 137-41, 154-61, 158

court education: debates and evolution of, 3-13, 165-73; postimperial politics and, 163-65, 174-75; Puyi and, 24-25, 165, 174, 175-81; Republic of China and, 163-65. *See also* Guangxu (r. 1875-1908); Tongzhi (r. 1861-1875); Xuantong (r. 1908-1912)

Crossley, Pamela, 5, 14-15, 176

Crystal Palace (London), 153

Crystal Palace (Shuijinggong), 152-54

Culp, Robert, 16

Dagong bao (newspaper), 123, 126, 128, 141, 160

Daily Lectures (*rijiang*), 9, 66, 77-80, 142

Daoguang (r. 1820-1850), 8, 167-68

Daoism, 36

datong (Great Unity), 146-48

Datong shu (Book of Great Unity) (Kang Youwei), 148
Daxue (Great Learning), 7, 133-34, 168
de Bary, Wm. Theodore, 166
dianxue (classical studies), 142
Diao Minqian (Dr. T. Z. Tyau, 1888-1970), 133
Dijian tushuo (Illustrated mirror for the emperor), 63
Diwang cheng gui, 43
diwang zhi xue ("learning of the emperor"), 8, 166-67
Dong Yuanchun (dates unknown), 30-31
Dongfang zazhi (*Eastern Miscellany*), 154-55
Du Shoutian (1788-1852), 9
Duanfang (1861-1909), 132
Duanhua (1807-1861), 28
Duara, Prasenjit, 15
Dudden, Alexis, 93

Eastman, Lloyd, 72
Edgerton-Tarpley, Kathryn, 200-201n4
education: Hundred Days Reform and, 61, 80, 99-104, 105-7, 145; in Japan, 13, 19-20, 81-82, 124-25, 129, 148-49, 160, 172-73; military examinations and, 75-76, 99; national school system and, 109, 129-32, 145, 154, 156-61, *158*; women and, 93-94, 110, 120-29, 133, 173-74. *See also* Civil Service Examination system; court education
emperorship: court education and, 5-8, 168-72; female rulership and, 32-34, 72, 114, 116-20; postimperial politics and, 163-65
empress dowagers, 30-34. *See also* Ci'an (1837-1881); Cixi (1835-1908); Longyu (1868-1913)
English (language): Cixi's education and, 119-20, 173; Guangxu's education and, 67-70, 83-93, 99, 104, 143; as language of international law, 93; Puyi's education and, 177, 178
eunuchs, 46, 62, 92
Exhortation to Learn (Zhang Zhidong), 172

female education, 93-94, 110, 120-29, 133, 173-74
female rulership, 32-34, 72, 114, 116-20, 134
Feng Guifen (1809-1874), 86
firearms, 69
Fletcher, Henry, 140
foreign press: on Cixi's education, 119; on female education, 126-27; on Guangxu's education, 66-67, 85-86, 87-89, 90-91, 171-72; on Meiji, 18-19; on Puyi's education, 176, 177; on Tongzhi's education, 47, 53-54; on Xuantong's education, 143-45, 159-60, 161-62
France, 98
Fubi jiamo, 43
Fujitani, Takashi, 19
Fukuzawa Yukichi, 205n99

Gakushūin (School for Nobles, Japan), 124
Gan Yonglong, 154-55
Gao Xieceng (1841-1917), 78-80
Garden of Perfect Brightness (Yuanming yuan), 50, 51-52
George V (r. 1910-1936), 150
Germany, 13, 19, 177. *See also* Wilhelm II (1859-1941)
Grand Council, 53, 71-72
Gu Hongming (1857-1928), 178, 212n29
Gu Yanwu (1613-1682), 18
Guangxu (r. 1875-1908): Boxer Uprising and, 113; celebration of birthday of, 129-30; Cixi's role and power and, 70-76, 101-7, 111-17; enthronement of, 55-58, 168-69; funeral of, 131-33; Hundred Days Reform and, 99-104, 105; marriage and concubines of, 91-92; place of scholar-officials in the emperorship and, 77-80; Sino-Japanese War (1894-1895) and, 91, 92-93
Guangxu (r. 1875-1908)—education: *bandu* and, 155; Cixi and, 57-58, 64-65, 67-68, 69-70, 73-74, 91-93, 98, 168-69; classroom for, 58-59; competing tutors and texts in, 2, 3,

Guangxu (r. 1875-1908)–education (*continued*) 5-6, 10-11, 15-16, 18-19, 58-62, 80-82, 94-99, 171-72; early days of, 62-65; Kangxi's example and, 65-66; language training and, 58, 61, 63, 64, 67-70, 76-77, 83-93, 99, 104, 143; study abroad and, 96-98; transition to personal rule and, 73-77; Western learning and, 61, 66-70, 80-81, 83-93, 99, 104, 171-72

Guarino, Marie, 7

guoxue (national learning), 142

Guozijian, 60

Haiguo tuzhi (*Illustrated Gazetteer of the Maritime Countries*) (Wei Yuan), 86

Hall of Literary Brilliance (Wenhua dian), 35-36

Hall of Mental Cultivation (Yangxin dian), 62-63

Hall of Preserving Harmony (Baohe dian), 109

Hall of Sages, 39, 64

Hani-i araha sain be huwekiyebure oyonggo gisun (Important speech admonishing good deeds, composed by the khan), 76-77

Hanlin Academy (Hanlin yuan), 42, 60

Hanyuan Hall (Hanyuan dian), 137

Harrison, Henrietta, 16

Haruko (Empress Shōken, 1848-1914), 124-25

Headland, Isaac Taylor, 89-90, 133

Heart Sutra, 75

Heshen (1750-1799), 1-2, 31

Hevia, James, 18

Hill, Joshua, 218n6

Hirohito (1901-1989), 148-49

Hong Xiuquan (1814-1864), 27

Hongde Hall (Hongde dian, Hall of Promoting Virtue), 35-36, 58-59

horsemanship: Guangxu's education and, 61, 68, 69, 171; Manchu Way and, 11; Tongzhi's education and, 38, 44-45, 48

Huang Zongxi, 95-96

Huang Zunxian (1848-1905), 81-82

huangzu nü xuetang (School for Women of the Imperial Clan), 124, 125-28

Hundred Days Reform (1898), 61, 80, 99-104, 105-7, 145

Illustrated Gazetteer of the Maritime Countries (*Haiguo tuzhi*) (Wei Yuan), 86

Imperial Academy, 81, 102

Imperial Astronomy Bureau (Qintianjian), 67-68, 137

imperial birthdays, 129-30, 156

Imperial Lecture (*linyong jiangxue*), 7-8, 9-10, 157, 168

Imperial University, 129, 131

Imperial Workshop, 70

international community in China: Cixi and, 103-4, 114-16, *115*, 117; Xuantong's education and, 140, 159-60. *See also* foreign press

Itō Hirobumi (1841-1909), 17-18, 93

Japan: constitutional rule in, 139; education in, 13, 19-20, 81-82, 124-25, 129, 148-49, 160, 172-73; emperor's birthday in, 130; funerals in, 132-33; imperial power in, 17-21; Puyi and, 179-80; Western learning in, 90, 92-93, 149. *See also* Russo-Japanese War (1904-1905); Sino-Japanese War (1894-1895)

Jiang Xizhang (1907-2004), 161

Jiaqing (r. 1796-1820), 8, 59, 167

Jing Yuanshan (1840-1903), 93-94, 111-12

Jinliang (1878-1962), 141

jinshi degree, 27, 59-60, 76

Johnston, Reginald (1874-1938), 178-79

Judge, Joan, 127-28, 202n25

junxue (military studies), 142

juren degree, 75-76

Kahn, Harold, 5, 9

Kang Youwei (1858-1927): Chen Baochen and, 145; Chongqi and, 111; *Datong shu* and, 148; on education, 15, 95, 97, 98-99, 101, 102-3, 104; Japan and, 81-82, 139; Weng Tonghe and, 106

INDEX 253

Kangxi (r. 1661–1722): celebration of birthday of, 130; Daily Lectures (*rijiang*) and, 9; on education, 95, 166–67, 174; female rulership and, 30, 31; Guangxu's education and, 65–66, 76–77, 78; military training and, 152; political tutelage (*xunzheng*) and, 74; *qiangang duduan* (the power of the sovereign is absolute) and, 94; Tongzhi's education and, 38, 43–45

Kaske, Elisabeth, 210n5, 213n51

Kazoku jogakkō (Peeresses' School, Japan), 124–25

Ketteler, Clemens von (1853–1900), 151

kexue (science), 141–42

Kuhn, Phillip, 8

Kungang (1836–1907), 128

Kuo, Ting-yee, 198n477

Kutcher, Norman, 202n27

"learning of the emperor" (*diwang zhi xue*), 8, 166–67

Li Ciming (1830–1894), 29, 71–72

Li Dianlin (1842–1916), 146

Li Hongzao (1820–1897), 37, 50, 51–52, 169

Li Hongzhang (1823–1901), 14–15, 60, 71, 77, 93

Li Wentian (1834–1895), 50

Li Yuanhong (1854–1928), 163–64, 177–78

Liang Dunyan (1858–1924), 151

Liang Qichao (1873–1929): Chen Baochen and, 145; on education, 15, 81–82, 93, 95–96, 98–99, 102–4, 106

Liji (*Book of Rites*), 148

Liu, Kwang-Ching, 197n49

Liu Dapeng (1857–1942), 172

Longyu (1868–1913): death and funeral of, 176–77; female rulership and, 134; Puyi and, 24–25; Sun Yat-sen and, 176; Xuantong's education and, 146, 153, 156, 162

Louisiana Purchase Exposition (St. Louis World's Fair, 1904), 117

Lu Runxiang (1841–1915): Imperial Academy and, 102; Puyi's education and, 176; Xuantong's education and, 144–45, 148, 152, 155, 162

Lu Shenpei (dates unknown), 1

Luo Zhenyu (1866–1940), 178

Major, Ernest, 67

Manchu (language): court education and, 12; Guangxu's education and, 58, 61, 63, 64, 68, 69, 76–77, 84; Manchu Way and, 11; Pujun's education and, 112–13; Tongzhi's education and, 15–16, 38, 48; use of, 69; Xuantong's education and, 144

Manchu Way: court education and, 11–13; Guangxu's education and, 61, 64, 69, 77, 80–81; Kangxi's example and, 43–45; Puyi's education and, 174; Tongzhi's education and, 35–37, 38–41, 43–45, 46, 52–53; Xuantong's education and, 142. *See also* archery; horsemanship; Manchu (language)

Manchukuo, 179–80

Mao Zedong (1893–1976), 179, 181

Martin, W. A. P. (Ch. Ding Weiliang, 1827–1916), 86–87, 90

Meiji (r. 1868–1912), 18, 19–20, 81, 90, 92–93, 132, 139

Metzger, Thomas, 223n19

Miankai (1795–1838), 167

Mianning (1782–1850), 167

military examinations, 75–76, 99

military studies (*junxue*), 142, 148, 151–52

Ming dynasty (1368–1644), 7–8

Ming tang (Hall of Light, Hall of Illumination), 153

mingshi (famous scholars), 94–99

Mingyi daifang lu (*Waiting for the Dawn: A Plan for the Prince*) (Huang Zongxi), 95–96

missionary community, 89–90

Mokros, Emily, 50

Mongolian (language): court education and, 11, 12; Guangxu's education and, 58, 61, 64, 68, 69–70, 84

Morrison, G. E., 132

Mukden Incident (1931), 180
Musgrove, Charles, 163–64

Nanshu fang (Southern Study), 60
National Assembly, 129, 135, 145
national learning (*guoxue*), 142
national school system, 109, 129–32, 145, 154, 156–61, 158
Neixing lu (Records of introspection), 64–65
New Policy Reforms (*xinzheng bianfa*), 120–22, 131
New York Daily Graphic (newspaper), 206n10
New York Times (newspaper), 85–86, 87–88, 89, 176, 177
Nian Rebellion (1851–1868), 72
Nicholas II (r. 1894–1917), 116–17
Ningshou gong (Palace of Tranquil Longevity), 75
Nogi Maresuke (1849–1912), 149
North China Herald (newspaper): on Cixi's education, 119; on Guangxu's education, 87–88, 171–72; on Meiji, 18–19; on Tongzhi's education, 47, 53; on Xuantong's education, 144–45, 159–62
Northern Song dynasty (960–1127), 6–7
Nü xuebao (Journal of women's education), 94

Official of the Hongde Hall (*Hongde dian xingzou*), 35–36
"On the Education of Women" (Liang Qichao), 93

Palace Examination, 3, 76, 109, 187n7
Palace of Heavenly Purity (Qianqing gong), 24–25
Palace of Tranquil Longevity (Ningshou gong), 75
Palace School for Princes (Shangshufang), 37, 39, 64
Pan Qinglan (1848–?), 95
Pang Hongshu (1843–1911), 142
Pavilion of Purple Light (Ziguang ge), 72–73

Pearl Concubine, 91–92
Peeresses' School (Kazoku jogakkō, Japan), 124–25
Peers College (Japan), 148–49
Peleggi, Maurizio, 210n3
People's Republic of China (1949–), 179–81
Peter the Great (1672–1725), 15–16, 96–97, 98, 104
photographs, 116–17, 132
Polachek, James, 37
political tutelage (*xunzheng*), 74
press: on Cixi's education, 119; on female education, 121–23, 125–28; on Guangxu's education, 62, 65, 66–70, 85–91, 99, 171–72; on Japan, 125, 173; on Meiji, 18–19; Puyi and, 180; on Puyi's education, 176, 177; on Tongzhi's education, 47, 53; on Xuantong's education, 139–41, 143–45, 146–49, 151, 155, 157, 159–62; on Zaifeng, 134
Prince Chun (Yihuan, 1840–1891): Cixi and, 72; Guangxu's education and, 61, 65, 69, 171; succession crisis (1875) and, 55–56; Tongzhi's education and, 15–16, 38–39, 43–45, 48, 51–52
Prince Duan (Zaiyi, 1856–1922), 111, 113
Prince Dun (Yicong, 1831–1889), 55
Prince Gong (Yixin, 1833–1898): constitutional rule and, 129; foreign policy and, 70–71; succession crisis (1875) and, 55; Tongzhi's education and, 35, 38–39, 40, 41–43, 50–52, 53; Xinyou Coup (1861) and, 31
Prince Qing (Yikuang, 1838–1917), 123–24, 125–27
Protect the Emperor Society (Baohuanghui), 106
Pujun (1885–1942), 111, 112–13
Puyi (1906–1967), 24–25, 165, 174, 175–81

Qi Junzao (1793–1866), 37–38
qiangang duduan (the power of the sovereign is absolute), 94
Qianlong (r. 1735–1796): calligraphy and, 36; Cixi as heir to, 72–73, 75; education and, 5, 6, 8, 9, 84; *qiangang duduan* (the power of the

sovereign is absolute) and, 94; Yuqing Palace and, 59
Qianqing gong (Palace of Heavenly Purity), 24–25
Qin (221–206 BCE), 96
Qin xin jin jian (Golden mirror for the instruction of the heart), 42–43
Qing Empire, 1–3, 7, 13–21. *See also specific emperors*
Qingliu scholars, 60
Qu Hongji (1850–1918), 196n27
Quanxue pian (Exhortation to learn) (Zhang Zhidong), 98

Renmin ribao (People's daily) (newspaper), 180
Republic of China, 163–65, 174–75
Rhoads, Edward, 11–12, 214n63
Richard, Timothy (Ch. Li Timotai, 1845–1919), 88–89, 91
Roskam, Cole, 219n65
Rowe, William, 1
Russia, 15–16, 19. *See also* Nicholas II (1894–1918); Peter the Great (1672–1725)
Russo-Japanese War (1904–1905), 121, 149

Sacred Edict (*Shengyu*), 76–77
School for Female Interpreters (Yiyi nüxue), 128
School for Nobles (Gakushūin, Japan), 124
School for Women of the Imperial Clan (*huangzu nü xuetang*), 124, 125–28
School of Combined Learning (Tongwen guan), 16–17, 42, 83
science (*kexue*), 141–42
Self Help (Samuel Smiles), 19–20
Self-Strengthening Movement, 65, 95, 168
Shang Yanliu (1875–1963), 109
Shangshu (*Classic of History*), 24–25
Shangshufang (Palace School for Princes), 37, 39, 64
Shen Duo (dates unknown), 83, 86–87, 87, 90, 91, 143

Shenbao (newspaper): on Guangxu's education, 62, 65, 67–70, 89, 90, 99; on Japan, 173; on Xuantong's education, 139–40, 144, 146–48, 149, 151, 155, 157, 161–62
Shengzu Ren huangdi tingxun geyan (Aphorisms from the familial instructions of the Kangxi emperor), 38
Shiduo (1843–1914), 61–62
Shimoda Utako (1854–1936), 125
Shixu (1853–1921), 137
Shuijinggong (Crystal Palace), 152–54
Shunzhi (r. 1644–1661), 7, 30, 75, 76–77, 95, 203n50
Siam, 98, 210n3
Sinclair, Marian Headland, 133
Sino-French War (1884–1885), 70–71
Sino-Japanese War (1894–1895), 13, 18, 84, 91–93, 149, 172–73
Smiles, Samuel, 19–20
Society for the Education of Women (Yukun wenhui; Yukun hui; Yukun zongxue hui), 122–23
Songgui (1833–1907), 61–62
Southern Study (Nanshu fang), 60
St. Louis World's Fair (Louisiana Purchase Exposition, 1904), 117
Strand, David, 174
study abroad, 15–16, 96–98, 177, 178, 212–13n43
Sun Jia'nai (1827–1909), 61, 64–65, 100
Sun Yat-sen (1866–1925), 110–11, 163–64, 174, 176
Sun Yijing (1826–1890), 60–61
Sushun (1816–1861), 28, 29–31, 36–38, 71

Taft, Marcus, 89–90
Taiping Rebellion (1850–1864), 2, 9–10, 27–28, 59–60, 72, 168
Taizong (r. 626–649), 6
Tang Shouqian (1856–1917), 134–35, 155
Temple of Goddess of Sericulture, 76
textbooks, 131
Thompson, Roger, 16
Tibetan (language), 84

256   INDEX

Times (newspaper), 132
Times of London (newspaper), 87–88
Tongwen guan (School of Combined Learning), 16–17, 42, 83
Tongzhi (r. 1861–1875): ascension to personal rule of, 47–49; death of, 52; enthronement of, 168–69; limits of imperial power and, 49–52; marriage of, 48; succession crisis (1875) and, 55–56; Sushun and, 29–31; travels and, 60
Tongzhi (r. 1861–1875)—education: after ascension to personal rule, 48–49, 50–51; *bandu* and, 155; Cixi and, 37–39, 41–42, 46, 47–48, 50, 53, 168–69; competing tutors and texts in, 2–3, 5–6, 10–11, 15–16, 18, 27–29, 34–45, 52–54; early days of, 39–43; Kangxi's example and, 43–45; struggles in, 45–47

United States, 81, 178

Veritable Records, 33, 52
Victoria, Queen (r. 1837–1901), 116–17
Vos, Herbert, 117

Wagner, Rudolf, 174
Wang Guowei (1877–1927), 178
Wan'guo gongbao (periodical), 88–89
Wei Yuan (1794–1857), 86
Wei Zhongxian (1568–1627), 31
Weng Tonghe (1830–1904): on decline of empire, 1, 2; dismissal of, 105–6; on education, 169, 170–71; Guangxu's education and, 59, 62–65, 75, 86; Tongzhi's education and, 40–42, 46–47, 53
Weng Xincun (1791–1862), 2–3, 37–38
Wenhua dian (Hall of Literary Brilliance), 35–36
Wenyu (dates unknown), 78
Western learning: Cixi's education and, 12–13, 119–20; constitutional rule and, 129; Guangxu's education and, 61, 66–67, 80–81, 83–93, 99, 104, 171–72; in Japan, 90, 92–93,

149; Kangxi's example and, 43–45; Puyi's education and, 174, 178–79; Tongzhi's education and, 35, 41–42, 43–45, 48, 52–53; Woren and, 16–17; Xuantong's education and, 141–45, 150–51
White Lotus Rebellion, 1–2
Wilhelm II (1859–1941), 19, 96, 151
Will, Pierre-Étienne, 4
women: Beijing's foreign legation and, 103–4, 114–16, 115, 117; education and, 93–94, 110, 120–29, 133, 173–74; rulership and, 32–34, 72, 114, 116–20, 134
Wong, Yong-tsu, 202n29
Woren (1804–1871): on education, 27, 169–70; Tongzhi's education and, 16–17, 37, 42–43, 48, 53
World's Chinese Students' Journal (*Huanqiu Zhongguo xuesheng bao*), 21, 121, 122, 134
Woshenhunbu (1797–1866), 38
Wright, Mary, 12, 14, 15
Wu Kedu (1812–1879), 56, 57–58
Wu Tingfang (1842–1922), 151
Wu Zetian (r. 690–705), 153
Wuchang Uprising (1911), 137, 162, 175

Xia Tongshan (1831–1880), 59–60
Xianfeng (r. 1850–1861): Cixi and, 32–33; education and, 9–10, 27–31, 37–38, 168, 169–70; Taiping Rebellion and, 2, 27–28
Xiangheng (1832–1904), 112–13
Xianzheng yanjiu suo (Constitutional Research Center), 129
Xiaojing (*Classic of Filial Piety*), 150
Xiaozhuang (1613–1688), 30, 31, 93–94
Xinyou Coup (1861), 29–32
xinzheng bianfa (New Policy Reforms), 120–22, 131
Xiyang tongshi jiangyi (Lessons on the comprehensive history of Western countries), 129
Xu Dingchao (1845–1917), 129
Xu Shichang (1855–1939), 178

Xu Tong (1819-1900), 46, 64-65, 111, 112
Xuantong (r. 1908-1912): enthronement of, 138, 168-69
Xuantong (r. 1908-1912)—education: *bandu* and, 155-56, 161-62; Cixi and, 168-69; competing tutors and texts in, 2, 3, 5-6, 10-11, 142-48, 147; constitutional rule and, 137-41, 154-61, 158; early days of, 137; language training and, 146-48, 150-51, 156; new curriculum and, 148-54

Yan Fu (1854-1921), 15-16, 95, 97-98, 104
Yan Yongjing (1838-1898), 86
Yangxin dian (Hall of Mental Cultivation), 62-63
Yeh, Wen-hsin, 16-17
Yijinga (1811-1866), 38
Yiketan (1862-1922), 144, 156, 176
Yiyi nüxue (School for Female Interpreters), 128
Yomiuri shimbun (newspaper), 92-93
Yongzheng (r. 1722-1735), 94, 95
Yuan Chang (1846-1900), 75
Yuan Shikai (1859-1916), 14-15, 130, 162
Yuanming yuan (Garden of Perfect Brightness), 50, 51-52
Yubei lixian gonghui (Association for Constitutional Preparation), 155
Yupi lidai tongjian jilan (Comprehensive mirror of dynastic history with imperial commentary), 33
Yuqing Palace (Yuqing gong, Palace of Nurturing Joy), 59, 64, 83
Yuzhi quanshan yaoyan (Imperially commissioned exhortations to good deeds), 77

Yuzhi wuti qingwen jian (Imperially commissioned mirror of the Manchu language with five kinds of script placed together), 84

Zaichun (1856-1875), 27. *See also* Tongzhi (r. 1861-1875)
Zaifeng (1883-1951): Puyi and, 24-25, 134-35; Xuantong's education and, 145-46, 149-50, 151-52, 155
Zaitian (1871-1908), 55-56. *See also* Guangxu (r. 1875-1908)
Zarrow, Peter, 15, 225n48
Zeng Guofan (1811-1872), 9, 56, 59-60, 169-70
Zeng Jize (1839-1890), 171
Zhang Deyi (1847-1918): Guangxu's education and, 83, 86-87, 87, 90, 91; Puyi's education and, 178; Xuantong's education and, 143
Zhang Jian (1853-1926), 155
Zhang Jiaxiang (1827-1885), 61
Zhang Xun (1824-1923), 178
Zhang Zhidong (1837-1909): Cixi and, 75; on education, 20-21, 98, 120, 127-28, 132, 172-73
Zhao Binglin (1876-1927), 133-34
Zheng, Xiaowei, 139
Zhiping baojian (Precious mirror for governance and peace), 33
Zhongyong (*Doctrine of the Mean*), 157
Zhu Xi (1130-1200), 8, 166
Zhu Yuanzhang (1328-1398), 7, 77, 163, 164, 175
Zhuangzi, 36
Zongli yamen (Office of Foreign Affairs), 44
Zuozhuan (Commentary of Zuo), 36

STUDIES OF THE WEATHERHEAD EAST ASIAN INSTITUTE
COLUMBIA UNIVERSITY

Selected Titles
(Complete list at weai.columbia.edu/content/publications)

Mobilizing Japanese Youth: The Cold War and the Making of the Sixties Generation, by Christopher Gerteis. Cornell University Press, 2021.

Middlemen of Modernity: Local Elites and Agricultural Development in Modern Japan, by Christopher Craig. University of Hawai'i Press, 2021.

Isolating the Enemy: Diplomatic Strategy in China and the United States, 1953–1956, by Tao Wang. Columbia University Press, 2021.

A Medicated Empire: The Pharmaceutical Industry and Modern Japan, by Timothy M. Yang. Cornell University Press, 2021.

Dwelling in the World: Family, House, and Home in Tianjin, China, 1860–1960, by Elizabeth LaCouture. Columbia University Press, 2021.

Disunion: Anticommunist Nationalism and the Making of the Republic of Vietnam, by Nu-Anh Tran. University of Hawai'i Press, 2021.

Made in Hong Kong: Transpacific Networks and a New History of Globalization, by Peter Hamilton. Columbia University Press, 2021.

China's Influence and the Center-Periphery Tug of War in Hong Kong, Taiwan and Indo-Pacific, by Brian C. H. Fong, Wu Jieh-min, and Andrew J. Nathan. Routledge, 2020.

The Power of the Brush: Epistolary Practices in Chosŏn Korea, by Hwisang Cho. University of Washington Press, 2020.

On Our Own Strength: The Self-Reliant Literary Group and Cosmopolitan Nationalism in Late Colonial Vietnam, by Martina Thucnhi Nguyen. University of Hawai'i Press, 2020.

A Third Way: The Origins of China's Current Economic Development Strategy, by Lawrence Chris Reardon. Harvard University Asia Center, 2020.

Disruptions of Daily Life: Japanese Literary Modernism in the World, by Arthur M. Mitchell. Cornell University Press, 2020.

Recovering Histories: Life and Labor After Heroin in Reform-Era China, by Nicholas Bartlett. University of California Press, 2020.

Figures of the World: The Naturalist Novel and Transnational Form, by Christopher Laing Hill. Northwestern University Press, 2020.

Arbiters of Patriotism: Right Wing Scholars in Imperial Japan, by John Person. University of Hawai'i Press, 2020.

The Chinese Revolution on the Tibetan Frontier, by Benno Weiner. Cornell University Press, 2020.

Making It Count: Statistics and Statecraft in the Early People's Republic of China, by Arunabh Ghosh. Princeton University Press, 2020.

Tea War: A History of Capitalism in China and India, by Andrew B. Liu. Yale University Press, 2020.

Revolution Goes East: Imperial Japan and Soviet Communism, by Tatiana Linkhoeva. Cornell University Press, 2020.

Vernacular Industrialism in China: Local Innovation and Translated Technologies in the Making of a Cosmetics Empire, 1900–1940, by Eugenia Lean. Columbia University Press, 2020.

Fighting for Virtue: Justice and Politics in Thailand, by Duncan McCargo. Cornell University Press, 2020.

Beyond the Steppe Frontier: A History of the Sino-Russian Border, by Sören Urbansky. Princeton University Press, 2020.

GPSR Authorized Representative: Easy Access System Europe, Mustamäe tee
50, 10621 Tallinn, Estonia, gpsr.requests@easproject.com

www.ingramcontent.com/pod-product-compliance
Lightning Source LLC
Chambersburg PA
CBHW022043290426
44109CB00014B/961